LESLEY CHAMBERLAIN is a writer and reviewer distinguished for her wide-ranging work from travel (*In the Communist Mirror*) to philosophy (*Nietzsche in Berlin*). In 2003 she published her first novel, *Girl in a Garden*. Her most recent book is *Motherland: A Philosophical History of Russia*.

'Lesley Chamberlain has a rare gift for animating philosophy through intensely human stories... A richly humane and complex book of enormous spiritual depth.' Michael Burleigh, *Sunday Telegraph*

'Moving, deeply thoughtful... Revel in the glorious spectacle of the failure of Lenin's attempts to murder art, history and faith. Hope, as they say, springs eternal.' Bryan Appleyard, *Sunday Times*

'Both learned and absorbing... Chamberlain's book is more than an elegy on the theme of exile. She explores the ideas that these Russians brought with them [and] has written a fine monument to a generation of thinkers who addressed questions of contemporary relevance and deserve to be better known.' *Economist*

'Chamberlain has dug up or reprinted some wonderful material from Soviet archives, including some marvellous interrogation records.' Anne Applebaum, *Spectator*

'Comprehensively and imaginatively researched... Chamberlain steers a highly unpredictable course between history, biography and philosophy and it works superbly... She makes particularly good use of a wide array of memoirs, allowing us to feel, at very close quarters, the mixture of astonishment, irony and, finally, dignified resignation with which the deportees faced their interrogators and their punishment... fascinating.' Liver Ready, *Moscow Times*

Тов. Ленин ОЧИЩАЕТ землю от нечисти.

'Comrade Lenin Cleans the Filth from the Land.' Soviet Poster, 1920.

The Philosophy Steamer

LENIN AND THE EXILE OF THE INTELLIGENTSIA

Lesley Chamberlain

Atlantic Books
LONDON

First published in Great Britain in hardback in 2006 by Atlantic Books,
an imprint of Grove Atlantic Ltd

This paperback edition published in 2007 by Atlantic Books

1 2 3 4 5 6 7 8 9

A CIP catalogue record for this book is
available from the British Library.

ISBN 978 184354 093 9

Printed in the UK by CPI Bookmarque, Croydon, CR0 4TD

Atlantic Books
An imprint of Grove Atlantic Ltd
Ormond House
26–27 Boswell Street
London WCIN 3JZ

www.groveatlantic.co.uk

Contents

List of Illustrations

Frontispiece: 'Comrade Lenin Cleans the Filth from the Land.' Soviet poster, 1920.

1. Semyon and Tatyana Frank honeymooning in Austria, summer 1908.

2. Cover of the first edition of Lenin's Materialism and Empiriocriticism.

3. Aleksei Peshekhonov addressing a political meeting, Petrograd 1917.

4. Dzerzhinsky and his twelve Cheka / GPU Apostles.

5. Maxim Gorky at a Petrograd station, bound for Moscow, 1920.

6. Yury Annenkov's 1921 portrait of the writer Zamyatin.

7. The Moscow GPU's File on Peshekhonov.

8. A convalescent Lenin hard at work in Gorky 1922. Photographed by his sister, Maria Ulyanova.

9. Chekists ready for action.

10. Prison photographs of some of the arrested intelligentsia, August 1922.

11. German press advertisement for pleasure cruises on the *Haken* and the *Prinzessin Sophie Charlotte*.

12. Foreign passport issued to Dmitry Lutokhin, Petrograd 1922.

13. The Philosophy Steamer: the 'small but stately' *Oberbürgermeister Haken*.

14. The Frank children in Berlin.

15. Advertisement for the Berlin émigré newspaper *Rul* ('The Rudder').

16. The critic Yuly Aikhenvald lecturing at the Russian Scientific Institute, Berlin 1924.

17. Staff at the Russian Scientific Institute, Berlin 1923–24.

18. Farewell to Berlin, 1923.

19. Advertisement in French and Russian for the film 'Nostalgia', playing in Paris, 1928.

20. Nikolai Berdyaev in France.

21. Berdyaev's study at his home in the Paris suburb of Clamart.

The author and publishers are grateful to the following for permission to reproduce images: frontispiece, 4, 6, 8, 9, David King Collection, London; 1, 14, 17, Peter Scorer; 3, 7, 10, 12, Russky Put; 5, Gorky Museum, Moscow; 13, Deutsches Schiffahrstmuseum, Bremerhafen; 15, 19, André Savine Collection, Wilson Library, University of North Carolina at Chapel Hill; 16, John Graudenz / Ullstein Bild, Berlin.

Acknowledgements

Thanks are due to Toby Mundy and Clara Farmer at Atlantic for their support, as always, and to my husband for his encouragement and wisdom. George Leggett took a helpful interest in the quest for sources and the Society of Authors made possible a visit to Szczecin, where the archivists at Archiwum Państwowe were most helpful. Mikhail Glavatsky sent me a copy of his important book. Peter Scorer supplied me with transcripts of his grandmother's memoirs and I also have him to thank for my introduction to Victor Frank in 1971. Katya Andreyev kindly advised me on sources for the emigration in Czechoslovakia. Rita van Duinen, of the André Savine Collection at the University of North Carolina, and Ivan and Misha Sovetnikov in Moscow helped bring the story alive with pictures.

A Note on Translation

All the translations from non-English material are mine unless otherwise indicated.

A Note on Transliteration

Names in the text are transliterations of the Russian originals, e.g. Lev Trotsky, not Leon. Exceptions are well-known anglicizations like Alexander (not Aleksandr). I have also preferred the ending 'y' to 'i' or 'ii' thus Dmitry not Dmitri, Dostoevsky not Dostoevskii. As a concession to easy reading in the text the soft-sign usually marked with an apostrophe has been omitted. References in the notes and the bibliography and Russian names quoted in non-Russian newspapers follow the style of individual publications.

Introduction

From midday on 28 September 1922, a small group of men, women and children, carrying what luggage was permitted, began to gather on the maritime quay of Vasilievsky Ostrov in northwest Petrograd.[1] The point of embarkation, the Kronshtadt pier, was opposite the Mining Institute on the Nevsky Embankment, what is today the Naberezhnaya Leitenanta Shmidta in St Petersburg. Throughout the afternoon and into the early evening, as queues snaked here and there, Lenin's political police, the GPU, carried out a smooth, impersonal 'operation'.[2] Their task was to deport around twenty-five Russian families. Forms were filled out in triplicate, customs officials searched for what they could confiscate or tax, and a policeman ruffled a child's hair in search of jewels.[3] There was no violence but the attenuated police procedures eventually added almost a day to the forty-eight-hour journey the deportees faced on their specially chartered German ship, the *Oberbürgermeister Haken*.

A second ship, the *Preussen*, carrying almost as many people again – mostly writers, philosophers and academics, and their dependants – sailed six weeks later. *Pravda*, the Communist Party newspaper, recorded the expulsion of a portion of the intelligentsia but the event was hardly mentioned again in Soviet times.[4] As this extraordinary story recedes ever further into history what has become known as The Philosophy Steamer remains little-known anywhere. Our ignorance is all the more astonishing since it was Lenin himself, the leader of the

Bolsheviks and the founder of the Soviet Union, who masterminded the deportations and chose many of his victims by name.

When *The Times* reported the event from Riga, it picked out some of the most prominent victims. There was Nikolai Berdyaev, 'a brilliant exponent of religious philosophy', Mikhail Osorgin, a writer and journalist who made his name as a foreign correspondent in Italy, and Professor Alexander Kizevetter, a distinguished historian and founder member of the Constitutional Democratic Party, the Kadets, which opposed Lenin in 1917.[5] Other big names by Russian standards included the philosophers Semyon Frank, Lev Karsavin, Nikolai Lossky and Ivan Ilyin, and a much-loved literary critic, Yuly Aikhenvald. I came to write this book partly because one of the expellees, Frank's eldest son Victor, aged thirteen when his family was forced out of Russia, was a friend of mine some years ago. His story struck me as an unforgettable experience of loss.[6]

Almost nothing was said in Russia at the time. The event seemed to frighten people into silence. The writer Kornei Chukovsky, for instance, who in the Soviet Union became a famous storyteller for children, made no mention of it in his private diary, despite the presence of several leading members of his Petrograd literary circle among the victims.[7] The event was a scandal. The deportees numbered amongst the best-known and most highly qualified men in Russia. They wrote the books and newspapers that the moderate majority was still reading in 1922. They taught at the universities, institutes and schools where Bolsheviks and Kadets alike still sent their children. They excelled at the academic and journalistic professions which had recently enjoyed a renaissance, having been liberalized and professionalized in the last decade of tsarism. Many were teachers and half a dozen were top university administrators, distinguished by their technical expertise and their public service.

'Philosophy Steamer' suggests it was philosophers who were forced to leave, and in all eleven 'philosophers' in the Russian style were deported. They included cultural critics and religious thinkers. Berdyaev was a mystical individualist, Frank an academic philosopher and critic, Karsavin a writer, teacher and historian of art and ideas, and Yuly Aikhenvald the translator of Schopenhauer into Russian and a popular and prolific literary critic. These thinkers clashed with Lenin and in an instant lost their homeland, because they were convinced that a new Russia would go astray if it did not enshrine religious moral values in its programme of social reform.

They were mostly conservative and religious in their thinking. Nevertheless, religious conservativism was not the only world outlook to be banished from Soviet Russia in the making. The young sociologist Pitirim Sorokin, for whom a brilliant professional future in America lay ahead, was a spokesman for global economic freedom and Christian-humanist cultural values, while Boris Brutskus was a liberal economist. In 1922, almost before it had begun, Brutskus was already delivering public lectures on why the planned economy of the Marxist-Leninists could not succeed in Russia, or indeed anywhere else. Brutskus's free-market economics so impressed an American professor of the subject seventy years later that, in 1990, as a new Russia struggled to emerge from the Soviet ashes, he sent a copy of Brutskus's 1922 article 'The Socialist Economy', to the cultural journal *Novy Mir*, to make a new generation aware of it. He recommended it as the most important Russian work on economics of the whole twentieth century.[8]

The story of how more than sixty such distinguished men as Boris Brutskus and Pitirim Sorokin, and their families, were deported by Lenin in the year the Soviet Union came into being, is the one I shall tell here. It is a slice of intellectual and political history with rich and occasionally devastating human consequences.

This book begins with an evocation of the world the expellees were leaving behind, followed by a detailed examination of the political manoeuvring that made the expulsions legally possible. It continues with a survey of the new lives the expellees made abroad in difficult times, with Europe hardly recovered from one war only to be confronted by another. The final part considers what the expulsions meant in the context of Russian history and the history of ideas.

I have touched on a wide variety of individual fates, while concentrating on a few specific figures like Berdyaev, Lossky, Karsavin and Frank. Where major cultural figures were, or felt themselves to be, involved in Lenin's selection, even when they did not leave on the two autumn ships, they have also been included. Sorokin, the poet Vladislav Khodasevich and his partner the writer Nina Berberova, and the theologian Sergei Bulgakov were among them. The philologist and literary theorist Roman Jakobson, having left two years earlier, also has a place on the fringe of the story. Jakobson was a modernist, in some ways close to the Revolution, but his life and career abroad mirrored the fates of those Russians who were forcibly expelled. He was also a successful émigré, whose work showed the potential for certain Russian ideas to be transferred fruitfully to Europe.

Though they could never have identified themselves that way, the 1922 expellees were the first dissidents from Soviet totalitarianism, whose fates would be connected with later individual victims of Soviet banishment like the writer Alexander Solzhenitsyn and the poet Joseph Brodsky. Together they embraced many varieties of dissenting belief. At least two of them were pacifist followers of Tolstoy with their own, non-Marxist idea of what the communal life should be. Brutskus, a Jew whose family had fled Russian anti-Semitism in the 1890s, had Zionist leanings. Sorokin was a non-Marxist sociologist who openly baited Lenin. Lossky was a Fabian socialist and somewhat reluctant participant in Kadet politics, whose main energy went on running the philosophy department at St Petersburg University and ensuring a good middle-class home life and education for his three sons. Father Abrikosov and his pupil Kuzmin-Karavayev were Eastern-rite Catholics. Sergei Prokopovich and his wife Ekaterina Kuskova were left-wing economists who preferred reform to revolution. Yuly Aikhenvald rejected the future Communist idea that literature existed as a vehicle of social improvement and argued that personality, and personal originality, were the source of well-being in society. Kizevetter admired Tolstoy's unheroic, sceptical view of history which focused on the relative strength or weakness of individual players and had no time for the supreme and impersonal historical process Marxism professed.

The expellees were shocked at their fate. Many were entirely innocent. After all, what had the mathematicians Polner and Selivanov done to harm the Bolshevik cause, apart from teach people to be numerate? Probably Sergei Polner, who taught the children of the Nabokovs and the Trotskys and the Kerenskys in Moscow, and who briefly became notorious for failing the fourteen-year-old future composer Dmitry Shostakovich in maths,[9] had done nothing worse than have a brother. Tikhon Polner had emigrated and was running an anti-Soviet press in Paris.[10] Sixty-seven-year-old Dmitry Selivanov was just as innocent.[11] He was nothing more dangerous than a man of aristocratic birth who became a world expert in algebra, a member of the Russian Academy of Sciences, an outstanding linguist and a great traveller. His fondness for attending international conferences only left him with a larger number of friends abroad than the closed new regime was comfortable with. Why the victims of 1922 were taken by surprise, however, was because they had no experience of totalitarianism. The idea that a single and total view of the world could be universally imposed by a brutal police regime was a new political fate in the modern world.

Apart from the prospect of the hardship they faced abroad, the expellees had every incentive to quit the new Russia. The five years since the Revolution had brought only hunger, social humiliation and imprisonment to the former ruling and culturally dominant classes. 'Let's exult in leaving', the forty-four year-old writer Osorgin who travelled on the *Haken* encouraged his fellow victims.[12] Yet almost none of the men – and one woman – on Lenin's lists wanted to go, because Russia was their homeland, despite the torments it inflicted. This reluctance to leave, felt by nearly all of Lenin's exiles, coupled with the fact that they had to go, determined the rest of their lives. It put a distance between them and the émigrés who went more willingly. The tension was in some ways unfounded, but it created the drama of the Philosophy Steamer and became the stuff of daily conflict when exiles and émigrés found themselves together, in a new invisible country called 'Russia Abroad' over the next thirty years. It made the future difficult and often lonely.

Like so many features of Soviet Russian life that would follow, the expulsions seemed barely credible. They were more suited to the ancient world than to the twentieth century. The Athenians used to vote to 'ostracize' certain members for three years and the voting process could be manipulated to get rid of political opponents. Lenin was doing something similar. Seen in a modern light the expulsions were equally incredible because they were realpolitik, not socialism. Lenin's action only followed the ways of modern empires, including imperial Russia. With deportation the idea of punishment was combined with getting rid of a social problem. This punitive cum problem-solving aspect of the nineteenth-century imperial ethos especially recommended itself to Lenin, in whose hands it took on an unprecedented form: building on tsarist practice. Even Plato only dreamt of banishing the poets, whereas Lenin made ideological banishment a reality.

In retrospect the expulsions marked off Russia as the territory where an as yet unique political experiment, which we now know to have failed, was about to begin. Lenin pioneered a division between a Western world that believed in freedom and a Russia that did not. The mass deportation of a large portion of the intelligentsia was a terrible act. In the bitter words of one Russian historian from the present day:

> There never [was] a pre-planned collective deportation of minds like this in history. [It was] a huge qualitative blow, coinciding with the lumpenization and conformatization of society and the spread of dogmatism and primitivism in social awareness.[13]

To excavate the story now is at once to fill in a missing chapter that confirms some of the darkest aspects of the early years of Soviet Communism and Lenin himself, and to evoke a lost world.

Of course for Russians the Philosophy Steamer has a special poignancy. What Leninism stripped out of the Russian fabric was what those ships carried away, in terms of cultural decency and intellectual independence. If, in forcibly modernizing a backward country, Lenin all but killed off the spirit of the old intelligentsia, today's Russians want at least to know what that world was like. In any case they are predisposed to admire it. The industry surrounding the rediscovered Philosophy Steamer is probably only just beginning.

The historian I quoted above, though, was bitter when the story of the Philosophy Steamer came to light in the 1990s. 'They threw away what was never theirs to give' was another writer's response.[14] The pity of the present rediscovery of the past is the way the event has been used to support all kinds of new irrationalism and national mysticism proclaimed in the name of the recovered Russian spirit.[15]

I've tried to take a more dispassionate approach to the lost Russian past, while benefiting from some of the spadework done by others in the past thirty years. In 1978 an émigré Russian historian, Mikhail Geller, published a groundbreaking article, in Russian and French, in which he recounted the story of the arrests and the ideological climate surrounding them, and made Lenin's personal role clear.[16] In 1988 the German historian Karl Schlögel published a study of what made postrevolutionary Russia 'modern', including a long chapter on the deportations. By the time the Soviet Union collapsed several Russian historians were uncovering the subject, and the wave of interest culminated in Mikhail Glavatsky's *Filosofsky parokhod* (2002). Most recently V. G. Makarov has published the GPU records of the 1922 Purge. All these sources have been useful to me, but I owe a particular debt to Glavatsky and also to the work done in the Soviet archives by the late Dmitry Volkogonov for the several volumes he published on Lenin in the 1990s.

My approach concedes that the expulsions, the product equally of Lenin's political cunning and his vision, were a relatively mild act in vicious times. His plan to 'rationalize' Russia and build an efficient modern state meant destroying all schools of thought opposed to Bolshevism, and as a priority removing the religious thinkers who spoke to the individual conscience of the people. This was a totalitarian project. But Lenin, who knew the West was watching, masked its true nature by, in this case, ensuring the non-violent removal of the philosophers.

The West accepted what it was told by Lenin about his own vision for Russia's future. For most of the twentieth century it was widely believed that Lenin, as a Marxist, stood for the culmination of Enlightenment in his country. Many historians accepted that he wanted to see reason triumph over superstition and to lay the foundations for a modern, egalitarian, in some sense democratic state. Since Lenin's aim to free Russia from an obscurantist religious past was one he would share with other world leaders of his day (Atatürk in Turkey was a great example), and with Western political leaders of several generations to come, it was readily intelligible. Quiet support for Lenin's rationalism seems to me why Western historians avoided tackling the subject of the Philosophy Steamer during the Cold War. The expulsions were primarily associated with expelling the last exponents of an outdated and harmful mysticism from Russia. Lenin went too far in his choice of means but surely, the implicit reasoning went, the advance of secularism was good.[17]

As a secularist I have a great deal of sympathy for this position. Yet clearly there was something wrong with making the outrage to human rights the only objection to the expulsions. To see the religious philosophers who fortuitously lent their name to the Philosophy Steamer as redundant idealists was to fail to appreciate the peculiar condition of religious thought in Russia.[18] Reason in that country took a perverse, political form in the twentieth century which became the foundation of the totalitarian system. It led to a militant and incriminating ban on all expressions of faith and an attempt to destroy individual conscience and human inwardness. To favour reason over religion, under such conditions, as the right choice for Russia in 1922, was not self-evidently correct, and certainly it is not from our vantage point today. On the other hand what makes our long-delayed familiarity with the story of the Philosophy Steamer all the more interesting is precisely the fact that behind its absence from the historiographical agenda lies a further story of the recurring conflict of reason and faith, and their political usefulness at different times in history.

This is still the only book on the subject available in English, and I hope it will be useful for two reasons. The first, obvious reason is that it documents a little-known moment in Russian history for those who don't read Russian. The context is a showcase for how the Leninist totalitarian state was created and what lessons Stalin could learn from it. The second is that I have taken a different approach from Russian historians, whose interest in the story has so far mostly been limited to what happened to Lenin's victims in Russia, and not what followed abroad. Russian commentators have also tended to see the significance of the Philosophy Steamer only in the context of Soviet history. They have concentrated on publishing 'secret' archive material and laid great store by the quantity of people expelled. My preference, in contrast, has been to consider the human story and its significance. I do speculate on precisely who was expelled, and when, but I have confined these thoughts to an appendix.

PART I

'…the Leninist bacchanalia…'

Victor Frank, 'Lenin and the Russian Intelligentsia'

'Never, of course, have I thought of
"chasing away the intelligentsia"…'

Lenin to Gorky, 13 February 1908

The Night Before

WHO WERE THE men on the Philosophy Steamer? Lenin thought of them as the class enemy, but how did they think of themselves, and what was their world like before it was so violently disrupted? The contrast between the machinery of the totalitarian regime and the lives of real people it affected leaps out of the reminiscences of writers like Berdyaev and Lossky.

The most famous name on Lenin's list of unwanted minds, Nikolai Berdyaev, was surprised at the extreme nature of his treatment by the Bolsheviks, because he thought that both he and they were socialists. But he became resigned, sold his possessions and, like his fellow professors, resolved to face his ill-wishers with courage and stoicism. On 27 September, by that well-known railway line which links Russia's 'Asiatic' with its 'European' capital, he arrived in Petrograd from Moscow. The first, easy stage of his irreversible journey abroad was now behind him. The trains were not in the best of conditions that year, but that was nothing new. As a Russian Berdyaev felt he belonged to a people more resilient than most, one which had shown in recent years that it could put up with almost anything. After his experience during the Revolution, when a bomb dropped in the courtyard of the family home and then again during the Civil War when a basement near his bookshop was blown up, nothing frightened him. A train without heating and without water he hardly noticed.

He was forty-eight. With him on his last Russian train were his fifty-one-year-old wife Lidiya Yudifovna, Lidiya's younger sister Evgeniya Rapp, estranged from her husband, and their mother Irina Vasilievna Trusheva. Though she would live another eighteen years, Berdyaev's mother-in-law was not in good health and walked with a stick. The Berdyaevs were a conscientious family of an old-fashioned kind, who looked out for each other, as well as for strangers in need.

Berdyaev's Petersburg colleague, Professor Lossky, not himself to be expelled for another two months, had offered to put up the party for the night. His address was Kabinetskaya Street, about ten minutes' walk south from where the Fontanka river flowed under the city's central thoroughfare, the Nevsky Prospekt, and about the same distance from the Moskva railway station. In fact the station was still referred to as the Nikolaevsky after the last tsar, Nicholas II. The tsar was murdered in 1918 but Russia was only slowly becoming Sovietized. At the station Berdyaev, a wealthy man while still in his own country, called a cab, while a few streets away preparations were made for his arrival.

Interesting Russian families from the pre-revolutionary intelligentsia came together in a subdued Petrograd that night: the Berdyaevs and the Losskys, and the Trushevs and the Stoyunins, the families into which the two men had married. The Berdyaevs, with their family seat in Kiev, were aristocracy. Nikolai's father was a military man, and his mother half-French. *Her* mother was the Comtesse Choiseul. French was thus one of Berdyaev's languages from infancy, and a maternal influence was Roman Catholicism, which took its place alongside his father's Orthodoxy. Berdyaev never disdained his privileged background. Instead, like two of Russia's most famous aristocratic revolutionaries, Alexander Herzen and Peter Kropotkin, he aspired to the classic imperative of *noblesse oblige.*[i]

Kropotkin was already an adult when he rebelled against his army background, but Berdyaev left military cadet school in his mid-teens. Like Herzen he studied philosophy and in the 1890s philosophy led him directly to Marxism, and thence to a repudiation of it and a clash with both the tsarist government and the upcoming Bolsheviks. For his part in revolutionary disturbances at the University of Kiev, Berdyaev found himself in a mild form of internal exile from 1902–4. Thereafter, and especially after the 1905 Revolution, he embarked on a packed career as a teacher, social campaigner and public figure that only ended with his death abroad in 1948. All this was consistent with Berdyaev's position as an *intelligent*, a member of the ultimately mixed-class intelligentsia. From cradle to cathedra, his task was to help the Russian peasantry and lower classes find their place in a more dignified and just social system than tsarism represented.

Berdyaev met Lidiya, the daughter of a notary, in Kiev in 1904, just after his return from exile and her release from prison. Both the Trushev girls were well educated, and had spent a year or so in Paris perfecting their accomplishments. But in the way of the educated Russian middle class Lidiya and Evgeniya were also socially aware, and had in their late teens naturally fallen into the Populist way of 'going to the people' and teaching both general subjects and political awareness in the backward countryside. After indulging in 'revolutionary activities' in 1903 they were held for three months in prison, where they went on a hunger strike.[2]

The meeting of Berdyaev and Lidiya fulfilled an idealistic yearning for love and understanding on both sides, and after Lidiya divorced her first husband in 1904 they married. Neither partner seems to have had a pronounced sensuality and according to Berdyaev their marriage was unconsummated, leaving him saddled for life with 'the fateful problem of sex'.[3] Nevertheless they forged a lifelong bond of shared religiosity and social commitment, coupled with the habits of leading a cultivated life. They read the classics, listened to music and followed political developments from day to day, and they lived frugally. Nikolai's character was stormy and solitary, Lidiya was nervous and sometimes hysterical, but somehow this quintessential pre-Freudian pair complemented each other perfectly. It is probable that Lidiya and Evgeniya when young were too hastily married off to men who were of the right class but were not choices of the heart, since

Evgeniya also left her husband, Rapp. As an unmarried woman, she became – rather like Martha Freud's sister Minna – part of her sister's family and a devoted friend of her brother-in-law. Indeed, when Lidiya died Evgeniya cared for Nikolai in his last three widowed years and he dedicated his autobiography to her.

The Losskys were both less political and less eccentric than the Berdyaevs. Nikolai Lossky's provincial origins were also far more modest, though not lowly. His paternal grandfather was an Eastern-rite Catholic priest and his father was a forest warden who became a district police superintendent. Nikolai was one of fifteen children. They lived in a small town near the Russian–Latvian border, in what was a largely Polish area. A bright, quiet boy, he made his way with ease through school until he ran into a political barrier. In his late teens he fled abroad from the repercussions of being a political critic of tsarism and began his tertiary studies in Switzerland. In his twenties he married into the educated middle class, what one might call Russian haute bourgeoisie.

Lossky was also a philosopher, but one in the academic tradition, which removed him, at least in manner, from the more individualistic and charismatic world of Russia's mystical thinkers. Berdyaev's warnings and predictions and visions concerning the social and spiritual life of his contemporaries never pretended to be scientific, whereas Lossky, in his quest for goodness and truth, laid stress on rationality and method and could expect to have his work reviewed in an international professional publication like *Mind*. Yet in practice the distance between the contributions to philosophy of Berdyaev and Lossky was not so great, because both were thoroughly Russian, working in a different time-frame from Anglo-American argument and differing also from Continental European philosophy. They reached back to structures of thought long discarded by mainstream rational thought in the West. At a time when Wittgenstein and Russell were insisting on the primacy of precise language coupled with mathematical logic, Lossky was trying to revive the work of the seventeenth-century rationalist and deist, Gottfried Leibniz. Berdyaev drew his inspiration, even more radically, from the mystical tradition born in Ancient Greece. His sources were Plato, neo-Platonists like Plotinus, the Greek Church Fathers, Nicholas of Cusa in the fifteenth century and the anti-rationalist Jacob Boehme two hundred years later.

In his *History of Russian Philosophy*, written in the early 1950s, Lossky would write of Berdyaev:

> Berdyaev is particularly concerned with the problem of personality. It is a spiritual not a natural category. It is not a substance, it is a creative act ... Some of his thinking is not in strict conformity with the traditional doctrines of the Orthodox and Catholic churches ...[4]

Berdyaev, paradoxically much more modern in spirit than Lossky, was interested in what today would be called performative acts of cognition. He was a maverick figure, who took chances and refused to belong to any particular time or tendency. His vocabulary was often vague and mystical but one of his achievements was to grasp the importance that twentieth-century thinkers would accord to subjectivity.

That September evening in 1922 the two philosophers sat for hours ruminating. There was much to report, Berdyaev was garrulous, and both were well informed. The city of St Petersburg, where Lossky had studied, married and was bringing up his children, was part of the family identity and a part of it which perhaps had taken the greatest battering of all in the last decade. 'Piter', as it was colloquially called, had been renamed Petrograd at the beginning of the war with Germany, because the tsar found the traditional name too Germanic. The linguistic move, though intelligible, was discomfiting, and became a token of the city's self-alienation in the early years of the Soviet takeover. Prior to having its status as capital city removed, and being further renamed Leningrad in 1924, Piter would be deliberately run down as the hub of European Russia, and something of that debilitation could already be felt.

In 1922 the philosophy department where Lossky had worked for sixteen years was under Bolshevik pressure to close. An Institute of

Red Professors was already working up a suitable sociology to underpin Soviet academic life. The St Petersburg girls' high school which Lossky's mother-in-law, Mariya Stoyunina, had founded with her husband and run in the family name for more than thirty years, had recently been forced to go co-educational and change its name to a number. As Gymnasium No. 1, however, it was still functioning, on the lower floors of the building where the Losskys lived in Kabinetskaya Street, and with its reputation for excellence intact.[5]

Amongst Madame Stoyunina's present pupils was the Losskys' second son Boris and his friend 'Mitya' Shostakovich, already a pianistic prodigy. Shostakovich's sister Mura also attended, as did Olga and Yelena Nabokova, sisters of the future novelist Vladimir Nabokov, before the family fled in 1919. The Nabokovs, a well-known conservative family, were in a dangerous situation following the Revolution, because Vladimir Dmitrievich Nabokov, the novelist's father, had been a minister in the Provisional Government which the Bolsheviks overthrew. Had Nabokov senior remained in Russia he would have been in danger of his life.

The Stoyunina school remained, for a few more months, one of the great clearing-houses for the children of the Russian pre-revolutionary professional class to establish themselves in their parents' footsteps. Before the merger of some establishments, and the closure of others, prior to the complete Sovietization of schooling, privileged boys had gone to the Shidlovskaya Academy. All the top people, across the political board, from the man who was briefly Prime Minister in 1917, Alexander Kerensky, to Lev Trotsky, now Lenin's Commissar for War, sent their sons there. But now in these mixed, transitional times, a *perekhodnaya situatsiya*, as Russians say, patterns were breaking. The Kerenskys had also fled abroad. No one could know what kind of world was about to emerge after November 1917, least of all the young Shostakovich whose life and music would be tormented by Soviet ways.

Daily life in 1922 had the character of a switchback. On the one hand things felt almost normal after the Civil War and the Famine, while on the other persecution, imprisonment and murder lurked around every corner. Despite the goods in the shops and the cafés and theatres restored to life, and happier faces on the boulevards, the political year had been horrific, with the show trials of the clergy from April to June, and the trial of the Socialist Revolutionaries (SRs), Lenin's former allies, in July. Sentences of death were passed on men whose only crime was to belong to the opposition. In the midst of the trials, in May, the head of the Orthodox Church was arrested. Patriarch Tikhon was held indefinitely while the Bolsheviks replaced his church with a more compliant model, called, with deliberate and heavy irony, *zhivaya tserkov*, 'The Living Church'.

The growing power of this fake institution enraged Berdyaev as he prepared to leave the country.[6] The very term was a typical Bolshevik ploy, meaning the opposite of what it said and designed to deceive simple minds. The way the Communists tampered with the Church, and murdered its priests, confirmed general suspicions about the nature of the revolutionary ruling ideology. The great Russian philosopher of the previous generation, Vladimir Solovyov, had warned, just before his death in 1900, of the coming of Antichrist. Frank, Karsavin, Ilyin, Vysheslavtsev, Aikhenvald, all prominent members of the intelligentsia, felt the spirit of Christian Russia was in danger. Lossky, a devout, lifelong believer, sustained by a personal God the way Berdyaev was not, did not express himself so passionately, but he had no doubt of the evildoings of the day which coupled with the usual human vices to blight the new era.

In his eloquent autobiography Lossky remembered how he had been forced to wait for a chair of philosophy in Petrograd until the relatively late age of forty-six. He was not a man to bear grudges, but he might have wished for an easier career path, especially as he was not the kind, unlike the flamboyant Berdyaev, to build his worldly adventures into his writing. The member of Faculty who had stood in his way for years, and who had even once told him, 'you get a chair over my dead body', or words to that effect, was now a leading member of the 'Living Church'. Every generation has its godless opportunists and the one in Lossky's midst was a moral philosopher – and priest – called Professor Alexander Vvedensky.

The Living Church member Berdyaev focused on, however, was Robert Yurievich Vipper. Vipper, a sixty-three-year-old historian and expert in religious studies, was the Bolsheviks' replacement for Tikhon as head of the new Church. Vipper had compared the present moment in ecclesiastical history with the great watershed in European history when Martin Luther dissented from Rome, but that to Berdyaev was an outrage. Far from being equal to the emergence of Protestantism, the phoney Living Church was an invention of 'the bureaucratic Petersburg mind' on which the whole phenomenon of Bolshevism could be blamed. On the eve of his departure from Russia most of Berdyaev's key ideas about the country's fate were already formed. This one concerned the harm Russia's modernization would wreak, if guided by 'the bureacuratic Petersburg mind' to follow Europe down a secular, rational and technocratic path.

It is a commonplace of Western political science that Soviet Communism evolved partly as a substitute for and continuation of Russia's traditional collective religosity. The ruthless wielders of political power in twentieth-century Russia, first Lenin then Stalin, derived at least some of their authority from the religious craving of the people for unity and belonging. But as an alternative to these theories, which highlight Russia's unique weaknesses, Berdyaev concentrated instead – half a century and more ahead of his time – on what European thinkers after the Second World War would call the danger of 'the Enlightenment project'. In his battle with Bolshevism and with Communism this was the message he repeated over and over, that without a sense of the transcendent it was difficult to see how humanity could remain in touch with its greater aspirations towards spiritual freedom and moral self-determination. Technology, the rise of a world entirely geared to human need, and in which nature appeared to be reduced to a convenience, was for Berdyaev likely to blunt the kind of sensitivity in human beings essential to their refined cultural survival.

And so Berdyaev had a heated exchange with the Losskys about 'the bureaucratic Petersburg mind'.[7] To any Russian it would be clear that Berdyaev was referring in part to the city's founder, Peter the Great, who built his stone palaces on the marshy banks of the Gulf of Finland against vast natural odds. The phrase also evoked the spirit of Pushkin's poem 'The Bronze Horseman' which dramatized the struggle of the humble individual against the mighty power of the ruler. One of its subtexts was the moment when the eighteenth-century tsar who opened Russia's window on Europe exposed his people to his 'Enlightenment' experiments with new 'technology'. Pushkin wrote about this fundamental clash of homespun Russian and modernizing Western values in the nineteenth century and Lenin enacted it again with his Soviet experiment in the twentieth. If there was such a thing as 'the bureaucratic Petersburg mind' it evidently spanned three centuries. In each case the problem was a process of Europeanization and rationalization imposed upon formless, suffering, traditional Russia. Lenin stood for reason as a principle of social order, and he stood for technological advance, but both of these worked in opposition to the traditional forces of religion and tradition – and a perverse kind of goodness.

Watching Berdyaev, with his long hair and hard, bright, visionary eyes, from across the table, Boris Lossky and his elder brother Vladimir, already at university, had their first intellectual taste of 'the magnificent figure of the Moscow oracle' that night. They resisted him, because he was not how they supposed a philosopher should be. A more plausible intellectual model was their father, a Fabian socialist and a Westernizer who loved England.

They considered Russia's recurring struggle between tradition and modernization. What Lenin had introduced to it was the Marxist class war. That was why both these distinguished families were on their way out of Russia. The Losskys were indeed Russian haute bourgeoisie, who led domestic and professional lives on a par with their counterparts in Berlin and Paris and represented a level of civilization the growing Russian metropolitan middle class could be proud of. They kept a French-speaking maid, Mazyasiya, and a governess for their children. They went to concerts and opera, they travelled, they knew languages and they kept abreast of international developments. Then suddenly, into this almost Proustian world, at a time when Lyudmila Lossky was expecting their fourth child, Leninism broke in. The day Andrei Lossky was born, in May 1917, the family could hear the sound of riderless horses galloping down neighbouring Ivanovskaya Street. The Bolsheviks had attacked and were seizing control of a 'bourgeois' printing press. A group of Cossacks sent to defend the printers was thrown into confusion when the raiders frightened their horses and caused a stampede. The incident was one of a series contrived by the Bolsheviks since the February Revolution to weaken the Provisional government and, coinciding with Lyudmila's confinement, it passed into family legend.

A year later, when the Losskys' ten-year-old daughter Marusya died of diphtheria in one of those outbreaks of disease which seemed already to set the seal on Russia's isolation from the world in 1918, the Losskys began to feel ever more vulnerable. Through 1920 and 1921, at the height of the famine which killed millions on the lower Volga and thousands in the cities, they only survived with the help of food parcels sent by a former Stoyunina pupil who had married in England. (Her name was Natalie Duddington, née Ertal, and she would earn a name as a prolific translator into English of Russian literature and philosophy.) Contact with abroad marked the Losskys out politically while they were still in Russia, but it helped them reshape their later lives. Three-year-old Andrei was so grateful for the gifts of tinned milk delivered to his family via the American Relief Administration (ARA), which was working to ease the Russian famine, that he fell in love with that notional Anglo-Saxon world where the word 'milk' originated and grew up an Anglophile. Meanwhile his father Nikolai wondered already if the family should not emigrate, when, hard on the heels of Civil War and hunger, he had to struggle to come to terms with the cold-blooded murder of several of his close colleagues and their wives, and one of the country's great poets, Nikolai Gumilyov, in the so-

called Tagantsev Affair of August 1921. The GPU, still known by its
pre-1922 name the Cheka, was growing in notoriety. Nikolai Lossky
knew he had to make plans to move abroad even if he was reluctant to
act on them.

Berdyaev would never have emigrated, had he not been forced. He
identified his whole being with something he felt to be Russian Truth,
and for which he needed to be in Russia to contribute. Berdyaev
believed in Russian exceptionalism, and in his own. He did not think
the Russians were a Western people and hoped the distinction would
work to their advantage. As things looked to him in 1922, Russia had
not surrendered itself to European civilization and 'the international
city'. It still had indigenous culture and religion, and could make a
world of its own. Its unique flower was still in the making, and,
although the internationalist Bolsheviks were trampling the seeds,
Russia was the country where he wanted to be. In fact, Berdyaev
agreed with much that had been said by the Austrian theorist of
history Oswald Spengler in his recently published *Decline of the West*,[8]
that Russia was the rising civilization in Europe, in the latest stage of
its history.

The urgency of Berdyaev's desire to rescue Russia from a great
mistake made him excited that September night and his voice grew
louder. The Bolsheviks were changing the streets, the institutions, the
university, the language. They didn't understand the sacredness of
traditional life. On the other hand Berdyaev was ready to concede that
the Revolution was good for the soul, that people needed shaking up,
so he didn't altogether disapprove of the present upheaval, only the
prospect of a barbaric outcome. A man waiting for the Russian people
to be reborn, he was a fiery type who might have been invented by
Dostoevsky. Always fierce, always angry that anyone should doubt he
was right, he was a fervent judge of the moral condition of the world.

Lossky, saner, more prosaic, couldn't agree. But at the same time he
simply couldn't understand who would want to destroy his way of life.
What had the Losskys and their kind done? His boys and their
friends, as they inherited the best of what Russia had to offer, helped

fill the world with talk of literature and music and art, and they led gentle lives. What was wrong with that? Another of the men on the boats, the writer Osorgin, would express exactly the same middle-class consternation in a novel he wrote a few years later, depicting the destruction of educated life after the Revolution.

Osorgin's *A Quiet Street* embodied and memorialized the social capital Bolshevism destroyed. Possibly modelled on the household of another future exile, the Moscow professor Alexander Ugrimov, it makes slightly unreal reading today, despite its realistic portraits of suffering. To its defenders like Osorgin and Lossky, Russia's pre-revolutionary culture was superior because it took the best from Russia and from an older Europe superior to the present. They defended traditional Russian culture despite the Empire's political weaknesses. Their country's unusual place in the world, and in European history, seemed to them a great good, because its ethos was not tainted by a misplaced faith in science and technology to solve every human problem. The most admirable Russian culture, shot through with educated Christian traditions, was still more a matter of idealism than materialism, and that distinguished it from the progressive West.

Lossky loved the culture that was slipping away from him, and he kept hoping to keep it alive. But then he remembered a story his son Boris, Borya, had told him, that one day a servant girl who worked for the family had rounded on them petulantly and retorted: 'All your Pushkin-Lyagushkins! They will go to the devil now, you see.' Boris had a good eye for detail and recalled many things. In his own memoirs he would recall how his parents and the Berdyaevs had supper on that unforgettable evening in September 1922.[9]

Lenin was an astute, silent presence among the gathered members of the two families. He probably could have traced the shape of the conversation in advance. He knew the intelligentsia he was part of. He knew he would have to bring the key aspects of private life, like the Church, and like the proud, Europeanized identity of St Petersburg, under state control. Russia had a natural maximalism which made it ripe for totalitarian control and Lenin felt no hesitation about exploiting that weakness and effectively taking over from God and the tsar, God's representative on earth. God was the people's superstition, their opium, as Marx said. Now Lenin would be their opium. The Russian masses would do as they were told, behave as he wanted them to, because Lenin was in God's place, and the tsar's. It was the intelligentsia that had to be tamed. In 1922 the intelligentsia was the great problem.

One difficulty outsiders always experience in trying to understand Russian history – and this despite reading Dostoevsky – is how in the end all individuals seem to be automatically caught up in political and religious conflicts. But commitment had been in the nature of an intelligent Russian life since the early nineteenth century. The moral imperative derived from the idea that no thinking person could be neutral in the face of tsarism. A good man was bound to fight against the autocracy. In the West it was a different, but related, idea that Marx pioneered, that the struggle for a decent life entailed a conflict between the bourgeoisie, which had power and capital, and the proletariat, which did not. As a result, every man either by virtue of his birth or his commitment pursued the interests of one class or the other in everything he did. What marked the last decade of nineteenth-century Russia was how these two ways of thinking coalesced. Every intelligent Russian had a stake in a better future for his country, whether he or she was Marxist or not. Reform was the world Lenin and the expellees shared, and it created the backdrop for the last passionate episode in the life of the pre-revolutionary intelligentsia.

The main reason why Marxism was so popular in university and journalistic circles in 1890s Russia, and why those who would change Russia would be Marxist, was the absence of any other way of thinking likely to bring about long overdue social and political change. The only real alternative, Populism, centred on a romanticized admiration of the peasantry and on Russia's unique social and historical circumstances. Its peaceful and specific nature was widely cherished. But the truth remained that Populism was a sentimental vision without a political engine behind it. Marxism was dynamic, global and presented itself as scientific. The theory of peasant socialism was still-born beside the vigour of Marxist economics. Sergei Bulgakov, Semyon Frank and Pyotr Struve all studied Marxist economics before breaking away.

In truth Berdyaev, Semyon Frank and others around them were always liberals. But their Western-style gradualism, with its eventual target of greater equality and justice for all, had no counterpart in Russia, and for a while they had to call themselves Marxists in the hope of getting something done. Their mature careers took shape around the realization that they would have to find a special Russian way of expressing the core human values upheld in the West by political liberalism. Their language couldn't be Marxist, but what it should be, in order to uphold Russia's peculiar political and moral needs, was never certain. For better, for worse, they chose the language of religion.

All the Russian liberal thinkers wanted reform and welcomed an end to the imperial order by one means or another. Only in philosophy they objected to Marxism's fundamental tenet, materialism, as both uncongenial and un-Russian. When Berdyaev published his first book, in 1900, with a long introduction by Struve, it was to make clear that Russia's social and political reform should be driven by spiritual values. There should be a revolution of the human person before all else. The idealists were distrustful of a materialist theory of history that made individuals less than men of Christian free will.

Berdyaev, Frank and Bulgakov combined aspects of political liberalism, philosophical idealism and socialism in their various ways of thinking. The importance of transcendent moral values made them Christian rather than secular socialists. They were closet liberals but who shared a quest for social justice with Marxism. Before the Revolution Berdyaev and Frank envisaged a very slow unfolding of socialism in Russia. Since that goal was likely to be far in the future, the country's immediate, relatively pleasing prospect was a long period of Russian closeness to the West. On the other hand Russia and the West would never be the same. The thrust of everything Berdyaev,

Frank and Bulgakov wrote from the turn of the century reflected a Russia politically compatible but spiritually distinct from Europe.

The religious philosophers were directly opposed to the international, but in effect isolationist, ideology Lenin was trying to impress on the newly awakened Russian people. Party organization and ideology aside, Lenin was their opponent from the moment he published his 'philosophical' position in 1909, when he made clear in *Materialism and Empiriocriticism* that he hated religion and its preachers. Lenin considered that spokesmen for religion were only one more arm of the 'bourgeoisie' which was anxious the world over to defend its property and financial interests against the proletariat and exploit that propertyless class which had no capital. The 'materialist' Lenin forced a class-war identity on his 'idealist' opponents in philosophy by branding them bourgeois apologists. But in fact Berdyaev and his kind resisted materialist economics because they believed that without religion moral standards were difficult to determine. Lack of concern with morality was a weakness of Marxism. There was nothing in Marxist materialism which guaranteed universally, regardless of social class, the sanctity of the individual. That was what made them anti-Marxists above all.

The two sides were competing on different planes. They had a conflicting idea of what philosophy and politics were about. Lenin's instruments were class warfare and historical inevitability, tools borrowed from Marx, combined with his own political machinations and scurrilousness. The idealists by comparison were politically naive, but they had philosophical learning and the history of Christianity and Western mysticism on their side.

For most of the period between 1903 and 1917, when the idealists built up an unprecedented cultural strength and influence, Lenin was in voluntary exile from Russia. When he returned there was bound to be a clash between Lenin, the self-styled Marxist internationalist, and these men of 'the Silver Age', many of whom had mystical visions of modern Russia. The mystical thinkers were teaching at the universities and philosophical-religious institutes and societies, and writing prodigiously in the press. They shared with some Marxists a passionate exploration of the philosophy of hope; but their focus was on the hope which underlay centuries of Christianity, not secular egalitarianism. Socialism was mainly a secular political movement in the West, but not so in Russia where Christian socialism was richly represented. The Russian religious idealists encouraged effort and conscience and imagination on an individual basis. With their adaptation of traditional Christian teaching, and also with a spiritual interpretation of land and labour, they aspired to make Russia a moral country, whereas Lenin, by contrast, believed in the 'science' of Marxism to make Russia an efficient, modern industrial society, secular and collective in character. It was in this sense that the two camps clashed – the religious men with their 'idealism' and Lenin with his 'materialism'.

On the night of 27 September the Losskys and the Berdyaevs ate a meal together, perhaps a *zapekanka* of baked vegetables and potatoes, plain food for old times' sake, drank their tea and went on talking about these intractable things. As Vissarion Belinsky, literary father of the nation, once said, 'We haven't yet solved the problem of God and you want to eat!' They hadn't yet solved the *cultural* problem of Bolshevism. How could they stop talking? The most obvious thing about Lenin was the tyranny of vulgarity he was pressing on Russia. He was the latest in a line of crude, violent upstarts in Russian history. He used vulgar language. No one in the history of philosophy had ever expressed himself so bluntly and with such violence. He spoke of religion as getting off on the dead.[10] The brutishness of what was being foisted upon educated Russia veered from the painful to the laughable.

Take the way, Lossky said, that they had hounded Kizevetter, whose history lectures were so popular. The Bolsheviks wanted to drive him out of the history faculty, indeed to banish him from the university altogether, so they stencilled a big poster saying 'COMRADES! AS MANY OF YOU SHOULD GO TO BUKHARIN'S LECTURE AS GO TO THE LECTURES OF PROKOPOVICH AND KIZEVETTER!' and hung it at the back of the room.[11] Prokopovich, forewarned that he would be banished, had already left

Russia. As for Kizevetter, he was arrested the same night as Lossky and Berdyaev and subjected to a miserable trick. He didn't want to leave Russia, and he was an eminent man, an elder of the academic community, on whom, perhaps, the Bolsheviks should not be seen to be inflicting such a fate. So they waited until he had sold everything, even his apartment, then offered him a reprieve. He could stay in his *beloved* Russia if he so wished. The sarcasm was typical of the ignorant executives recruited by the political police to carry out operations like the 1922 purge. The truth was Kizevetter could hardly stay in Russia with no job, no possessions and no apartment. The trick reduced him to despair.[12]

Lyudmila Lossky wondered how Piter struck her guests. Many visitors found the city half-dead in 1922, but Lyudmila felt loyal, and hopeful that the New Economic Policy (NEP) would pay a social dividend. The 'War Communism' which had prevailed until the previous year had almost destroyed the country by freezing commerce with the outside world. But these days things had loosened up to such a degree that the Nevsky Prospekt, the main Petrograd thoroughfare, was being called the NEPsky.[13] Thanks to the NEP the trams were running, the shops were full, people had time to stop and talk, it was almost like the old days.

Neither she nor they were quite convinced. Indeed, Lossky reverted to the story of his illness after the appalling Tagantsev Affair, which had deprived him of several of his colleagues. That was when he and Lyudmila had seriously thought of leaving the country as a family. Someone had told them of a trick worth trying. First Nikolai had to escape over the border into Finland alone, then Lyudmila should go down to the morgue and identify some poor tramp as her husband. That done, she would be free to travel with her children abroad without arousing suspicion. But either the scheme didn't sound too convincing or they weren't desperate enough. So instead they hung on to a useful contact abroad in Tomáš Masaryk, who had visited them in 1918 and was now the founder and first president of Czechoslovakia.

Masaryk, the author of a vast, unfinished work on the history of Russian thought, sympathized with the plight of the liberal intelligentsia in Russia, and had offered to make it easy for Lossky to visit the spa of Karlovy Vary for rest and recuperation. So when the GPU called midway through August, and asked Lossky to come down to its headquarters on Gorokhovaya Street, the professor thought it was to pick up his Czechoslovak visa. What a fool he was! No sooner was he down at the GPU office, the counterpart of the Moscow Lubyanka, in fact just around the corner from Kabinetskaya Street, than he found himself arrested. On the other hand the mindset and the modus operandi of the political police, by no means always violent, not even always primitive, was unpredictable. Berdyaev told the story of how he had been arrested in 1920 and interviewed in the Lubyanka by the chairman of the Cheka himself and been treated rather well. Chairman Dzerzhinsky had even listened politely to Berdyaev's lecture on why Communism wouldn't work.

Berdyaev was brave, sighed the Losskys. But lucky too. Everyone these days needed luck, whatever their moral character.

Luggage, Lyudmila began. How did you manage to pack everything? But the Berdyaevs didn't have much between them because in addition to duty being payable on certain items, there were strict regulations governing what they could take out: two complete suits of clothing, plus whatever they travelled in.[14] Lenin's victims planned to beat the restrictions by getting on the *Haken* wearing as many layers as they could manage, with every pocket filled with something or other, and of course wearing a hat. But they could hardly take their books. Also absolutely forbidden were icons, gold and jewels. Berdyaev grew gloomy and wondered how they could survive abroad without broaching the deeply alien activity of 'speculating in stocks and shares'.

He really didn't want to emigrate. One horror in prospect for the moral exiles was to be confused with the decadent émigrés like the conservative poet and mystagogue Dmitry Merezhkovsky and his wife, the poet Zinaida Gippius. Those two, tsarist exiles but supporters of the White cause in the Civil War, and who had owned a flat in Paris since before the Revolution, were out of a different world, at least as Berdyaev saw it. Nor could he do anything but argue with Pyotr Struve, who had also fought with the Whites and now lived in Masaryk's Prague. For the left-leaning Berdyaev the proper thing would have been to stay in Russia and battle it out with the Bolsheviks over what Communism really meant. His politics were a shade of red, full of contempt for the bourgeois materialist West, and therefore they should let him stay. But with a mixture of self-importance and resignation he recited what they told him down at the Lubyanka. 'They hope in the Kremlin that when you find yourself in Western Europe you will understand on which side justice lies.'[15] The Bolsheviks believed they were teaching the dissenting intelligentsia a lesson. The expulsions had something to do with that.

Berdyaev didn't like being taught a lesson and was already working out how he would retaliate. He would found a journal, and an academy abroad. He would set up a rival Russia to question every Bolshevik move. And when the Leninists died of their own poison the exiles would be on hand to restore true Russian culture. Emotionally Berdyaev and his idealist colleagues would take the spirit of Russia with them in their suitcases. No customs man could ask them for a receipt for that. Nor stop them. They would take with them the invisible and the ineffable essence of Russia and preserve it for eternity.

Privately, Berdyaev was a troubled man. His mother had suffered from liver disease during his childhood and her cries of pain at night had left him traumatized. He was a disturbed adult, who, with the addition of further unknown psychic ingredients, could seem possessed. He was like one who held the clue to a transfigured world no one else could inspect. With his consciousness pre-secular and bizarre, he was, in his way, a prime symbol of the mystical world the 'rational' Lenin wanted to banish. Moreover he had an unfortunate tic, which gave him the appearance of a Dostoevskian epileptic.

We wanted to shake hands with him, when he suddenly lurched to the right and thrust out his palm as if to push us away. First his mouth opened like the jaws of a lion and his tongue hung out, then for five to ten seconds he struggled with himself, making something like hypnotic movements with his hands, pointing his fingers, as if trying to chase the tongue back into its proper position.[16]

Boris Lossky also remembered that once a young woman came to his father, asking how to defend herself from the harmful rays emanating from the Berdyaev spirit. She said they had entered her like the devil. This was the kind of case that Freud studied in his day, and which he wrote up as the case of the deeply troubled, indeed insane, Dr Schreber. Somehow Berdyaev's tic expressed everything that was wild, woolly, neo-medieval and deeply inconvenient about his religion of creativity. And still his way of thinking had some merit because it embraced imagination and freedom.

The problem with appraising what Russia was losing or gaining by expelling Berdyaev was almost the whole problem of what modern Russia should become. It had both positive and negative sides. As Freud showed, in the days when some degree of religious or mystical thinking was second nature to most people at the end of the nineteenth century, the morbid imagination tended to conjure up wild spiritual-erotic scenarios to explain the 'truth' of existence. Perhaps Berdyaev's talk of creativity and the divine amounted to no more than that. Perhaps it was perverted because born of a politically frustrated culture, as well of a sexually frustrated man. Yet in despotic Russia, as Dostoevsky knew, it was the disturbed man who spoke out for the sacredness of the person. Berdyaev had huge weaknesses. His writing style was prolix and his philosophy was not an argument but a statement of belief. His gift was not analytical. Freud and Lenin – with Nietzsche and Marx four of the half-dozen great architects of the twentieth century – were properly Berdyaev's enemies (though he had a great admiration for his own version of Nietzsche). Still Berdyaev spoke for something decent and good, at once radically modern and medieval, and he was wise about Russia. He knew the country could not give up its Christian hope, and its mysticism, without risking losing its humanity altogether.

Left alone in Lossky's study Berdyaev ran his eyes over the rows of fine Russian volumes on the shelves: Igor Grabar on the history of art, the Wanderer painters, Pushkin, Tolstoy, Dostoevsky, the latest history by Ivanov-Razumnik. In his diary he wrote with a typical excess of words: 'Now that the moment comes to take leave of my country... the experience is more agonizing than I would myself ever have thought possible.'[17] What is to become of Russia? Supposing Spengler got it right when he said that historical fate, the fate of a culture, exists only in the sense that fate exists for a flower. If this is true then what we in Russia are losing is not even tragic, it is simply over. Ashes to ashes, dust to dust.

Berdyaev had a seizure in the night which made him cry out. The maid Mazyasiya sleeping next door had a terrible night. 'He's a monster, madame. You should have heard him shouting. I could hear these cries of "No! No!" I thought someone was being murdered. I'll never sleep next to him again. Never! If he stays, I'm leaving. S'il reste, je pars. Tant pis!'[18] But, since they were all going, it didn't really matter.

And so the time came. At two in the afternoon on 28 September, in accordance with the Russian custom governing all departures from home, the Losskys and the Berdyaevs sat for a moment and collected their spirits. The two wives said prayers, Lyudmila almost silently, Lidiya ostentatiously crossing herself. Then the large party went downstairs – five flights – to where three droshkys were waiting, and left in convoy for the Kronshtadt pier.

The Paper Civil War

THE PATRIOTIC BUT critical men about to be expelled from Russia had been in conflict with Marxism, and with Lenin and Bolshevism, since early in the century, but they didn't expect the heightened clash of opinions after the Revolution to end like this. Berdyaev and Frank hoped for constructive dialogue, as before with the tsarist government so now with the Bolsheviks, and more self-criticism on the part of the intelligentsia. They looked forward to cooperation, not schism, in line with views on Russia's way forward they had long since set out. *Landmarks*, a book of essays by them and others, published in 1909, subsequently became famous as the moment when these thinkers defined themselves against collectivism. *Landmarks* urged upon Russia the lessons of Western freedom, reason and respect for the individual. After February 1917, when Nicholas II abdicated and Kerensky formed his Provisional government, many of the *Landmarks* writers resurfaced writing for the liberal-conservative paper *Russkaya Mysl* ('Russian Thought'). Thus far they joined forces with Pyotr Struve, one of Lenin's most prominent critics, who had founded the paper the year after the 1905 Revolution.

For liberals and conservatives alike the task through 1917 was to prevent the democratic process being derailed ahead of free elections later that year. In June the veteran *Landmarks* writer Alexander Izgoev joined with Struve, Berdyaev, Frank and Sergei Bulgakov, to form a new association, *Liga russkoi kultury* (The League of Russian Culture), to try to hold a moderate Russia together in the face of extremist threats. Close to the Provisional government and including several of its members, the League took the view that Bolshevism, violent and anarchic, threatened the Russian state and the interests of the people. Insisting that 'freedom' from the old imperialism was no excuse for lawlessness, it demanded that political novelty be balanced against continuing patriotic duty. This appeal had little effect on subsequent events in Russia, but when the Bolsheviks used force to destroy the Provisional government and the intellectual dialogue only a few months later at least the men of the League knew that their fears were well-founded.

Kizevetter, who edited 'Russian Thought' with Struve, was one of the most compelling moderate voices of the day. Through most of 1917 he also wrote weekly articles for the liberal *Russkie Vedomosti*, ('Russian Gazette') in which he criticized Kadets and Bolsheviks alike for being 'enemies of the people'. When the Bolsheviks seized power he was incensed, decrying 'all this wild and destructive fanaticism unleashed on Moscow and Russia by a handful of Russian citizens who do not refrain from unheard-of evil acts against their own people, intent on securing power in their own hands at any price, violating with the most unlimited shamelessness those very principles of freedom and brotherhood which they blasphemously shelter'.[1]

Since Lenin had clamped down serially on the free press from the first days after the Revolution, the chances to say such things publicly were numbered, but while he could Kizevetter repeatedly encouraged fissiparous moderate forces to stand together to keep Russia open and lawful, while comparisons between Bolshevism and tsarism at its most repressive sprang to mind. Izgoev was one of many *intelligenty* who denounced the reinvention of the old repressions by the very party that had set out to liberate Russia from the imperial oppressor. At the end of 1917 he founded and edited a new newspaper, *Borba* ('The Struggle'), to carry on the battle against the Bolsheviks as long as he could.[2]

The issues that pitched Kizevetter and Izgoev against the followers of Lenin were both of-the-moment and matters of general political theory. They believed that not only Bolshevik violence but the very idea of socialism, by which they meant Marxism, threatened the Russian state. The problem with this imported doctrine lay in its abstract nature. It was not specific to the nation and had no actual positive action linked to it. The socialism the Bolsheviks were putting into practice was destructive of the Russian state and alien to the Russian people. For Izgoev it would be better to return to the principles of private ownership, albeit 'with certain restrictions on big business'.[3]

The war the Bolsheviks and their critics fought in the press in the first years after the Revolution needs a name to underline its importance. It may be called 'The Paper Civil War' in so far as it was a prelude to the Civil War (1917–20), the military conflict that would tear Russia apart over the next three years. To highlight this battle of ideas is to see the bitter fight between the Red and White armies as at the centre of a larger campaign – lasting from 1917 to 1922 – to destroy opposition to Bolshevism generally among the people and specifically among the intelligentsia. It is the historical-political framework I am suggesting in this book to make sense of the expulsions. Only when Lenin deported the liberal intelligentsia in 1922 did the overall conflict end. This shift of perspective is necessary to understand the neglected topic of the fate of the intelligentsia in the early Soviet years.

Almost every man on Lenin's future list of political journalists, economists, literary critics, philosophers and publishers, owed his place on the ships to his part in the paper anti-Bolshevik campaign. If he wrote for the other side, then he was likely to be deported. But this did not make the opposition all of a piece. Because the Bolsheviks controlled the historical view of the times for so long, and manipulated its popular image also in the West, much remains to be corrected about who opposed the Revolution and why. Resistance to Bolshevism came from many quarters, and certainly not just from one 'Whiteguardist' and 'reactionary' element as Lenin maintained. Libertarians, patriots, nationalists, Christian socialists, cooperatists, European-style Social Democrats all joined in pre-Communist Russia's final agony.

To consider the Christian protest first: in April 1918 when, at Struve's instigation, the *Landmarks* group published a new collection of essays, *Iz Glubiny* ('From the Depths'), the philosopher Semyon Frank expressed deep Christian reservations over what was happening in the country. The title of the collection alone, which was his inspiration, expressed a biblical 'cry from the depths' that the Revolution was 'the suicide of a great nation'.[4] For a theocrat like Frank the country's salvation could only lie in a religious conception of the state and the people. Frank's views roughly aligned him with Berdyaev's Christian Socialism and with Sergei Bulgakov's reform Orthodoxy. Bulgakov was a former Marxist who had written a poetic *Philosophy of Economy* inspired by the needs of the Russian soil, and had recently been ordained in the Orthodox Church. With hindsight Frank also bears comparison with Boris Vysheslavtsev, a writer who has stirred some renewed interest fifty years after his death, and who was Frank's best contemporary interpreter.[5]

The Church and Christian belief in post-revolutionary Russia supported various strands of anti-Bolshevik feeling. At the point closest to the institutionalized Church, an unshakeable buttress of the monarchy, stood for instance the Trubetskoy family, although the soon-to-be-exiled Sergei Evgenievich seems to have been more drawn personally to Eastern Catholicism by the time he left Russia. Sergei Bulgakov meanwhile was involved in an extensive reform of the Orthodox Church to give it a social conscience and make it more answerable to the people. The All-Russian Church Council set up to pioneer these reforms was in session when the Revolution broke out. It had left its reforms too late.[6]

The other Christian philosophers were more vague in their allegiance to the Church as an institution. On a rough scale, to show their distinctiveness, Berdyaev was mystical and idiosyncratic, Bulgakov active as a priest, Frank a pantheist inspired by Spinoza and Goethe, and Aikhenvald an impressionistic humanist who admired 'the ethical pathos of Christianity' and read Christian values into literature and art. But as 'idealists', all these thinkers were deeply attached to the moral values underpinning traditional faith. They cared above all for the sanctity of nature and the sacredness of private experience, values they couldn't derive from any other source capable of impacting on Russian life.

In 1918 Aikhenvald, sometime literary editor of 'Russian Thought', published a book entitled *Nasha Revolyutsiya, nashi vozhdi* ('Our Revolution, Our Leaders'), and later wrote a second, *Diktatura Proletariata* ('The Dictatorship of the Proletariat'). His two commentaries on contemporary history offered a consistent Christian personalist defence of freedom of speech and conscience. He valued the individual creative personality and turned his back on the impersonal power of history which the Marxists favoured. He also stressed equality before the law, which challenged the Marxist-Leninist idea of guilt according to class.[7]

The attitudes of all these liberal humanists were both valuable in themselves and might also have guarded against the rise of totalitarianism, had they been general to Russian culture and strongly enough rooted. Therefore it was not surprising that the Bolsheviks closed in on them consistently and ruthlessly from 1917 to 1922. First their publications were hit and then their lives. The editorial team who had produced 'From the Depths' now hid their stock in a warehouse to protect it against the rising 'Red Terror'. Eventually all of it was confiscated. Aikhenvald's *Our Revolution* was seized and destroyed and *The Dictatorship of the Proletariat* never published. 'Russian Thought' survived until late in 1918, when Struve fled to join the White Army,[8] but in the end no oppositional publication could survive Bolshevik thoroughness. The same year saw the closing of both the 'Russian Gazette', in existence since 1863, and the Kadet Party organ *Rech* ('Speech'), a paper jointly founded by a team including the conservative V. D. Nabokov and the leading liberal and Provisional government Foreign Minister, Pavel Milyukov. *Sanktpeterburgskie Vedomosti* (the 'St Petersburg Gazette'), which first appeared in 1728, published its last number in 1918. The monthly organ of the Popular Socialists, *Russkoe Bogatstvo* ('The Wealth of Russia'), also closed.[9] On a rough count at least ten of the 1922 expellees were prime movers behind and contributors to these censored organs which were suppressed across the political spectrum in the first year or so after the Revolution.[10]

And so the new mood of the times was established. In practice the three main political groupings unable to reconcile themselves to Lenin's ways were the SRs, the Kadets and the Popular Socialists. To these main parties could be added many writers and thinkers whose loyalties either fluctuated or couldn't be pinned down.[11] To conflate them into one 'reactionary' group, as the Bolsheviks did, was a distortion of Russian history. The Popular Socialist Party, semi-Kadet, tried to represent the people on the level of land ownership and agriculture, issues which mattered greatly in Russian politics. The Popular Socialists believed in a native form of peasant socialism for the country and defended the interests of small landowners or *kulaks*. This was the class already loathed by Lenin and which, fifteen years later, Stalinist collectivization would starve to death.[12] The religious philosophers' political loyalties were not tied to any particular party, although the Kadet Party, which embraced a range of opinion from liberal to conservative, offered most of them a passing anchorage. As its name suggested, its direction was, rarely for Russian politics, constitutional and democratic (the military-sounding connection with 'cadet' was fortuitous).

Frank was never at home in politics, but was active with the Kadets after 1905.[13] Lossky overcame his dislike of political activity to write a Kadet manifesto for the 1917 elections in Petrograd, and Kizevetter did the same in Moscow. Neither associated with the right wing of the party. Left-leaning Bolshevik opponents included the sociologist Sorokin, who was a young SR and an activist both before and after he became secretary to Kerensky in 1917, and the economists Prokopovich and Kuskova. At the turn of the century this husband-and-wife team had dismayed Lenin when they tempered their Marxism in line with the Austrian Eduard Bernstein's criticism of the historical inevitability of revolution.

The Bolsheviks, who suffered from a Marxist-internationalist interpretation of themselves, fashioned their image in the world as the
unique force that had ousted tsarism. But after 1905 that was the programme of all the main Russian parties, not least the Kadets, who
largely formed the Provisional government twelve years later. Indeed,
almost every man Lenin expelled had spent years campaigning against
tsarist social evils and had done so publicly from within Russia, unlike
Lenin himself who had worked abroad and underground. Osorgin,
Kuzmin-Karavayaev, Sorokin and Aleksei Peshekhonov, a socialist
economist, had all suffered a great deal more in tsarist jails than Lenin
himself. When Peshekhonov was arrested in 1922 he was therefore
appalled at the injustice of his situation. He complained in a sarcastic
police deposition asking for his release that 'I spent time often enough
in prisons under the old regime...'[14]

Lenin's many oppponents came from very varied social backgrounds. The aristocratic Berdyaev conformed to the class stereotype
peddled by the Leninists, but Lossky did not. The Franks were established middle-class intelligentsia, Jewish on Semyon's father's side and
German-Russian-Christian on his mother's, but, unlike Lenin's
family, made up of similar ethnic ingredients further back in its
history, they owned no land. Bulgakov came from a very poor family
of priests who nevertheless gave him the incentive to study. Sorokin's
father was an itinerant church restorer, which is how Sorokin first
came to be educated in a provincial seminary. Kuzmin-Karavayev, the
poet who would become a bishop, was born into wealthy hereditary
aristocracy, as was one of Lenin's most vociferous early economic
critics, Dalmat Lutokhin, and the university astronomer who was also
a banker, Vsevolod Stratonov. These three aristocrats all behaved quite
differently politically. Yet all were exiled under the same anti-
Bolshevik rubric.

In the five-year 'Paper Civil War' Russia would lose some of the
finest minds it had ever produced. A contemporary historian has
called the process the 'deliberate negative selection' of an intelligentsia
that was erudite, professional and cosmopolitan as never before.[15]

Here, for instance, was a generation touched but not formed by the Chernyshevskian social activism, democratic and utilitarian, which dominated the mid-nineteenth century. It consisted of men who in many cases had been partly educated abroad, which gave them the scope and experience to think about Russia's problems in a much wider context than previous generations. Aikhenvald, who before he became a literary critic studied philosophy and was a devoted interpreter and brilliant translator of Schopenhauer into Russian, took the almost unheard-of measure of writing about Russian literature in terms of art for art's sake. His attempt to abandon the tradition of art as social concern, very much part of Chernyshevsky's world, and replace it with a 'principled impressionism' caused a scandal but was a much-needed move towards the creation of a cosmopolitan middle class in Russia, which held a variety of views on what was of value to society. One of the hallmarks of the Silver Age, which began about 1890 and was carried into emigration by the generation born between 1875 and 1895, was the way in which its best minds strained to make Russia an open-minded world-class culture and not an obsessive backwater.

To add misfortune to tragedy, those opposed to Lenin were deeply committed to their country and to the Russian people, far more than Lenin himself was. Just as the military civil war squandered lives, so in the paper civil war many patriotic and constructive impulses towards the well-being of the country were stifled. There was hardly a man on Lenin's expulsion list not marked by the strong Russian Populist tradition of public service which committed him to work for his country as an organizer and teacher. Lenin and the future Communist state would be able to benefit from this voluntarist tradition and it became one of Communism's most admirable features, except that under Communism voluntarism was no longer voluntary.

The description *obshchestvennyi deyatel* – literally 'social activist', but perhaps better translated as 'public figure' – fitted many of the expellees and is still how they are best described. They belonged to a world before the Populist ethic was harnessed to Soviet Communism.

The men of the Silver Age were as ready to 'go to the people' as the intelligentsia had been fifty years earlier and, in that way, a Western reader might well see them as men created by the kind of nineteenth-century Russian literature, of Turgenev and Tolstoy above all, which is still so much admired across the world and often associated with a form of nineteenth-century socialism. Since, in the main, they were not socialists, however, the Russian reformers of the Silver Age may best be understood more loosely, as seeking a new kind of moral world through what could be made of the unique, still mostly pre-industrial condition of Russia. The banished writer and philosopher Fyodor Stepun noted of Aikhenvald what applied to nearly all his cosmopolitan contemporaries and himself, that they loved above all provincial Russia, which for them was a moral country.[16] After 1917 this was the Russia which for them had been reinvigorated and to which they wanted to devote themselves.

The idea that Russia was a universal moral force was another image fostered by the liberals and the conservatives, and which Lenin and Communism would borrow and politicize in the name of the Party. Even though they turned Russia into nothing of the kind, the ideological descendants of Lenin managed to manipulate the Soviet 'socialist' moral image worldwide for almost the duration of the twentieth century and make millions of sympathizers believe it. Yet what Soviet Russia became, and what post-revolutionary Russia might have become had the liberal intelligentsia not been forcibly removed, were not opposites. Related through old ideas of communality and service, they reflected each other. One might say the Communist phenomenon debased the true national coinage, because most of its real weight, embodied in the culture of its liberal-conservative patriots and religious men, was sent abroad.

Those who stood out for their Populist commitment in 1917–18 included Aikhenvald, who toured the provinces giving lectures on literature; Kizevetter, who gave popular lectures on history and his pet love, Russian theatre, and wrote textbooks for self-education; and the young Ivan Ilyin, a brilliant philosopher who put aside his work on

Kant and Hegel to chair a regional election commission and join a peasant executive committee. The prose writers Evgeny Zamyatin and Aleksei Remizov, and the poets Khodasevich, Yury Annenkov, Nikolai Otsup, Nikolai Gumilyov, and Alexander Blok and Kornei Chukovsky all gave their services in similar fashion. Within the regime Gorky and Lunacharsky worked with a similar devotion to the cause. No doubt because of the sense of national emergency which the Revolution inspired, the five years after 1917 produced a moving display of moral unity among an intelligentsia about to be forcibly divided.

Though the fact is far less well known because the Bolshevik version also prevailed in the West through the Soviet period, the lectures and other efforts of Aikhenvald and Ilyin and many other writers and poets in the provinces were the non-Bolshevik answer to agitprop. The intelligentsia 'went to the people' out of a love of culture and social and political idealism, something qualitatively different from the Party utilitarianism which motivated Lenin. Their aim was to teach and encourage an appreciation of Russian culture and help spread its benefits to the long deprived and illiterate masses. The hope was to disseminate a quality of culture which in turn would make a life without freedom unbearable. With the installation of the Provisional government this enthusiasm became government policy and Kizevetter was engaged as an official provincial lecturer.

Why the Bolsheviks and their liberal enemies were not wholly divided from each other was that the Russian 'spiritual-intellectual culture' which many of the non-Bolsheviks, but particularly the philosophers, were propagating and defending, was nevertheless not designed to make Russia a *culturally* Western country. In many ways Communism was the more Westernizing force. The alternative post-revolutionary cultural project emanated from the historical-philological, philosophical and juridical faculties of the universities and its purpose was to spread a 'spiritual' idea of Russianness which could be retained in partnership with a liberalized political system. But the spiritual or idealistic tenor of this way of thinking was its political weakness. Lenin was able to denounce it as 'reactionary' above all because of its frequent association with religious faith. Through that connection he could then link it with an old and unjust Russia.[17] Lenin's argument was dishonest but since Russia's 'spiritual-intellectual' culture was a rival source of national pride and hope, in competition with Marxist-Leninism, it was not surprising that he resorted to it.

What Lenin needed to crush was powerful but amorphous. Even those brought up steeped in its ways had difficulty defining it except in terms of a national distinctiveness from the West. A recipient of a typical Russian spiritual-intellectual education rooted in nineteenth-century traditions recalled many years after he had moved to England that 'My Russianness ... the way I feel about myself, my Russianness in literature, religion, music, culture, conversation ... the word *dusha* comes to mind and there's no English equivalent. The word spiritual is wrong – it doesn't mean the same thing at all.'[18] *Dusha* in literal translation is spirit or soul, but it is probably better rendered in terms of its effect within the Russian cultural context, where it encourages individual awareness, artistic refinement and conscience. The Russian spiritual tradition impelled those brought up in its ways to lead carefully examined moral and cultural lives and made them responsible for the quality of social and intellectual life round about.

This powerful and affecting Russian attitude, so elusive to foreigners, so strongly determinant of the Russian sense of moral and social duty, was what the men of the turn of the twentieth century wanted to see replicated in a democratic modern Russia. They leaned on Russia's Christian tradition to make it happen. A critic who emigrated defined the Silver Age as when spiritual Russianness reached new heights of self-awareness in philosophy, art and music and the country showed itself to the world as a primarily Christian and mystical force. The very term 'Silver Age', he claimed, belonged to Berdyaev, whose Russian personalism taught 'the freedom of creativity [based on] the Christian feeling for God, personhood and freedom'.[19] Lenin had to suppress the idealist philosophers who taught these values because they offered themselves as alternative national moral leaders.

Christianity was a strong tradition to set against Marxism. Yet when it persuaded some of the philosophers to put a moral-religious construction on the Revolution, it showed up the typical weakness of the idealists' political culture. The typical Silver Age outlook bred exaggerated hopes for Russia as a moral country. When the editor of *Landmarks*, Mikhail Gershenzon, claimed he 'accepted the Revolution because he sincerely believed that the devastating revolutionary storm would free the modern soul from the progressive scales of excessive culture and knowledge', he seemed to set the seal on a Russian cult of moral anti-rationalism which could only put obstacles in the way of modernity and progress.[20] Political effectiveness in Russia was not be gained by this means. Gershenzon was not exiled, but the rest of his life in Soviet Russia – a matter of a couple of years – was spoilt by his being torn both ways.[21] He became a martyr to the great truth about Russian history, that political effectiveness was not to be gained by moral means.

Left to its own devices the Christian humanist programme in Russia was naive because it lacked a sense of political reality. Frank's theocracy was impotent. When Berdyaev hailed the Revolution as a potential revolution in human nature, he was declaring in effect that he had no *political* programme, only a moral vision.[22] His attachment to spiritual freedom, as he called it, made him powerless. The Christian humanists needed the Kadet Party to enter politics at all and that broad church of a party collapsed under the weight of its own internal tensions. As early as 1917 Frank wrote a haunting indictment of his generation which fatefully anticipated the place 'between worlds' where Lenin would confine the 'spiritual' intelligentsia:

> Our weak intelligentsia souls are simply incapable of conceiving abominations and horrors on such a Biblical scale and can only fall into a numbed and unconscious state. And there is no way out, because there is no longer a motherland. The West does not need us, nor does Russia, because she no longer exists. You have to retreat into the loneliness of a stoic cosmopolitanism, i.e., start to live and breathe in a vacuum.[23]

Frank's generation was in the end an easy target for a totalitarian regime. At the same time the cruelty of history ensured that many of the Silver Age's moral and social preoccupations helped to give Marxist-Leninism its appeal in Russia. Communism adopted those preoccupations in a politically controlled, censored 'proletarian' form.

A small number of the endangered intellectual class was nevertheless spiritually less encumbered and more prepared for violent political action. Sorokin, the active SR turned university professor, headed north in the summer of 1918 to try to foment an armed anti-Bolshevik insurrection amongst the peasantry. He was caught and thrown into a provincial Cheka prison, where he faced the possibility of a fatal bullet fired in his direction by a malign or confused police agent. The horror of this prospect was enough to drive him to make a public recantation. He wrote to a local paper that he was renouncing politics to dedicate himself to his true academic calling. When his letter was reprinted in *Pravda* it elicited a response from Lenin himself and Sorokin was released 'on Lenin's orders'. He then remained free until the summer of 1922. It was an unusual chain of events that would come back to haunt him abroad.[24]

The second prominent anti-Red conspirator was the aristocratic Prince Trubetskoy. He became both a military enemy and the embodiment of everything the Leninists despised. Not only were the Trubetskoys high-born and pious, but they had made an outstanding contribution to Russia's 'spiritual-intellectual' culture at the end of the nineteenth century.[25] The young Prince's uncle, Sergei Nikolaevich, was vice-chancellor of Moscow University until his premature death in 1905. The Prince's father Evgeny Nikolaevich wrote a famous book on philosophy and icon-painting called *Umozrenie v kraskakh* ('Speculation in Colours') and held high office in the Orthodox Church. The family member who was to be deported, Prince Sergei Evgenievich, having studied philosophy at Moscow University, was destined to follow his father in the subject when the Revolution came. With his surname and background the latest Trubetskoy coolly wondered why he was not arrested sooner, all the more as another uncle of his, Grigory, who would become a famous coordinator of anti-Soviet opposition in exile, was fighting with the White Army in southern Russia. But somehow Sergei Evgenievich was left three years of freedom, from 1917 to 1920, during which, having failed to rescue Tsar Nicholas and his family from Bolshevik detention in Siberia, he became the brains behind the underground White organization, Tactical Centre.

The Cheka eventually arrested Sergei Trubetskoy early in 1920. The story of his survival of a year and a half in prison and his release thanks to well-wishers amongst his university colleagues, as well as the British government, is one of the most interesting stories of the post-revolutionary interregnum to have been published in the last twenty years. When he was finally deported along with the unwanted intellectuals it was not as a conspirator but for his active religious beliefs.[26]

A third activist was the editor of 'The Wealth of Russia', Venedikt Myakotin, who after October 1917 declared the Bolsheviks to have usurped power and, as leader of the Union for the Regeneration of Russia (SVR), associated himself with the White opposition. After he was arrested in December 1920 in southern Russia his release was brokered by the veteran Populist writer and contributor to his newspaper, V. G. Korolenko. This intervention took place at a time when distinction earned in the old campaign against tsarism evidently still counted for something – just – with the new regime.[27]

But even with these examples of men who actively conspired and took up arms against the Bolsheviks, even with five years of paper conflict and the occasional brush with the Cheka, the expulsions of 1922 which finally divided the intelligentsia into obligatorily pro- and anti-Lenin branches were wholly unexpected. Sorokin and Trubetskoy were more prepared to receive a bullet than a one-way exit visa. The traditional intelligentsia couldn't conceive of the kind of machinations that Lenin would perfect and the lengths to which he would go to divide and control them, precisely because his moves were so new. Totalitarianism was a political novelty Berdyaev would spend the rest of his life explaining – thirty years before Hannah Arendt undertook the task.[28] (Even so, many people in the West would never associate a 'socialist' country with inhumanity, let alone the evil that later happened under Stalin.)

The physical emergency of the Civil War and the Famine at first disguised the totalitarian Bolshevik project. The decline of industry, the rise of hunger, the chaos of social reorganization, all laid the country desperately low. Like most of the population the intelligentsia was traumatically affected by the highly restricted, state-directed economy of War Communism imposed from 1918 and which, unbeknown to them, gave an extreme foretaste of the Soviet command economy to come. The policy of commandeering agricultural produce and not allowing the peasants to trade their grain – in combination with unfortunate harvests – eventually brought famine to the Volga in 1920–21.[29] In Petrograd many writers, academics, redundant journalists and discarded bourgeois families struggled to keep themselves alive. But the idea that the Revolution and suffering were good for Russia, and somehow necessary, invited their forbearance. Thinkers toying with a new Russian, and possibly world, order did not confront what was happening as unequivocally wrong. Influenced by their Christian heritage they rationalized the benefits of suffering.

Frank's wife Tatyana left moving memoirs about how she coped in the years 1918–21. Berdyaev wrote of how he became inured to material hardship and also of how a man of his class deserved to learn the use of a shovel.[30] Solidarity with the people was integral to the Russian idea that the intelligentsia preached and made them want to adapt and share in the suffering that had befallen the whole country after 1917. It has rightly been suggested that one of the key attitudes of the Silver Age philosophers was their resistance to any of the kinds of material improvements to daily life which, in the early twentieth century, industrialization was at last bringing to Russia. They feared material ease would destroy their moral country. In this sense they saw War Communism as almost good for them, and when it subsided they hoped the moral country would be the better for it and resume a new, even exemplary, twentieth-century life.

While the Russian people and the Russian intelligentsia did not yet fully understand their potential enemy in Lenin, Lenin and Bolshevism were equally feeling their way, appraising the possibilities, looking for opportunities, testing international opinion over how they could establish their total authority in Russia. Although Lenin had no doubt what he wanted, for the duration of the Civil War the new regime lacked the muscle to wage war on its own citizens internally as well as fight the Whites, who had Allied assistance and were attacking on three fronts. In that respect, the intelligentsia benefited through 1918, and to a certain extent right up until March 1921, from a policy of cooperation. They even received some material aid specifically as a class. They might have been alerted by the harsh terms in which Lenin stated – in two *Pravda* articles in 1918 – that this policy of cooperation was *temporary* and *expedient*. But because it was their nature to hope and keep faith they were not.

Lenin, who was addressing Party workers concerned as to what their attitude to the old intelligentsia should be, was hardly ambiguous in his statement of intent:

> The slogan of the moment here is not to fight these sections [of society] but to win them over…Political distrust of the members of a bourgeois apparatus is legitimate and essential. But to refuse to use them in administration and construction would be the height of folly, fraught with untold harm to Communism…After all, even backward Russia produced…capitalists who knew how to make use of the services of educated intellectuals, be they Menshevik, Socialist-Revolutionary or non-party. Are we to be more stupid than those capitalists and fail to use such 'building material' in erecting a Communist Russia?[31]

Still the old intelligentsia didn't take this as a warning.

The story of the expulsions shows Lenin's remarkable qualities as a brilliant strategist in pursuit of his ideological goal. His passing co-operation with the traditional intelligentsia, while masking his ultimate aim, reflected the Marxist view that socialist revolution needed advanced capitalism and bourgeois life as its foundation and springboard. It couldn't develop out of nothing. Lenin also conceded the fact that temporary cooperation was practical in terms of cultural manpower, because the traditional intelligentsia boasted too much talent for the Bolshevik Russia to ignore in its first uncertain years. Thus the final battles of the Revolution on the cultural front were pushed into abeyance.

Nevertheless the Revolution had meanwhile stirred a class war at grass-roots level which Lenin was hardly interested in curtailing and for that reason alone the five years after 1917 were a difficult time to be 'bourgeois'. Five years of 'Red Terror' created a climate from which expulsion might eventually seem like an act of mercy. Trotsky would even instruct the Western press to see the deportations like that. The Marxist class war, nominally of proletarians against the bourgeoisie, motivated and excused the violence of the political police against almost anyone they chose to victimize. The Cheka, or Vecheka to give it its full name, was a new kind of Russian officialdom trained to view the 'bourgeois' intelligentsia as its collective enemy. Its behaviour was embraced in the more general term for the nastiness and pettiness of the new authorities, *sovdepiye*. The term, which literally meant the phenomenon of living under the 'Council of Workers' Peasant and Red Army Deputies', expressed middle-class Russia's first encounter with Red Terror.[32]

Osorgin's *A Quiet Street*, about the frighteningly straitened days a professor's family led when 'the people' commandeered the family home, might have been cynically subtitled 'Adventures in *Sovdepiye*'. The young man who terrorized the professor's household was the brother of their former servant. He was a familiar figure who was transformed into a dangerously unpredictable man by the gift of power. His weak, opportunist character was suggested by his desertion from the army: many of the conservative Russian middle class disapproved of Lenin's curtailment of the war against Germany as a case of moral desertion. During the course of the novel, houses, books, food and even a professional composer's piano were confiscated.

Worst of all a friend of the professor's family, the philosopher Astafiev, was arrested by the Cheka and executed in the basement of the Lubyanka prison, the place known the length and breadth of Moscow as 'The Ship of Death'. In this sequence of events Osorgin conflated what might have happened to the men of 1922, but didn't, with the fates of well-known victims of the Red Terror, in the academic community and the clergy.

What was extraordinary over the period 1917–22 was the way the intelligentsia mostly held together in body and spirit, despite this ideological offensive coupled with wartime adversity. Maxim Gorky, the great Soviet proletarian icon, author of a superb three-volume autobiography besides some lesser works, achieved a small miracle when he urged his friend Lenin to have pity.[33] Viktor Shklovsky, later to become world-famous as a pioneer literary structuralist, called Gorky in these years 'the Noah of the Russian intelligentsia'.[34] He saved many of his peers, regardless of their political persuasion. Gorky, the balance of whose reputation desperately needs to be reassessed after a decade of post-Soviet dislike, created the World Literature publishing house, and also a journal of the same name, to employ as many writers as he could. Much of the work he put their way was in translating the world's classics and thus perhaps Gorky also tried to keep some stability in Russia through stressing its links with world culture. He personally put a roof over the heads of many potential refugees from Bolshevism. Two stranded Romanov Granddukes and the poet Khodasevich were among the temporary beneficiaries. He obtained permits for his fellow writers, found food, jobs, milk for babies, medicine for the sick. His Commission for the Improvement of the Living Conditions of Scholars, and three autonomous institutions created by government statute, the Dom literatorov (House of Writers), Dom iskusstv (House of Arts) and the Dom uchonykh (House of Scholars), protected poets, academics, writers and journalists as a class from 1918, when they opened, up until 1922, when they were forced to close.[35]

The 'Houses' gave the intelligentsia a meeting place and provided subsidized rations throughout the Famine, though some writers and scholars still died. Sorokin fondly remembered as 'true science' the work of one professor who calculated that he would burn off more calories walking to the House of Scholars than he could recoup from eating the bowl of thin soup he would get by waving his pass.[36] Nevertheless Gorky's good influence was evident and remained in play until he himself was driven out of Russia for over-zealous criticism of Bolshevism in September 1921.

Another man to whom the intelligentsia looked for help in the transitional years was Anatoly Lunacharsky, who had been a playwright and spent many years in foreign exile close to Lenin, in consequence of which he found himself the first Soviet Commissar for Education and the Arts. He was able to cut through the first growths of Bolshevik bureaucracy to rescue independent literary initiatives and in one or two cases after Gorky's departure even saved lives. For instance, he seems to have intervened to remove the philosopher Gustav Shpet[37] from the 1922 lists. Shpet appealed to the memory of the boyhood, school and university years he had shared with Lunacharsky in Kiev. He made the wrong decision not leaving Russia when he could. But in 1922, because he had the right contacts, he gambled on the future going his way.

Lunacharsky was a weak character, something of an actor, who, never having achieved much in artistic or philosophical terms, relished the importance of his office and power in the Kremlin and paraded in a luxurious fur coat in times of desperation for others. Many *intelligenty*, while appreciating his efforts on their behalf, felt uneasy. Lunacharsky seemed like a portion of *sovdepiye* in himself. But it was characteristic of those times that the intelligentsia were caught between turning to uncertain friends and succumbing, if not to gratuitous meanness or life-threatening barbarity, then to a fair degree of stupidity from the Soviet regime's new worker-officials, and they needed their own kind to protect them from that additional threat.

Tolstoy's daughter Alexandra (aka Tolstaya) recorded a typical encounter with *sovdepiye* when she found the new regime trying to turn her father's estate into a collective farm. Tolstaya, who might have been a candidate for the 1922 lists but did not emigrate until 1929, went to see Lunacharsky in 1919 to protest at the proletariat's unsuitable plans for the Tolstoy heritage. She told him: 'I think that the Tolstoy estate ought to be not a Soviet farm but a museum, something like Goethe's home.'[38] Lunacharsky responded by instantly making her a Commissar for the Tolstoy Estate and giving her control over any changes. But as she wrote with hindsight, she knew she was lucky that day and might just as easily find herself in prison next morning.

Another kind of stupidity which undermined 'bourgeois life' was the new censorship the Bolsheviks started to impose. Zamyatin, who loved anecdotes and appreciated the anti-totalitarian power of laughter, liked to tell in public the story of how Aikhenvald had argued with a zealous censor who wanted to delete some lines from *Hamlet*.[39] This was not yet Stalin's Russia, when telling the wrong joke could land a man in the Gulag, but one of the things that has become clear since the end of the Soviet Union, when the archives were unlocked, is how much the immediate post-revolutionary terror which Lenin orchestrated laid the foundations for the worst Soviet institutions fifteeen years later. Thus even at the time resisting *sovdepiye*, calling a spade a spade, took courage. According to Tolstaya, her father's last secretary Valentin Bulgakov was brave to a fault when he told the Bolsheviks to their faces that they seemed to have lost the habit of free speech. Valentin Bulgakov would end up on the expulsion list.[40]

Both Berdyaev and Nikolai Lossky went on lecturing during the Civil War, the former at the Religious-Philosophical Academy he opened in Moscow in 1918, the latter at St Petersburg University and elsewhere. Memorable instances of *sovdepiye* which they encountered were recalled in their autobiographies. When Lossky lectured at the Dom iskusstv on 'God in the System of an Organic World Outlook' the audience comprised those keen to hear a refutation of atheism as well as 'sailors and members of the Red Army who came late and had to stand'.[41] The times were fertile in breeding a new mixture of opinions across the social classes. Nevertheless Lossky was struck by the degree to which religion was reviled by the common man who had been 'knocked from his senses by the Bolsheviks'. He recalled a still worse recent instance when someone in the audience at a Rakhmaninov concert took a shot at the soloist singing a religious text. In his view an ignorant fanaticism was forcing society apart at the seams.

Berdyaev had several memories of 1918. One was of taking part in a massive public procession, headed by the Supreme Head of the Russian Church, the Patriarch, affirming the Church's central role in Russian life. The occasion, led by Patriarch Tikhon, was a protest against the Bolsheviks' forcible division of Church from State that year. The regime did not interfere that time, but there was a demented hostility in the air among some sections of the newly liberated people: 'The Soviet order had by then not yet been fully worked out or put into practice … it was full of contradictions and inconsistencies.'[42]

At the Academy Berdyaev lectured on history and gave a seminar on Dostoevsky, both well attended, and didn't feel intimidated. 'In the presence of what looked like a young Cheka agent, invariably sitting in the front row and looking at me with a blank gaze, I always spoke freely … the debates which followed were equally outspoken.' As for 1919, the year he became professor of philosophy at the University of Moscow, 'for a year I gave lectures on which I openly and without hindrance criticized Marxism'. Berdyaev also held gatherings at home every Tuesday on Maly Vassilievsky Lane, which were not stopped or otherwise interfered with.[43]

But then he could encounter a public meeting like this:

As I entered the crowded hall, I had an almost physical sensation of terrific tension in the air. The crowd contained a great many Red Army men, sailors and workers. The whole atmosphere was significant of the elemental forces behind the Revolution, exulting in the downfall of intolerable restraints, wanton, unbridled, ruthless and frank to the point of naked shamelessness. One worker read a paper on the Gospel, in which he affirmed as a scientifically proved fact that the Mother of God was a prostitute and Jesus Christ the illegitimate son of a Roman soldier – a statement that was greeted with wild applause from the audience. He also dwelt incessantly on the 'contradictions' and 'inconsistencies' in the Gospels. [This man] ... produced, in what sounded like unprintable slang, some incredible hotch-potch of science, gnosticism and the Gospels. He finished by proclaiming that, since the maximum social programme had already been put into practice, 'the cosmic resurrection of the dead' will occur at any moment. This statement provoked an uproar of laughter in the audience. The next speaker, and the best of them all, was an anarchist ... I said what I expounded later in my pamphlet 'On the Worth of Christianity and the Unworthiness of Christians'. At first the audence was extremely hostile and drowned my words with hisses and derisive ejaculations. But gradually I gained control.[44]

All the more striking about Berdyaev's memoir is how he persuaded himself that the times conformed not to the vindictive anarchy apparent all around but to the exalted cultural ideal of free creativity he carried in his head. As I suggested earlier, the spiritual Russian intelligentsia had this great weakness: it could not see how little it possessed of political power.

The Russia of 1917–22 where the *intelligenty* continued to live and work was full of *sovdepiye* both absurd and menacing. Corresponding to Berdyaev's and Lossky's remembrances are figures giving the numbers of clergy murdered by the Cheka in the same years: as many as a thousand priests and twenty-eight bishops.[45] But the intellectuals had difficulty conceiving of themselves as a threat to the regime and candidates for imprisonment and murder, when, as it seemed to them, all they wanted was to help regenerate the country.

Amongst us, professors and writers, you will find representatives of all disciplines and orientations, but you will search in vain for politicians who are dangerous to the usurpers of power in Russia. What have they expelled us for? What is it? Stupidity or fright? I think both. The rulers of Russia, not to speak of how despicable they are, are such cowards that they are afraid of every independent and honestly expressed opinion, and out of stupidity they are exiling us to where we will have every opportunity to express the truth they want to hide from themselves and the whole world. Leaving Russia with this feeling, I hope to use my exile like a business trip and continue to serve the Motherland, which is alive and will not perish.[46]

Such were the thoughts of Boris Odintsov, a landowner and aristocrat by background, a professor of soil science by training, who from a young age had wanted to contribute to the reform of Russian agriculture – the burning question of the ownership and efficient working of the land. He regretted that *sovdepiye* had deprived him of his homeland.

A number of writers and philosophers in Moscow and Petrograd, including Berdyaev, Frank, Kizevetter and Aikhenvald, survived War Communism by running cooperative secondhand bookshops under the protection of the All-Russian Writers' Union. They were shoring up the old culture, not preparing to leave it. Their stock was particularly appreciated after the Bolsheviks nationalized all the new bookshops and controlled what they sold. Book cooperatives were a way for the educated classes to exchange their libraries for money and for the many *intelligenty* who hung around the shops, as customers, staff and well-wishers, a chance to stay in touch with the old world and its increasingly hidebound values. According to the writer Anatoly Mariengof, who remembered Berdyaev's and Osorgin's shop in Moscow, 'Provincial intellectuals with Chekhovian beards would walk out of the shop moved to tears – like old women leaving the presence of the wonderworking Iverskaya icon'.[47] Here was traditional Russian culture, albeit under duress, but not yet destroyed.

Osorgin left both a fictional portrait in *A Quiet Street* and a brief memoir of that shop, another of whose partners, Boris Zaitsev, would emigrate in mid-1922 and become a well-known literary figure in émigré Paris.

At 9 o'clock in the morning the shop was opened by a figure in felt boots and a lambskin cap, the young historian Boris Griftsov. Sometimes a cashier managed to arrive earlier – A. A. Dilevskaya, possessor of beautiful soprano voice and future opera singer, very nearly losing her voice in the freezing shop. Taking turns behind the counter were Boris Zaitsev and the philosopher Nikolai Berdyaev... These made up the most constant complement of shareholders... Khodasevich was such only for a short time.

The shop was on Leontievsky pereulok [No. 16] and later moved to Bolshaya Nikitinskaya [later Ulitsa Gertsena]. Mostly Griftsov and I ran the business. He lived with me in Chernyshevsky pereulok, almost next door. We handled all the routine tasks: bought books and priced them, worked the cash register, split wood, made the fire in the stove and kept an inventory. Yakovlev... hauled books by sledge for us... All the qualities of business impracticality and commercial lack of talent were combined in Boris Zaitsev, who managed the department of *belles letres* (where his knowledge allowed him to be reasonably competitive). Berdyaev, who took a very serious attitude towards the enterprise, never once managed to tie a package properly. But in the department of books on philosophy he had no peers...

We bought books by the wagon and the truckload. With the daily decline in the value of the currency such active trading 'throughout all Russia' gave us the possibility of feeding ourselves on millet and sometimes even horsemeat and of helping needy families of writers and professors.[48]

Over the five years they remained in business, Osorgin and Berdyaev and their partners bought useless books to keep the starving alive. At the same time, because books were needed by those who were contributing to their destruction, the secondhand shops ended up supplying the new workers' libraries and clubs. The proliferation of secondhand bookshops was matched by ventures in cooperative publishing which, in some cases having begun before the war, now expanded prolifically. Petropolis in Petrograd was both a shop and a publishing firm run since 1918 by Abram Kagan, the Pro-Rector (Deputy Vice-Chancellor) of the Petrograd Agricultural Academy and a future expellee.[49] The corresponding firm in Moscow, with a branch in Berlin, was Zadruga, whose founder and editor-in-chief since 1911, Sergei Melgunov, would become famous as the first man to write a world-renowned, bestselling account of 'the Red Terror'. Zadruga, oriented towards the Popular Socialist Party, attempted to tread a middle path as a cooperative enterprise rather than a full-blown commercial firm. It was a joint stock company owned by about 500 members and its deliberately chosen name meant, in south Slav, a communal enterprise, what the Russians called *obshchina*.[50] The host of future exiles and émigrés who subscribed to Zadruga included Berdyaev, Valentin Bulgakov, Osorgin, Kizevetter, Kuskova, Prokopovich, Remizov, Stepun, the archivist Alexander Izyumov, the agricultural economist A. A. Bulatov and others. Lenin considered all cooperatists enemies, though because of their socialistic tendency he pretended the opposite. Melgunov was arrested and given the opportunity to leave the country independently in 1922, while his deputy, Vasily Kudryavtsev, was expelled on the *Haken* with Izyumov, Bulatov, Berdyaev, Osorgin and Kizevetter. Zadruga came to an end when its type was 'nationalized' in 1922.

The bookshops, presses, philosophical societies and literary groupings of roughly 1917 to 1921 were, as Berdyaev recalled in retrospect, a sign that the Bolsheviks had not consolidated their programme. Paradoxically the bookshops created a wonderfully free atmosphere so infused with the shock of the new that occasionally it must have seemed as if Berdyaev's and Gershenzon's dream of a great spiritual renewal of mankind were taking place. In the Osorgin/Berdyaev bookshop Einstein's theory of relativity was pasted on the wall of the shop to cater for the huge interest it had aroused. Freud was another popular subject, in which Vysheslavtsev was an expert.

In Petrograd new ideas were discussed at Andrei Bely's Volfila – The Free Philosophical Society – and back in Moscow again at Berdyaev's

Academy where Vysheslavtsev and Frank also taught. Psychology, which the Bolsheviks would later suppress, was particularly popular. The literary equivalents of these centres for ideas were organizations like Opoyaz, the Society for the Study of Poetic Language, in Petrograd, and its counterpart Moscow School of Linguistics founded by the young poet and literary theorist Roman Jakobson. Gumilyov's conservative, craftsmanlike Tsekh poetov ('Guild of Poets') was depleted, but for those wanting to venture radically to the left in art Gorky and Lunacharsky were still mentors of the Proletkult group ('Proletarian Culture'), which they had founded in September 1917 and affiliated after the Revolution with Lunacharsky's Education, Arts and Culture Commissariat (Narkompros). Russian writers could also join, and might well have done to increase their own safety, the country-wide Union of Writers, of which Berdyaev was President in 1919, and another deportee, Viktor Iretsky, in 1921. The Union helped protect the cooperative bookshops and members in difficulty.

The poet Osip Mandelstam's wife Nadezhda kept a cool head about the real state of affairs:

> There was never any question of tolerance. It was simply that the
> State had not yet got around to dealing with literature – it was still
> too busy with famine and war. Leningrad [as Petrograd was
> renamed] was the centre of these pipe dreams. Gorky demanded
> that the intellectuals there be 'preserved' on the grounds that they
> knew *so much*. Such was the argument by which Gorky hoped to
> appeal to the new State: the *amount of* their knowledge. This is
> something that always impresses certain types of self-educated
> people... As for 'tolerance' and the taking of 'counsel', selected
> members of the intelligentsia, together with their charming ladies,
> were assigned to cultural duties and given translations to do... the
> intelligentsia was thus kept busy with so-called voluntary activity.[51]

Mrs Mandelstam found that the Guild of Poets had become a shadow of its old self and 'the old men from the Religious-Philosophical Academy were quietly dying off in the corners'. 'The cheerful goings-

on [at the House of Arts] seemed ominous against the background of
the subdued and dying city.'

To their credit, from the moment the Cheka began to pick off the
class enemy, Gorky and Lunacharsky expressed horror at the violence
of the new world, so lacking in respect for the word and for democracy.[52] In one of the 1917–18 essays that would drive Lenin to evict him
from the country, Gorky wrote:

> We are destroying the spiritual capital of the Russian people…We
> are breeding a new crop of brutal and corrupt bureaucrats and a
> terrible new generation of youth who are learning to laugh at daily
> bloody scenes of beatings, shootings, cripplings [and] lynchings…
> Petrograd…the centre of our intellectual life…is a dying city.[53]

When in later life Tatyana Frank wrote down what she remembered of
those difficult years her telegrammatic style produced a devastating
summary:

> The war years in Petersburg – shame and pain back home, sorrow
> on the front, the loss of loved ones, the search for them, finally
> establishing their loss for certain. A presentiment of catastrophe,
> stifling heat, meeting with great-men-and-patriots, their fear for our
> country. The Revolution, attempts, last attempts to save it, and all
> the stages these attempts went through and finally the collapse of
> the huge Russian colossus – and we are all beneath her shards.
> The rescue began, flight – some people went abroad, some into
> the country, some with the White Army, each went where he
> could…Russia hid, took flight, everything went dark. Everyone
> found a hiding-place, began to go hungry. Death from typhoid
> became a common occurrence. Friends and acquaintances passed
> away. Every experience possible on this sorrowful earth was vested
> on poor Russia, our homeland.
> And we saved ourselves by going into the country, somehow to
> save the children, and there were four of them, from hunger. Often
> in the area there were deaths from typhus and from the madness of

the crowd – both Greens [local bandits] and Reds. You could be hanged here and hanged there, or thrown into prison, but the hand of Providence led us through all these trials and further and further on. Arrest, release – finally freedom, we were beyond the frontier of this satanic, shameless regime, but before that we said goodbye to mother, we didn't think, didn't believe it was for ever. We left brothers, a sister behind too...[54]

In autumn 1917 Frank was asked by the Provisional government to set up a historical-philological faculty – an Arts Faculty – at the University of Saratov on the Volga. Since it was Tatyana's home town the family went willingly and perhaps saved their lives. Semyon Lyudvigovich had plenty of experience of *sovdepiye* at the university. In 1921, in a telling example of how Lenin's war in philosophy was translated into the criminalization of religious belief, three Saratov professors were jailed for suggesting that not everything in the world could be explained by material phenomena alone and perhaps there was a God.[55] No non-Russian reader and no reader in the twenty-first century should misunderstand what this offensive against religion, superficially justified as an attack on superstition, actually meant. One of the key aims of Bolshevism was to destroy religion in Russia, both in terms of the Church as an autonomous institution and in terms of Christianity as a source of popular authority. To this, Marxist-Leninist philosophy added an objection to religious faith because it sanctioned an 'inwardness' which in turn allowed for freedom of thought. Soviet totalitarianism meant denying individuals the possibility of a discrete 'inner' life. Everything had to be rendered to Caesar.

Because of the difficulty of getting food in overcrowded Saratov, Tatyana Frank went into the countryside to live, where the local Volga German colonists, who knew her, brought her what she needed. Thus she and her children survived the famine. Fifty-five years later she could still see the frantic, hungry eyes of a woman who arrived from Petrograd to help look after the children, and to whom she was able to give a meal of cooked ham. But starvation was only one threat to the

Franks' well-being. Civil War violence surrounded them. The local resistance to the Bolsheviks came from 'Green' bandit gangs as well as Whites, and the Franks found themselves caught between the three. On one occasion Tatyana and the children barely escaped with their lives when for once friendly Bolsheviks gave them three men and a sledge to move themselves – and their cow – to a safer village. 'I saw for the first time how you put a cow on a sledge. You tie up the legs and hoist her up and she lies on her side.' Later, with three children aged between ten and twelve and a fourth still suckling, Tatyana moved on by camel and finally got back to Saratov. When refugees began pouring into Saratov to avoid the Famine which was now devastating the countryside the Franks returned to Moscow. The date was autumn 1921 and Frank was able to join Berdyaev teaching at the Academy.[56]

The one consolation for the philosophers in these years was that against the Bolshevik diktat their lectures on a spiritual understanding of human existence actually proved more and more popular as people from all walks of life became tired and distrustful of atheist propaganda, or so they claimed. The ructions Berdyaev and Lossky faced in 1918–19 seemed to be fading two years later. Sorokin agreed that there was a religious revival after 1920.[57]

The year 1919, however, was when the first arrests took place in the capital involving the kind of public figures – the *obshchestvennye deyateli* – whom Tatyana had referred to as great-men-and-patriots. Kuzmin-Karavayev, Peshekhonov and Osorgin were arrested and it took a visit from Berdyaev, in his capacity as Writers' Union president, to the most amenable Bolshevik, Lev Kamenev, to get Osorgin released.[58] These arrests were not the outcome of popular vindictiveness nor even ideological warfare, but were early manifestations of Soviet state paranoia. In the summer the Soviet government had become suspicious of any contacts between its citizens and the International Red Cross. These three, who had been involved in Red Cross help for the relief of political prisoners during the war,[59] were now viewed as potential traitors, since in the Civil War the Red Cross had given humanitarian help to the stranded White Army in the south. The reasoning was terrifying.

The Cheka received a reprimand for excessive zeal in the matter of the Red Cross arrests.[60] But by the end of the 1919 his political police proved their mettle to Lenin by uncovering National Centre, the chief underground organization supplying political and military intelligence to the White Army. Simultaneously they closed in on National Centre's clandestine sister organization, the Union for the Regeneration of Russia (SVR), and thirdly on Tactical Centre, which coordinated both. Big fish were caught: Trubetskoy, who ran Tactical Centre 'although the life of risk did not suit my character',[61] Sergei Melgunov and Myakotin of the SVR. Kizevetter was also detained as a suspect in connection with National Centre, then released.[62]

The activists of National Centre, mainly military men, were summarily executed. On 23 September *Pravda* announced that the death sentence had been carried out on sixty-seven members of a counter-revolutionary and espionage organization.[63] The sympathetic intellectuals who in August 1917 had formed a kind of anticipatory intellectual arm of the National Centre, the *Soyuz obshchestvennykh deyatelei* (SOD), were fortunately not treated so harshly.[64] Nevertheless their association with National Centre was one way in which Lenin could identify their beliefs and tag them for the future. The SOD, a council of conservative intellectuals concerned to restore civic order, included such prominent anti-Bolshevik figures as the ubiquitous Pyotr Struve, Sergei Evgenievich's father Evgeny Trubetskoy, the former Duma deputy Vasily Shulgin, Kerensky's Foreign Minister Pavel Milyukov, the last tsarist ambassador to Paris Vasily Maklakov, and Berdyaev.[65]

The organizers of Tactical Centre were put on trial. Sergei Trubetskoy thought the fact that he and his membership were not immediately executed, like their National Centre colleagues, was the result of public pressure abroad, in particular from Britain, one of whose intelligence agents, Paul Dukes, had worked with Tactical Centre. The organization, however, was betrayed from its own side in another symbolic split of the intelligentsia paving the way for Lenin's 1922 gesture. Professors S. A. Kotlyarevsky and N. N. Vinogradsky revealed to the police the names of many of their associates in the SOD and the SVR, such as Alexandra Tolstoy.[66] The rank and file including Tolstaya were arrested and released, as was the biologist Professor Mikhail Novikov, Rector of Moscow University, after two weeks' detention.[67] Novikov would be among the 1922 deportees.

The four chief organizers of Tactical Centre were tried and given a death sentence. But the executions were commuted to ten years' imprisonment and Trubetskoy and Melgunov were amnestied the following year. Lenin seemed to be playing games with international opinion in 1920–21, now that the Civil War had been won and Soviet Russia's quest for international diplomatic recognition had begun. But if that was so, it was as deliberate and calculated as everything else Lenin did. The point was to deliver a mixed message, to demonstrate to what degree the Bolsheviks were flexible. They could show clemency if it helped their image, but they remained endlessly suspicious of public figures who had foreign contacts and/or belonged to the intelligentsia. The prosecutor in the Tactical Centre trial, Bolshevik Party member since 1904, Nikolai Krylenko, stressed in his summing up that the defendants belonged to the intelligentsia and the intelligentsia was the enemy.[68]

Yet when Berdyaev was arrested during the investigations into Tactical Centre it was not strange for him to be treated with great courtesy by the Cheka. This pre-Soviet Russia was unfinished, its tone uneven, its brutality unfinessed. The times were dangerous but the worst age of repression was yet to come. The top brass of the Cheka listened politely while Berdyaev lectured them on their philosophical errors as Marxist-Leninists, after which chairman Dzerzhinsky worried for the professor's safety as he travelled home at midnight through a lawless city. 'Mr Menzhinsky, it is late and there are plenty of bandits about; would it not be possible to take Mr Berdyaev home by car?' Berdyaev recalled: 'There was no car available, but a Red Guard took me home, with my luggage, on a motor-bicycle. When

I left the prison the governor asked if I had "enjoyed" my stay with them.'[69]

The great change came when, in February 1921, NEP formally replaced War Communism and after more than three years of hardship Russia was once more free to trade with the world. This temporary economic liberalization went so much against the ideological grain within his own party that Lenin had to defend it as a temporary expedient and show there was no risk of losing control of the country.[70] Fear that the Bolsheviks might lose their grip was confirmed when the sailors stationed on the island fortress of Kronshtadt, in the Gulf of Finland, mutinied on 1 March 1921. They were protesting at the siege economy and the ideological repression that had descended over the past four years. In the final showdown 15,000 defenders of the island faced 50,000 Red Army and Cheka troops, who did not acquit themselves well. 'A reasonable estimate put the total Communist losses in dead, wounded and missing at 10,000; the rebels' losses were probably in the region of 600 killed, over 1,000 wounded, and about 2,500 taken prisoner. Some 8,000 rebels fled over the ice to Finland.'[71]

The truth of the NEP was that it combined 'deep military and political repression with very marginal economic reform'.[72] Lenin deliberately tightened the ideological hold of Bolshevism while he eased up on the economic front. A note from Lenin to Kamenev first spelled out the policy in March 1922: 'It would be the biggest mistake to think that the NEP put an end to terror. We shall return to terror and to economic terror.'[73] Yet according to Sorokin, Zinoviev, the Politburo member in charge of the Petrograd Soviet, had given the same message to a meeting of Communist officials there on 2 May 1921, almost a year earlier:

> Comrades, the hydra of counter-revolution is raising its head again. Either these heads must be cut off or we shall be devoured by the monster. We must demonstrate that the machine of the Red Terror still exists and works efficiently.[74]

Already in the spring and summer of 1921, therefore, Lenin's personal strategy for the survival of Soviet Russia was to liberalize the economy temporarily but keep a tight control on the intelligentsia. In this spirit 1922 would become the Janus year in modern Russian history.

The intelligentsia could not believe that such a savage policy existed, although when the poet Nikolai Gumilyov was arrested in Petrograd in June 1921, prompting the unfolding of the Tagantsev Affair, some of his fellow poets wisely took fright. The Tagantsev Affair was a Cheka invention which cost sixty-one innocent lives. It took its name from a geographer at Petersburg University who was declared to be the ringleader of an unprecedented anti-Bolshevik conspiracy. The accused were academics, intellectuals and others. Apart from Gumilyov and Tagantsev, who was the son of Russia's most distinguished lawyer of the last years of the Empire, they included one of Russia's best-known sculptors, Prince Sergei Ukhtomsky, and a leading philosophical writer and literary critic, A. A. Gizetti and his wife. Ukhtomsky was a relative of Nina Berberova's and his work was widely commissioned, including by the Lossky family. The Rector of Petersburg University, N. I. Lazarevsky, a prominent minister in Kerensky's government, was another victim of the Tagantsev Affair. Others similarly charged and despatched from life were naval officers, sailors who had fought in the Kronshtadt mutiny, members of the bourgeoisie, workers and peasants. They were shot in woods outside Petrograd on 24 August 1921.[75]

For the journalist Nikolai Volkovysky, who was to be expelled from Russia on the *Preussen*, the events surrounding Gumilyov's murder were the most significant of his life in Russia. In the summer of 1921 he confronted the evil of what was happening. Gumilyov's fate was tightly linked with the life and survival of members of the Petrograd Dom literatorov, whose protector Gorky was himself under pressure to leave. Volkovysky was head of the Dom literatorov and acted on behalf of its members. Together with Nikolai Otsup, a poet who would emigrate a few months before the expulsions, Volkovysky spent weeks campaigning to get their friend and colleague released from prison. While he was detained, another celebrated poet and member of their circle, Alexander Blok, died. Blok's early death was natural, but hunger and lack of care had played such a strong part in it that it seemed to be a double crime to lay at the door of the new Soviets. The nineteen-year-old Nina Berberova turned up at the Dom literatorov and found it silenced by Blok's death and Gumilyov's arrest:

> I walked along Basseinaya to the Writers' House. It was Sunday (and the eve of my birthday), about three o'clock. I hoped to meet someone and learn something new about those who had been arrested the same morning as Gumilyov – amongst others Uncle Seryozha Ukhtomsky, the publisher of Rech named Bak, Professor Lazarevsky, all of whom I knew personally. I went in at the front door. It was empty and quiet. Through the glass door that opened on to the garden, the tree foliage was visible. (The Writers' House, like the House of Arts, was a former private residence.) I saw an announcement in a black frame hanging among others: 'Today, 7 August, Aleksandr Aleksandrovich Blok passed away.' The announcement was still damp, it had just been stuck there.
>
> I was seized by a feeling, which I never again experienced, that I was suddenly and sharply orphaned. The end is near... We will remain alone... The end is coming. We are lost. Tears spurted from my eyes.
>
> 'What are you crying about, Mademoiselle?' asked a thin little man with a huge hooked nose and beautiful eyes. 'Blok?' This was Boris Khariton, whom I did not then know... He went out into the street. I went after him.[76]

As Osorgin explained in his incorporation of the event into *A Quiet Street*, 'A hearse was out of the question; even a simple cart was not to be thought of. In these days the poor were taken to be buried in quite unpretentious ways – on little sledges in winter and hand-barrows in summer. The body was carried if there were enough people.'[77]

Otsup took up the factual narrative from the cemetery where he, Volkovysky and others had carried Blok's coffin.

We carried Alexander Alexandrovich's coffin to the cemetery
ourselves. Our shoulders were aching with the heavy burden, our
heads were spinning with incense and bitter thoughts, but we had
to do something. They weren't releasing Gumilyov. There at the
cemetery Sergei Oldenburg, the late Akim Volynsky, Nikolai
Volkovysky and I agreed to go to the Cheka with a request to release
Gumilyov into the custody of the Academy of Sciences, of World
Literature and a whole series of not very loyal organizations.
We agreed at the last moment to add to these institutions the
thoroughly loyal Proletkult and three others where Gumilyov gave
lectures.

Volkovysky described their visit to the Cheka.

The Cheka said Gumilyov had been arrested for abuse of his post.
One of us replied that Gumilyov didn't hold any post. The
Chairman of the St Petersburg Cheka was clearly irritated that
anyone should argue with him. Our delegation was told to call again
on Wednesday. When we phoned that day we were told we would
have the answer the next day. But that day the whole of Russia
already knew that he was dead. A few young poets and students who
took a parcel to Gorokhovaya Street for him every day found that
on Tuesday evening their delivery was not accepted. On Wednesday
we began to search all the prisons to find Gumilyov. We managed
to get inside the courtyard of Shpalernaya [the longer-term
investigative prison], go upstairs and ask someone on duty
where Gumilyov was. Answer: "They took him last night to
Gorokhovaya." As we ran away a voice pursued us: "Heh, who are
you anyway? Stop! Stop!" That evening the St Petersburg GPU
chairman [Bakaev] who had received our delegation disclosed to a
closed session of the Petrosoviet that Tagantsev, Gumilyov etc. had
been shot and the rumour began to spread through the city. Secret
witnesses described how Gumilyov faced death – but we didn't need
them to tell us that Gumilyov died a death worthy of his reputation
as a brave and steadfast person.[78]

Nikolai Lossky, for whom Lazarevsky and Tagantsev were colleagues and Ukhtomsky a family friend, was deeply distressed. This was the moment when the family considered escaping from Russia. But like so many they were deterred by the hope of Russia's recovery.[79] Zamyatin wrote that Gorky had taught the intelligentsia to overcome its doubts and have faith and that was indeed how they lived.[80] Since they could not yet know of Lenin's true policy their hopes were cruelly raised by the NEP, a painful irony of the day. 'To all intents and purposes life seemed to be on the mend and to many it even seeemed to be booming... the streetcars were running, the shops and markets were open.' Even Nadezhda Mandelstam was partly seduced, although 'every day brought something new to fill us with horror and destroy any hope of recovery'.[81]

The Soviet side was constantly calculating, pitting its image abroad against its real needs at home. The greatest problem that the NEP brought for the regime was the presence of foreigners who might undermine its authority or give it a bad press. Archive material has revealed how Lenin didn't want the League of Nations High Commissioner for Refugees and future Nobel Peace Laureate Fridtjof Nansen in the country in late spring 1921, for fear that 'he'll catch us napping'.[82] The request of an American journalist to visit in July 1921 was turned down for the same reason. Above all the Bolsheviks were adamant that no one at home or abroad should believe they had changed their policies and were giving way to capitalism. If the West sensed too much relaxation it might encourage France and Britain to mount an anti-Communist crusade.[83]

But journalists and other foreigners were not in Russia to check up on the progress of the NEP. By summer 1921 the whole world had been alerted to the Russian famine, and many came to see how they could help. The disaster of 1921 would claim five million lives. Prominent Russians founded the All-Russian Public Committee to Help the Hungry (VKPG), while Gorky issued an appeal to the world: 'I ask all honest European and American people for prompt aid to the Russian people...'[84] An immediate response came from US

President Herbert Hoover and the American Relief Administration (ARA).[85] Lenin, under pressure from Gorky and other public figures, had little choice but to accede to the creation of the VKPG, otherwise known as Pomgol, which came into being on 21 July, though he immediately imposed conditions to keep it under political control. Likewise he was extremely wary of the ARA.

Pomgol had seventy-three members, including leading cultural figures, liberal politicians, an ex-tsarist minister, famous agronomists and engineers, doctors and 'Tolstoyans', followers of Tolstoy's views on the communal economic life. Twelve of them were prominent Communists imposed to prevent any drift into political activity. It was the first and last independent public body established under Communism and it lasted six weeks. Hoover replied to Gorky's appeal on 23 July with conditions for America's provision of aid which included the release of Americans from Russian prisons and 'full liberty to come and go and move about Russia' for representatives of the ARA. Hoover expected the ARA to be free to provide aid 'without regard to race, creed or social status', in exchange for which it would refrain from political activity. Lenin was furious at having these conditions dictated to him and once American aid was secured closed Pomgol down. That move was followed on 27 August by the arrest of all its public members except Gorky and Korolenko.

Of those who would be expelled abroad in autumn 1922 or left shortly before at least five were Pomgol members: Prokopovich, Kuskova, Osorgin, Alexander Ugrimov and the Tolstoyan Valentin Bulgakov. A sixth, the agronomist Pavel Velikhov, would be regarded as so dangerous that, once arrested as a possible deportee, he would never be released abroad. Prokopovich, the former minister for Trade and Industry in the Provisional government, with his wife Kuskova, were the prime movers of the public side of the committee, and prime targets. But all sixty-one of Pomgol's non-Communist members were arrested. As fabrication was piled upon fabrication, Bolshevik newspapers attacked the aid committee as an anti-Soviet terrorist organization with links to the late Tagantsev. The problem on Lenin's side was evidently the contacts Pomgol members had with foreigners. In the first week of September Prokopovich, Kuskova and Osorgin, along with the other three members of Pomgol's six-man presidium, were in fact sentenced to death. They were held in that basement of the Lubyanka otherwise known as the Ship of Death (which is how Osorgin came to collect his copy for the philosopher's death in *A Quiet Street*). When Hoover and Nansen protested to Lenin at the sudden disappearance of so many important Russian public figures the death sentences were commuted – but with what terrifying cynicism – to exile 'in a famine region'.[86] Osorgin first spent three months in Moscow in appalling conditions before being sent to Kazan a sick man in November. He owed his freedom and his life to a friendly Kazan doctor who signed a medical order allowing him to return to Moscow in April 1922.

In the event Prokopovich and Kuskova left Russia in June 1922, as did rank and file Pomgol member Boris Zaitstev, who would become a well-known émigré figure, around the same time. Osorgin, Ugrimov and Valentin Bulgakov, who made no plans to leave under their own steam, were all on Lenin's list and were shipped out, respectively, in September 1922 and March 1923. Of still other Pomgol members who came close to expulsion[87] Alexandra Tolstaya remained in Russia until the chance came to escape in 1929. The agronomist N. D. Kondratyev was a rare figure drafted on to the autumn 1922 list but then pardoned.[88] Meanwhile Patriarch Tikhon prompted his later arrest by giving the famine committee his blessing.

The combination of the Tagantsev Affair and the persecution of the Pomgol members persuaded at least some of the intelligentsia to leave the country while they could. Andrei Bely, Aleksei Remizov and Gorky were three who moved to Berlin in the autumn of 1921. The artistic exodus of that year, which the NEP made possible, has sometimes seemed like a coming up for air. Here were writers like Pasternak and Ehrenburg, Mayakovsky and Esenin, refreshing themselves with a taste of Europe after the confinement of the Civil War and the famine. Health grounds were frequently cited for their trips abroad. But health was also a euphemism for uncertainty as to what the Red future meant and who should remain to enjoy it. Already in the winter of 1921 Nikolai Trubetskoy, another member of that illustrious family who had emigrated and who was to become world-famous for the new start he gave to the study of linguistics, advised his friend Roman Jakobson not to go back to Moscow, since the chances of ending up in the Lubyanka were high.[89] When the poet, novelist and mystic Bely arrived in Berlin he had recently attacked the death of Andrei Blok as a symbol of the terrible conditions under which the Russian intelligentsia had to exist, and it seems highly possible that his protest was the reason why he got a visa to travel.[90] By the same token, however, he would have to negotiate his return with a fair amount of grovelling eighteen months later. Critical intellectuals weren't wanted in Soviet Russia but the country was not yet a totalitarian state: there was still some scope for individuals to make a personal decision about whether to leave or stay.

Indeed, because the Soviet state was still in the making, what characterized the extended Berlin–Moscow axis of the intelligentsia from around 1921 to as late as 1927 or even 1929 was a two-way process of experimentation and negotiation to establish who, both psychologically and politically, could bear to live where. For Russian intellectuals, while Lenin was alive, and for the time his influence continued, the Bolshevik message was: this is how things are, either accept them or get out. Lenin had endured similar conditions set by tsarist Russia and now he was passing them on in a new political context. Under Stalin things were different again. Almost no one could get out. There was at least that difference between Lenin's and Stalins' Terror.

Gorky was one prominent figure whose criticisms got too much for Lenin in July 1921. He delivered a naked threat to his old friend. 'You're doing nothing to look after your health … push off abroad … if you won't go then we'll have to send you.'[91] That terse exchange, another discovery from the recent investigation of the archives, puts paid to the idea that Gorky left Russia because he was embarrassed over how the Soviet government had persecuted Pomgol.[92] Rather, Lenin gave him a hearty push, leaving him no alternative.

Years later Berberova, who would leave Russia in 1922 with poet Vladislav Khodasevich, asked:

Could we at that time foresee the death of Mandelstam on a rubbish heap, the end of [Isaak] Babel, the suicides of Esenin and Mayakovsky, Party politics in literature aimed at destroying two if not three generations? Could we foresee twenty years of silence on [Anna] Akhmatova's part? The destruction of Pasternak? The end of Gorky? Of course not. 'Anatoly Vasilievich will not allow it.' This opinion about Lunacharsky was in the air at that time. But if Anatoly Vasilievich is himself poisoned? Or even if he dies a natural death? Or if he is removed? Or if he decides one day not to be a Communist aesthete any more but to become a hammer, forging the Russian intelligentsia on the anvil of the Revolution? No, such possibilities dawned on no one, but doubts that it would be possible to survive swarmed in Khodasevich's thoughts for the first time during those months. That one would be seized for no reason, jailed and annihilated then seemed unthinkable, but that one would be crushed, tortured, have his mouth shut and either be forced to die (as later happened with Sologub and Gershenzon) or give up literature (as Evgeny Zamyatin, Mikhail Kuzmin and, for twenty-five years, Viktor Shklovsky were forced to do) began dimly to take on more distinct shapes in one's thoughts.[93]

Shklovsky, who spent 1922–3 in Berlin, was Jakobson's friend and over several years relations between them carried a subtext of indecision over whether they should live abroad or remain in Russia. The same applied to relations between Jakobson and the radical poet Vladimir Mayakovsky. The problem for these men was to balance their Russian and left-leaning sympathies with the reality of the Terror. Gershenzon came to test the German waters and returned within a couple of months. The actor and theatre director Nikolai Evreinov hesitated over what to do, to the extent of sailing on the *Preussen* as a

free man, with his wife, on the same November voyage that carried
Lossky and his colleagues into exile. The Evreinovs returned to Russia
and then left again in 1926. The circumstances of Shklovsky's return,
like Bely's and both in autumn 1923, confirmed that going back to
Russia was as complicated as leaving. Berberova spoke of their
'petitioning for return'. Shklovsky was readmitted because he was
vouched for by Lunacharsky, Kamenev and Zinoviev.[94] He then
begged Jakobson publicly to return to Russia, but to no avail.[95]

Jakobson eventually explained why he didn't go back in his celebrated essay of 1931, 'On a Generation that Squandered its Poets'.

> Gumilyov (1886–1921) was shot, after prolonged mental agony and
> in great pain; Blok (1880–1921) died, amid cruel privations and
> under circumstances of inhuman suffering…after careful planning
> Esenin (1895–1925) and Mayakovsky (1894–1930) killed themselves.
> And so it happened that during the third decade of this century,
> those who inspired a generation perished between the ages of thirty
> and forty, each of them sharing a sense of doom so vivid and
> sustained that it became unbearable.[96]

Did Jakobson want to leave? He realized as early as 1920 that
Russia was no place to continue with academic work.[97] But still the
emotional answer was no. Did Gorky want to leave? Equally, no. And
this same reluctance would characterize almost all the men on the
1922 ships. Gorky was perhaps the least equivocal member of the
intelligentsia trying to see whether he could live abroad and escape his
Russian conscience. Lenin wanted Gorky to stop interfering with the
Bolshevik plan for a new Russia, but from the moment he arrived in
Berlin on 29 September 1921 Gorky continued where he left off at
home, campaigning to help the starving Russian people and the
degraded intelligentsia. He instantly told the world that the intelligentsia, whose number he put at 9,000, was under siege. 'An
insignificant number for so huge a land and for the cultural work
needed in Russia', these men were vital because they were 'the leaven
which leaveneth the whole lump'.

They are the best brains of the country, the creators of Russian science and culture, people more needed in Russia than in any other country. Without them it is impossible to live, as it is impossible to live without a soul. These people are a precious thing on a worldwide, general and human scale.[98]

Eventually in 1928 Gorky would lose the battle with himself and go home anyway.

Why individual Russians were prompted at different times to leave Russia between 1917 and late 1922 would repay a dedicated study. For the academics, sweeping overnight changes in the universities had begun in summer 1918, when professors who had taught at the same institution for ten or more years were dismissed, higher degrees were abolished and juridical and history departments closed. The situation worsened under the NEP when in deadly combination the coopera-tive bookshops went to the wall and prices rose overnight. Nikolai Lossky recalled being paid for one lecture with bread before finally losing his job. In autumn 1921, however, just as men like Lossky were being forced to leave the universities, the regime realized it could not do without academics and specialists entirely, and so Trotsky, the Politburo's unofficial media- and culture-watcher, forwarded to Lenin a recommendation that the state take measures to protect a group of 'real scholars' from dying off.[99] The distinction was specious, but there was a genuine problem lurking behind it, namely what to do with the other, unwanted staff dismissed for their ideologically unpromising views. Forwarding this request to the President of the Soviet of People's Commissars, Nikolai Gorbunov, Cultural Commissar Lunacharsky presented it as primarily a case of welfare. He observed that, with four thousand million roubles having been set aside entirely for Petrograd academic staff,

We would willingly arrange recuperative leave abroad for the sick and exhausted, but we draw your attention to the fact that we are inhibited by two factors: in respect of foreign currency subsidies and restrictions on the part of the organs of the Cheka.[100]

Was there not then already a plan being considered – in November 1921 – to send abroad en masse all the unwanted thinkers and academics who had not yet gone willingly? It seems possible from this memorandum of Lunacharsky's that Lenin had already discussed it with him and with Trotsky. But generally Russian historians think not. They date the expulsions from January 1922, when Lenin first tasted the solution of forced exile, began to focus on his enemies in the press one by one, and looked to how he could systematically remove the legal and financial barriers Lunacharsky mentioned.

3

The Janus Year

L ENIN WAS NO stranger to the idea of deportation. He had hardly seized power before he was inciting Bolshevik communes 'to show initiative and inventiveness in devising ways of cleansing the Russian land of noxious insects, scoundrel fleas, bedbug rich...'[1] In his correspondence he increasingly talked either of 'chucking people out' or more gently suggested that certain people would be better off abroad.

In January 1922 an opportunity arose for a dress rehearsal. Some 2,000 members of the Menshevik Party, veteran critics of Lenin, including their leader Fyodor Dan, had been arrested in the first ten weeks or so of 1921 and accused of helping to foment the Kronshtadt uprising. That they were in prison before the event may have encouraged Lenin to resist Zinoviev's request to execute them. But a year later the legacy of this fleeting act of fairmindedness was that hundreds were still being held and Lenin didn't know what to do with them. He was also needled. The Mensheviks, who had consistently insisted on legal means in their opposition to Bolshevism, excelled at making an international fuss.[2] They had been impressively vocal abroad about the Red Terror ever since their founder Yuly Martov was forced to emigrate in 1920. Mindful of their imprisoned colleagues, the Berlin-based Mensheviks now did everything they could to discredit the Bolsheviks in the run-up to the Genoa Conference in March, when Russia was scheduled to meet its former Civil War enemies Britain and France for the first time across the negotiating table.[3]

In his correspondence Lenin kept up a furious tirade throughout January, demanding that the Cheka mete out ever more severe punishments. He delivered an explicit call to the Politburo 'for reprisals against the Mensheviks to be intensified'.[4] But at the same time, secretly, he made preparations for the Mensheviks' 'administrative exile', including to Germany. Thus on 5 January 1922, Dzerzhinsky's deputy at the Cheka, Iosif Unshlikht, was instructed to find Russian towns where the Mensheviks could be exiled; but also not to object to their going abroad. Pravda meanwhile confirmed that the Mensheviks 'were all going to be thrown out once and for all (and would even be given money for the journey) to join their friends Martov and Co.'[5] Unaware of the precise nature of Lenin's plans, the detained Mensheviks went on a hunger strike in Butyrki prison, protesting against the threatened removal of some of their number to Turkestan. The strike, publicized in the West, brought Lenin under such pressure that on 26 January he arranged for Dan, his close associate Boris Nikolaevsky, and eight others to leave Russia for Berlin, via Riga.[6]

The despatch of the Mensheviks abroad was doubly interesting because it presupposed the already functioning cooperation of Germany, on which the autumn expulsions would depend. To formalize good relations with Weimar in the international sphere and deport his critics at home, Lenin's two peak achievements in the year he spent consolidating the Soviet state, were already in his sights as 1922 began. While the Treaty of Rapallo was signed on 16 April and the Soviet Union created on 31 December, exactly midway between those two dates the dissident intelligentsia was arrested following Germany's agreement to take them. The date of the arrests, 16/17 August, was uncannily, though surely accidentally, precise.

The domestic plan took shape when between January and May Lenin began to compile a mental list of journalists and publishers, university teachers and economists whose views didn't accord with Bolshevism. The particularly irritating publishing industry (which included journals and newspapers) moved him to tell Gorbunov 'strictly confidentially' on 6 February: 'Also have a secret talk about how and what kind of supervision of this business is organized on the part of the... All-Russia Cheka.'[7]

Around this time Lenin also focused on an economist called Peshekhonov, whom the Politburo had removed from his job in the Central Statistical Bureau in Ukraine on 20 January. In a special letter to Kamenev, written some time close to 25 February, Lenin ordered the renegade to be given statistical work 'in trade and sanitary matters', where he could do no harm, and for Unshlikht's men to watch him at all times. Above all Peshekhonov should stay out of politics. Lenin's tone suggested he was aware of Peshekhonov's talent but that 'preventative' measures were needed to keep him loyal to the Party line.[8]

The staff at the Moscow Technical University meanwhile enraged Lenin when they went on strike in defence of their academic autonomy, and to protest over poor working conditions and salaries. Towards the end of February he told fellow Politburo members Kamenev and Stalin that he would like to get rid of between twenty and forty professors 'who were making fools of us'.[9] No names were mentioned but come late August *Pravda* would refer to the strike – 'resistance to the form of higher education' – as one reason why certain academics were being asked to leave the country.[10]

The professors were big bourgeois fish for the Bolsheviks to fry. To take just two of them, Vsevolod Stratonov was the country's most distinguished astronomer and had until recently been adviser to Narkompros, the Education Ministry, on all scientific publications in the country. Alexander Bogolepov was a specialist in law and the history of the Church, who had been President of the Republic under Kerensky's government and whose ministerial portfolio in 1917 had included overseeing the election process. When Lenin fingered him he was Pro-Rector (Deputy Vice-Chancellor) of Petrograd University.[11]

It was also in February that Lenin realized Sorokin would have to go, after he made a quite unacceptable public speech on freedom, culture and individual responsibility. The occasion was the 103rd anniversary celebrations of St Petersburg University. As the speaker remembered:

> In my speech I pointed out the new guideposts which would
> be followed by the young generations. Individual freedom,
> individual initiative and responsibility, cooperation, creative love,
> respect for the liberty of others; reform instead of revolution, self-
> government instead of anarchy – these were now and should ever
> be our social ideals.[12]

Furious personal denunciations of Sorokin by Lenin and Zinoviev, the head of the Petrograd Soviet, followed in the Communist press the next day, 22 February.

Lenin retaliated further on 12 March with a contribution to the newly founded Communist philosophy journal *Pod znamenem marksisma* ('Under the Marxist Banner'). His 'letter', 'On the Significance of Militant Materialism', called in battering terms for militant atheism and atheist propaganda to characterize Soviet intellectual life and set an example by lambasting the journalists, including Sorokin, who published in *Ekonomist*. These 'advocates of serfdom, reactionaries and graduate flunkeys of the popery' had no right to take government money to educate young people. They would be better off living in bourgeois countries. 'The working class in Russia, having seized power, would long ago have told such teachers and members of learned societies to hop off to the countries of bourgeois "democracy", had they known how to use that power.'[13]

Lenin's winter of anti-dissident fury was rounded off when Berdyaev, Frank, Stepun and Struve's pupil Bukshpan,[14] put together a collection of essays entitled *Oswald Spengler and the Decline of the West*. In a 'secret' letter of 5 March Lenin accused them of being 'White Guards'[15] and returned obsessively to these men, with their non-Marxist view of history, two months later.[16] Deportation, and a list of men who might be subject to it, was now Lenin's *idée fixe* and the only problem was to how to implement it legally.

The obvious way was to follow long-established tsarist Russian practice and have the political police exile awkward subjects under a law which bypassed the judicial process. But, as Lunacharsky had noted the previous December, it was exactly the power to do that that the Cheka presently lacked. Whether or not this curtailment of its powers was a genuine punishment or just a temporary measure to impress critical opinion abroad, the Cheka had acquired a reputation for acting unlawfully, which made it an unsuitable agency for such a high-profile action.

From the time the Cheka chairman Dzerzhinsky was despatched on an urgent 'transportation' matter to Siberia for three months in December 1921 it was obvious that efforts at reform of at least the image of the political police were underway. They culminated on 6 February when the Cheka was officially dissolved and the GPU created in its place. The new organization was placed under the control of the People's Commissariat for Internal Affairs (NKVD) rather than Sovnarkom, The Council of People's Commissars, but since it retained its old personnel the Mensheviks rightly jeered at the change. Indeed, the only area where the GPU's scope was restricted was the measure Lunacharsky already knew of several months earlier, and even that seems to have been staged to create a false impression, since already on 10 May Dzerzhinsky's deputy Unshlikht was writing to the General Secretary of the Russian Communist Party, asking him to restore the GPU's power of administrative exile.[17] This was exactly what Lenin needed, and with the formal, but entirely hollow, makeover of the political police complete, the way was cleared for him to ask Dzerzhinsky on 19 May to prepare 'the deportation abroad of writers and professors who are helping the counter-revolution'.

Lenin took care to muddy the trail of actions and decisions leading up to the sailing of the Philosophy Steamer. So far as the informed Russian public knew, no law existed by which Russian subjects could be exiled *abroad* without trial. The requisite change in the Penal Code would not be announced until August, just a week before the deportees were arrested. Nevertheless Lenin, trained as a lawyer, had been secretly working on such a move all winter.

George Kennan (1845–1924), the American writer and traveller to Siberia, who was Chekhov's friend and who travelled in Russia in the early 1890s to see how administrative exile worked under the tsars, gave the more familiar form of Russian banishment the following description.

> Exile by administrative process means the banishment of an
> obnoxious person from one part of the empire to another without
> the observance of any of the legal formalities that, in most civilized
> countries, precede the deprivation of rights and the restriction of
> personal liberty. The obnoxious person may not be guilty of any
> crime...but if, in the opinion of the local authorities, his presence
> in a particular place is 'prejudicial to public order' or 'incompatible
> with public tranquillity' he may be arrested without a warrant...he
> may be removed by force to any other place within the limits of the
> empire and there be put under police surveillance for a period of
> from one year to ten years. He may or may not be informed of the
> reasons...in either case he is perfectly helpless.[18]

Kennan observed from the large number of such cases recorded in his notebooks that very many of the exiles under the tsars were writers, editors, journalists and people with contacts abroad and that 'The whole system is a chaos of injustice, accident and caprice.'[19] 'Administrative exile...is directed against ideas and opinions from which criminal acts may come...It is designed to anticipate and prevent the acts by suppressing or discouraging the opinions...the pretence that administrative exile is not a punishment but only a precaution is a mere juggle with words.'[20] Clearly Lenin was about to build on more than a century of corrupt tsarist practice, and knew that he was. The key to the practice of administrative exile lay in one term: *neblagonadyozhny*, which meant politically unreliable. Everything turned on whether the subject was 'politically reliable' or not. Russian governments had been asking the intelligentsia to be *blagonadyozhny* since Catherine the Great's reign in the mid-eighteenth century, and Lenin took over the practice wholesale. Thirty years ago Western Sovietologists reeled in horror at the suggestion that the Soviet Union was substantially a continuation of tsarist Russia, only so much more punitive, but a close study of Lenin's procedure over the deportations confirms it in this respect. Lenin, who was himself exiled to Siberia in the 1890s, asked of the new Soviet intelligentsia exactly what he himself had once refused to give to the leaders of imperial Russia. He took over the doublet of imperial requirement unchanged: the choice was either reliability or exile.[21]

The deportations of 1922 were made legal with the addition of a single clause to Article 57 of the Penal Code. Lenin suggested to the All-Russian Central Executive Committee – VTsIK – nominally the highest organ of state, that administrative exile abroad could be offered as a legal alternative – and effectively an act of mercy – to those whose potential or actual crimes otherwise condemned them to death.[22] The sentence could be for a fixed time or indefinite and if the guilty men returned without permission they would be shot. In fact the Politburo had agreed to Lenin's proposals soon after he had set them out in a letter on 15 May to Dmitry Ivanovich Kursky, the People's Commissar for Justice. The VTsIK was then invited to wield its rubber stamp.[23]

The revision of Article 57 was integral to the 'Janus year', in that it allowed Lenin to show his twin faces of terror and clemency simultaneously, both at home and abroad. The death sentence could be handed down to ideologically 'guilty' men, and yet without fear that Russia would incur the wrath of the world by actually slaughtering its unwanted intellectuals. Meanwhile the change in GPU regulations meant Lenin could instruct the political police to carry out a purgatorial operation without precedent.

In the light of all the extra material that scrutiny of the archives has produced, it is clear that Lenin's letter of 19 May to Dzerzhinsky was as much a summary of how far his personal idea had progressed as it was a programme for a busy GPU summer to come.

Comrade Dzerzhinsky!

On the question of deporting the writers and professors
helping the counter-revolution. This needs more thorough
preparation. Without it we shall make ourselves look silly. Please
discuss these preparatory measures. Call a meeting of Messing,
Mantsev and I don't know who else in Moscow. Entrust the
Politburo members with devoting 2–3 hours a week to looking
through a number of periodicals and books, verifying execution
[of the task], demanding reviews in writing and securing the
despatch to Moscow of all non-Communist publications
without delay.

Add to this reviews by a number of Communist writers
(Steklov, Olminsky, Skvortsov, Bukharin, etc.). Collect systematic
information about the political record, work and literary activity
of the professors and writers. Assign all this to an intelligent,
educated and scrupulous man at the GPU.[24]

My opinion on the two Petrograd publications: Novaya
Rossiya No 2. Closed down by the Petrograd comrades. Perhaps
it has been closed down too early?[25] Circulate it to the Politburo
members and discuss more thoroughly. What is its editor Lezhnev?
Is he from *Den*? Could information about him be collected? Of
course, not all the people working on the magazine are candidates
for deportation.

The Petrograd magazine *Ekonomist*...is another matter. I think
this is clearly a White Guard centre. Its No. 3 (only No. 3!!! nota
bene) carries a list of its members on the cover.[26] These I think are
almost all the most legitimate candidates for deportation.

These are all patent counter-revolutionaries, accomplices of
the Entente, an organization of its servitors and spies and corrupters
of the student youth. We should make arrangements to have these
'military spies' caught and once caught constantly [*sic*] and
systematically deported.

Please show this confidentially, without making any copies, to the Politburo members, returning it to you and to me, and inform me of their opinion and your conclusion.

Lenin

Gorky in Germany claimed to know of the GPU's operation as early as April, perhaps from Rykov, the Politburo member with whom he was in touch, so it seems possible Lenin was already discussing his intentions well before mid-May.[27] The significance of the April date, when there is otherwise a hiatus in the evidence for the expulsion plan going forward, would be that it coincided with the green light given by the Treaty of Rapallo. With this, the first recognition of the Soviet government by a foreign power, Lenin had at last secured an international partner of whom he could ask favours.

From Lossky's memoirs we know the Weimar government was prepared to grant visas that summer. Chancellor Wirth disdained the idea that Germany be seen the world over as a second Siberia. But, war-ravaged and diplomatically cold-shouldered, his country was committed to helping Russia in exchange for the gifts of Rapallo, which included Most Favoured Nation trading status and extensive trade agreements, plus cancellation of war debts and pre-war claims. Germany did not have much scope to say no.[28]

How much Lenin nevertheless depended on German cooperation can be seen from what happened at the end of 1922, after the *Haken* and the *Preussen* had sailed. The Weimar government introduced immigration restrictions in December 1922, to bolster the falling Reichsmark against the mass of incomers living off foreign currency, and from that moment the Soviet expulsion project collapsed. German complaisance in Lenin's project was crucial. The seventy-seven names on the Ukrainian list were not expelled abroad because the Soviets left it too late. No other country was willing to be party to Lenin's scheme except Czechoslovakia, and in that case Lenin was deterred because he did not want to add brain-power to Prague's already thriving anti-

Soviet Ukrainian university.[29] But the Ukrainians were the only glitch. A high-ranking German diplomat was sceptical about what Rapallo brought Germany but thought it a brilliant Russian achievement, which was right. Nineteen twenty-two, the Janus year, was a triumph for Lenin as the founder of the Soviet Union.[30]

In accordance with Lenin's letter of 19 May the GPU set to work collecting and assessing materials to draw up credible cases against the suspect intellectuals. A new regulation requiring all professional organizations to re-register with the police produced a useful list of names and addresses. But the GPU men were not up to the task, just as Lenin feared. They lacked the expertise to undermine the work of distinguished scientists and philosophers. History would uncover their primitive mentality when some of the files they compiled were opened seventy years later.

The brilliant, energetic Lenin remained the one person who could make the totalitarian gesture succeed. He read every journal and had the annual conference of every profession watched for signs of something less than docility;[31] anything he could use against his perceived ideological adversaries he did. He was also almost demented in his sense that anti-Bolshevik conspiracy lurked round every corner, and pounced on anything that seemed like criticism of his power. Already at their congress the previous October the agricultural cooperatists had shown some resistance to Bolshevik bullying, and Lenin subsequently marked down all those who favoured or taught or participated in economic cooperatism, even though he feigned approval of their ideas in public. He also lined up for expulsion a number of engineers like Nikolai Kozlov, who became a friend of the Franks, and the railways specialist Efim Zubashov, because they were members of a welfare organization campaigning for better conditions for their profession. These men were to be deported despite the skills they could offer a needy country. Out of a similar paranoia, when the independent-minded agronomists met in March, and the doctors and the geologists in May, Lenin quickly put the GPU on their trail. By the time a report on the doctors' recalcitrance by People's Commissar for Health Nikolai

Semashko reached him on 21–22 May, the Politburo knew what was required of it and voted on 24 May to ask Dzerzhinsky and Semashko for a joint plan of action on curbing professional independence. When, the next day, 25 May, Lenin suffered the first of the series of strokes which would render him powerless by the end of the year, he could not have organized things better. No doubt it was a coincidence, but the campaign against the intellectuals now had its own momentum and could be left to run.

The engine of the campaign was the notion that 'an anti-Soviet intelligentsia' – an institutionalized counter-revolution – was threatening the state and had to be stopped.[32] Such a motive body didn't necessarily exist, but the GPU was primed to create the impression, which it did amongst the Soviet public, by carrying out appropriate arrests. If criminal intent could be shown, then punitive action could be justified.

There has been disagreement among historians over whether Lenin targeted individuals or their ideas in his purges, but surely the notion of an anti-Soviet intelligentsia makes his tactics clear. Lenin was always furious at being personally humiliated, as he felt he was, for instance, by the professors' strike in February. He could make it seem as if a political offence was a personal insult. But there can be no doubt that his primary target was ideas. For Lenin individuals were politically acceptable or not by virtue of the ideas they held. If their views were inimical they had to be got rid of.[33] When the GPU 'interviewed' the deportees and sentenced them to administrative exile, the only real charge against them was that they would never come round to a Bolshevik way of thinking. Yet Lenin's attitude was not only the result of his paranoia. There was genuine Marxist reasoning behind it. Individuals could be marked out by the conscious views they held, or, according to Marx, by their socio-economic background, which inspired those views unconsciously. Thus some men worthy of deportation might be active campaigners against Bolshevism, while others would have to be removed from any future Communist society because they were unwitting tools of a redundant class.

The Soviet class-war mentality was classically defined in 1918 by Martyn Latsis, one of Dzerzhinsky's two right-hand men at the Cheka.

> We are not waging war against individual persons. We are exterminating the bourgeoisie as a class. During the investigation, do not look for evidence that the accused acted in deed or word against Soviet power. The first questions that you ought to put are: To what class does he belong? What is his origin? What is his education or profession? And it is these questions that ought to determine the fate of the accused. In this lies the significance and essence of the Red Terror.[34]

For Lenin similarly it was not who men were but what ideological force they generated that mattered. One can see this in the letter of 19 May, the way he asks of the editor of *Den*: 'What is he?' On the other hand, Lenin was less purely ideological than he might have been, in so far as he gave every Soviet citizen the chance to save himself from trouble. At the Tenth Party Conference in 1921 he openly advised those critical of the October Revolution to 'make an effort to hold back from expressing your views'.[35] Perhaps he wasn't a wholesale convert to Marxist inevitability after all.

A key GPU man involved in preparing the deportations was Yakov Saulovich Agranov, who had directed investigations of all the important cases against perceived anti-Sovietism over the past two years – National Centre, Tactical Centre, the Kronstadt uprising and the Tagantsev Affair. It was Agranov's memo which allowed Unshlikht to write his report 'On Anti-Soviet Groupings Within the Intelligentsia' and move the whole process on while Lenin was ill. That report finally proposed that lists of people guilty under the revised Article 57 and therefore ripe for deportation, be drawn up by a special commission.[36] The Politburo discussed the matter on 8 June.

From the last week of May the campaign was steered by the three-member Kamenev Committee, or Commission, on which Kamenev represented the NKVD, Unshlikht the GPU and Kursky the Justice Ministry.[37] One of their first tasks was to precure visas, and one assumes that this was when they approached the Germans on a state level and were rebuffed by Chancellor Wirth's insistence, later recorded by Lossky, that Germany would only deal with individuals, not act as a dumping ground for the Russian government; at least not openly. Through June the three Leninists then blundered their way through a case prompted by the medical profession's annual conference. This, twenty-five years before Stalin would create a farrago of a similar name, was the case of the 'anti-Soviet' doctors. On 21 June Unshlikht informed Josef Stalin, as Chairman of the Sovnarkom, that sentences of administrative exile had already been carried out on doctors Granovsky, Manul, Vigdorchik and Livin, next day adding that questioning the culprits had produced increasing evidence of anti-Soviet conspiracy. Unshlikht then used the existence of the 'doctors' plot' to urge his colleagues to get on with the main 'operation' – the deportations – quickly. In fact the doctors, not yet despatched anywhere, were eventually sentenced to internal exile because they were too useful to their country to be deported. But their cases remained mixed up with the foreign deportations right into the autumn, and more doctors were arrested along with the main purge of the intelligentsia in August. Above all, the GPU was keen to build up a sense of anti-Soviet conspiracy in the air.[38]

Stalin entered the deportation story halfway through 1922, thanks to his steady rise to power through the Party. The arrangements made for the Philosophy Steamer to sail would not be his crime so much as an opportunity for him to learn. He had a rougher lesson in terror from watching the staging of the two show trials against the Church, and a third against the SRs, between April and the end of July 1922.[39] But Lenin copied him in on his memo about wanting to throw out the professors in February, and once Stalin became General Secretary, all the key documents regarding the expulsions passed over his desk. Stalin thus became one more functionary from whom Lenin could demand action to implement his plan, and he was the first person to whom Lenin turned when, in the third week of June, he began to recover. Immediately he fired off a letter asking why the new 'Gensec' was dragging his feet on the expulsion issue.

Comrade Stalin,

On the matter of deporting Mensheviks, Popular Socialists, Kadets and so on from Russia, I'd like to raise several questions, seeing that this operation, which was started before I went on leave, hasn't been completed even now. Has the decision been taken to 'uproot' all the [Popular Socialists]? Peshekhonov, Myakotin, Gorenfeld, Petrishchev and the others? In my opinion they should all be expelled. They're worse than any [Socialist Revolutionary] as they're more cunning. Also A. N. Potresov, Izgoev and all the staff at *Ekonomist* (Ozerov and many, many others). The Mensheviks Rozanov (he's an enemy, a cunning one), Vigdorchik, Migulo and anyone else of that ilk, Lyubov Nikolaevna Radchenko and her younger daughter (I hear they're sworn enemies of Bolshevism); N. A. Rozhkov (he has to be expelled, he's stubborn); S. L. Frank, the author of *The Methodology*. Mantsev's and Messing's commission must draw up lists and several hundred of such gentlemen must be expelled abroad without mercy. We're going to cleanse Russia once and for all.

Like all the people on *Ekonomist* Ozerov is the most relentless enemy. All of them must be chucked out of Russia. It should be done all at once. By the time the SR trial is over, not later, and with no explanation of motives – leave, gentlemen!

All the authors in The Writers' House [Dom literatorov], *Mysl'* in Petrograd; Kharkhov must be ransacked, we have no idea what is happening there, it's abroad to us. We must clean up quickly, no later than the end of the SR trial.

Pay attention to the writers in Petrograd (their addresses in Novaya russkaya kniga No. 4 1922 p37) and also to the list of private publishers (p29).

With Communist Greetings,
Lenin[40]

Writing this letter, Lenin, despite having suffered a stroke, jumped straight back to where he left off on 19 May, even using the same heading.[41] Having been, as he put it, 'on leave', he showed no sign of intellectual disability, only an increasing focus on which names should be listed. Familiar generalizations about his health suggest it was impossible for Lenin to mastermind the sailing of the Philosophy Steamer in 1922 because he was too debilitated, but close attention paid to the timetable and detail of his illness shows how he managed. The first stroke of the year briefly confused his mind and immobilized the right side of his body, but while his body would never fully recover and his emotions remained fragile his intellect quickly refocused.[42] Above all he stuck to his plan to *cleanse* Russia once and for all of dissenting elements. 'Cleansing' was what he was already doing to the Church[43] and, in passing, was one of the key lessons Lenin provided for Stalin.

Stalin was slow to take up the initiative in Lenin's eyes, but Trotsky was not. While Lenin was ill he stepped forward to play his part in the expulsion campaign without prompting, though it was an odd move. Perhaps it was most in line with his own interests as a writer. On 2 June he published an anonymous article in *Pravda* fiercely denouncing Yuly Aikhenvald, a cultural figure whom Lenin might not otherwise have come across.[44] Headlined *Diktatura, gde tvoi khlyst?* ('Dictatorship, Where is Your Whip?') Trotsky's article declared it a political offence for a book like Aikhenvald's recent *Poety i poetessy* ('Poets and Poetesses') to be published in the new 'Workers' Russia'.

Aikhenvald was close to the men of Dom literatorov who had begged for Gumilyov's life, and, like Berdyaev and Frank, his way of thinking was idealist rather than Marxist-materialist. Aiming to make him seem pretty awful as a critic by any standards, Trotsky decried Aikhenvald's sentimentality and lambasted his essays praising Blok and Gumilyov. But chiefly he claimed to find a political machination behind every one of the critic's aesthetic judgements. As Lenin had already purported to show in his philosophical work, 'idealism' was one of the means by which the bourgeoisie shored up its power, helped by the Church, so there was no question but that Aikhenvald was a class enemy. Now Trotsky showed how the critic used his literary judgements to further a political agenda.[45] He had 'a political taste for monarchy and reaction' – a reference to his support for Gumilyov – and he was 'a philosophical, aesthetic, literary, religious sponger, that is, he's the dregs, trash'.[46]

Trotsky's article heaped personal abuse on Aikhenvald in that unmistakably snide and abusive style pioneered by Lenin which came to typify official Soviet journalism. A typical ideological-stylistic device was to seize on a proper name and make it plural, thereby falsely extrapolating an organized political faction out of an alleged individual case. Thus Trotsky now decried 'the Aikhenvalds' of this world just as Lenin had sometime decried 'the Berdyaevs'.[47] Once they were depicted as organized and plural it was only natural that the whole lot of them deserved to be deported.

Stalin chaired a series of Politburo meetings through July, when the selection of deportees was finessed.[48] As many as thirty discussions took place, during which time Lenin suggested that the following categories of men be banished:

> Professors of 1st Moscow University
> Professors of Petrovsko-Razumovsky Agricultural Academy
> Professors of the Institute of Railway Engineers
> [Those involved in] the case of the Free Economic Society
> Anti-Soviet professors of the Archaeological Institute
> Anti-Soviet figures connected with the Bereg publishing house
> People involved in Case no. 813 (Abrikosov Group)
> Anti-Soviet agronomists and cooperatists
> Physicians
> Anti-Soviet engineers
> Writers
> Petrograd writers
> A special list of anti-Soviet members of the
>   Petrograd intelligentsia.[49]

When files began to arrive from the GPU naming and shaming specific people in these categories, the Politburo, perhaps alerted to Lenin's fear of 'being made to look silly', sent them back with a request for more attention to be paid to the distinctiveness of the individual cases. They had to look convincing. This was difficult, of course, because each case had to be fabricated.

Meanwhile Unshlikht finally got round to the money needed to send the unwanted intelligentsia abroad.

> All notable individuals will be arrested and offered the chance to
> leave the country at their own expense. If they refuse the GPU
> will pay.

At the same time he placated Lenin by telling him that the counter-revolutionary newspapers *Vestnik sel'skogo khozaistva* ('Agricultural News'), *Mysl'* ('Thought') and *Ekonomicheskoe vozrozhdenie* ('Economic Rebirth') would be closed for publishing anti-Soviet and idealist views.[50]

The Philosophy Steamer is in its way a neglected chapter of Lenin's biography. The detailed story of the expulsions yields the richest possible material to help us understand his tainted genius. It shows his propensity for evil, and his tactical brilliance. As he masterminded preparations for the expulsions through July, he continued, as always, to combine violent rhetoric with cool calculation.[51] He meted out verbal death and destruction to every least and last ideological opponent, and he had no aversion to letting their deaths happen.[52] Nevertheless he was not a maniac, nor a 'gibbering wreck', precisely because he was in control, even to the extent of worrying what posterity, the only possible inspecting eye, would one day think of the thin, bogus cases being dreamt up against the philosophers.[53]

Lenin's procedure that summer included both the right presentation of the expulsions in the press and a judicious review of exceptional cases, which in at least two present instances he carried out himself. A terminally ill man unlikely ever to function politically again was the Menshevik Nikolai Rozkhov, whom in June Lenin had called 'stubborn' and a prime candidate for eviction. When less than six weeks later he learnt Rozhkov was in the final stages of tuberculosis, he removed him from the list and gave him a flat and a pension to see out his last days. A fellow Marxist from Lenin's Petersburg days, Nikolai Korobko, was also reprieved because he was suffering from the same disease, and, quietly, the son of another colleague from those days was also allowed to leave Russia to join his father.[54] The men whom Lenin excepted from punishment in 1922 further support the claim that his targets were not men in themselves but their capacity to embody and spread unacceptable ideas. Other instances of Lenin's sympathy towards Party workers and opponents alike can be found in earlier years. His evil is not diminished by utilitarian actions which were also charitable, and perhaps sympathy is too strong a word for what swayed his judgement, but one has to take his inconsistent behaviour into account. Even evil men are not machines.

It is also clear that Lenin never contemplated shooting the likes of Berdyaev, Frank, Aikhenvald and Kizevetter, however much he despised them, and here two reasons suggest themselves. The first was that once again he was wary of what the West might think if leading members of the intelligentsia were executed. In July he would be deterred from carrying out the death sentences passed on the SRs for just that reason. The SRs – of whom fourteen were initially sentenced to death – were treated much more roughly than the intelligentsia because they were seen as a military enemy. The SRs had been useful to the Bolsheviks so long as they helped against the Whites, but were regarded as enemies once the Civil War was over. On Trotsky's advice, their death sentences were commuted to five-year prison sentences. The SR prisoners didn't benefit since they were forgotten in jail and shot when Stalin's purges began. But at least the world could see that they were not shot by Lenin. An interesting archive document published since 1991 is a letter Gorky in Berlin wrote to Rykov of the Politburo on 1 July, saying that 'if the SRs are killed the crime will lead to a moral blockade of Russia on the part of Socialist Europe'. If this advice was passed on Trotsky and Lenin may well have heeded it.[55] So I am inclined to disagree with the view that Lenin had 'a personal phobia' which made him fear assassination.[56] He was simply much too cunning to associate himself directly with killing.

But the greater reason why the intelligentsia was spared was surely that Lenin was prepared to treat them with a minimum of civic dignity, as his equals on the defeated side. The liberal philosophers and journalists were originally of the same class – educated men of mixed social origins – as Lenin, and for a century the Russian intelligentsia had been defined by its concerted desire to rid the country of tsarism. Also the intelligentsia was not, except in isolated cases, violent. Circumstances only changed when the intelligentsia split, and one faction of it seized political power by force. Then real power came to matter more than winning arguments and, just as the tsar had driven out the anti-imperialist Lenin and Lunacharsky to keep his empire intact, so now Bolshevism would oust its critics to the same purpose.

In fact although the GPU was several times warned by Lenin that it would have to make its cases against the intelligentsia convincing, it never managed to do so.[57] Bright members of Narkompros were called in to help fabricate arguments but failed to make things better. Characterizations in the files which were supposed to be incriminating, and which we can now read for the first time since the event, focused on irrelevant information like 'knows a foreign language', 'only explains himself and teaches in Ukrainian' and 'is ironic and fools about in his lectures'.[58] To be criticized for being 'close to the Americans – the representatives of the ARA', and 'organized fund-raising balls for the Whites' was not irrelevant but hardly a sufficient offence if expulsion was really to be justified. Every file contained a sentence saying one way or another that this was a harmful person and an enemy of Soviet power, who had invidious contacts, or was in a position to stir up anti-Soviet feeling among others, above all students. But little rang true.

Lossky and Karsavin were alleged 'to have received in 1920–1921 financial support from White organizations through the leader of

Tagantsev organization'. Sorokin and Karsavin were blamed for their religious convictions and teaching. Frank was judged 'to have the capacity to join in counter-revolution on the part of the Church'. He also 'opposed higher education reforms' as did Yasinsky, who took part in the Professors' Strike. Karsavin and the journalists Khariton and Volkovysky were alleged 'to do nothing' professionally – the future Soviet charge, yet to be codified, of parasitism – or they were said like Yasinsky to be unimportant in their contribution. Aikhenvald 'prevaricated', Khariton and Volkovysky were 'cunning and devious'. 'If we got rid of them,' said the file on these two organizers of the Dom literatorov, 'we could get at that cell which is taking up a position against us.' The GPU commended Aikhenvald for praising Trotsky – some misunderstanding there – but reprehended him for praising Gumilyov. Berdyaev 'belonged to The Black Hundreds', an accusation which was the equivalent of calling a man a Fascist today. To say of Stepun meanwhile that 'he would feel very well abroad' begged the question. The paragraph on Izgoev was packed with absurdly innocuous details:

> He's a rightwing Kadet and an old Vekhi man. A fairly powerful figure. He always was a Bolshevik-eating Kadet. That's his dangerous side. His 'Little Fools and Clever Chaps' is a very good pamphlet against the Bolsheviks. He's a clever and cunning writer. Up until now he's avoided all contact with us and persists in his work at the House of Writers. He is the soul behind all the protests and resolutions introduced there. Comrade Stekov [sic] observes that Izgoev has suffered all deprivations and still hasn't gone abroad.

A file compiled on the writer Zamyatin was more vicious and even more fantastic:

> Works for the *Letopisi* [*Doma literatorov*] ('The Journal of the House of Writers') and *Literaturnye zapiski* ('Literary Notes'). A secret and inveterate White Guard. He is the author of an illegal resolution, which he introduced to a meeting of the House of Writers, in which

he denounced Andrei Bely for his defence of Soviet Russia. In his literary work he takes an entirely anti-Soviet line. He's in close touch with Remizov who ran away. Remizov himself is a definite enemy. Zamyatin is the same. If we send him abroad he'll become a dangerous leader. We have to send him to Novgorod, or to Kursk, but not under any circumstances abroad.

The Kamenev Committee also wrote comments on the files as to what 'punishment' would be appropriate. 'Send him abroad regardless of the outcome of the investigation' was one such recommendation, entirely in Lenin's own spirit.[59]

There was now an almost slapstick quality in the way all those who wished to impress Lenin were showing off their competence and commitment to the coming expulsions. Zinoviev marked the Twelfth Conference of the Russian Communist Party (B) with two articles in *Pravda*. On 8 August he told the story of how, with the reawakening of social life at the end of the Civil War and the transition to the NEP, 'chains of [hostile] molecules had formed…' In a mirror image of what the Politburo was doing, Zinoviev accused the regime's opponents of trying to exploit the 'legal possibilities' of the Soviet regime. His article of 9 August named areas in which the new state was particularly vulnerable: the cooperative movement, higher education, literature, publishing, and the professions of medicine, engineering, agronomy. All these were potential sources of opinion-formation which needed to be dealt with on a preventative basis. Zinoviev spoke of a 'system of combined measures' and of 'preventative surgery'. He referred to the strike of the Moscow professors, the various professional congresses during the year, and the periodicals *Ekonomist* and *Utrenniki* ('Matinees') to which Izgoev, Sorokin and Berdyaev contributed. He singled out Brutskus among the agricultural economists. Thus he very neatly prepared the way for the signing into law of the change to Article 57 on 10 August, the revision on which the Politburo had been acting since May.

It was made public in a decree of 10 August, building awkwardly on the established imperial legal framework dealing with internal exile:

The All-Russian Central Executive Committee resolves that:

1. In the interests of isolating individuals predisposed to counter-revolutionary acts, in relation to whom the All-Russian Central Executive Committee is requested to permit their isolation for more than two months, in those cases where there is the possibility of not resorting to arrest, to implement expulsion abroad or to defined places within the RSFSR by administrative order.

2. Questions relating to the expulsion of individuals may be lodged with the Special Commission of the People's Commissariat for Internal Affairs [NKVD] acting under the direction of the People's Commissar for Internal Affairs and the People's Commissar for Justice, as endorsed by the Presidium of the All-Russian Central Executive Committee.

3. Decrees relating to the expulsion of each individual person must be accompanied by detailed indications of the reasons for the exile.

4. The exile decree must show the place of exile and the duration.

5. The list of places for exile prepared by the Commission is to be passed by the All-Russian Central Executive Committee.

6. The period of administrative exile is not to exceed three years.

7. Those sentenced to administrative exile for the duration of their exile lose active and passive voting rights.

8. People exiled to named regions will come under the surveillance of the local branch of the State Political Administration [GPU], which will determine where the person shall live within the region of exile.

9. Escape from the place of exile or on the way there will be punished before a court according to Article 95 of the Criminal Code.

On the basis of the present decree the People's Commissariat for Internal Affairs will give detailed instructions to local authorities.[60]

Even now the decree's contents were veiled with regard to reality: Article 95 entailed the death sentence. Nor, *pace* paragraph six, was it for three years that the unwanted intellectuals and their families were about to be sent away. Here was the legal means to banish Lenin's ideological opponents indefinitely.

Zinoviev's articles during the Party Conference reiterated all of Lenin's pet hatreds and made them public. They echoed Lenin's March policy statement on the need for terror: 'In the economic sphere the retreat remains, in the political the assault continues.'[61] Their unique new feature was to refer to the expulsions as 'preventative surgery'. That is how the expulsions would be presented to the Russian people at the end of the month.

4

Arrest and Interrogation

THE ARRESTS TOOK place, simultaneously in Moscow and Petrograd, overnight on 16–17 August, though it would take weeks to round up the few whom the GPU could not immediately find. Stratonov was arrested on the 17th after a document was sent to his place of work but Stepun and Myakotin were harder to locate and there was no sign of Ilyin before 4 September.[1] Many families like the Franks and Osorgins were at their summer dachas and the Stepuns had been living in the country, growing their own food, for the past four years. The Ukraine arrests happened twenty-four hours later, on 17–18 August, although Lenin felt he 'knew nothing' about the operation there because the location was 'almost abroad'.[2]

The GPU swoop was accompanied by a flurry of paper exchanged between offices, with figures for each city and names of who was being held where. Documents undersigned by Stalin went every few days from the Politburo to Lenin to keep him informed. By this route Lenin heard from Unshlikht on 18 August:

> In accordance with your instructions I enclose lists for the intelligentsia in Moscow, Piter and Ukraine as endorsed by the Politburo. The operation was carried out in Moscow and Piter on the night of the 16/17, and in Ukraine on 17/18. The Moscow public will learn today of the decree on foreign deportations and [how those deported will be] warned that arbitrary entry into the

RSFSR is punishable by execution. Tomorrow we will sort out the question of the visas. I will send you a report daily as to how things are going with the deportations.

Communist greetings.
Unshlikht[3]

In fact the public would first learn of the deportations thirteeen days later, on 31 August, from a front-page story in *Pravda* headlined 'The First Warning'. Simultaneously the story would become news in the West.

Given that nothing in practice is quite what it seems on paper, the arrests went remarkably smoothly. By 23 August two senior GPU men could report to Stalin that of the sixty-seven names on the Moscow list, all but two were accounted for.[4] One of those turned out to be already in prison, otherwise the breakdown of the figures was as follows. Out of a total of forty-six arrests, twenty-one of the detainees had already been released, having undertaken 'to go abroad at their own expense'. They included Berdyaev, Aikhenvald, Frank, Stratonov, the journalist and painter Iosif Matusevich, the cooperative publishers Vasily Kudryavtsev and Vladimir Rozenberg and the cleric Father Abrikosov and his disciple Kuzmin-Karavaycv. Eleven wanted men were in other towns, where they would be picked up by local police. Eight were known to be in the Moscow area but had not yet been found. That left some twenty-five men in prison.

Possibly a delay in completing the interrogations prompted the longer detention of these men who included Novikov, Kizevetter, Ugrimov and Osorgin. One who initially refused to go abroad was Trubetskoy, because he suspected a GPU trick. He remained in prison for two weeks. A second man, not released because he absolutely refused to emigrate, was Leonid Naumovich Yurovsky, a financier and pupil of Struve. This old friend of the Frank family would eventually die in Stalin's purges.[5] Velikhov was another who remained in prison.

For Petrograd, thirty arrests were announced in the report of 23 August, including Brutskus, Selivanov, Lapshin, Zamyatin, Karsavin and Lossky. Passed on to Moscow as 'a summary', the report did not specify whether any of those detained had been released, although it did note that the last three names, plus four other well-known figures – Pumpyansky from *Ekonomist*, Izgoev, and Volkovysky and Khariton from Dom literatorov – had agreed to paid the journey into exile themselves.

The report of 23 August is evidence of how difficult it is, even today, to pin down the exact number of deportees. That key document named ninety-seven individuals, of whom the vast majority were sooner or later arrested, but as many as forty-six of them were not in the end expelled abroad. Zamyatin was one, Lenin's former St Petersburg Marxist colleague, Nikolai Korobko, still listed though already reprieved, another. An uncertain number, but at least the four people specified, who were all doctors, were treated as their professional colleagues had been in June and exiled internally 'to the Eastern provinces where their specialities can be of use'. In compensation for the lack of exact figures, what we have are some remarkably detailed accounts of some of the detainees' last days of freedom.

Nikolai Lossky, who with his wife and family was an almost perfect representative of bourgeois academic life in pre-Soviet Russia, remembered it as a busy and interesting summer, though otherwise nothing out of the ordinary. He, Lyudmila, her mother and the children had gone to stay out at Tsarskoe Tselo, the 'Tsar's Village' situated about sixteen miles south of St Petersburg. The nearby imperial palace of Pavlovsk, built in the mid-eighteenth century, and the presence of an elite school where Pushkin had studied, had helped to create a summer resort popular with men and women of culture. The Bolsheviks went some way to try to undo that image when they used this privileged village to house orphans from the Revolution and the Civil War. These were 'wild' children who had taken to roaming the country in gangs. The move prompted a change in the name of the village to Detskoe Tselo, 'The Children's Village'. Lenin's wife Krupskaya and the Cultural Commissar Lunacharsky were among many prominent figures who tried to deal with the huge social problem of the *bezprezornye*, literally 'the children with no one to care for them' out at Detskoe Tselo. Later again the name of the village, easily accessible from St Petersburg by train, was changed to Pushkin.

That summer our family was staying out at Tsarskoe Tselo. The writer Ivanov-Razumnik was staying at his own house in the town. He invited Maria Nikolaevna [Stoyunina] and me to come and spend the evening of 15 August [*sic*] with him, so we could meet the poet Klyuev and the writer Olga Forsh. Klyuev read his poem to us which was a very vivid depiction of peasant life in the north of Russia and Olga Forsh told us about an anti-religious meeting she had attended. The priest Alexander Vvedensky had spoken up in defence of religion and the existence of God...

Vvedensky was of course the man who for so long had been Lossky's head of department and who had blocked his professorship. Yet Lossky was not a man to bear a grudge, all the more as Vvedensky had become a man almost to be pitied by those who knew him. The Bolsheviks had dismissed him from his academic post after he had called pro-Bolshevik students 'sheep', and he had used the religion that was permitted under the auspices of the Living Church to work his way back into a public position.

In fact what remained uppermost in Lossky's memory of his last summer holiday in Russia was his own political naivety.

Next day I received a communication which said I was to appear in Gorokhovaya Street at the Headquarters of the Cheka... Thinking they were calling me in over some formality regarding my foreign passport I had no qualms in going. But as soon as I entered I realized I was under arrest. They took me to one of the upper floors and sat me on a bench in a corridor, outside a door, with an armed guard alongside. 'Have them bring in Karsavin.' Just next to me they took Lev Platonovich into the room I was sitting alongside. After half an hour Karsavin was led out and I was led in.[6]

Although the GPU agents were not always very bright, amongst the intelligentsia there was not much scope for being clever at their expense because Lenin's political police had such a powerful hold on the country. Vera Aleksandrovna Ugrimova, aged twenty, soon learnt. She was at home in central Moscow on the evening of 15 / 16 August 1922, when the knock on the door arrived. Her immediate thought was not to betray to the police where her father was.

> They came when father was in the country (in Uskoe) and my main
> thought was how to stop them finding out where he was. The
> address was beside the telephone but fortunately they didn't see it. I
> was able to get word to him what had happened. Next morning I
> met the Berdyaevs' maid in the Arbat. She told me there had been
> many searches in the night: Novikov, Vysheslavtsev, Kizevetter, Ilyin,
> Trubetskoy. When Father came back he reported voluntarily to the
> Cheka. He said there wasn't much point in resisting.

One consolation felt by nearly all the detainees was the realization that arrest was not happening to them alone. They felt solidarity and tried to help each other.

> It was difficult to get German visas, but my father was able to help
> the whole group, because through a happy coincidence we had
> a German visitor at the time, a colleague of Father's from the
> University of Leipzig called Videnfeld. Videnfeld handed over
> the visa requests personally at the German Consulate.[7]

This for the young Ugrimova was a matter of some pride.

For her part Tatyana Frank left an animated and typically defiant account of the months leading up to the expulsions, when she was aged thirty-five and the mother of four children. Her grandson Peter Scorer invited her to recount her memories forty-three years later and recorded them on tape.

> When did we go to Moscow? They expelled us in '22. By that time
> we had already been two years in Moscow. So it must have been in

1920. [It was autumn 1921.] Yes, that's it, yes. Semyon Lyudvigovich [Frank] had joined the social security department of the local Soviet and with the job he got two rooms in a large house. It was a communal house, where one day, not understanding the situation at all, I said to a Communist woman with a Lenin brooch, why are you wearing that scoundrel? Two rooms, one of which was called the bedroom, the nursery, the drawing-room and the dining room. We slept in the other room with [our younger children] Natasha and Vasya, and in the first were our two boys and our cook Maria Aleksanna. So the manager calls me upstairs. He's sitting there. We haven't anything apart from what Sofia Lyudvigovna [my husband's sister] sends us [from Paris]. Nothing else at all. [The manager]'s sitting there, eating caviare, doesn't ask me to sit down, nothing. He says, tell me, please, are you an intelligent person? I said I used to be, I don't know about now. 'How can you permit such an absence of understanding of hygiene?' I say: 'In what respect?' 'How can you keep your cook in the corridor?' 'And where should I put her, according to your standards of hygiene? In my flat? We have two rooms and there are seven of us.'

The reference to 'hygiene' was a peculiar Soviet circumlocution, a mixture of primness and ignorance on the part of a minor official who really had in mind 'decency'. Tatyana evidently enjoyed leaping on that piece of verbal idiocy. But just like Professors Lossky and Ugrimov she recognized from the outset that she was powerless to resist the Sovietization of her life in any more meaningful way. And so, on grounds of 'hygiene', the cook was dismissed.

I just had to let her go, there wasn't enough room. [The manager] called me in again, without Semyon Lyudvigovich. I always gave him the same response, 'What do you want me to do? How are we supposed to live?'

We decided to stay in Moscow, we couldn't get away anywhere else, we settled the children in a wonderful school, of the kind which still existed then. We survived the winter, then went out to Akulovka, a village on the banks of a wonderful little stream, and there we spent a grand summer....

It was one of the memorable features of the arrests, that they happened in the middle of the dacha season, the time of the year when the cities were abandoned for the countryside and Russian life was most glorious. For several years the Franks had been sharing their summer holidays, renting wooden cottages on the banks of the Moscow river, with Mikhail and Rachel Osorgin.

It was there that these gentleman came out to see us in a big car. The housekeeper woke me in the morning and said, they've come for your old man, but they've got stuck in the marshes, they missed the road. So we had time to get up meanwhile. I wrapped all the jewellery I had left just in a handkerchief and threw it into the patch of nettles outside. I saved it like that. They arrived, three men and one peasant woman wearing a red scarf. Alyosha went straight over and sat with them, that sort of thing. [He was 12.] They sent him to him to buy them something to eat. And then they took Semyon Lyudvigovich away.

Tatyana could barely write a word without recording the obtuseness and crude manners of the Bolshevik officials who despised men and women of her class and whose state-sanctioned task it was to confiscate their valuables and houses. She was too spirited and resourceful to be afraid, but looking back the element of unpredictability on the other side was menacing. In the event she lived from hour to hour.

People said 'Your flat is empty, you can go back.' I arrived and found the flat sealed. So there I was with nowhere to go. I had to go to some office, I don't remember where, to get them to undo the seal and open it. That was all. The same day Berdyaev telephoned and said: 'They've questioned and released me. They'll question Semyon Lyudvigovich tomorrow and he'll be back with you in the evening, because they're not keeping us after questioning.' Well, he spent two or three nights in prison with Trubetskoy, Evgeny's son, and with the Bishop of Kazan, I've forgotten what his name was. He ate absolutely nothing, he couldn't. There was cabbage, but, as he said, 'I couldn't, then we waited and waited.'[8]

The day they came for Tatyana's 'old man' it seems that Mikhail Osorgin had gone fishing. With the same justified fatalism as all of Lenin's other earmarked victims, he knew his luck only gave him a temporary respite. He used it to say a proper farewell to the Russian countryside he loved.

> I see the village of Borvikha near Moscow… on the Moscow river…Where we were staying there was a square field about one verst each side surrounded by a forest. In the middle of the field was a small island of young pines, and within that little wood was a tiny meadow.
>
> If it had rained the night before and the sun came out hot in the morning, then a miracle occurred: an invisible vapour of mint rose up from the field…The same vapour, a mist of mint, enveloped one on the downslope of a shallow green ravine some distance away… And there was a pine forest… A primeval pine forest, never logged and completely untended…
>
> I once walked through the forest in order to keep from returning home.

There was something of a mythical tone to Osorgin's memoir of the fateful summer of 1922, written much later, after he had settled in France. The fragments evoking his earlier life in Russia were amongst the best things he ever wrote, because he was able to combine his view of events from a great distance, which evoked pathos at the fate of individuals making their insignificant way through history, at the same time as he seemed to be re-hearing the voices and re-viewing the images of yesterday.

At home – at the dacha – certain people dressed in overcoats had arrived, insisting they had brought 'a letter from Narkompros'; it was absolutely necessary to deliver it in person. But it was not nor had I ever been in correspondence with any sort of Narkompros. From the top of a little hill my people waved a handkerchief, and I understood the signal. As though going fishing, I went off with my rod and reel along the forest path. Where the path came out near a road, I met an automobile. In it sat two insolent young men, wearing red stars on their cloth helmets bordered in black. Nothing happened. They went on past, not letting down their hooks, although they would soon have been winding in their reels.

Now Osorgin too experienced what Tatyana Frank, and professors Ugrimov and Lossky had felt, namely that these unintelligent lieutenants of Bolshevism, whose job it was to arrest them, were so easy to deceive, and yet, at the same time, it was impossible to escape from them.

I climbed up on the steep bank and looked for the last time at the Moscow river… And for a long time I walked through the pine forest. As luck would have it, that very day a mass of huge white mushrooms had burst through the forest floor. One could not help but pick them and it would have been a pity to throw them away. I hid my fishing rod at the edge of the forest under a bush and carried my mushrooms in a handkerchief to the nearest village. There I stayed overnight with good friends.

For three days I wandered in the forest and gathered mushrooms; on the fourth day I went to Moscow.

'Are you looking for me?'

'Yes.'

'Well here I am. I'm turning myself in.'[9]

Had escape been possible, the clever and resourceful Pitirim Sorokin, surrounded by equally quick-thinking students and family, would surely have managed it. Russian families and groups of colleagues and friends had in those days, as they did all through the Soviet period and still today, a sense of needing to band together, positively to get what they need in terms of goods and services, and negatively to defend themselves against sudden encroachments by the state. Under Soviet influence half of Europe would come to know the need for that kind of carefully maintained private life, in order to survive in a totalitarian system. Sorokin had honed those skills, and they brought him a little extra time to prepare his departure.

On 10 August, 1922 I left Petrograd for a few days in Moscow. From the station I went directly to the apartment of Professor Kondratyev, who invited me to stay with him. We had breakfast and parted, arranging to meet at five o'clock in his apartment...

I returned but my friend was not at home. At six he had not come and I became a little uneasy. At seven a student came, asking for my friend's wife. I told him that neither he nor she were at home... He looked at me fixedly and asked: 'Who are you?' I introduced myself and he said: 'Professor, get out of the apartment. Your friend is under arrest and the Chekists may be here at any moment.'

I took my bag and left... A few hours later we learned that professors Kizevetter and Frank, Berdyaev and Yasinsky, Sofronov and Ozerov, Myakotin and Peshekhonov, Osorgin and many others... had been arrested. A great terror was evidently beginning and might be starting also in Petrograd. All doubt on this score was removed the following day when I read a telegram sent by my wife to a friend in Moscow. This telegram read: 'Please detain my son. We have scarlet fever in our house.'

Sorokin's wife was as cunning as Vera Ugrimova tried to be. But her husband, with a characteristic sense of what his service to his country was worth, and what the Bolsheviks were about to deprive themselves of, quickly made up his mind: 'As soon as the fate of my arrested colleagues became known I decided that my own banishment abroad was the best thing that could happen to me. I could do nothing more for my country.'

He set off for the same village refuge just outside Petersburg where, like the Losskys, he and his wife were accustomed to spend the summer.

It was a lovely September morning when I reached Tsarskoe Tselo. My wife was away from home so I began to prepare my prison bag myself, packing it with food and linen and with two or three books…When my wife returned she tried at once to dissuade me…She showed me copies of 'The Petrograd Pravda' and 'The Red Gazette' in which I was furiously assailed and threatened. On the way we met friends who joined my wife in considering me quite mad to venture into Petrograd. 'If Zinoviev and his crew do not shoot you at once,' they said, 'you will be banished to Siberia and not to any foreign country.'

Finally I agreed that it might be better for me to be arrested in Moscow, and next morning I returned there. With my prison bag I presented myself at the Cheka…

'My name is Sorokin,' I said. 'Your comrades in Petrograd want to arrest me but I was here in Moscow. I have come to know what you wish to do with me.'

The Chekist, with the white face of a cocaine addict, waved his hand, saying: 'We have plenty of people in Moscow we don't know what to do with. Go back to Petrograd and let the Cheka there decide your fate.'

Thank you, I said. 'I will not go back to Petrograd. If you want to arrest me here I am.' After a moment's thought he said, 'Well, all university people are to be banished abroad. Sign these two papers and in ten days leave the territory of the RSFSR.'

I signed willingly and asked where I was to apply for my passport.[10]

Arrest brought fear at the unknown and, for every man concerned, relief when he saw that he was not alone. Initially Trubetskoy and Frank shared a Lubyanka cell, as Tatyana recalled, 'with the Bishop of Kazan'. Later Trubetskoy, Velikhov and Peshekhonov were held in the so-called 'inner prison' where more severe conditions applied.[11] In Petrograd Lossky shared with Odintsov and a Pole whose name he couldn't remember, in fact Professor Stanislav Visloukh, who appeared on the final GPU list.[12] The memoirist, socialite and collector Count Valentin Zubov recalled being detained with Professor Lapshin and the journalist and House of Writers member Afanasy Petrishchev. Zamyatin was also in their cell, according to Petrishchev.[13] It was a time of fear, but also wry amusement, for those who found themselves together in the early hours in Gorokhovaya since many of them had only recently parted company after an evening at the Petrograd House of Writers, and hardly expected to meet again before breakfast.[14]

All the Petrograd detainees were first held in Gorokhovaya, but moved within a week to the larger Shpalernaya prison. The move was initially unfortunate. The detainees had to march in convoy a kilometre throught the streets of Petrograd, east from the Admiralty along the Neva embankment, carrying their belongings and being hurried along and shouted at by their guards.[15] Some of the older men found this a torment and the experience triggered Lossky's heart trouble. Shpalernaya didn't solve the problem of overcrowding either and the detained intelligentsia were kept three to a cell in spaces meant for solitary confinement. Yet both Lossky and Zubov agreed that their time there was relatively painless. 'The prison had a rather good library and we took out books and spent the days reading. In the evenings we took it in turns to give lectures on our specialities.'[16] Selivanov would stay a month, Izgoev three months and Zubov, who was not deported, four months. This was not the worst fate Bolshevism could deal innocent men.

Meanwhile the interrogations began.

I said: 'Why am I here?'
     'You've been attending religious meetings.'
     But I could tell that wasn't the real reason [wrote Sergei Trubetskoy]. They put me in a general cell with others. The

combination was unusual, though it was only what we had come to expect from the Cheka. There was the philosopher Semyon Frank, a member of the Cooperative economic movement, a churchman – Metropolitan Kirill Kazansky – and an artillery officer. We had been arrested on the same night, and Frank had seen a number of cars bringing other detainees, so perhaps there were more of us. When Berdyaev and I crossed paths on the way to the interrogation room I realized they were having some kind of check-up on philosophers.

'What is your attitude to Soviet power?' The Chekist asked.

'I'm watching its development with interest.'

'So you sympathize?'

But he wasn't really interested in my answers. He told me I was accused of having been at Father Abrikosov's, which entailed the highest penalty. Nevertheless, instead of being shot would I care to go abroad? I was astonished, and on my guard. It was impossible for the most harmless citizen to get a foreign visa in those days.

'Go! he said. 'Think of what you'll face here. You'll go under, whereas over there, you can be with your brother and uncle. They respect you. They'll welcome you with open arms. Just sign this form to apply for a visa at the German Consulate and you can go.'

I thought I was being set up. If I signed they might produce it as proof that I was a traitor to Russia trying to escape. So I waited. But by the end of the week I was the only one left in prison. Berdyaev signed. Frank signed. Semyon Lyudvigovich said that since the Bolsheviks could do what they liked with him anyway, he had nothing to lose by signing, and it meant he could go straight home.

Prince Trubetskoy's reluctance to do a deal with the GPU was so understandable that it seems remarkable not more of the detainees were moved to resist. On the other hand his suspicions had been finessed in underground work during the Civil War, experience of a kind of which the philosophers and journalists around him were inno-cent. In any case the outcome for Trubetskoy was not the best, because it initially resulted in his being moved to the harsh 'inner prison' unlike the other detainees, most of whom were released once they had signed away their right to remain in Russia. He had to wait two weeks before he got a second chance.

> About two weeks later a top Chekist called Artur Khristianovich
> Artuzov came to see me. I said I would sign if they let me write on
> the visa form that I was applying at the invitation of the Cheka.
> Also I insisted on taking my mother and sister and my cousin and
> her child with me. A deal was struck. I signed a second paper
> accepting that I would be shot on sight if I returned to the country,
> and I undertook to report daily to the Cheka until I left. They let
> me go.[17]

It was not, as it would be during Stalinist times, that the interrogations in Lubyanka and Shpalernaya were violent. They seem by all accounts to have been routine bureaucratic 'interviews'. What stuck in the minds of the detainees was rather the unpredictability of the occasion, often predicated on the whims of the single GPU policeman across the other side of the table.

Lossky remembered:

> A woman was sitting inside, carrying out the duties of judicial
> investigator and interrogating the members of the intelligentsia
> arrested on 16 August. I think her name was Ozolina. She was so
> stern that, had I met her in the forest, I would have been terrified.
> She set out before me the charge laid before all of us who had been
> arrested on 16 August...essentially that...we had not seen our way
> to agreeing to the ideology and the power of the RSFSR [Russian
> Soviet Federal Socialist Republic] and that in the time of external
> difficulties (i.e. war) we had increased our counter-revolutionary
> activity. I paled reading the charge as I understood that I was
> threatened with being shot, and I waited to be interrogated as to
> whom I knew, which gatherings I attended, where we organized our
> conspiracies against the government, that I was there and so on. In
> reality no such questions were put to me or anyone else: the

> government knew that we had not taken part in any political
> activity…After a week they moved us from the Cheka to the prison
> on Shpalerna Street…[18]

Lev Karsavin had what could only be called a bizarre experience face
to face with his interrogator. His sister Tamara, already world-famous
as a ballet dancer, recalled the story he told her when they re-met 'after
years of separation'.

> He told me of an incident that had happened during his prison
> days. In the night he was awakened and summoned before the
> Cheka. These nocturnal examinations were particularly ominous
> and my brother had incurred their special wrath. The Commissar
> was stern; he put before my brother one of the incriminating
> points. 'You are in correspondence with abroad. Who are your
> correspondents?' 'My sister.' 'What's her name?' 'Same as mine.
> Karsavina.' 'You are the brother of Karsavina!' The Commissar
> veered round in his revolving chair. 'Giselle is her best part, don't
> you think?' 'I can't agree with you,' said my brother. 'I consider
> the Firebird one of her finest achievements.' 'Oh, do you?' The
> conversation wandered on to the principles and aims of the art; the
> prosecution was forgotten. 'Won't you write to your sister?' asked
> the Commissar at parting. 'Tell her to come back. Tell her she will
> be received with honours.' My brother's sentence was to be exiled
> with all his family, the government paying all the expenses.[19]

These various accounts suggest the GPU agents did not have a consistent attitude. Some were thugs. Zinoviev, as Chairman of the local
Soviet, was particularly feared after his master role in the Tagantsev
Affair. Gorky thought him cruel to the point of perversity.[20] Other GPU
officers were dangerous because they were believers. They believed that
their enforcement of the Revolution was just. Some of them, probably on Zinoviev's orders, had murdered Metropolitan Venyamin in
prison just a few weeks earlier. It was never clear what they would do
next, with what legitimacy. Now the more primitive among them

surrounded the detainees in an atmosphere of faint ritual humiliation.

After he was released, but while he was going from office to office getting the requisite paperwork for the journey stamped, Nikolai Lossky encountered the former blacksmith Kozlovsky, who with 'his simple-mindedness, his unconscious cruelty and his injustice' declared he would have shot the professors rather than give them the chance to leave.[21] Boris Lossky heard the same thing from his barber.[22] In the corner of his GPU office Kozlovsky had what looked like an icon but proved to be a photograph of Chernov, the imprisoned SR leader found guilty in the other show trial that summer. Kozlovsky told Lossky that he and his colleagues had nicknamed Chernov 'the Selyansky Mother of God'. Here once again was that mixture of childish vindictiveness, political ruthlessness and lethal stupidity which Osorgin and others called *sovdepiye*. Lenin's political police force had been primed to think of Christianity as a kind of alternative, reactionary sect to Bolshevism. To these primitive men the class war was 'outsourced', to be fought no questions asked.

Boris and Vladimir Lossky had a brush with two agents who arrived to search the apartment in Kabinetskaya Street. The GPU men ridiculed the number of books they were using for their academic work. 'They're studying to be scholars,' said someone on their behalf. 'And why [are they] not [studying to become] cobblers, eh?' came the mocking reply.[23]

Writing with hindsight, referring to what would happen when the Nazis took control in Germany, Zubov called events in Russia in August 1922 a *Gleichschaltung*, literally a 'switching on to the same tracks' which imposed an absolute conformity of thought and action on public life.[24] He was particularly moved by the arrest of the schoolteachers around him. This was the moment when Russian citizens tempted to remain independent-minded had to accept proletarian 'equality' or suffer the consequences.

The 'interviews' which began on 17 August followed a strict format. They formally explained the new balance of power in the country, and delivered the regime's uncompromising terms to each man concerned. The interviews were held in the middle of the night, which conveyed the gravity of the occasion, and the questions, asked simultaneously in both capitals, were roughly of two kinds. The more specific ones referred to events in 1922 which Lenin regarded as particularly provocative to the government, such as the strike the academic staff had staged in February. The others referred to perceived anti-Soviet groupings like the 'Savinkovite' forces in Czechoslovakia under the leadership of a former SR terrorist, Boris Savinkov.

1. What are your political views?
2. What is your view of the structure of Soviet power and of the proletarian republic?
3. What is your view of the role of the intelligentsia?
4. What is your attitude to the Savinkovites, the 'Change of Landmarks' people and the trial of the SRs?
5. What is your attitude to the professors' strike, to sabotage and other similar ways of fighting against the Soviet regime?
6. What is your view of the Soviet regime's policy towards higher education and to the reforms taking place there?
7. How do you see the prospects of the Russian emigration abroad?[25]

By setting these various questions side by side the Bolsheviks insinuated the reality of a concerted anti-Soviet effort, both inside and outside the country, which justified their totalitarian response. They tried to link the expellees with various individuals and organizations they found suspect. Hence the attention paid to the 'Change of Landmarks' movement, which had support in Russia but was mostly taken up by White émigrés abroad. 'Change of Landmarks' recognized that Lenin and the Bolsheviks had restored Russian national pride and strength after the war and recommended that patriotic Russians drop their opposition to the Reds and return home. But the movement's very existence as an alternative political organization was enough to spark Bolshevik paranoia.

Myakotin replied to questions 2 and 3 that he could never approve of a dictatorship. Berdyaev, never one to express himself briefly where an excess of words could be deployed, told the men across the table that he could never take a 'class' point of view and considered the ideologies of the nobility, the peasantry, the proletariat and the bourgeoisie 'all equally narrow, limited, and self-seeking'. 'I stand for the point of view of mankind and humanity...'[26] On the question of Savinkov, who would eventually smuggle himself back into Russia and die in a Soviet prison in 1925, both Myakotin and Berdyaev excused themselves for lack of knowledge. On the 'Change of Landmarks' men, the *smenovekhovtsy*, both also distanced themselves, Berdyaev more stridently. Both he and Myakotin criticized the severity of the SR trial. Looking ahead Berdyaev said he saw the position of the Russian emigration as difficult to bear.

The records available suggest that all the arrested members of the intelligentsia took their interrogators at face value and answered sincerely, though not without irony. As Trubetskoy recalled, when asked 'What is your attitude to Soviet power?', he replied: 'I'm watching its development with interest.'[26] None of these men knew whether or not they were about to be shot. After the questions were asked, all the detainees, regardless of their answers, were accused under Article 57 of the Soviet Penal Code of not reconciling themselves to Soviet power and persisting in counter-revolutionary activity. They were then told that they faced the death sentence but could opt to leave the country.

In archive material that has come to light since 1991 the charges trumped up against each deported individual make interesting reading.[28] A substantial number in Petrograd were accused of receiving 'material help from Tagantsev'. They included Selivanov and Lapshin. The accusation was all the more ludicrous since the Tagantsev Affair was itself a fabrication. Amongst his friends Lapshin was well known for having no political interests whatsoever. The writer Viktor Iretsky was accused of 'destructive anti-Soviet activity'.

Peshekhonov, perhaps because of Lenin's early intervention in his case, was treated as specially problematic and detained under a higher degree of security than most of the others. His GPU file contained 'masses of' handwritten material by Genrikh Yagoda, Stalin's future henchman, who deputized for Unshlikht at this stage of his career. Dzerzhinsky and other top people also annotated the file, according to Russian investigators who examined it in 2002. Yagoda personally forbade the release of Peshekhonov from prison until the moment of departure. A report in Kamenev's name, apparently a direct answer to the accusations which led to Peshekhnov's removal from his job in February 1922, quoted the victim as saying 'I haven't been active in politics for more than two years and I served the Soviet government with a clear conscience in Ukraine.' The GPU file noted that in answer to 'What do you think of the Soviet regime?', Peshekhonov answered: 'I recognize the Soviet government... but I don't consider it ideal in the sense of coming close to self-government by the people [*narodovlastie*]. I have always taken a negative view of all dictatorship, personal or class.' Another GPU file recently made available for examination, that of Prokopovich and Kuskova, was characterized by investigators in 2002 as 'a haphazard collection of letters, textual fragments, introductions, articles etc., which the Chekists called the material of "counter-revolution".'

It is evident from the files alone that, regardless of their answers to questions, prefabricated excuses were used to justify ousting the deportees. Often these were based on alleged defects in their moral character. Lev Karsavin especially was marked down as an idler, the kind of man the new society should not tolerate: the GPU styled him 'a philosopher-mystic and man of the Church. He's gone over completely to mysticism and doesn't do any work.'[29] This sort of charge anticipated one of the classic accusations against dissidents in the Soviet Communist world, that they were 'parasites' who refused to work. (In fact they were denied work.) The way the GPU operated in autumn 1922 created a blueprint for Soviet practice over the next seventy years. Now and in future, the political police fabricated cases against rebellious members of society by taking one or two key facts and distorting them, but not quite unrecognizably.

In Karsavin's case one could trace a line back from the accusations to the true facts about his life, and see how they were wilfully misconstrued.[30] He was not exactly a mystic but his mother was directly related to Aleksei Khomiakov, the founder of modern Russian religious thought, and her son was brought up to perpetuate that tradition that was anathema to Lenin. Karsavin excelled as a student of history at St Petersburg University and then did research in Italy and France, working on medieval religious belief in the twelfth and thirteenth centuries. His popular book of 1911, *On the Medieval Monastic Life*, first brought him his reputation as a writer for a larger audience. His great admirer was a fellow medievalist turned literary critic, Pyotr Bitsilli, who would become one of the most respected writers of the emigration, and he was also the favourite teacher of Vladimir Lossky. Karsavin was not actively religious in his early academic years, but after the Revolution he changed and could be found delivering sermons in churches. He defended the traditional Orthodox Church against the politically submissive 'Living Church' and on one memorable occasion publicly took on Robert Vipper to thunderous applause in the former hall of the City Duma.[31]

As for the allegation that Karsavin 'did nothing', certainly he had lost his job when the university closed. But there was also the matter of his love affair, which may or may not have distracted him from his work. Everyone remembered Karsavin's twenty-five-year-old student lover Yelena Chaslavna Skrzhinskaya, who said she would follow him anywhere in the world, and did, into exile. Karsavin used to ride her bicycle along the extensive corridors of the Faculty building known as 'The Twelve Colleges'. An unusual, experimental book Karsavin wrote in 1920, *Noctes petropolitanae*, in the style of a medieval tract and exuding a sense of loneliness and of the tragedy of the world, imagined the end of their love affair while it was still very much alive. 'His erudition was enormous and poured out in unforced conversation which never tired the listener,' said Karsavin's university colleague Count Zubov, who added that he found Karsavin 'one of the most interesting and pleasant men I have ever met'. Boris Lossky described

Karsavin as terribly popular with the students during his time, 1918–19, as Rector of the university.[32] But the 'hygienic' Bolsheviks formed the opposite impression and worked it into a reason for his enforced exile abroad.

When all the 'interviews' had been conducted, the GPU sent Lenin a list summarizing the results. It wasn't comprehensive but it detailed each individual case where the way forward was clear. Since the leading Moscow and Petrograd philosophers were described as at liberty, and Berdyaev was 'kept for about a week'[33] it must have been compiled between 24 and 31 August.

Stratonov V. V.	To be deported. At liberty.
Artobolevsky I. A.	To appear before a revolutionary tribunal. Accused of agitating against the seizure of church valuables.
Tyapkin N. D.	Keep under surveillance.
Velikhov P. A.	Keep under surveillance.
Korobkov N. M. [*sic*]	At liberty. In last stages of TB.
Lossky N. O.	To be deported. At liberty.
Kondratyev I. D.[*sic*]	Accused in connection with SR activity. Deportation order suspended for the time being. Keep under surveillance.
Frank S. L.	To be deported. At liberty.
Aikhenvald Yu. I.	To be deported. At liberty.
Osorgin, M. A.	To be deported. At liberty.
Stepun F. A.	Not found.
Sorokin P. A.	Arrested. To be deported.
Zamyatin E. I.	Deportation postponed until further notice.
Ermolaev N. I.	Not to be sent abroad. To be brought to trial.
Visloukh S. M.	Arrested. To be deported.
Berdyaev N. A.	To be deported. At liberty.[34]

A news report corresponding to this list appeared in *The Times* on 29 August.

News of the intended deportations was first given to the Russian general public indirectly, when Trotsky 'gave an interview' to a token Western journalist in *Pravda* on 30 August. He set the scene by recalling the crucial events of the 'Janus' year, from the international Genoa Conference to the positive economic outlook for the new workers' state, the move towards disarmament after the Civil War, the justice of the SR trial, and finally the deportations. *Pravda* gave the last topic a special sub-heading, 'Farsighted Humanity', which in turn was just the right headline to promote a two-faced interpretation of the deportations. From Russia they were to be seen in terms of prudent government, whereas from abroad the critical West was urged to view the deportations as an act of clemency.[35]

You ask me [said Trotsky] what the explanation is of the decree to expel abroad elements hostile to the Soviet regime. And does it not mean that we are more afraid of them within the country than on the other side of the frontier?

My answer will be very simple. Recently you witnessed the trial of the SRs, who, during the Civil War were the agents of foreign governments fighting against us. The court judged them as warranting the death penalty. Your press, for the most part, conducted a despairing campaign against our cruelty. Had we got the idea straight after October [i.e. the Revolution] to send the SR gentlemen abroad we could have saved ourselves from being called cruel. Those elements whom we are sending or will send [abroad] are politically worthless in themselves. But they are potential weapons in the hands of our possible enemies. In the event of new military complications – and these, despite all our love of peace, are not ruled out – all these unreconciled and incorrigible elements will turn into military-political agents of the enemy. And we will be forced to shoot them according to the regulations of war. This is why we prefer in a peaceful period to send them away in good time. And I hope that you won't refuse to accept our far-sighted humanity and will take it upon yourself to defend it in the face of public opinion.

The woman who 'interviewed' Trotsky was Louise Bryant, 'correspondent of the International News Service', and not by coincidence she was the widow of John Reed, the sympathetic US reporter who had witnessed the October Revolution and published *Ten Days That Shook the World*. A supporter of the Soviet cause, Bryant was the ideal Westerner of whom Soviet Russia could publicly ask a favour.[36]

For the Russian public, the Communist Party newspaper withheld its direct message on the expulsions until the following day, 31 August, and then delivered it with a bang. The unsigned front-page article, headlined 'A First Warning', was clearly aimed at the remaining intelligentsia. It picked out Kadet and SR connections, the professors' strike earlier in the year, the proliferation of new magazines in Petrograd, and implied that such activities and connections should be avoided. The thinking classes had better pay attention if they wanted to survive in the new Soviet state.

> Imagining that the NEP would give them a new chance for counter-revolutionary work, the Kadet and SR circles of our intelligentsia have been pursuing that kind of thing all the more intensively, maintaining close links with Whiteguardists abroad. The Soviet government has shown far too much patience. Now it has finally sounded a first warning: the most active counter-revolutionary elements amongst the professors, doctors, agronomists and others are being exiled partly abroad and partly to the northern provinces. For the workers and peasants all this will serve as a reminder that they will soon need their own worker-peasant intelligentsia.

Soviet newspaper writing was an art of its kind, able to compress many damaging allusions into a few declamatory lines which appeared to be based on fact but were often told in the manner of a fable so no one could accuse the writer of lying. One had to read description as reprimand and reportage as moral example. Writing in such a tone already in 1922, *Pravda* justified the expulsions using all the themes and tricks Lenin and the GPU had worked up, including allusions to the expellees in the same breath as the 'guilty' SRs.[37]

Pravda tried to stir up popular feeling against the ousted men by depicting them as either spies for foreign powers or scroungers on the state. The expellees belonged to groups 'out of which up until now foreign Whiteguardist newspapers have been recruiting their correspondents and providing false and slanderous information to the foreign press'. *Pravda* thought it scandalous that in recent hard times such men had continued to receive food and other subsidies from Narkompros. 'If these gentlemen don't like it in the Soviet Union then let them revel in all the joys of bourgeois freedom beyond its confines.'

The article of 31 August wove a tissue of false hints and accusations around the blatant lie that 'amongst the expellees there are hardly any big scientific names'. It ended by stating the uncompromising terms the Bolshevik government was offering to any possible future Soviet intelligentsia:

> The expulsion of active counter-revolutionary elements from the
> bourgeois intelligentsia is the Soviet government's first warning
> in relation to these classes. As before, the Soviet government will
> continue to value highly and support in every way those
> representatives of the old intelligentsia and specialists who will
> work loyally with the Soviet government, as the best part of the
> specialists are working with it now. But as before it will destroy
> root and branch every attempt to exploit Soviet possibilities to wage
> secret or open battle against the government of workers and
> peasants aimed at restoring the regime of the bourgeoisie and
> the landowners.

Suddenly the tone sounded reasonable again, as if the policy of cooperation had not changed, only the quality of the men involved. But this was not the case in mid-1922, when the nascent Soviet Union was closing the door on all individuality and all unauthorized discourse. When the article said that the time had come to create a new, more appropriate 'worker-peasant' Soviet intelligentsia what it meant was to create a servile brain-force in a one-party state. Not by coincidence the state agency that would oversee the censorship of literature and the press for the next nine years, Glavlit, was founded on 6 June 1922, as part of the same measure to tighten intellectual control.

The *Manchester Guardian*, which had carried news agency stories on the arrests, remained silent on the announcement of the expulsions because, as Lenin personally appreciated, so long as it was fed the right material it was disposed to think well of the new Soviet regime.[38] But *The Times* was outraged. It rounded out a series of brief reports on the arrests and first arrivals abroad with a fierce editorial on 6 September.

The East Wind

The news from Russia is significant of a curious change. There is no real change in the policy and aims of the Bolshevists. Their aim is power for their little group and for its sinister associates. The fiction that the activities of the Bolshevists can, in any possible sense, promote the welfare of labour, should be finally exploded. The present state of Russia is a sufficient illustration of the terrible effects of their rule and their system on those whose life is spent in a hard struggle for the wherewithal to live. The working men of this country do not yet realize the condition of the Russian working man under Bolshevism. The famine, the typhus, and the cholera that have laid millions low are the direct result of methods ostensibly applied in the interest of the working man and in the name of an implacable war against capitalism. What has really happened is that the workman has seen the industries in which he was employed crumble away and the liberties of which he had begun to dream snatched from his grasp, while a new and grosser form of capitalism has arisen from the corruption fostered by Soviet rule...

They are primitive and barbaric tyrants, and to associate their name with the ideals of democracy or social reform is an absurd and dangerous illusion. After their futile attempts in the course of this year to array themselves in a garb suitable for European Conferences the Bolshevists have now reverted to the more congenial habits which they never really abandoned. They continue with unabated

vigour the persecution of the Church, to which the Bishop of
WAKEFIELD referred in his sermon last Sunday, and priests are
murdered daily.

The so-called extremists of the Communist Party are now
definitely gaining the upper hand, and Zinovieff, the President of
the Third International, who was recently called to account by his
own party for unexplained expenditure, has come into the
foreground as a leader in Russia. At his instigation a fresh campaign
has been started against the intellectuals, and hundreds of these,
including several very distinguished scholars, have been arrested and
are now being expelled from Russia – their families being kept
behind as hostages ... the stubborn remnant of the Russian educated
class is thus being eliminated.

The only satisfaction Lenin might have drawn from this subtle,
accurate and justly ferocious criticism was the lack of association of his
own name with the expulsions, and the success of using Zinoviev as a
willing scapegoat.

The Soviet response to foreign criticism was at once crude and
scathing. An article in the New York-based propaganda organ *Soviet
Russia* began with the words 'The bourgeois press has raised a great
clamour...' and followed them with a reprise of the *Pravda* article, the
whole now headlined 'A Warning to Counter-Revolutionary
Intellectuals'.[39] The piece ought to have scored an own goal, advertis-
ing Soviet injustice ever more widely, but those Soviet sympathizers
who read *Soviet Russia* had already made up their minds in Lenin's
favour while others were either not in a position to sort the lies from
the truth or did not want to know.

Gorky wrote to Lenin on 15 September expressing his concern at
the evictions which were now only days from being put into operation. Lenin replied, admitting that mistakes had been made but
otherwise conceding nothing to liberal concern. He resorted to his old
Manichean-scatological vocabulary to distinguish the discarded intelligentsia from the proletarian lifeblood of the new Russia.

The intellectual forces of the workers and peasants are growing and getting stronger in the struggle to overthrow the bourgeoisie and their accomplices, the intellectuals, the lackeys of capital, who think they're the brains of the nation. In fact they're not the brains, they're the shit.[40]

The expulsion of the Moscow group was delayed six weeks and the Petrograd group waited a further ten. The visas expected in mid-August were not to hand until late September or after. On 17 September Lenin wrote impatiently to Unshlikht: 'Please be so kind as to arrange for all the documents to be sent back to me with comments as to who has been deported, who is in prison, who has been excused deportation and why. Make short comments on this letter.'[42] On 18 September, Yagoda as Unshlikht's deputy replied to Lenin: 'In accordance with your instruction I enclose your lists with comments on them and the names of people (listed separately) who have remained in Moscow or Petrograd for one reason or another.' Yagoda added that the first contingent would leave Moscow on Friday 22 September.[42] This official target was probably the source of a misleading report in *The Times* that Berdyaev, Frank and others had arrived in the Latvian capital Riga on 26 September. The only person known to have arrived in Riga on that date, by train, was Sorokin.

Weimar's insistence that the deportees apply for their visas individually took a lot of time. It quickly led to the strategic release of senior detainees to speed up the paperwork. The GPU wanted to get the business over. The Moscow group representatives were Berdyaev and Ugrimov, in Petrograd Lossky and the journalist Volkovysky. The latter knew many people through his role at the House of Writers and had worked for years with the journalists Khariton, Pumpyansky and Petrishchev. Now it became his role to help his friends fill out a visa application form, on which they would leave their thumb print behind. The group elders then took the applications to the Consulate of the Weimar Republic on St Isaac's Square, in the former embassy of the Reich, or, as it seems happened in

Moscow, submitted it through the good offices of Ugrimov's friend Videnfeld.

The more urgent business dealt with, Lossky and Volkovysky sought better terms for the departure of the Petrograd group.

> The group of us who were released had to worry about a great many other things besides visas. For instance, anyone going abroad at the time could only take very little bedlinen and clothes; only one sheet per person; no books, particularly dictionaries were considered national treasures which had to be kept in Russia. To obtain more favourable conditions...we had to go to many Bolshevik institutions.[43]

Eventually the Petrograders were allowed to take three sets of clothes, including those they were wearing, any books and other objects they could carry, but still no icons.

Money caused delays. Indeed, the issue created so much anxiety that, as was noted earlier, Zinoviev had to come forward publicly a few weeks before the Petrograd expulsions to say that the GPU would pay for the tickets.[44] Lunacharsky had suggested almost a year earlier that the sending of awkward members of academe abroad was unfeasible because of the non-availability of funds. Now that Lenin had forced the measure to become reality, the sums involved remained too great for individuals to manage, although still no Soviet institution wanted to pay.

Fyodor Stepun begged the help of neighbours with foreign relatives, a difficult request since providing Russians with foreign currency was technically illegal. He had been quoted the figure of six pounds sterling for the journey from Petrograd to Berlin, which did not take into account the money that would be needed to begin life abroad. Each expellee was allowed to take out a maximum of twenty-five pounds per head.[45] The well-off Losskys sold all their possessions and raised one thousand million roubles to pay for their family party of six to travel. But the Karsavins, with two older children and a new baby, couldn't possibly raise what they needed and even Prince

Trubetskoy lacked funds, though in mustering the cost of the longer journey from Moscow he encountered unexpected charity:

> It was difficult to raise the money, which by the standards of the day was a considerable amount. The figure of eight or eleven pounds sterling comes to mind. We were permitted valuables of up to twenty-five gold roubles per person, which was almost nothing. Inevitably we had to try, illegally, to get the money from abroad. Then quite unexpectedly my colleagues at the State Agricultural Syndicate came to my aid. My former boss, a man called Demchenko, arranged back-pay for all the time I had been in prison plus my salary for two months ahead – the entitlement of anyone made redundant. He took a considerable personal risk doing this and I begged him not to. He showed me there could be highly decent people among the Communists too. He and his staff threw me a party with 'best wishes for your new life!' and only one Chekist and a few bourgeois who feared for their skins avoided me.[46]

If paying for one's own passage into exile sounds like paying one's own hangman, it's important to remember how wary the intelligentsia were of the political police. When the interrogators asked the *expulsanty*, as they became known in bastardized Russian from the French *expulsé* stamped in their passports, whether they would pay for themselves or travel courtesy of the GPU, most immediately suspected a trap and said they would pay for themselves. They distrusted the GPU and concentrated on getting away as quickly as possible. Even Karsavin *agreed* to pay, knowing he could not.

On the other hand, it seems clear that the GPU was not so much playing tricks as not thinking straight. Lenin had adapted the sentence of 'administrative exile' from tsarist practice without his agents realizing it entailed inappropriate legal paraphernalia which would have to be deleted in the case of expulsions abroad. Under the Empire those sentenced to administrative exile were offered a choice of the means of travel to Siberia: they could go by train, if they had the money, or on foot – 'in convoy' – if they didn't. Such a choice was well known to Lenin himself. When he was sentenced to go east, he and his family journeyed by rail in relative ease and once they reached Siberia were free to choose a pleasant rural way of life. Siberian exile became synonymous with suffering only in the cases of those who, for lack of means, had to walk. It was the long trek east 'in convoy' that cost lives.

When Kozlovsky, the former blacksmith, and his kind applied themselves to the deportation paperwork they followed the precedent for adminstrative exile. That meant that every prisoner had to be offered the chance either to go on foot – *pod konvoem* – or to pay his own passage. The fact that there were no foot convoys going from Russia to Germany was irrelevant, because the rule was the rule. The *expulsanty* took it as such and scraped together what means they could.

A few well-placed individuals didn't even wait for the autumn ships. Sorokin took up the offer of immediate release from prison if he left within a week, and was gone by 23 September. Melgunov and Peshekhonov also left by their own means at the end of September or the beginning of October: Peshekhonov was destined in the first instance for Riga and Melgunov for Warsaw. The economists Prokopovich and Kuskova, whose names only appear on early drafts of the expulsion lists, went in June without even tasting arrest. Other independent travellers, in the end, were the *Ekonomist* editor Dalmat Lutokhin and the agrarian expert Aleksei Bulatov.[47]

Kuskova was the only woman expatriated in her own right. Her Social Democratic economic *Credo*, a pamphlet published with her husband in 1899, earned her Lenin's lasting contempt. Subsequently she featured on the wrong side in 1917, when she was involved in the last days of the Provisional government, and again when she was active in Pomgol. Like Sorokin, she and her husband left Russia by train, crossing the border at Sebezh and thence to Riga and Berlin.

A man who helped a number of Russians leave by this route was the Lithuanian ambassador in Moscow, Jurgis Baltrusaitis. Baltrusaitis has been called 'the Lithuanian Schindler' in comparison with the German businessman Oskar Schindler who, twenty years later, would rescue some 1,200 Jews persecuted by the Nazis. The comparison is exaggerated because of the small number of Russians involved and the less than total threat to their lives. But that does not detract from Baltrusaitis's quiet and admirable contribution to the expulsion story.[48]

He was a poet who wrote in Russian and had lived in Moscow for several years before the Revolution. Aikhenvald so admired Baltrusaitis's Symbolist poetry that he included it in his classic three-volume *Silhouettes of Russian Literature*. When Lithuania won its independence from Russia in the post-war settlement of 1920, Baltrusaitis became his country's ambassador to Russia, which left him in a position to issue entry visas into his country. The evidence is only circumstantial, but it seems Baltrusaitis might have been involved in helping Sorokin, since Sorokin wrote in his autobiography that at the railway station in Moscow 'I carried our two valises into the Lettish [Lithuanian] diplomatic car.' (The American 'car' was in English a railway carriage.)[49] One couple definitely helped by Baltrusaitis were the poet Khodasevich and his girlfriend Berberova.[50]

The Stepun family also made a unique journey out of Russia. During his interview with the Moscow Cheka, Stepun insisted that he did not want to emigrate but changed his mind when, obliged to inquire at the German consulate, he found that the consul was an old friend from Heidelberg. He would remember for the rest of his life that, when the consul invited him to dinner, he realized how far he and his wife Natasha had sunk from their old lives. They were living in a prison. They paid for their own train tickets and left Russia on a 'windy, damp, dank' day some time in October or November.[51]

The last *expulsanty* of 1922 to leave were two unrelated men with the same surnames, Sergei and Valentin Bulgakov. Though registered in Moscow, Sergei Bulgakov, an economist, philosopher and ordained priest, was teaching and worshipping in Odessa. The time it took the authorities to find him meant that he did not leave Russia, via Constantinople, until the last day of December 1922.[52] Valentin Bulgakov travelled out by the same route in March 1923.

5

Journey into Exile

THE LENGTHY WAIT for the visas gave some of the Petrograd group time for farewell parties and ritual leavetakings. Boris Lossky and his friend Dmitry Shostakovich got so drunk on vodka at a party at the Shostakoviches' that sixteen-year-old Dmitry passed out. Boris and Vladimir Lossky later waved a bird's-eye farewell to their native city from the gallery of St Isaac's Cathedral. Their regret at leaving Russia for Europe was not great and when more was expected of them they became ostentatious and insincere. Boris kissed the ground in imitation of what Raskolnikov did in Sennaya Square, in Dostoevsky's novel *Crime and Punishment*, and Vladimir – Volodya – went along with his grandmother's suggestion that parting was most sorrowful for him because he was in love with a girl in his class.[1]

The older generation had more genuine emotions to expiate. Lyudmila Lossky and her mother Maria Stoyunina visited the chapel in the wooden house of Peter the Great, 'on the Petersburg side', and lit a candle to the Saviour. Lossky senior went to tea with his old rival, the Living Church representative, Alexander Vvedensky. Lapshin and Karsavin were also invited to call on their long-time colleague at his home on Vasilevsky Ostrov, close to the university. Lossky and his colleagues weren't sorry to see Vvedensky go because they could finally claim their overdue Chairs, and when Vvedensky managed to re-instate himself they coexisted uneasily. But they also sympathized with the way the Bolsheviks had made his life impossible, and the mixed emotions all round made the farewell tea-party memorable. 'They discussed Plato's *Symposium* and the behaviour of Aristophanes, and they also looked at a map on the host's wall of Europe with its new post-Versailles borders, and the new outlines of the new states. The parting was friendly, despite old enmities.'[2]

Prince Trubetskoy said two farewells, one in Moscow and the second in Petrograd, with an amusing train journey in between.

> The English mission – there was not yet an embassy in Moscow after the Revolution – offered me a car to the station, on the grounds that transport was very difficult. But I turned it down because I feared it would annoy the Cheka. Instead we went in a cooperative truck arranged by a friend. I had mixed feelings about leaving: both *Heimweh*, as the Germans call homesickness, and what our nineteenth-century poet Tyutchev called *Rausweh*, the longing to get out.
>
> The authorities had reserved a Third Class carriage for us, and throughout the journey no one else was allowed to get in, though from the beginning a few other passengers were already installed. One was a woman with a baby at her breast wrapped so tightly that neither its face nor hands could be seen. She didn't feed it the whole journey and it made no sound. When we stopped at a station we weren't allowed to get out, but we could go along the corridor for hot water any time. So I had the chance to look out of the window into the station buffet. I saw our 'mother' knocking back a few drinks with some Chekists in uniform, while her 'baby' was propped up against a chair on the floor.
>
> When we arrived in Petrograd we found that the steamer wasn't leaving until the day after next. We needed to stay somewhere but anyone who put us up was at risk from the police. The Director or the Deputy Director of the Public Libary did us a great kindness since his Jewish relatives had suffered at the hands of the White Army. I did as I had done in Moscow. I went round the city saying goodbye: to its views, to its monuments, to the Hermitage. Moscow

was battered, but intensely alive. Life was new, strange and spiteful, yet all the same the city was vital. But Petrograd was dead. It was half-empty, like a grand house abandoned by its owners. There was grass growing in the streets. On the other hand the air of neglect gave the palaces and statues a rare and peculiar beauty.

I stood in front of the statue of Peter the Great. I thought surely his spirit can chase out this degenerate bunch. Surely his spirit can fight against Bolshevism. But the spiritual plague gripping Russia was also in [Peter's] soul, the way he departed from the Church, the way he cut loose from traditions. It was in his wild coarseness, his brutality, his tricks, the sadistic way he treated his son and executed the Streltsy [his elite military bodyguard]. No, I decided, the spirit of Peter is not destined to fight Bolshevism. The Bronze Horseman doesn't have the spiritual strength to spur his horse against that slant-eyed Lenin who has debased and destroyed Peter's nation. Suddenly I felt a sharp burst of *Rausweh*. I could do nothing here. There was nothing left but to run, to run ever faster and with closed eyes, like Pushkin's Evgeny.[3]

Another double farewell, first from Moscow, then from Petrograd, was remembered by Vera Ugrimova:

The day we left we took our leave of grandmother and said a prayer for the road. To cheer up babushka Father said: 'We'll be back in a year, Granny' and we all believed it. The coachman came and drove us to the Nikolaevsky Station. Quite a few people came to see us off, which was daring. One of my girlfriends brought me sweet peas, my favourite flowers, which I dried and kept with me in Berlin for a long time after. Early next day we arrived in Petrograd, and then two days later we left in tears for Stettin.

Lev Karsavin and his wife, and the Losskys and others came to see us off, already knowing that they would be travelling a month later. The Captain refused to let Father take the violin which was a family heirloom. So we gave it to someone. From the deck I looked back to the quay. It was dark but there were lights on inside the departure shed. The face of a male friend of mine was suddenly picked out there through a window.[4]

The evening the *expulsanty* boarded traumatized the writer Evgeny Zamyatin. He too went down to the quay, with fellow writer Yury Annenkov, who remembered the occasion.[5]

There weren't more than ten people about. I guess people were afraid to be associated with the deportees. We weren't allowed on the boat and when we arrived they were already in their cabins, where we couldn't see them. We didn't manage to say goodbye.

The confusion of Zamyatin, a leading experimental writer and author of the novel *We*, which helped inspire Aldous Huxley to write *Brave New World*, came about because he was reprieved from expulsion at the last minute. Having been arrested on the night of 16 August, on his release from Shpalernaya prison five weeks later he went to the Smolny building to collect his exit visa. To his surprise, when he got to the former Institute for Noble Young Ladies, now the headquarters of the Petrograd Soviet, he found his permit to leave the country had been cancelled. The story of what actually happened to Zamyatin in the six months from August 1922 to January 1923 is one of the most interesting to have been clarified by archive material published for the first time after 1991.[6]

Two days after the first Philosophy Steamer sailed – without him on board – Zamyatin told a joke at the House of Arts, before a packed gathering of Petrograd's most fashionable writers, which revealed his shock at what had happened, though it gave no clue as to whether he was relieved or disappointed to remain in Russia. 'You know what?' he told fellow writers Boris Pilnyak, Vsevolod Ivanov, Kornei Chukovsky and others: 'We like writers so much in this country we even export them abroad.' In fact he was in turmoil, because the friends who, while he was in prison, had petitioned the Politburo for his reprieve, had completely misunderstood his wishes. This in turn left others

ВЛ. ИЛЬИНЪ.

МАТЕРІАЛИЗМЪ
и
ЭМПИРІОКРИТИЦИЗМЪ

критическія замѣтки объ одной
реакціонной философіи.

ИЗДАНІЕ „ЗВЕНО"
МОСКВА
1909

Cover of the first edition of Lenin's *Materialism and Empiriocriticism*. Lenin first attacked Idealist philosophy and then thirteen years later expelled the Idealists themselves.

Semyon and Tatyana Frank honeymooning in Austria, summer 1908. Lenin regarded the educated and cultured Franks as typical 'bourgeois intellectuals'.

Aleksei Peshekhonov addressing a political meeting, Petrograd 1917. The men deported abroad included some would-be political allies of the Bolsheviks.

Marked 'Do Not Copy' and stamped by the Supreme Soviet of the USSR, this rare photograph of Dzerzhinsky, seated centre, and his 12 Cheka /GPU Apostles, was a blasphemous Bolshevik version of Christ's Last Supper. Unshlikht is seated third from left, with Menzhinsky on Dzerzhinsky's far side. Standing, third and forth from left, are Yagoda and Latsis.

Maxim Gorky at a Petrograd station, bound for Moscow, 1920. Gorky actively championed the cause of the persecuted intelligentsia before he was himself driven out in 1921.

Yury Annenkov's 1921 portrait of the writer Zamyatin highlighted the modernist style and contacts abroad which complicated Zamyatin's relations with the Bolsheviks.

The Moscow GPU's File on
Peshekhonov. The accompanying prison
photograph is dated 5 September, 1922.

A convalescent Lenin hard at work in Gorky, sometime
between August and early October 1922.
Photographed by his sister, Maria Ulyanova.

Chekists ready for action. Incribed on the reverse: 'Experience in tactics and technique
required. As you can see from the picture, implementation of the directives of the Centre
is quite up to scratch.'

Prison photographs of some of the arrested intelligentsia, August 1922. From left to right, top row:
N. P. Kozlov, B. I. Khariton, I. I. Lapshin. Second row: L. P. Karsavin, A. S. Kagan, S. I. Polner. Third row:
A. B. Petrishchev, A. S. Izgoev-Lande, I. I. Yushtin. Forth row: N. O. Lossky, N. M. Volkovysky,
D. F. Selivanov.

German press advertisement for pleasure cruises on the *Haken* and the *Prinzessin Sophie Charlotte*, before it was renamed the *Preussen*.

Foreign passport issued to Dmitry Lutokhin, Petrograd 1922.

The Philosophy Steamer: the 'small but stately' *Oberbürgermeister Haken*, named after Stettin's most famous mayor.

The Frank children in Berlin. From left to right: Aleksei, Vasily, Natalya and Viktor.

Advertisement for the Berlin émigré newspaper *Rul* ('The Rudder'), in its ninth year in 1928. The masthead listing the founders still bore the name of Nabokov's father, murdered in 1922.

The critic Yuly Aikhenvald lecturing at the Russian Scientific Institute, Berlin 1924.

Staff at the Russian Scientific Institute, Berlin 1923-24. Front row, left to right, starting fourth from left: Frank, Yasinsky, Berdyaev, Aikhenvald, Prokopovich, Karsavin.

Farewell to Berlin, 1923. Standing, second from left, Vladislav Khodasevich and, centre, Mikhail Osorgin. Nina Berberova is seated front left. Front right is Andrei Bely, who returned to Russia.

Advertisement in French and Russian for the film 'Nostalgia', playing in Paris, 1928. 'The whole auditorium applauded when the Russian flat was unfurled in a burst of gunfire,' according to the conservative émigré paper 'The Latest News'.

Nikolai Berdyaev in France. His sister-in-law
commented: 'This was a typical expression.
A great likeness.'

Berdyaev's study at their home in the Paris suburb of Clamart.
He died at his desk on 23 March, 1948.

guessing where his political loyalties really lay. His personal correspondence suggests he also didn't know.[7]

Literary Petrograd had pulled out all the stops to help Zamyatin from being consigned for export. Annenkov, shortly before he emigrated himself, told Chukovsky he'd seen a request to reverse the decision to deport Zamyatin addressed to Comrade Messing, Chairman of the Petrograd Cheka. It had gone something like 'It is hereby respectfully requested that Evgeny Ivanovich Zamyatin, writer, shouldn't be deported abroad but be allowed to go to Moscow instead.' Pilnyak, a novelist and short-story writer who was enjoying a brief, precarious period of Bolshevik favour, reminded the authorities that Zamyatin had been a member of the Party until 1917, and asked what more proof they could want of his undying loyalty. (To have left the Party because it resorted to violent revolution was hardly a sign of loyalty to Lenin but Pilnyak got away with his trick.) Pilnyak finally addressed a personal appeal to Kamenev, although the letter Annenkov saw was delivered to the Politburo in Zinoviev's handwriting. Whichever member raised it, an appeal at Politburo level was unlikely to be refused. Distraught, Zamyatin immediately made a fresh application for permission to leave the country. This was granted early in 1923.[8]

Zamyatin's widow always maintained that her husband was unequivocal in his desire to go abroad in 1922, and that his friends had indeed misunderstood. But Zamyatin's correspondence with Pilnyak and Voronsky, insisting that he was neither White nor Red, has finally provided proof of his uncertainty. It is also clear that the Zamyatins might once again have left Russia in 1923, although they eventually delayed their departure until 1931. Trotsky was probably the most astute judge of Zamyatin's character in relation to Russia when he accused him of naturally inclining towards 'inner emigration'. He arrived at this judgement while Zamyatin was still in Shpalernaya. The perceptive Trotsky seems to have coined that phrase 'inner emigration' for intellectuals who despised the regime, but were not against the original aims of the Revolution, several decades before it came to characterize the situation of thousands of dissident intellectuals who chose to remain in totalitarian countries over the seventy years that the Soviet Union lasted.[9]

The Losskys left Kabinetskaya Street, for the last time, on the afternoon of Wednesday 15 November. They had a *taksomotor*[10] to carry the luggage, the women and five-year-old Andrei down to the Nikolaevsky Embankment. Boris, Vladimir and their father followed in a droshky. The route inevitably took them on a tour, for the last time, of some of the great sights of the city – the Admiralty, St Isaac's, Falconet's statue of Peter the Great – but Lossky senior, more worried about the bags falling off the new-fangled vehicle ahead, didn't have time to appreciate it. Fresh snow was falling as they arrived at the embankment where about a hundred friends and wellwishers had gathered, some with tears in their eyes. Embarkation followed the same routine as with the earlier ship: passengers on board the evening before, departure at dawn.

Police guarded the ships through the night while the deportees slept. Someone was there to wave to Boris Lossky at dawn, watched by a wary policeman ready to bar the way. Then the ship's engine started up and slowly it turned in the direction of the sea. Every one of the memoirists remembered the sequence of events though only the Losskys paid attention also to their greater surroundings. To Boris's eyes the buildings of the embankment – the classical portico of the Mining Institute, the silhouette of St Isaac's – looked fabulous as they rose pink out of the early-morning mist. He saw his home town, for the last time, with the eyes of a future art historian.

As the *Preussen* glided seawards the beautiful sights became more ambivalent. Down the Neva Sound, near the Kanonersky Islands, the confiscated imperial steam yacht *Shtandart* stood marooned, 'waiting for a new designation'. Boards had been laid against it so that the inside was not visible. Was this because the yacht was too luxurious for proletarian eyes to see without inspiring envy? Had this opulent vessel been half-hidden by its captors, like the high-street shops full of imported food for Party members which would be screened off in years to come? Probably it had simply been looted, not a pretty sight. There were other less ambiguous signs of post-revolutionary violence round about. The journey out to Kronshtadt, past small round fortresses on the riverbank, was peppered with gunshot souvenirs of the abortive anti-Bolshevik uprising.

For Trubetskoy the final hours in no man's land before the ship's engine started up dragged interminably.

> I was afraid something would prevent our departure. Until the last minute I had the sense of something supernatural and unreal. Then they started loading our luggage. The *Oberbürgermeister Haken* was standing at the Nevsky jetty. There was a customs search after we had handed in a list of the goods we were exporting. We boarded during the day, but the boat was only due to depart early next morning. Chekists in uniform got on with us, keeping all the passports in their possession.
>
> Departure was delayed. The Captain couldn't get the requisite permission. I remember waking and realizing we had not moved. Then the ship turned and began to chug down the Nevsky Sound. As Kronshtadt [Island] and the Tolbukhin lighthouse came into view a motor-launch pulled away with the Chekists on board. Our boat picked up speed. 'Jetzt können Sie ruhig Ihren Kaffee trinken,' said the Captain. 'Now you can drink your coffee in peace!' He tapped his pocket. 'I have your passports.' I thanked God. Slava Bogu![11]

Somehow very few people were aware that the GPU men were on board; that they were still holding the passengers' Soviet passports, with their German visas, until the ship reached Kronshtadt. But the moment when the police agents left the ship everyone felt the change. Tatyana Frank recalled in old age:

> On the steamer at Kronshtadt the steamer sounded its horn, you know? Our reception on the ship was incredibly cold, the captain

didn't say hello to us, nothing. We felt as if we had been just cast
aside. I found Semyon Lyudvigovich on the deck, and he was
sitting, crying. I asked him why. 'I'll never see my homeland again,'
he replied. Only Alyosha stuffed himself with every kind of sweet
stuff he could lay his hands on, then was sick, and started
again... But at Kronshtadt the steamer turned for some reason. It
began to summon a small boat, and the boat approached and three
people got off. When they had disappeared the captain said:
'Congratulations, now the Chekists have got off, I can say hello to
you.' It seems they had been travelling with us. 'Please understand
why I had to be careful,' he said. 'No one knew what was going on,
and anyone could have uttered God knows what kind of slander.'
After that the captain became incredibly kind, and fed us
fantastically.[12]

Once the ideological navigators disembarked the ship was free to
enter international waters and pick up speed.

There are hints in one or two memoirs of a wary curiosity on the
part of the German crew and a readiness on the Russian side to be
offended. On the November ship, the Lossky boys, who shared a six-
berth cabin on the lower deck with the two older Karsavin children,
felt they were treated 'highhandedly' because of their nationality.
Some guidebooks used to observe the extreme constrast between the
orderly German ships and the disorderly Russian port they served, so
there were certainly prejudices to summon up.

One thing the Germans must have taken in was that the Russians
were hungry. The NEP had relieved them of an existence at subsistence
level but not re-established comfortable pre-war norms. Alyosha
Frank, aged twelve, ate all the sweet stuff in sight. Tatyana established
a more contemplative sense of European luxury by admiring the
starched napkins in the dining room. It was true that the Germans
were always so good at formality. Every honest Russian knew it. Good
at catering too. Vera Ugrimova, aged twenty, rated as 'plusquamperfect'
her 'thoroughly German breakfast' of eggs, bread and butter and jam.

It's a painful fact of life that terrible things happen alongside the banalities of bread and jam. Ugrimova was on her way to breakfast, as the *Haken* picked up speed, when she noticed a moving detail about the departure of the GPU agents. 'At Kronshtadt the customs officers got on board and checked all the papers again and then, something strange, they bid us an emotional farewell. We stood on deck and for a long time they waved their caps at us from their launch. Someone cried: 'We are all Russians. Why is this happening?''[13]

There was no clearer evidence that Russia was being divided against its will than this picture of the GPU agents raising their caps to the departing intelligentsia. As the moment came to leave Russia, Berdyaev was enraged and Osorgin and Frank cried. Aikhenvald had to leave without his wife and sons, and the journalist Boris Khariton and the economist Peshekhonov without their children. The Ugrimovs and the Franks left elderly parents. Parting was pure sorrow and even for those who didn't have children troubling enough. Berdyaev mourned his dog, Shulka, while the poet Khodasevich thought of the millions of Russians who remained:

> Your fate is to accept the yoke,
> To live in bitterness and woe.
> But I have packed my Russia in my bag,
> And take her with me anywhere I go.[14]

The *Haken* entered international waters on the morning of Friday, 29 September.

Berdyaev recorded: 'There were twenty-five of us, and together with our families about seventy-five. The ... *Oberbürgermeister Haken* ... was entirely occupied by our party.'[15] It was a slender, elegant German vessel designed to carry both freight and passengers, which made a weekly round trip between the German Hanseatic port of Stettin and St Petersburg, a standard commercial route before the advent of popular air travel. Guidebooks also recommended taking it as a cruise in summer. According to the company's advertisements, the *Haken* and its sister ship the *Preussen* boasted 'every comfort, large elegant salons, spacious cabins, bathrooms etc. with all modern conveniences and equipped with wireless telegraph'.[16] The young at least could enjoy themselves, while their parents were comfortable. The Lossky parents and the Karsavins both travelled first-class, in two four-berth cabins on the *Preussen*, while their children amused themselves on a lower deck.

Years later passengers remembered the weather on the same journey quite differently. Some recalled endless grey, others focused on the rough weather as the *Haken* turned, on day two, into the Baltic mainstream. It was a tiny ship compared with today's ferries – a mere 1,000 compared with 12,000 tonnes – and couldn't guarantee its passengers a smooth ride. Berdyaev wrote: 'The voyage across the Baltic was wonderful; the sea was calm and smooth; the sun beat down from an unclouded sky, and the nights were mild and starry.'[17] He needed the sensation of peacefulness so probably he invented it.

His great limitation, as a modern thinker, was that he wasn't self-conscious. He didn't suspect *himself* of invention, only others of error. He was also a kind of philosophical anarchist; he didn't like concepts; and this was a difficult enterprise for a philosopher. But he wanted to convey the idea that concepts act as a prison, limiting perception, making change difficult, clogging up the mental room with too many bulky souvenirs, and that made sense of his philosophical anarchism. He felt what Osorgin knew for certain after his painful times in prison, that life had to be defended against all encroachments. They shouldn't have expelled Berdyaev because he represented, in Russian philosophy, a form of checking and balancing that might have stopped the Soviets building a conceptual prison; although had he remained in Russia he would surely have succumbed to Stalin's purges. What can one say? In any case, he was free now to take his ideas abroad.

My inner world has the likeness of a desert, a waste land bare of all but stark and solitary rocks. The moments of greatest exultation in my life are devoid of all adornment, of all frills and furbelows, and

> their closest symbol is to be found in a bare flame. I feel most akin
> to the element of fire; and am therefore a stranger to the elements of
> earth and water. I have therefore seldom felt life to be well-grounded
> and secure, or relished it in the living.[18]

He was a mystic, and, like many mystics, he preferred to look beyond
the world of human creation at the consoling plainness and coldness of
essential existence. In philosophy he suggested that to give up the fixed
contours of rational concepts might be as attractive and as compelling
as letting the mind flow with the unpredictable but somehow patterned
heaving of the sea. His way of thinking may seem extravagant and intellectually self-indulgent today, but there is no doubt he was bringing a
welcome anti-materialism to the West, while embodying a repressed
Russian tradition of respect for the individual person.

Truth dawning at the vanishing point of human endeavour was an
idea which appealed to all Lenin's unwanted philosophers: Berdyaev,
Frank, Vysheslavtsev and Ilyin on this boat, Lossky and Karsavin on
the next. Many of them associated the unreal with man's fragile efforts
at civilization, above all in Russia. Russian writers and poets, especially Gogol, had traditionally felt a special unreality about St
Petersburg, Peter the Great's dubious 'European' creation. Peter's city
was unreal because it defied nature, and nature always seemed poised
to remove it from the map for its hubris. Westerners educated on the
guidebook myth of the Venice of the North cannot easily grasp this
mystical-nihilistic Russian view of Petersburg, but Pushkin made it
the mood of *The Bronze Horseman*, which described the devastating
floods of 1824, and Blok, who had only been dead a year when the
Philosophy Steamer sailed, seemed to concur when he said St
Petersburg was the point of departure for infinity.[19]

The capacity of philosophy to console is almost its defining mark.
The difficulties of the practical life, the well-being of their families,
and their own unquenchable sentiments of home threatened to invade
all minds during the inactivity of the forty-eight-hour journey, but the
philosophers tried to remain stoical in their waking hours. Each had

his book. Osorgin was reading the *The Meditations* of the Stoic Roman Emperor Marcus Aurelius, a treasury of early Christian consolation. God deals with us rationally. It is our fault if we cannot see how clearly enough. So we must try to see the sense of things, be reasonable, love those close to us, do our civic duty, resist idleness, and remember that we are each of us only a speck in time. Osorgin picked out his favourite apothegm: 'Soon you will have forgotten the world, and soon the world will have forgotten you.'[20]

On another page Marcus offered an encouraging sentiment in particular to those monarchists among the expelled men who had run into bitter conflict with Lenin and his spurious socialism, now claiming the moral high ground on behalf of the entire modern world. 'Where life is possible at all, a right life is possible; life in a palace is possible; therefore even in a palace a right life is possible.'[21] Osorgin had monarchist leanings, though as everyone knew, he had passed through almost every possible political position in his lifetime. In Paris Lidiya Berdyaev would dismiss him as a philosophical dandelion whom it was impossible to take seriously, not what Marcus had in mind at all.[22]

The unshakeable monarchist on board the *Haken*, however, was the Hegel expert Ivan Ilyin. What many on the political right have since found attractive about his thinking from the 1920s is the way he defiantly retained an ethic of good and evil and incited others to fight back against Lenin, rather than turn the other cheek. They admire the first and most famous book he wrote in exile, *On Resisting Evil with Force* (1925). Professor of Philosophy in Moscow until his expulsion, Ilyin was a 'Right' Hegelian. At a time when Marxists everywhere believed Hegel had been turned 'the right way up' Ilyin resisted. He disagreed with Marx that material conditions change the world. Hegel's version, that ideas are the motive force, seemed much more plausible to Ilyin. He was philosophically an idea-l-ist, not a materialist. For Marx and Lenin what mattered were economic conditions and the tension between economic classes, and if philosophy, as they said, as well as understanding the world was also going to transform it, then it had to understand economic power. Ilyin, however, saw Christian reason and its institutions as the source of progress. Two such men as Lenin and Ilyin could not live in one world harmoniously. They had to believe, as they did, in necessary conflict; a battle to the end.[23]

Frank believed something of what moved Ilyin, but he was not prepared to fight for it, except on paper. They had been colleagues and friends for years, but eventually Ilyin went too far for Frank, who couldn't bring himself to accept the reality of evil. People said it was a weakness of his philosophy, as it was of Solovyov, the great father of Russian religious thought, that they didn't account for evil. Berdyaev, who did, and who, frighteningly to some, borrowed from the mystic Boehme an Ungrund, a foundation of nothingness to life, was more sanguine. However, Frank was subtle, and one of the subtlest things he ever said, something prophetic for the intellectual century just taking shape in his day, concerned morality and politics. He said that the Left – by which he also meant Lenin – had so deftly associated itself with what was morally good that men of the Right, even where their ideas were correct, would always secretly feel themselves inferior.[24]

Frank was one of the least political men on board the *Haken*, neither for nor obdurately against the monarchy, a natural moderate democrat. What consoled him was, like Marcus Aurelius, a sense that the world in its highest form, the world God shared with man, was ultimately reasonable. He believed that human nature properly understood was governed by the same mathematical rules as made God's universe. This divine orderliness of things, of which human beings were part, spoke to Frank in the first instance out of nature. He encountered a reflection of that faith in all his favourite writers and philosophers: Plato, Spinoza, Goethe. He had to admit that even Marx had first struck him this way. 'When I read in Spinoza's *Ethics* the sentence: "I will talk about human passions and vices as if they were lines, planes and bodies," I found there expression of the same cherished mood which I felt on studying Marx's theory.'[25] As for Goethe, he always put it so beautifully:

Und alles Drängen, alles Ringen
Ist ewige Ruh in Gott dem Herrn.

(And all our days of strife, all earthly toil
Are peace eternal in God the Lord.)

'No efforts of thought help us think; good ideas come to us suddenly of themselves, as God's free children, and say: "here we are".' Reason is God's gift, if only we can see it. This was Frank's refined and judicious view.[26]

There must have been impassioned conversations on the *Haken* between a calm, pale, prematurely old Frank and an impatient, cigar-smoking Berdyaev, who believed that at all costs a good world had to avoid the social and economic determinism of socialism.[27] He and Frank agreed that the target was socialism as philosophy, by which they meant the social, political and spiritual ramifications of Communism. They were not attacking charity, nor the principle of human equality, both of which were the essence of Christianity. The problem was determinism, and the removal of the spiritual dimension as a guarantee of human freedom. Where Berdyaev criticized Frank was over the kind of determinism Frank inherited from Spinoza. Although it was based on the highest conception of reason, it was dangerous. It was too close to something Marxist materialists could build on and it figured human beings as too passive. A man who thought like Spinoza wouldn't be in a position to defend anti-Communist values strongly enough.[28]

The two leading Russian philosophers of their day had conducted this debate many times before: in the corridor of the Religious-Philosophical Academy where they both taught in Moscow, in the lecture room, and now on the high seas. Berdyaev was always ready to engage in mental combat. The debate went on, whatever the place. His aim was to tease something subjective out of Spinoza and thus find an exit into the freedom of the mind. 'I mean it's almost comical to imagine that Spinoza claimed to attain knowledge in *modo geometrico*; the true origin of Spinoza's philosophy, as indeed any other philosophy, is intuitive. It begins with "I".'[29] That was Berdyaev's consistent point, that everything good can be created by men out of their own efforts. It takes only free, creative personality to make a good world. 'Whatever the truth of and prophetic power of Marx's critique of bourgeois society and its assumptions, it is still the ultimate freedom of the spirit which is the truth of philosophy,' he wrote. Frank persisted. 'I felt early on [in Spinoza] something which touched the deep essence of my personality. Philosophy is just that, Spinoza's "intellectual love of God".'[30]

Berdyaev was modern in the way he wanted to dynamize philosophy, give it the force of action, not accept a definition which rested on the power of contemplation. In this way he had an affinity even with Lenin. Also he had read Nietzsche and he knew about the dream of philosophy as dynamite, of 'philosophizing with a hammer' to change the world. Frank, on the other hand, was gentle, unassertive, an almost feminine man, for whom Spinoza's philosophy made it possible 'not to cry, laugh, hate but to understand'. Spinoza was the philosopher whom he lived with, who mattered vitally to him.[31]

Berdyaev and Frank would never grow close, but they agreed that perception of the truth could not be rational in a narrow sense. It was not only a matter of computation and evidence. In this way they could cooperate. They could form a team to teach. Moreover, that they had these fundamental Russian religious beliefs in common ensured that they were both on board the *Haken*, not staying in Lenin's Russia. Lenin and his Great October, the fifth anniversary of which was approaching, had no truck with these fanciful, profound, old-fashioned, poetic, religious-minded relics of the bourgeoisie. Marxism-Leninism wasn't interested in sharing a roof with stoics and idealists and it rejected philosophical pessimism.

So it disdained Aikhenvald too, a scholar whose translation of *The World as Will and Representation* people said was just what a Russian Schopenhauer would have written.[32] Schopenhauer thought of the world as a rough, cruel, relentless place, in which it was difficult for a thoughtful person to be at home. Human existence was subject to the laws of the jungle, except in two things. One was art and the other was the capacity to feel pity. Schopenhauer said we should devote ourselves to these things until our time is up, or until we decide to shorten it.

It is worth emphasizing that Lenin's expelled human cargo were among the last generation in Europe to believe in tragedy in the classical sense: to picture human beings struggling for meaning and for love against often impossible metaphysical odds. They believed metaphysics had something to do with human fulfilment, not only the barriers of money and class. They expressed something which it often seems only poetry can express these days.

From the mere look of the passenger list, did the German captain notice how many of his brilliant Russian passengers had German or German-Jewish names? The Russian intellectual emigration had the same high proportion of Jewish blood as did the first Bolshevik regime. It was a cross-section from the same tree, the top now lopped off, transported for possible transplant, though who knew or cared if the cutting would take. Looking at the two shiploads together, Matusevich, Khariton, Volkovysky, Pumpyansky, Aikhenvald and Frank were Jewish (and, on the lists, also the poet Khodasevich). But blood did not mean religion. Jews by birth, Aikhenvald and Frank had both converted and become assimilated.[33] To my knowledge, Brutskus, whose surname was Polish, was the only practising Jew on board. As for the German-sounding names among the deportees it was true that their families were originally Baltic German, but Kizevetter's foreign roots lay so far back that he did not speak German, nor feel any affinity. The names of these Russians were therefore a little misleading when first glimpsed by an outsider, although many spoke French, German, Polish, English, whatever their varied backgrounds and brilliant education had brought them. In sum, they were cosmopolitan, but no less Russian for that.

Twenty-year-old Vera Ugrimova was walking about the ship when she heard laughter coming from the Trubetskoys' cabin. Perhaps they were looking through the ship's Visitors' Book, dwelling on the mistakes in Russian grammar, and the imperfect German. Her teacher-father always pointed out such things to her. In fact the laughter disguised Sergei Evgenievich's low spirits. He ought to have been happy, he had tricked the Bolsheviks into letting him bring his sister-in-law out, and she was overjoyed at the prospect of joining her husband again in Europe, and so grateful to him. But his sense of his own plight, as a patriot, as a man forced to abandon his heritage, was overwhelming. He was thirty-two years old.

> Hopeless grey sky, grey sea ... even the seagulls are grey. Sadness, homesickness, hopelessness. But that's Russia, the land of our fathers and grandfathers. I feel a tremor in my heart. Is it really for ever? I put on a mask of good cheer for others, and perhaps above all for myself.[34]

At least Trubetskoy was fortunate to be travelling with his family. Aikhenvald's wife and two sons had refused to come. Not only that, the sons were Bolsheviks. His wife may have stayed because of them, but possibly too because she had a bad experience of the West when she 'worked for the Americans' in Moscow.[35]

Ugrimova heard more spasmodic laughter from the Franks' cabin, where Semyon was ridiculing the Bolsheviks' use of acronyms. There was only one word in Russian for the language of *sovdepiye*: it was *podly* – mean, base, ignoble.[36] Take the word for the new Soviet-style government Ministry – *narkom* – made up of two shortened words, 'people' and 'committee'. (In English the word would sound like the 'Peopcom'.) To critical Russian ears *narkom* sounded like *narkoz*, a drug. Or, in an even worse association for the fate of Russia, it sounded like *sarkom*, a sarcoma, a cancer on the body of the motherland. Worst of all, words like *narkom* had no etymology and therefore no history, no national or world roots.[37] They were just what these insane Communists wanted for their RSFSR – their Really So Fantastic Soviet Republic, as Sorokin called it.[38] The exiled philologist Roman Jakobson supplied a variant interpretation of what the new state's initials stood for: *Redkostny sluchai fenomenalnogo sumashestviya rossii*. It was 'A Choice Instance of the Complete Madness of Russia'.[39]

And yet everything about this split, mad Russia had two sides by definition, and the other side of the language story was that it co-incided with an astonishing renewal of poetry in Russia, and new ways of thinking about language and literature that would change the twentieth century. The carrier of that true linguistic revolution to the West would be Jakobson, somehow combining criticism and admiration for all that belonged to the intellectual revolution in Russia. There are two stories about when Jakobson was travelling on *his* boat out of Russia, thinking about words, back in 1920. He was travelling voluntarily, to take up a minor post at the Soviet consulate in Prague, but he had an inkling he wouldn't return. In one version, en route for Stettin, Jakobson was reading Czech poetry and comparing the language to Russian with such growing fascination that he sought out a Czech speaker among the passengers and asked him to read the poems of the celebrated Karel Hynek Mácha out loud so that he could assess the difference between the two Slav languages by ear.[40] In another version, he was listening to a Latvian speaker and hearing about Latvian literature.[41] Both stories are told by Jakobson himself, to capture the symbolic value of his exit journey, and they give the dry, esoteric flavour of the intellectual passions which seem to stalk his work in emotional disguise. He found a way of writing the sounds of his native language into a new science which preserved their unique-ness. It was a science which said 'no one can take away my Russianness, my freedom to be Russian through my ears'.

Jakobson suffered from his fate as an exile. He missed his homeland terribly and plunged himself into work to escape the pain. He caught up with ordinary life by being a big drinker. When he got to Prague one of his first pieces of published work was a long, five-part book review, almost a book in itself, on the ways in which the Bolshevik Revolution impacted on the Russian language. It ended with an implicit comparison between Bolsheviks and Jacobins, and an expression of horror at tyranny. In Soviet Russia they had a new word for the guillotine, he reported, and it started with the first syllable of the Che-ka: the *cherezvechaika*, the cheka-otine, was its name.

Unlike the men on the *Haken* and the *Preussen*, however, Jakobson's potential for loneliness centred on the fact that in spirit, and above all in art, he sided with the new. Born in 1896, he was an atheist with a lifelong passion for the innovations in Russian poetry pioneered by Velimir Khlebnikov and Vladimir Mayakovsky. Like them, syllable by syllable he was ready to take apart the nineteenth-century legacy and open up a twentieth-century world of sensibility and expression. The avant-garde poets called their innovatory, invented, human-all-too-human language *Za-um* or 'trans-sense'. The religious philosophers could never have accepted such free thinking. Their inclination was to believe, with the German anti-rationalists of the eighteenth century, that language was on loan from God, in which case how could it be discarded or reinvented at will?

Now clearly Russia's misfortune after the Revolution was the loss of a rich cultural life which could accommodate both these points of view and many in between. The country was extraordinarily creative in the two decades Lenin plotted to seize power, but when he succeeded in grasping it the culture began to shrink. Lenin's insistence on intellectual conformism was why later critics would lament the 'lumpenization' and 'banalization' of the country after 1922.

The Franks in their cabin began to sing.[42] They had often cheered themselves up by singing at other difficult moments of their lives, such as when they were in Saratov during the Civil War, because it helped to create a warm family atmosphere and a feeling of shared pleasure. So why not now? Possibly that night, waltzes, especially from Tchaikovsky's *Eugene Onegin*, a great favourite, took their minds off the Baltic swell and a rotten fate, although Victor most loved Schubert songs.

Ugrimova went up on deck and stared down at the sea. She was joined by Ilyin, whose Hegelian faith in cultural synthesis persuaded him that even the White cause was a disease Russia had to suffer, before a good life was possible again. The country had to get beyond both Bolshevism and anti-Bolshevism.

'Verochka, do you remember how in the liturgy we sing "of real things in the distant sea"? It's about Plato, you see. "Of real things and the distant sea."[43] Plato's man of virtue spends his life approaching the ideal and the eternal and does finally see it reflected in the sea.'

'Yes, Ivan Alexandrovich, I see now.' Ugrimova was embarrassed. Ilyin was unfair. Only a philosopher would have picked up the echo of Plato in the Eastern Church rite, and this was just a child. But he was so lonely he had to ask this impossible question of a child, to have an excuse to speak of infinite things.

Something in Tchaikovsky's music urged Semyon and Tatyana to go up on deck alone after Vasya fell asleep. They stood under the stars, holding hands and considering their lives. As a destination Germany had a certain awkward symbolic value because in earlier life Semyon had enjoyed a long illicit love affair there with the wife of a friend.[44] The thing had gone on too long, six or seven years, and it had tortured him before he met Tatyana and had the courage to end it. 'The woman in green', his wife would call her, after the first time they met.[45]

'I thought I was in love with her, but as I see now it couldn't have been true love because it was based on a lie.' Marriage was a sacrament, and to love outside it was to defy that sacred truth. Tolstoy tried unconvincingly to preach this vision in *Anna Karenina*, that love is only true love when it has true Christian-social foundations, but admirably the Franks lived it and believed it.

As the *Haken* ploughed on through the darkness and the philosophers couldn't sleep for worry, they felt the debt they owed to their strong wives. Boris Vysheslavtsev depended on his Natasha. Osorgin needed his Rachel. Semyon Frank let himself be guided by the inimitable Tatyana, who also kept an eye on poor, good Aikhenvald. Kizevetter was so close to his wife that he would not want to live after she died. The youngest wives there were Rachel Osorgin, née Ginzberg, thirty-seven, and Tatyana, thirty-five. Both were educated. Rachel had a degree and knew foreign languages. Tatyana, though no intellectual, was a former pupil of the Anglophile Lapshin, and also of

Lossky, at Stoyunina's academy. She was fast becoming a feisty matri-
arch with a sharp tongue.

They awoke on Saturday, 30 September 1922, to rough weather. Those
who followed in November would have a similar experience. When
the ships emerged from the sheltered Baltic channel along the
Estonian coast they were immediately buffeted by the North Sea. The
Preussen passengers put their chess pieces on a board at the bottom of
a heavy, deep-sided box and continued to play, while every now and
again spewing with the wind. Boris Lossky spent all night on deck
talking to the captain who spoke to him kindly in 'really rather good'
Russian. Still most people retired to retch in the stuffy privacy of their
cabins. On the *Haken*, when the waves rose in the early morning,
people ran gagging from the dining room.

Osorgin, who never felt sick, breakfasted with the Trubetskoys in
the emptied salon. They raised their coffee cups. Two name-days in
the family fell that day. 'We'll have a party, shall we? This afternoon?
And invite the captain? There can hardly be a luckier day on the
calendar than one which has four saints.'[46]

After lunch they crowded into the Trubetskoys' cabin. His sister
Sofya, his mother Vera, and another woman called Nadezhda were the
centre of attention. Trubetskoy remembered: 'Osorgin delivered a
flowery speech in their honour. He said Sofya, Vera and Nadezhda are
with us. Only Lyubov is not here. Lyubov has been left behind in
Russia.' Joyfully the name-day party explained to the captain that the
names doubled as common nouns in Russian, so what Osorgin was
actually saying was: Wisdom, Faith and Hope are with us. Only Love
is not here. Love has been left behind in Russia.

Misha Osorgin was, to judge solely by appearances, outstandingly
attractive. Yet any woman who drew close to him must have realized
there was something missing. Saddened by his past, he never knew
which political course to steer, what to believe in. Also he had no
children. First with one wife, now with Rachel, fortune denied him a
family. Altogether he spent too much time thinking of the path his life

had taken. His emotions got in the way of his fiction. He would never be a great writer, but his life was extraordinary, worth writing down in itself. In exile he would often recall the times when he was 'secretly reading Italian novellas, waiting for the knock at the door'.[47] Then again, when he wrote that he still believed that exile was glamorous.

Who was the architect of the intelligentsia's nemesis? The Philosophy Steamer seethed with speculation. The two *Pravda* articles in August suggested Zinoviev. (*The Times* in London took this line.) Nikolai Lossky argued that Zinoviev's reports as head of the Petrograd Soviet positively showed he was to blame.

> [Zinoviev] wrote that various groups of the intelligentsia were beginning to found journals and societies; that for the time being their activity was uncoordinated but in time would be united and would then entail a significant force. Thereupon the Moscow government decided to carry out arrests right across Russia of eminent academics, writers and public figures, which then took place on 16 August 1922.[48]

The journalist Khariton also blamed Zinoviev.[49] But others thought that Trotsky was responsible, and Aikhenvald even blamed a poet, Valery Bryusov, to whom he had given a bad review.[50]

The other persistent question was what had they done wrong? Efim Zubashov, who was a chemist and academic administrator who had been a Duma member before the Revolution, wrote in his diary during the *Preussen* voyage:

> The vast majority of expellees are either criminals or heroes. In relation to myself neither is apt: I have committed no crime, I have also shown no sign of heroism, my expulsion is the outcome of a misunderstanding, and, maybe more likely, Soviet power's inevitable debt to demagoguery. In the first revolution I was expelled from Tomsk (in 1906) as a revolutionary. Now they are driving me to the West, beyond the borders of Russia, as a counter-revolutionary. In both cases I have been tarred with someone else's feathers.[51]

Zubashov's assessment of his fellow victims as either criminals or heroes was not correct. His self-portrait was pitiful. But pity a man whose only 'crime' was to have written for *Ekonomist*.

Karsavin decided that by taking away his country God must be punishing him for his affair with Yelena.[52] His colleague Ivan Lapshin, thinker, psychologist, musicologist, was equally troubled. Lapshin was a dapper Anglophile and probably suspect for being just that. He had garnered some very un-Leninist views from having an Anglo-Swiss mother and from reading William James while studying in England. As a result he was interested in a wonderful, completely unacceptable Jamesian subject, namely 'the psychology of metaphysical need'. When the ship's Visitors' Book was passed around in the middle of his voyage out on the *Preussen*, Lapshin borrowed the words of Pushkin's Don Juan and wrote: 'Look here, I'm not a state criminal!'[53] Meanwhile he and his fellows were touched to see, on an earlier page of the same book, a cartoon by the great Russian baritone Shalyapin, with the inscription: 'I'm not afraid of anything.' Shalyapin had not been forcibly hounded out. On the contrary Soviet Russia wanted to keep him, for the sake of the country's artistic prestige.[54] But when Shalyapin got an exit visa on trust he felt lucky to escape that mean, stunted world-in-the-making and had no intention of going back.

The night of 30 September, the second and last for the *Haken* at sea, closed in. Lithuania, a speck of a country newly liberated from the Russian Empire, passed invisible to port side. Invisible to starboard lay the southwest coast of Sweden. The children following the journey on the map beside the reception desk mentally ticked off the East Prussian port of Königsberg. The older ones managed Danzig before their eyes closed. The map of Central Europe redrawn by the Treaty of Versailles after the First World War had conspicuous oddities. The German enclave of East Prussia was like an island trapped on three sides by unfriendly blockades. The only way out was the sea. A thin strip of Poland separated East Prussia from its mother Germany. The flèche of Polish land, slim and sharp at the tip and lying inert and proud between rivals, resembled the sword between Siegfried and

Brünnhilde on their wedding night. It was unnatural to keep apart two human forces which were bound to rush together sooner or later – with terrible consequences.

Of course no one could foresee the course European politics would take over the next twenty years: the rise of Hitler and Stalin, a war that would take the Germans to Petrograd under another name, a campaign ignited by German fear of Bolshevism and the ragged 'East', and supported by Mussolini in Italy. But there would be a startling foretaste of what was to come when the party from the *Preussen* arrived in Germany on 18 November 1922. They bought newspapers at the railway station in Stettin, only to find that the Wirth government had resigned over its failure to curb inflation, Hitler was already Leader of the National Socialist Party and Mussolini had marched on Rome. Brutskus's wife drew everyone's attention to the story of a National Socialist opponent of the Weimar government poisoned in prison by his own party in case he betrayed them.[55]

Victor (Vityusha) Frank was thirteen when he sailed on the *Haken*, and this would be the European geography, and the beginning of a chain of events, that would shape his fractured world. During the 1939–45 war both sides would have killed him, if they could, since his blood was Jewish and his passport Soviet. Stalin had no tolerance of Russians who lived outside Russia, no matter how they got there. But Victor survived, by happy chance, because he managed to get to England. He was to continue studying European history in Oxford, after Berlin and Prague, but then the war broke out and he joined the BBC instead, monitoring foreign radio stations to gain insight into the mind of the enemy. Later, in over twenty-five years as a professional broadcaster, he made it his task to try to keep Soviet and émigré Russia in touch. He aimed to mend the divorce which blighted his childhood. His father's seriousness combined in him with his mother's Catholicism. He believed there were metaphysical reasons why things happened, which gave him comfort when he had to face the death of three of his loved ones in quick succession, in the middle of his life. He wrote a book of essays on Russian literature and heroically translated Joyce's *Ulysses* into Russian. He was also a great opera-lover, who would have appreciated the connection between the passion of Siegfried and Brünnhilde and the tragic geography of post First World War Europe.[56]

That night, as the *Haken* steered a course along that fateful coast, the professors met in the empty dining room. We only know there was a meeting. No one kept a record of what happened, still less took a photograph. The photograph would not have been very exciting, but history would be happier if it existed. It would have been one of the dull institutional kind the professors usually appeared in. At first glance, with the exception of the much younger Trubetskoy and the moustachioed but beardless Osorgin, the unwilling academic exiles seemed to be of strikingly similar appearance, each one owlishly wise behind his round, steel-rimmed spectacles and, in Orthodox or Rabbinical fashion, sporting a wizard's beard. Possibly Lenin had chosen to exile men of a certain physiognomy. Anything was possible in the new Europe in the making. But these were redundant men, and the writing on the back, in a careful Cyrillic hand, would leave no doubt of the century to which they belonged – Vysheslavtsev b. 1877, Ilyin b. 1883, Frank b. 1877, Berdyaev b. 1874, Kizevetter b. 1866, Osorgin b. 1878, Trubetskoy b. 1890, Aikhenvald b. 1872, Ugrimov b. 1874. The writing might even be in the old orthography, if, for instance, Ilyin had been charged with keeping the record. One of the first 'modern' shocks Russia felt after Nicholas II abdicated was a change in the written language introduced by the Provisional government. Those who mistakenly associated the move with the Bolsheviks took an especially long time to get used to it. The orthographic reform, to remove a very common but superfluous letter, was trivial. The modernized Cyrillic orthography did for the printed page what sanserif typefaces did for English, they made it cleaner and sharper. But what in England was an easy transition was difficult for Russians because of the huge political upheaval of which language seemed to be part. Some of the exiles went on strike for fifty years. No man on the 1922 ships was quite so stubborn, but they were sailing to join communities where the new orthography would be resisted until 1970.[57]

By the time he reached his early twenties Victor Frank would realize that his father's generation marked the end of a world, not the beginning of a new one.[58] Old Russia was left behind in the wake of the *Haken*.

Berdyaev wanted the meeting of the professors because as a group they would need to have a speech prepared for their arrival in Stettin. Their expulsion from Russia was an extraordinary moment and history should not be disappointed by a lack of self-awareness on the victims' part. The German Red Cross and other relief organizations alerted to the professors' status as effective refugees would come to meet them officially and would need to be answered. Also the press would be there, and would need to be advised of the political significance of the event. Ideally Chancellor Wirth, who was still in office when the *Haken* arrived with its cargo of intelligentsia, would make a statement. In short Berdyaev wished to know what he should say when they arrived in Germany, because it was clear he was the man to do the job.

Left to himself Berdyaev would not mince words over the way the Russian intelligentsia had let the evil of Lenin happen, had even invited it or at the very least was inseparable from it. He and his colleagues were partly to blame. But could he really say that now? He preferred to insist that now revolution had finally taken place, the revolution for which they too had longed, it didn't make sense to be travelling in the opposite direction. Tsarism was over. Rule for the people by the people had been promised. The task of the intelligentsia was to act as spiritual watchman over Bolshevik proceedings. But where are we? Not there! Somewhere else! They pushed aside the question of the speech. Their own fate was too pressing.

Ilyin intervened. 'We shouldn't treat with criminals. They must be caught and punished and the monarchy restored, and then we'll see.'

'But you would surely agree, Ivan Aleksandrovich,' Aikhenvald entered the fray, 'that the revolution was our brainchild and that, just as we have seen the triumphant birth of new beginnings in art, so we have to accept the misbirth, the *Mißgeburt*, of a new form of tyranny over the people.'

'I would add,' said Berdyaev, 'that if Ivan Aleksandrovich does not feel sympathy with the failings of the intelligentsia of which he is part, then surely he can see how the Church has failed Russia? Christians ought to have embodied the truth of Communism; had they done so its false aspect would never have prevailed.'

'Russia is in the grip of a disease she must work through. Both the Red and White movements are to be left behind,' replied Ilyin.

'Then Russia will have no blood at all,' joked someone. 'No red parts, no white parts, you see...'

Aikhenvald sat trying to muster his gloomy spirits. He wanted to remind himself that it was art and artists, and above all the great poets, who had the answers in Russia. 'Perhaps it would be appropriate to recite a number of poems on our arrival tomorrow, for the sake of a memorable ceremony. You know the classics, gentlemen. I don't have to remind you of Lermontov's tortured love for his country – "I do love my country, but with a strange love..." (*Lyublyu otchiznu ya, no strannoyu lyubovyu...*). Lermontov sometimes struggles to convince himself of that love, as some of us do now. When we left yesterday you surely heard his "Farewell to Unwashed Russia" in your head. I did.'[59]

> *Proshchai, nemytya Rossiya,*
> *Strana rabov, strana gospod,*
> *I vy, mundiry golubye,*
> *I ty, im predanny narod.*
>
> (Goodbye unwashed Russia
> land of slaves, land of lords
> goodbye you sky-blue uniforms out there
> and you, you devoted hordes.)

'Who has had time to read poetry in the last two years?' someone cried. The crumpled figure of the critic replied that poetry was his job.

And he cited the poet Sergei Esenin who even now was in Berlin allowing love to push aside his inky addiction to bridges and departures and farewells: 'Now we are going step by step/to the hushed land of bliss.' Yes, Esenin had married a dancer called Isadora   Duncan, and she had whisked him abroad.[60]

If only our departure were like that! As Esenin often said, 'to die, but not yet'. Poetry is like setting out on the last journey. It has the allure of life lived as if in the last moment, the allure of language possibly spoken for the last time. Poetry is penultimate. It expresses the moment before the moment which will finish us, but which we cannot finish. Osip Mandelstam was in deep melancholy when in 1920 he wrote his invitation to the unfinishable dance. It began, 'In Petersburg we'll meet again/We buried the sun there, didn't we…' And then a year later, just last year, Mandelstam took us to the railway station to hear music we could dance to. Something he saw and heard made him believe he could bring hope to the endless departures and farewells, and the deaths, and the deaths of the spirit that afflict us these days in Russia. He called his poem 'Concert at the Station'.

> It's impossible to breathe and worms infest the land
> And not a single star breaks,
> But God can see where music is: up there, a band.
> The station is shaking from aeolian sol-fa,
> Engines are repeatedly whistling
> and the torn violin air is rippling.

'It's impossible to breathe', yes. *Nelzya dyshat*. Gumilyov felt it too. 'It's hard to breathe and painful to live.' '*I trudno dyshat i bolno zhit*.' Who can be Russian and not echo Lermontov: '*I skucho i grustno*', 'I'm worn-down and sad'. Poetry is a whore like the rest of us, she allows History to make use of her, but sometimes she, and we, are more memorable for that.

A dozen heads bowed as Aikhenvald began:

I was walkin' down a street unknown
when crows started crowin'
I heard a lute-ish sound and distant thunder
A tram had gawn and wrenched itself asunder.

'ow did I leap on the runnin' board?
I some'ow made a try.
The tram had left a fiery swaid
Across the daylight sky.

Like a dark, winged storm it soared; astray
it raged in a timeless ferment.
Stop tramdriver, stop this tramway!
Stop tramdriver, please, why so intent?

It's too late...

...

I ask my heart: where am I?
Can you see the station? It replies. In it –
– it is a dark and fearful reply –
They have tickets to the India of the spirit.

A shop-sign...lettering splashed with blood
Announcing greenstuff – but I know then
That instead of cabbages and spuds
They sell the heads of dead men

In a red shirt, with a face like an udder,
The hangman also cut off my smile
It lay there with the others
In a slippery box, beneath the pile.

There's a fence, down an alleyway,
There's a house, three windows, a grey grass ascent,
Stop tramdriver, stop this tramway!
Stop tramdriver, please, why so intent?

Mashen'ka, this is where you used to live.
Where you sang and wove me a rug. My bride!
My bride! Are your voice and body no longer yours
     to give?
Can it be that you have died?

You sighed at home with frustration
Whilst I powdered my hair with a view
To meeting the Empress: for a presentation.
Now I'll never see you.

Then I understood: our freedom is light
But reflected from afar
People and shadows stand right
In the door of the zoo of the distant planet stars

Straightaway a warm and gentle wind lists
And beyond the bridge flies
A horseman with an iron-gloved fist
And the two hooves of his horse strike my eyes

As the true firmament of Right Belief
St Isaac's towers up and stands out bold
I'll have prayers told
There for Mashen'ka; and a mass, so that I too may
     rest in peace.

And still my heart is weighed down in eternity
It's painful to live and hard to breathe…
Mashen'ka I never knew the verity
Of how hard it is to love and grieve.[61]

The smooth chug of the steam engine was suddenly all the sound to
be heard in the dining room of the *Oberbürgermeister Haken*. The reliable heart driving the ship through the Baltic darkness hummed on.
The ship was alive like a huge warm-bodied creature on which they
were leaning and resting.

Trubetskoy said Gumilyov was answering Pushkin's 'Bronze Horseman'. He was reliving the Petrograd nightmare, linking the great flood with the power of autocracy established by Peter, and now the Revolution. He mentioned that Pushkin had almost called the city Petrograd too. 'Stand firm in your beauty, city of Peter, stand unshakeable like Russia': '*Krasuisya, grad Petrov, i stoi/Nekolebimo, kak Rossiya*'. Others took up the murdered poet's image of freedom as reflected light, which allowed them to link Plato and Russia and feel the greatness of their inheritance in the Russian style of philosophy, in poetry, and in the Orthodox rite. 'Was not Gumilyov suggesting he found all freedom in this world illusory?' objected Vysheslavtsev. 'Not an illusion, but creative and spiritual in character, not to be found in nature,' replied Berdyaev. He sounded his old tune. Freedom reflected the divine potential in man. Gumilyov's idea of freedom was not sufficiently creative and positive.

'This debate is so Russian,' moaned Aikhenvald. 'Every man milks the poem for his own philosophical nourishment, or to fight some publicistic battle. Gentlemen, please, spare our culture! In any case, if you read the poem again I think you will agree that Gumilyov preferred his faith blind. You know how it is, when you prefer medicine taken with closed eyes.'

'I can't put that in my speech,' said Berdyaev.

Of course, yes, Berdyaev would make the speech in Stettin. No one else was so wise to the mechanisms of publicity. No one else could formulate yesterday's events as such persuasive history. The professors assented to his choice of himself because none of them sought the limelight. They just wanted to get on with their work. Frank saw that it was natural and useful for Berdyaev to adopt a certain swagger. He wasn't sure he liked him, but having such a figurehead could work to all their advantage. Osorgin cut a fine figure of a man, but he was not a commanding speaker. Aikhenvald was subtler in his speech, but his posture and therefore his delivery were poor. He mumbled into his rabbinical boots. Trubetskoy was too young, Kizevetter too old, Vysheslavtsev too undemonstrative. There was little doubt who should represent them. The professors nodded as Frank spoke.

'In any case you'd better not mention freedom. It's too difficult to know what is meant.'

'And instead? What will the world think?'

'Talk about history. It's an equal mystery,' said Ilyin.

Berdyaev wrote hastily in his notebook. 'For myself I did not doubt the utter inevitability of Russia's experience of Bolshevism. "Historical inevitability" is, admittedly, often a grand name by which people seek to fortify themselves and sometimes even to paralyse their antagonists: but this was a different inevitability, showing a decisive experience in the inner destiny of the Russian people and ushering Russia into a new world in which she was enabled to speak the full truth about herself. There is no return to what was before the Bolshevik Revolution, and all attempts at restoration, even of the principles of the February Revolution, appear to me as both powerless and harmful.'[62] He went on, that after the experience of the Communist Revolution there could only be a forward movement. But it was no excuse for the Terror.

The company clapped. It would certainly do as a speech.

Suddenly the oldest man in the group, Alexander Kizevetter, wanted to speak. Everyone deferred. 'Gentlemen, as you know I am an historian. As you may not know, but I am quite willing to admit, I have never read Hegel and at the age of fifty-six I do not intend to do so. What concerns me is the concrete inadequacy of almost every approach to Russian history I have ever read. The facts are not enough to explain the life of the people. But on the other hand, the so-called life of the people attracts far too much speculation and often contradicts the facts and is spun into a myth. As we move towards making our new lives in the West we will have to counter many ignorant and untrue images of our country, and it would be a sad loss of opportunity if we encouraged those mistaken views.

'Some of us love Lermontov's farewell to the sky-blue uniforms and the subordinate horde. But do we really think that Bolshevism has conquered Russia because the mass of people are inert, and have no character of their own? Do we really think that Russians cannot do otherwise than be ruled by an autocrat? I would rather argue that the nature of imperialism was such that the people would in the end support any force in opposition to it. Autocracy was a poor political education and ultimately an incitement to any violence to get rid of it. The fact that tsarist autocracy has been replaced by Bolshevik autocracy is not evidence of the hopelessness of the Russian people. It is only deeply unfortunate that in their ignorance and lack of democratic practice they have been misled.'[63]

Trubetskoy drew a breath, reflecting on how close the Whites had been to winning the Civil War in 1919 and how that defeat had devastated everyone in his circle. Sustained British and French support might have tipped the balance. But Berdyaev said he had always been against foreign intervention and remained so with hindsight, even if it had led to the present tyranny.

Kizevetter continued: 'The other theory I think we must beware of is the idea that Russia is an eastern country. If my memory serves me that idea comes in Lermontov's very next stanza, something about serving the pasha. The fact is Russia has as much in common with West as East. It depends on who is doing the looking. Nor has it an Oriental idyll to look back to in its pre-Petrine experience. The wisest view of Russian history, the one we should endeavour to make known in the West, is the view of Lev Tolstoy. I have been remarking to myself this evening how incredible it seems that Lev Nikolaevich only died twelve years ago; also that, had he gone on living, he would surely be with us today on this ship, if the Cheka had not killed him. Tolstoy takes the view that the world can be divided into two kinds of players: those who strut on the stage and aim at public notice and acclaim, and those whose goal is inner fulfilment through love of their fellows. For Tolstoy, history comprises the impressions we leave on each other, and the way these impressions cause us to act this way or that, aiding, interfering with, resisting some inevitable unfolding of our existence in time. The prime mover of that existence remains unknown and unknowable. Through love of our fellow men and our nation, Tolstoy suggests we can nevertheless make sense of how to live. In other words, for the good life and for the good of history the development of human character based on sympathy for our fellow men is everything. All else in life is vain and accidental.

'Tolstoy was rather ambivalent about whether we should think of ourselves as nations, with a destiny. He said no to the politicians who used the idea to wage war, but yes to the people who felt their personal destiny bound up with their past and their land. In the end he encouraged us to think of ourselves as a country – and even more as a people, a wandering and searching people, whose fate lay in God's hands.'

On that calm note struck by Kizevetter, and with the speech for the morrow pretty much written, the professors retired to their cabins. A new parallel, however, between their Russian fates and the eternal Jewish fate stuck in the mind of Aikhenvald, who would begin to discover his Jewish heritage in Germany.[64]

'Quick, quick, Verochka, we're arriving in Stettin.' Professor Novikov's daughter Yelena was banging on the Ugrimovs' cabin door. 'Yelena came to fetch me,' Vera Ugrimova remembered sixty years later. 'We could already see the town from our cabin. Then we all went up on deck.'

Like so many ships on so many routes, however, the *Haken* and the *Preussen* were scheduled to approach their home port at dawn, so crucial sights were missed by most of the passengers. When the engines slowed for the turn into the Oder Estuary at Swinemünde, the art nouveau lighthouse went unnoticed. Up close the Baltic coast of Western Pomerania consisted of a strip of white sand with greenish scrub behind it. The scenery was uneventful, like a coastal version of Levitan's flat, watery Russian landscapes with birch trees. The sea ran to meet the land in long flat wavelets. A few people were fishing on the shore.

The *Haken* glided smoothly through the natural bay of the Kleines Haff and down the narrow Oder channel, flanked first by a couple and then by many tethered boats. Cranes towered over shipyards. Seagulls screamed and flew ahead as if to pilot the ship into port; as if their life's task was to bring home a captive, or a trophy, or a hero warrior's body. They would have done the same had the Trojan Horse risen from the sea: piped it home with their shrill cries, not understanding that home was more than just a place where ships docked and that they might have piped in an alien object by mistake. Finally, some forty miles inland, the *Haken* docked at its mother port.

When the Losskys arrived six weeks later Borya and Volodya did notice the lighthouse and the handsome shipbuilding city hugely impressed them.[65] The way its medieval and neo-Gothic redbrick churches, its true Gothic spires and Renaissance royal residence swept back up the steep hill from the river, the way its majestic wharfs lined the route from the sea, was not only a regal confirmation of eight centuries of beauty and enterprise but also an indispensable location for international trade. But, oh, in spirit, so far from Russia!

Vera Ugrimova, who lacked their education, recorded her first impressions:

> We arrived in Stettin in the early morning. On the wharf, which
> was well-constructed, stood a few drunken Germans with fat beer
> bellies. [My cousin] Sonya Sherbakova observed: 'Look, the
> Germans didn't lose weight in the war.' Of course this hasty
> judgement wasn't true – much had changed in Germany. But for us,
> coming from a country which had been through a cataclysm, less
> intensive changes in other countries could seem to us immaterial or
> even non-existent.

She stared about her, at the majestic medieval redbrick home of the Pomeranian kings, but the sight conveyed to her nothing more than her own alienness.

Trubetskoy instantly noticed the skill with which the wharf was constructed. This place couldn't be Russia. Mayor Haken, celebrated as the great late nineteenth-century beneficiary of Stettin, had modernized the riverbank and given his name to the Haken Embankment where the Russians landed and to the very ship they travelled on. Everything in Germany was so modern and efficient.

Vera needed an object to stare at, to steady herself. The tall, Renaissance-gabled warehouses on the far side of the Oder spelt out the superior – but unfriendly – form of the West as if in a huge foreign alphabet. It was all so foreign. She burst into tears. Then the Philosophy Steamer anchored between the Baumbrücke and the Lange Brücke, and the group disembarked.

Berdyaev set his floppy felt hat in place for the first time since the voyage began. His dark flowing locks sprouted from either side. His eyes glistened. For a moment his teeth bared themselves, but the spasm subsided. He scanned the length of the deserted Haken embankment. Not that he expected the late Mayor Haken, of course, but what about his successor, or his successor's successor? 'There doesn't seem to be anyone.' He wrote later, hurt above all: 'No Russian émigrés came to meet us.'[66]

The reception of the *Preussen* passengers was better organized and included a medical parade. 'It consisted of an old, kind-hearted doctor looking into the eyes of every passenger as he or she passed by in single file and wishing them well.'[67] Tatyana Frank even recalled for her grandson how she and Semyon were reunited in Stettin with the young painter Lev Zak, Semyon's half-brother who had 'gone through an epic ten times worse than ours'.

[In Stettin] Lev didn't recognize us. Silent, very quiet when he did speak, he kept looking around him. He left the Crimea after a terrible pogrom, when they went from house to house butchering people, and they were to be butchered themselves the next day, they gave a list to the yardwoman, the doorman's wife, of everyone's address, Mikhail Lyudvigovich, Sofya Lyudvigovna and grandfather Vasily, and her mother was with them too, and once they had torn the rings from their fingers, and it was time to do away with them, Sofya's mother shouted: 'What are you doing? Just think what you're doing! Have you gone mad? The Lord be with you, please God that

such a thing –' They replied: 'Go to the devil, you Jews,' and left.
And so they were saved. They were all there, you know, Machno,
Petlyura [anti-Semitic Ukrainian militants], it just went on and on.
From the Crimea he [Lev] got to Italy.[68]

But at eighty-eight Tatyana was probably mistaken, and the meeting
with her Jewish brother-in-law, who had been lucky to escape the
White Army with his life, seems more likely to have taken place in
Berlin. The Russian parties really only passed through Stettin, remaining as long as it took to get their luggage to the station and the Berlin
train to arrive.

The station was close to the river, just eight hundred metres from
where they disembarked. Ugrimova remembered vividly the short trek
they made with the luggage:

> My father was very cheerful and hired three handcarts which were
> loaded with coal. We put the luggage on top. Professor Novikov's
> son and my brother Alexander, both fifteen at the time, rode on top
> to guard the things. Behind the carts came the professors walking
> hand in hand with their wives down the middle of the road. The
> parade through Stettin resembled a funeral procession. The boys on
> the cart were killing themselves with laughter at the way there were
> these people in Stettin who took care of the wharf, they wore white
> trousers and were washing the riverbed with mops. After all we had
> been through in five years in Moscow, this activity seemed to us
> inconceivably stupid. The Germans looked at us as if we were
> mad ... Finally we got to the station. No one was waiting for us
> there either.[69]

The problem was it was Sunday, the day of rest in the Protestant
and Catholic world of northern Europe. The previous week a group of
Mohammedans from Bokhara at the heart of the Russian Empire had
stepped off the *Preussen* on a Wednesday, when the port was in full
swing, and excited huge attention with their exotic costumes. But the
professors on the *Haken*, with no particular costumes to identify them

except here and there a certain eccentricity, had arrived on 1 October, a Sunday, when all the shopkeepers were at home and the port quiet. The accident of a delayed timetable probably accounted for the absence of any welcome, and any surrounding life.

The result was that, for the first time, the passengers disembarking from the Philosophy Steamer actually felt like refugees. When they boarded their train it was evident that some preparations had been made on their behalf, but that didn't help.

> When the train arrived some coaches were reserved for our group. We found some Germans sitting in them. When my father explained the situation we heard them reply: 'Damned Bolsheviks, now they're barging in here too.'
>
> We travelled in the same compartment as Osorgin. While Father explained to my brother and me the principles on which German agriculture was organized – fields and market gardens were speeding past the window – Osorgin sat limp and weeping, and his wife comforted him.

Ugrimova went on:

> That evening we arrived in Berlin. Again there was no one to meet us. We sat at little tables [at the station], not knowing what to do, where to go. A boy appeared with newspapers. Someone bought a copy of the émigré Russian newspaper *Rul*, where they found a small notice saying that a number of professors and their wives and children were being exiled from the Land of the Soviets. Some were named. But then a very nice German from the German Red Cross arrived and put us in pensions and cheap hotels. Ours smelt of gas and sauerkraut and I went to sleep under a bright yellow feather-quilt.

Trubetskoy remembered: 'In Berlin they expected us refugees to arrive looking wretched and hungry and were surprised to find us spruce. I think they imagined that we would look as we used to when they moved us from one prison to the next. But we arrived in Germany looking middle-class.' Lidiya Berdyaeva recalled: 'We arrived in Berlin yellowish-green and looking like ghosts. But spiritually we were much strengthened and rebellious. And that's the most important thing for us as Christians.'[70] A well-wishing German observed that the deported Russians at least had their identity as a group to sustain them as they found their feet in Europe. Berdyaev replied furiously that he could not abide groups. 'I am a free man and a philosopher of freedom. I do not respect groups. I respect particular men and women.'[71]

The arrivals on the *Preussen* had it better. After the four-and-a-half-hour rail journey, about forty people came to meet them at Berlin's now demolished Stettiner Bahnhof, once the Euston or King's Cross of Berlin. They included members of the September group, and Olga and Yelena Nabokov, who came to see their old headmistress Mariya Stoyunina. The new arrivals from Russia transferred to the same pensions and cheap hotels and found that many from the earlier group were still there. This time too *Rul* ('The Rudder') had the proper measure of the story. Its front-page editorial on 5 October spoke of 'a grimace of history'. It took issue with Fridtjof Nansen who had just told the League of Nations that Russian émigrés no longer faced danger in their country and could return. This was laughable, said 'The Rudder'. At the present time in Russia 'no one can feel safe from the arbitrariness and surveillance of the regime'. The Russian intelligentsia were only grateful to the Western European countries which had taken them in.

The element of fear was strong among the *expulsanty*. Nabokov would say that Russians abroad would never lose the sense of the long arm of the Russian political police ready to interfere in their lives.[72] Lossky refused to speak about Russia in public.[73] Sorokin, who soon after he arrived in the West noted that 'it became clear that I had left none too soon', must have tried to laugh off the news he received from a friend back in Russia: 'Our grandmother is very sorry for having let you go without giving you her last and eternal blessing.'[74] There were many popular codes for referring to GPU murders. 'Our grandmother's' activities was one.

Nevertheless many of the *expulsanty* were ready to talk. Berdyaev, Aikhenvald, Stepun, Myakotin and Sorokin himself delivered public lectures and gave interviews from their very first days in the West. The November arrivals brought with them the latest news on the Sovietization of Russia which fascinated everyone. At the same time arrival in Berlin remained a sad and confusing occasion for individuals in their hearts. Osorgin confided to his diary:

> A steamship rolled underway in the Gulf of Finland... and now I am in Berlin. The tea is bad but the dregs in the saucer are still the same: a long journey. (I once had my fortune told by a French woman on the Italian riviera.) I dream: perhaps the return journey? But there is no hope of that, and even my desire is not all that strong.[75]

As Tatyana Frank put it:

> Exile – *vysylka* – was completely unexpected, but none of those exiled foresaw that it was a departure from Russia for good. Many consoled themselves with the thought that Russia would soon be liberated and we would return.[76]

But it wasn't, not for seventy years.

PART II

'The way we have scurried to and fro in the twentieth century, trapped between Hitler and Stalin!'

Nadezhda Mandelstam, *Hope Against Hope*

'I was told: "They hope in the Kremlin that when you find yourself in Western Europe you will understand on which side justice lies."'

Nicholas Berdyaev, *Dream and Reality*

'I saw the Russian shore for the last time and I burst out crying. An oppressive feeling overwhelms me… How the journey differs from others. There is terror and darkness ahead…'

Vera Muromtseva-Bunina, from her diary, quoted in Thomas Marullo, *Ivan Bunin From the Other Shore*

'A reversal: in the Soviet Union the cooks began to run the state, while abroad, in exile, the intellectuals became the cooks…'

Andrei Sinyavsky, *Soviet Civilization*

6

Joining the Emigration

THE IMMEDIATE DOMESTIC arrangements in Berlin were trying. 'The Rudder' had advertised for temporary accommodation on behalf of the new arrivals but most of them ended up in hotels which were cramped and a drain on the little foreign currency they had. Wives and friends searched the city for more suitable places to stay, and when Berdyaev announced 'My womenfolk have hurled themselves into the abyss' he meant they were following up columns of advertisements offering accommodation. The Franks had six different flats over a short space of time when, according to German law, foreigners could only be sub-tenants and thus had little stability. Nabokov's last and greatest Russian-language novel, *The Gift*, opened with what became a classic scene of émigré life in Germany: a Russian family moving in or out of rented accommodation. Two more of the novels, *Mary* and *The Eye*, and many of the Berlin short stories, featured life in small pensions.

The editor of 'The Rudder', Iosif Gessen, had a sharp eye for how his compatriots were living. 'The cheap pensions were often run by widows or divorcees, which gave way to not a few German–Russian marriages – one to a very short-sighted Jewish-Russian professor-cooperatist with a famous name...'[1] One myopic professor who fitted this description was Aikhenvald, and there were not many other candidates. Yet in his Berlin years Aikhenvald was generally remembered as a man alone, so was it he who made this impulsive move on first arrival?

The Losskys would surely have noticed any liaison formed in the Hotel zur Ostsee (Baltic Hotel) on the Bahnhofsplatz, and if they didn't, there were plenty of other eyes and ears temporarily unoccupied with work. Packed into rooms on two floors of the Hotel zur Ostsee were, besides the Losskys, the Karsavins, the Kozlovs, Professors Zubashov and Yushtin and, from the Moscow group still, the Stratonovs and Professor Zvorykin. The building housed half the brains of tsarist Russia, all recently made redundant. Boris Lossky remembered that the name of the owner, under whose roof they spent their first month abroad, was Herr Schönrock – 'The man with a fine jacket'. Nabokov did not have to look far for the sad comedy and linguistic irony of his stories.[2]

Battered by the recent war, the enterprising former German capital was displaced from itself by poverty and suffering. It was energetic and unhappy with a German loss of face in the world which many thought the Weimar government was encouraging rather than repairing. In particular the Rapallo agreement struck many Germans as giving far too much away to Lenin's Russia. Right-wing extremists retaliated by assassinating the Foreign Minister Walther Rathenau that summer, and just before the *Preussen* sailed the Wirth government fell as a consequence of the economic crisis and general unpopularity. The Russian influx added to German despondency. There were now so many Russians in Berlin – around 250,000 – and so many small businesses and presses catering for them that a German doorman in Charlottenburg hanged himself out of longing for his German homeland – or so the joke went. Bus drivers called out '*Russland!*' at the stop where scores of émigrés got off.[3]

Locals hearing the Russian language complained out loud. The Losskys, who benefited from having their money in pounds sterling, were denounced as *Valutenschweine*, 'pigs with foreign currency'. Berdyaev responded: 'Germany at that time was a very unhappy country. Berlin was crowded with disabled soldiers; the Mark was falling at an incredible speed; and "*Deutschland ist verloren*" [Germany is lost] never left the lips of the Germans.'[4] That foreigners could take advantage of the weak Reichsmark helped the Russians in the short term but didn't make them popular.

Nor clearly would it sustain them. 'How do you Russians manage financially?' asked a German professor. 'Quite simple,' replied Karsavin. 'Frank and I constantly borrow money from each other.'[5] The academic families were suitably adept and disciplined at managing their resources over a short period, but what would happen if their circumstances continued to be difficult? The German government had already introduced a new tax on furnished rooms since their arrival. Tatyana Frank, ignorant of the strain to come, recalled: 'It was a cruel life away from our homeland, everywhere everything was always strange, we had to struggle on behalf of the children, they had to grow up, somehow they had to be educated and sent out into life not empty-handed. They had to live in such a way as not to distract their father from the most important thing in life which was his work – work devoted to ideas and creativity.'[6] Picture then the Karsavins in November 1922, immediately organizing their hotel room so that father, the only potential breadwinner – his recent adultery forgiven – could work undisturbed down one end, with Berlin's Russian newspapers heaped up beside him.[7]

Lossky senior treated his family to a good time. They spent the last days of November and the first of December following the recommendations of a 1901 Baedeker and their evenings at the opera. But the St Petersburg philosophy professor who loved Wagner was quietly appraising the situation. After the social dust raised by rounds of fundraising dinners and tea-parties to help the newcomers had settled, it was unclear how so many Russian thinkers abroad could earn their living. While the journalists might just about manage, it was clear that, since 'I'm not a writer, I mainly deal with specialized philosophical problems and I write slowly…',[8] Lossky would not stay long in a vibrant but problematic city.

In fact the writers among the exiles restarted their professional lives with deceptive ease. Within days of the Moscow group's arrival, its members were cashing in on their value as messengers. On 3 October, at the Logenhaus, Kleiststrasse 10, Sorokin lectured a packed audience on 'The Present and Immediate Prognosis' in Soviet Russia. He detailed the collapse of the economy in many areas, including health, but ended on an optimistic note, predicting that the country would put itself to rights. On 11 December Stepun raised the tone when he lectured on 'Tragedy and Today'. 'The tragic sense of life' was the opposite of a life lived casually from day to day. Berdyaev, Bely, Kuskova and Aikhenvald took part in a sceptical panel discussion afterwards. Brutskus spoke in early December on economic issues and Aikhenvald on the French writer Romain Rolland. The men on Lenin's ships were figures from public life. There was hardly one who could not adapt to public speaking. Just as they had taken their bearings in Moscow and Petrograd from the branches of Dom literatorov and the Union of Writers, their lives now revolved around the *Soyuz russkikh pisatelei i literatorov v Germanii*, 'Union of Russian Writers and Journalists in Germany', which acted as an events forum and general meeting place. On 6 November Prokopovich, Kuskova, Sorokin and Osorgin attended a meeting which brought them together with already established big names from the emigration like the former Duma deputy and friend of Nabokov, Vladimir Zenzinov, and the writers Mark Aldanov and Don Aminado. The exiles' other centre of gravity was 'The Rudder', which advertised and wrote up all these events and unified and galvanized the community.

'The Rudder' was the finest of the émigré newspapers, but a pall of sadness hung over it in its second year, after the murder of Nabokov's father, one of its three founder editors. In March 1922 fanatical Russian right-wingers had shot at Milyukov, a potential liberal leader of émigré Russia, on a Berlin platform and Vladimir Dmitrievich Nabokov had leapt to defend him. His son, later a world-famous novelist, was stricken with grief as at few other times in his life,[9] and his widow was left helpless and penniless. 'The Rudder' established a V. D. Nabokov Memorial Fund which helped new arrivals from Russia, while regular memorial services, and extensive coverage of the trial, kept the memory of a fine man alive. But the tragedy of March 1922 was both a real and symbolic blow to the émigré community, for it presaged how heavily Russian politics would continue to affect the exiles from afar, almost for the rest of their lives, at the same time as they could barely escape developments in Germany. They were about to suffer every available European fate between the years 1920 and 1948.

In August 1921 Soviet propaganda described the Russian emigration as comprising 'dispossessed nobles and capitalists who have taken refuge in capitalistic countries and are seeking the overthrow of Soviet Russia'.[10] Reinforcing that image, 'well-dressed bourgeois ...who go to balls' were certainly much in evidence in the early years in Paris and Berlin. A German cartoon of the time shows overweight, champagne-slurping, cigar-puffing diners turning away an appeal to 'help the starving Russian children' with the words: 'Thank you, we're Russians ourselves.'[11] Nevertheless the Bolshevik picture was vastly unfair. Even a writer sympathetic to Bolshevism, Ilya Ehrenburg, was 'amazed by the mixture of humanity thrown together by fate' in Berlin of the day:

> Some had fled out of terror, others because of hunger, others
> because they had simply shot their neighbour. Who emigrated and
> who remained was often a matter of chance...chance decided the
> fate of millions of people.[12]

Looking back ten years later, Izgoev found that the community he came to know didn't resemble at all this ideological caricature of idlers and vultures defending their class interests against the noble proletarian takeover. What had been driven out of Russia was 'a solid, middle-class, educated milieu lying between the millions of illiterates and the handful of aristocrats and capitalists' and which was essential to build a flourishing society.[13]

In 1921 the most numerous groups in the Russian emigration, not equal to the ousted landowners (17 per cent) but almost on a level with army officers (9 per cent), were soldiers, technicians and nurses, teachers and students. The emigration also comprised an unquantifiable number of illegal workers, many of whom, having settled in Paris, would find work at the Renault car factory in Billancourt or at its Citroën counterpart in the 7ᵉ arrondissement, behind the Eiffel Tower. The writers and thinkers whose lives would be played out against the background of a much larger and more amorphous 'Russia Abroad' comprised only 0.1 per cent of it, a figure to which Lenin's deportations added, but hardly substantially. What they changed was the intellectual substance. Their arrival was enough to create a second cultural 'Russia Abroad'.[14]

The largest communities in 1921 were in Berlin, Prague, Paris, Belgrade and Kharbin, followed by groups in Poland and the Baltic States. Major emigration to the United States did not follow until after the Second World War. Kharbin, a Russian city of recent origin which had grown up alongside a Chinese fishing village in Mongolia, centred on the railway industry and was more isolated than the European communities.[15]

Anti-Soviet feeling fuelled all the old Russian outposts, but each had distinct characteristics. These were partly determined by the host economy and partly by the kind of Russians who predominated. In Kharbin and Belgrade many remnants of the White Army gathered. The Serbian capital also sheltered the most conservative members of the Orthodox Church. Neither city became a centre of intellectual and artistic Russian culture in emigration and it seems that none of Lenin's unwanted intellectuals was tempted to go there. The availability of work and lodgings would take Myakotin to Bulgaria, where he became a lecturer in Russian literature at Sofia University. Sergei Trubetskoy joined family in Baden, Austria. But by their qualifications and politics the vast majority of Lenin's exiles were inclined to join, or work on the edge of, the largest cultural communities in Prague, Berlin and Paris.

Pyotr Struve coined the term *russkoe zarubezhye*, literally 'Russia beyond the frontier', to capture the uniqueness of Russia post-1917 as a world historical event. What had happened was 'a mighty and unprecedented exodus resulting from the grandest historical cataclysm' and 'a mass phenomenon...of an extraordinary impressiveness'. With the Turkish deportation in 1915 of 1.75 million Armenians in mind, he spoke of a rival 'Russian Diaspora'.[16] Russia Abroad, never one country, might yet be one political force. But its problem was it never settled on a leader. This produced a charged, factional atmosphere and a rather unlovable notional country which between 1920 and 1939 was constantly undermined by its own quarrels and demoralizingly outwitted by Soviet underground manoeuvring. The GPU pulled off some real cloak-and-dagger successes when it repeatedly lured 'White' agents on to its own territory or trapped them abroad.[17]

In a tense, schismatic Russia Abroad, Lenin's exiles were marked by their greater experience of Bolshevism. They had spent three crucial years longer in the country than either Nabokov or the other great writer and cultural figurehead celebrated by the emigration, Ivan Bunin, so they could claim superior insight. They could also honestly insist that they never wanted to leave. This fuelled a kind of snobbishness which gave them a special place in the community. Their calling card combined superiority of insight and reluctance at having left. But it also put them in a difficult position when they first arrived, as White Russian circles jumped to the conclusion that in 1922 Lenin had sent a Trojan Horse to infiltrate and destroy Russia Abroad. They accused the men on the ships of being GPU plants.[18]

Another source of tension was attitudes to the West. One or two of Lenin's exiles retained sufficient sympathy for Soviet Russia, and felt so out of place in the economically much more advanced West, that they soon returned anyway, despite the death sentence hanging over them. Peshekhonov and Lutokhin, former editor of *Ekonomist*, led the way, which makes one wonder about the circumstances of their departure in the first place.

Those who remained abroad continued to follow a path somewhere between Soviet and Western extremes. Brutskus and Sorokin had no trouble finding their place in respected Western traditions of thinking. But most of their fellow expellees, especially the journalists and the specialized academics, were only inclined and equipped to write for their own community in their own language. The writers and thinkers who took 'the human soul' as their subject were often oddly placed in the West and although Berdyaev transcended this limitation and became internationally one of the most translated 'philosophers' of his day, who also wrote and lectured in French, he was a good example of a thinker few could classify and whom some non-Russians suspected of being a fake.

He was a Christian socialist, but even then very much of his own kind and not in the English tradition. His socialism didn't make him Communist and his Christian faith made him abhor the Soviet regime. From a Western point of view it was difficult to take in that he was anti-Soviet at the same time as he was 'anti-bourgeois'. Solzhenitsyn would encounter the same problem when he was forced west fifty years later. Solzhenitsyn is, as Berdyaev was, a Russian moral thinker in a particular national tradition. Berdyaev used the term 'bourgeois' not in a Marxist sense to denigrate a class by birth but to attack a petty, materialist, acquisitive outlook which might be held by anyone. Whole books on his equal disappointment with a despotic Russia and a soulless West would follow his arrival in Berlin and his eventual move to Paris.[19] Certainly they were not Oxford philosophy. They were closer to the work of the French idealist Henri Bergson or the Jewish philosopher Martin Buber.

In one way, what disconcerted many soulful Russian intellectuals, who were plain-living puritans even by the standards of their own culture, was that the West was materially and technically more advanced than anything to which they could become accustomed in their lifetimes. Middle-aged and older when they arrived in the West, they had no use for, and only found culturally detrimental, what seemed to them over-provision, excessive comfort and superfluous luxury. The future Cambridge historian Nikolai Andreyev was not of their kind, but from a Russian family in Tallinn he came out of a similar intelligentsia milieu and was in a position to notice the differences soberly. Aged only twenty when he arrived in Stettin en route for an émigré academic life in Prague, and a far less obsessive man than Berdyaev, he was nevertheless struck, as a Russian arriving for the first time in the West in 1928, by the technologically advanced state of Germany, which intimidated him.

> As soon as we approached Germany there was a huge increase in constructions of a technical kind. Everywhere you looked factory chimneys towered and shipbuilding yards sprawled...We got ourselves on to the train to Berlin...and saw all the time...very many things being built, all of them individual: telephones, pipelines and electric beams everywhere.

This memory of being impressed by hugely advanced technology blended with his first sense of German as a technical language, as opposed to the poetic language he knew. There, he claimed, an element of apprehension joined with his other impressions. Something alienated him.

> Stettin struck us not only with the quantity of its ships, which we expected, not only with the high humber of its openly mercantile or technical buildings, which catered to the needs of the port, this was also understandable, but also with its extremely long German words, which were written on various signposts, and on the walls of the factories and quays. These grandiose technical words frightened me somewhat...[20]

It is easier to admit to being afraid of words than of life itself. Or perhaps what gets written down as a memory is only what one is prepared to acknowledge. It seems to me that in Andreyev's case twentieth-century Western technology was ready to overwhelm a young and sensitive Russian soul and produce a fierce reaction – and he was only a very mild case. To understand much of what Russian philosophers would write in exile, from Berdyaev's essay 'Man and Machine' (1932) and his book *The Fate of Man in the Modern World* (1934) to Frank's *Religion and Science* (1924) and *The Spiritual Foundations of Society* (1930) and Vysheslavtsev's *The Crisis of Industrial Culture* (1953), one has to grasp that twentieth-century modernity made an ugly and bewildering impact on essentially nineteenth-century Russian minds. Lenin's exiles were not Communist, but they believed in a world of Christian spirituality. The advanced materialism of the West struck them as diabolical, rather as it does extreme, disaffected elements in the Muslim world today. It was only long experience of their native country that stopped the philosophers of 1922 believing Russia was a better place, rather than merely diabolical in its own way. Away from their homeland they sometimes grew unsure.

Some of this 'Russian philosophical' attitude, rather like a cultural religion, also shaped the reactions of the exiled journalists and economists and their families. Ugrimova at twenty was not bound by deep thought. But as a result of a traditional Russian intelligentsia upbringing and a few impressionable extra years spent in Bolshevik Russia, she remembered the disgust she felt when she first arrived in Berlin. The cause was her own countrymen, the sect which could be labelled 'Russian monarchists'. After 'The Rudder', read by everyone in the community, had carried the names of the new arrivals from Moscow, 'next day my old schoolfriend Sandra Volkov came to find me. Her family was closely connected with the imperial court.' A first meeting with the Volkovs and people of their ilk, over tea in the famous Berlin avenue Unter den Linden, revealed to Ugrimova that 'These people were stupid. They asked silly questions. They were absolutely primitive in relation to the revolution and everything that was happening in Russia.'[21] Even the mild and gentle Frank would be forced to say something similar of his friend, now rapidly becoming a former friend, Pyotr Struve. The problem seemed to be that Struve did not remain in Russia long enough to know the Russianness of Bolshevism as Frank did.[22] As for the impetuous Berdyaev, he and Struve had a furious row the instant Berdyaev arrived in Berlin and only met again once in their lifetimes.

Some émigrés, including the exiles, found their fellows too anti-Bolshevik in their politics. But others, and this time mostly 'voluntary' émigrés like Nabokov and Roman Jakobson and briefly Viktor Shklovsky, detested the remnants of Russian mystical religiosity forced to leave in 1922. It made no sense to Jakobson and Shklovsky to block Russia's way forward in the modern world, as the idealist philosophers seemed to do, though Nabokov was perhaps a more ambivalent case. The gradations and distinctions from one man to the next were always fine and a matter of pride and self-belief. In Paris some of the edgier artistic figures, but also Berdyaev, would feel uncomfortable with pre-revolutionary émigrés like Merezhkovsky and Gippius. Separately, Nabokov and Berdyaev would turn up occasionally at what became the Green Lamp salon, but only not to lose essential ties with the Paris Russian world.

It was a difficult life to be a Russian abroad, sustained by pride and political fury, and a sense of really only belonging elsewhere. Nabokov spoke of the 'crude and irrational contempt that Russian émigrés had for the natives'.[23] Here were Russians who could not accept that Pushkin was dead and that the light emanating from Yasnaya Polyana – Tolstoy's country estate – was extinguished. Nabokov often gave that kind of yearning to his characters, made them long for Russian snow, Russian smells, Russian language, all dreams which belied the placelessness of their real lives. Such things could move simple and complex Russian souls in limbo to joy and tears. Educated Russians abroad felt they were bearers of a special sentimental heritage being destroyed in Russia, and which they should preserve, even at the cost of their own alienation.

These émigré tensions, whose surface expression was a proliferation of competing periodicals and many personal feuds over the next fifteen years, can seem in retrospect, to outsiders, to exemplify Freud's 'narcissism of small differences'. But they were felt at the time as psychologically profound, which made them so. This was the Russian way of intellectual and spiritual existence, as Dostoevsky immortalized it: to fight for the moral and political nuance. Ultimately the tensions mapped out religious differences, only the object of faith was not God but the ideal Russia. The need to discuss and work for this Russia never left anyone's mind, not on the rough Baltic Sea and still less in the cafés of Charlottenburg and Wilmersdorf, where smart pre-war Berlin became home to ousted middle-class Moscow and St Petersburg.

The Losskys were the first to move on from Berlin. Nikolai Onofreievich received a letter from Pyotr Struve with an irresistible offer almost immediately after their arrival. Frank, who went to Heidelberg to see his old friend, heard the same news there. Struve then arranged to come to Berlin for a general meeting of the exiled émigré community which Berdyaev accommodated in his flat. (His 'womenfolk' did him proud by finding a suitably spacious base so quickly.)

It was a stormy occasion which quickly moved on from practicalities to a battle for the Russian soul. Berdyaev was enraged when Struve laid out White plans 'to overthrow Bolshevism by military intervention' and denounced the plan as a monstrous farce and preached moral regeneration from within instead. He insisted – as would be his theme for the first year in exile – that the Revolution was good for Russia and would eventually bring her to her true vocation. The despicable Whites never for a moment considered that they might have been wrong, and implicated in Russia's tragedy. They wanted room for themselves, but not freedom as such. 'Freedom of thought was recognized no more among the émigrés than in Soviet Russia.'[24]

According to Frank there were a number of White émigrés at the meeting, as well as Izgoev and Ilyin from the ships. Ilyin was 'one of the few arrivals from Russia who was an unconditional supporter of the White Movement' and delivered an impressive speech on the right to die for one's country. He attacked the premature First World War peace the Bolsheviks had concluded with the Germans at Brest-Litovsk. 'Struve caught fire at these words…and found they encapsulated everything he wanted to say to us.' Otherwise-minded, Berdyaev began shrieking, accusing the Whites of 'Godlessness' and 'materialism'. Struve embraced him and tried to calm him down and failed, because, according to Boris Lossky, Berdyaev objected to Struve's encouragement of foreign powers interfering in Russia's fate but even more fiercely he rejected the idea that, should the Whites regain power, they would be right to punish those members of the intelligentsia who had cooperated with the Bolsheviks.

Nevertheless, in the midst of the evening's turmoil Struve managed to come to his other point, which was to encourage the professors to leave for Czechoslovakia. Struve lived in Prague, from where he brought the news that the government of President Masaryk was offering to support the exiles by creating or extending existing Russian institutions in the country. The Czechoslovaks would provide the Russians with a generous wage and living allowance; accommodation would also be found. Masaryk's underlying idea was the hope that an egalitarian, democratic Czechoslovakia, and a future democratic Russia, once Bolshevism collapsed, could be similar places.[25]

Berdyaev and Frank didn't warm to the idea. As Lossky senior recalled: 'They decided to stay in a big world centre like Berlin, to found a journal and pursue their literary careers. They invited me to join them... Then I went to Professor Kizevetter to find out his decision. He said he was going to Prague and advised our family to accept the offer of Czechoslovak citizenship.'[26] Lossky took that advice. Aged nearly fifty-three, he had a large family to support, and Prague was the obvious place to go. Masaryk's terms were exceedingly generous to promise both him and seventy-five-year-old Stoyunina, as a retired schoolteacher, 2,000 crowns a month. The whole family left in time for Christmas.

From the *Haken* and the *Preussen* others who took up the Czechoslovak offer were Lossky's colleague and friend Ivan Lapshin, and also most of the scientists on the Philosophy Steamer. Out of nineteen physicists, biologists, engineers, mathematicians, economists and sociologists forced to emigrate, twelve would move to Prague by 1925. Novikov, Odintsov, Selivanov, Sorokin, Stratonov and Zubashov almost immediately took the chance to work in a secure environment in their own language.[27] Sorokin meanwhile claimed he came on the personal invitation of Masaryk.[28]

Word of mouth encouraged those who prevaricated to give Prague a try. Sorokin invited Lutokhin, who, when he finally arrived in Berlin in February 1923, was also encouraged to move on by the Prague-based White émigré Vasily Shulgin. 'It's not bad here, there are a lot of us, do come!' Thus Lutokhin arrived in the Czechoslovak capital in May 1923.[29] He was followed in 1924 by the law professor Bogolepov, the journalist, economist and historian Rozenberg and the economist Peshekhonov, and that same year the economists Kuskova and Prokopovich also transferred their work to Prague, where they employed Rozenberg. Finally the archivist Izyumov, invited by Kizevetter, moved to Prague in 1925. All the writers and historians apart from Lutokhin found scholarly and academic posts.

Those who worked in the humanities were attracted in the first instance by the chance to continue in their own language. Kizevetter had been offered a chair of history in Leipzig but feared he could not lecture in German. The journalists needed employment somewhere and the expansion of the Russian presence abroad provided it. Izgoev moved to Prague as the correspondent for 'The Rudder' and the Riga émigré paper *Segodnya*. Myakotin (whose Sofia appointment lay in the future) got a job as a history professor where he was soon joined at the Russian university by Valentin and Sergei Bulgakov, arriving in Prague from Constantinople. As many went to Prague, some stayed in Berlin and a few began to drift towards Paris. Lenin's exiles were soon dispersed all over Europe, where they began to establish new lives.

7

Prague

P RAGUE WAS A BEAUTIFUL, architectural treasure trove of a city on
the Vltava: a capital of dreaming spires at the head of a small
newly independent country eager to make its name as egalitarian, cosmopolitan and peaceful. The 'Russian Action' which invited Russians
to live there after the upheaval in their own country was a gesture of
unrivalled generosity. From 1921 to 1928 Czechoslovakia spent more
than all other European nations together on Russian refugees, on
Masaryk's initiative.[1]

Masaryk, a Professor of Philosophy at the Charles University and
longtime observer of Russian affairs, expected Bolshevik power to collapse shortly, leaving a political and cultural vacuum which academics
and liberal politicians would fill on their return. While the exiled
Russians waited for better days, Czechoslovakia would keep alive their
knowledge and skills and feed, house and educate their families, along
with thousands more Russian refugees from the Revolution and Civil
War. The aim of Russian Action was a stable, democratic civil society
in both Russia and Czechoslovakia. It reflected an ideal for a liberal
state which Masaryk and Pavel Milyukov, who were old friends,
shared. For the Czechs it was also a way of looking to a better Russia
as a future ally.

The Russian-born Georgy Katkov, who would work at the Charles
University before moving to Oxford, evaluated the enterprise more
sharply with hindsight:

The Czech government thought that the Bolsheviks wouldn't hold their ground. Four months, six months, maybe a year, but they couldn't possibly hold out any longer than that. Who were these Bolsheviks? Nobodies. Trotsky? Lenin? Why, Russia is a great country, a brilliant country… You've got professors who are émigrés… While back there you had just an insignificant gang of thieves and robbers… They reckoned that within a year, or two at the most, the old regime would be reinstated, all these old émigrés would become bigwigs in Moscow and would want to show extreme gratitude.[2]

Evidently Czechoslovakia wasn't just being altruistic. The Germans to the West were always a force to reckon with, and culturally, after two centuries of German-language culture centred on Vienna, it was both prudent and desirable to let elements of pan-Slavism inform a Slav-oriented Czechoslovakia. 'The Czechs also felt a need to fill the ranks of the intelligentsia with brother Slavs, to replace the Germans now that Czechoslovakia had freed itself from the Austrian Empire.' Fifteen million Czechoslovaks occupied a conspicuously artificial state created out of opportunities presented by the First World War. The country, which was always a balancing act, would soon want to lean West. Meanwhile thousands of uprooted Russians stood to benefit from genuine Czechoslovak interest in their world.

A peculiar sequence of events had left the new state indebted to the White Russians.[3] During the Civil War a legion of Czechoslovak troops, former prisoners of war released by the Bolsheviks, had rebelled in Siberia and taken up arms against the Reds. The Allied Command in Paris counted the Czech Legion among its most effective forces, but when the Czechoslovak Republic was declared in October 1918, the Legion just wanted to go home. They had given up fighting when they let the French persuade them to guard the TransSiberian railway between Omsk and Irkutsk against pro-Communist attacks. 'While guarding the TransSiberian they amassed much wealth in the form of industrial equipment and household goods, which they stored in 600

freight cars.'⁴ It is said that the Czechs were thinking of their needs at
home, but what followed was a scandal that has hung over them ever
since. When the White Army collapsed and was driven out of Omsk by
the Bolsheviks, the White leader Admiral Kolchak left by rail for
Irkutsk, carrying half the gold reserves of the Russian state. When the
French ordered the Czechs to delay Kolchak's train (for reasons which
have never become clear) the White leader became an effective prisoner
and was eventually betrayed by the French and Czechs together. A deal
was struck whereby Kolchak and the Russian gold were handed over to
the Bolsheviks while the Czechs got a safe passage to the port of
Vladivostok together with their booty. Because the Czech Legion was
party to inflicting one of the gravest blows of the Civil War, possibly
Masaryk felt a debt to White Russia. Money amassed in the Legiobank,
some of the capital of which was derived from trade with the Legion,
was certainly used to fund Russian Action.⁵

But there were also good domestic political reasons for the
Czechoslovak government move. A high number of returning troops
and former Russian prisoners of war sympathized with the Bolsheviks.
The idea was that their pro-Communist influence might be tempered
by inviting liberal and conservative Russians into the country.
Hungary and Bavaria had briefly been declared Communist republics.
Masaryk did not want Czechoslovakia to go the same way. 'The
Rudder' noted the expulsion of suspected Russian Communists from
Czechoslovakia in autumn 1922, just as the President was welcoming
the constitutionally minded academics.⁶ However, because the
Czechoslovak leadership as a whole was more ambivalent about which
Russians were desirable, the country became home to a range of exile
loyalties. Masaryk supported the SRs, while his Prime Minister, Karel
Kramař, admired tsarism.⁷ One result was that old-world conservatives like Pavel Novogorodtsev and representatives of the ancient
noble house of Dolgoruky could live out their days in hospitable surroundings in Prague, their beliefs unsurrendered, while the President
dined with the modern-minded Sorokin and the pro-Bolshevik
Lutokhin and Peshekhonov kicked their heels in the hills.

Russian Action supported a vast range of people, and peoples, from within the Russian Empire, and especially from Ukraine. They included every class and political grouping, and every level of expertise from illiteracy to near genius. Some 5,500 new arrivals were officially registered in 1921–4 but by the middle of the decade the Czechoslovak authorities reckoned with a Russian population five times that number, including more than 3,000 who described themselves as intelligentsia. The Czechs actively encouraged eminent men and women to come. In January 1922 Foreign Minister Edvard Beneš sent 5,000 French francs and an invitation to the writer Ivan Bunin in Paris. Bunin declined to move, but noted in his diary for 27 January that year: 'I took the money with tears almost of sorrow and shame...' Here was the precedent for the invitations Struve brought with him to Berlin ten months later.[8]

Prague provided a passing home to a great Russian poet, Marina Tsvetaeva, and some lesser-known writers.[9] But essentially it was the academic centre of the emigration in its early years.[10] In April 1923, financed by the Czech government, Russian academic and pedagogical groups from throughout the diaspora held their first meeting in Prague. By the end of the same year, thanks to the efforts of Mikhail Novikov, who became its first head, a Russian People's University (Russky Narodny Universitet) opened in Prague.

The most important faculty of the Russian university was Law, and when Novgorodtsev at its head died in 1924 Bogolepov moved from Berlin to take up the job. Several hundred Russian students enrolled each year. Lossky taught logic there and other aspects of philosophy in the historical-philological department. Lapshin was also on the faculty. Meanwhile Prague in 1924 became the first city outside Russia to sustain a world-class think-tank on Russian issues. When Prokopovich's Economic Bureau, transferred from Berlin, 'aimed to produce an analysis of the USSR which could distinguish between the different elements of dogma and ideology... and the natural processes of the evolution of the regime, [Prokopovich] realized that both émigrés and foreign specialists required accurate information in order to assess the situation and to make realistic predictions.'[11] This independent-minded institution became so successful that Prokopovich and Kuskova became special economic advisers to the Czechoslovak government. From 1940 the Economic Bureau moved to Geneva and was funded by the Carnegie Foundation.

The social lives and general well-being of exiled Russians were cared for by Zemgor, 'The Union of Russian Zemstvos and Towns in the Czechoslovak Republic'. The organization was endorsed by Kerensky and became the channel through which Czechoslovak government subsidy of the Russian community flowed. It funded schools, universities and Prokopovich's Economic Bureau, as well as social clubs, health care and housing.[12]

In autumn 1924 the greatest collection of scholarly Russian work outside Russia, the Slavonic Library, was assembled and subsequently housed in the Baroque Klementinum in the historic centre of the city. Meanwhile the facts of the great Russian exodus mattered. The best Russian historians of their generation, including, from the Philosophy Steamer, Kizevetter, Rozenberg, Ugrimov and Myakotin, created a much-needed Archive of the Russian Emigration, which would one day help tell their own story as well as the fate of Prague in the Second World War. Apart from continuing the education of an upcoming Russian generation, defending the integrity of history was probably Russian Action's greatest achievement and it was performed in stark contrast to the way in which the Soviet regime either doctored Russian history or rendered it irrelevant. On a minor note, a Museum of Russian Culture was created in rural Zbraslav, twelve miles outside Prague, with Valentin Bulgakov as its curator and a strong input from Novikov.

Besides the academic life, the institution which featured highly in the emigration was of course the Orthodox Church. In 'Russia Abroad' generally the Church would yield to political infighting as nasty as anything which happened in the secular sphere. But everywhere it functioned it generated congregations which looked to it for emotional support and a feeling of national belonging. The man who early on created a genuine Russian religious life for the many uprooted Russians who craved it in Prague was Sergei Bulgakov. He lived in the city with his wife, adult daughter and teenage son for eighteen months and worshipped in the church of St Nicholas, borrowed from the Catholics on the Old Town Square. There Father Bulgakov buried Pavel Novgorodtsev, married Kizevetter's daughter to a Maximovich from the Russian Archive and baptized Tsvetaeva's third child, Georgy. It was Easter 1923 or 1924, in an improvised chapel on the ground floor of the Svobodarna refugee hostel, when he made Russian Easter memorable for scores of cooped-up families.

> At two in the afternoon Father Sergei, taking it upon himself to observe the services of the Passion...performed the rite of the Weeping Woman Being Led Away. He also found the strength to hold the all-night service of the Burial of the Body of the Saviour. I will never forget the luminous sight of the priest as he stepped smartly towards the door at the end of the service and inhaled to the depths of his lungs to greet the dawn of Holy Saturday. I also remember the Easter Sunday service which he celebrated with rapture, abandoning himself to gathering together and edifying many of the inhabitants of the Svobodárna...[13]

Bulgakov, much missed, moved on from Prague to Paris in September 1925, just as the Russian community began to build its own church in the southwest district of Olšany.

Russian Action was funded by the Czech government, with additional personal contributions from Masaryk and his President's Office. Further money came from the US philanthropist and personal friend of Masaryk Charles Crane, whose son Richard, as the first American ambassador to Czechoslovakia, created an American mission predisposed to helping the Russian emigration. Masaryk's personal role in Russian Action, though it stands to be defined more precisely, can't be overestimated.[14] 'It was his own money – or rather the Czech government gave it to him to use in whatever way he chose. He didn't take anything for himself. He was a very modest man,' Katkov remembered.[15] Beneš as President from 1935 continued the tradition. Both the Losskys and the Franks would receive special donations from the President's Office, even after Russian Action was over.[16]

Local conditions in Prague, especially at first, were not particularly comfortable. The beautiful but medievally cramped inner city meant high rents and few vacancies. Svobodárna, where the intelligentsia and workers alike were lodged on different floors, was a vast building surrounded by factories on the edge of the city, in the working-class district of Libeň. The Losskys had two, then three rooms there, which meant a difficult life for five adults and a young boy. From spring 1924, however, they could at least spend their summers in Zbraslav, which was pleasant and green, on the Vltava river, and eventually, in 1929, when a special Professors' House was finished, they returned to Prague, to the leafy, middle-class suburb of Bubeneč, which became known for its high number of cultured Russian residents.[17] For those who could not bear Svobodarna, one way round the difficulty of finding accommodation in Prague was to accept defeat and stay right out in the country. The Sorokins lived for their whole ten months in Czechoslovakia in Černošice. The Peshekhonovs lived, as did Tsvetaeva, in Všenory.

Consistent with their behaviour everywhere in the world, the Russian arrivals in Czechoslovakia did not necessarily get on with each other, nor with the locals, nor the locals with them. Peshekhonov deliberately isolated himself from his compatriots who didn't approve of his politics. As for the link between Czechs and Russians, on the immediate social front it was no easier than with any other nation, despite pan-Slavism. The Czechs spoke a Western Slav tongue, which made their language, with its own tortuous grammar, about as close to Russian as Spanish is to French. To a Russian ear, Czech sounded extremely odd, as Roman Jakobson once said, as if every Czech was either whining or preaching.[18] Underlying the linguistic difference the Czechs had a quite different European history from the Russians and a culture nourished by Roman Catholicism and the Renaissance. The cultural difference was compounded by the Czech experience of two hundred years as part of the Austrian Empire. Finally, the look of central Prague, as different from Moscow as London from Peking, cemented this distinction. It was a Gothic, Renaissance and Baroque European city, entirely lacking in the Asiatic characteristics of Moscow, and sharing only superficial similarities with 'European' St Petersburg.

Given all these differences, and many tokens of Bohemia's long history and civilization, it was galling for Czechs to have to endure the Russians' exalted belief in their own cultural and spiritual superiority. As Katkov remembered: 'Educated Czechs see themselves as Europeans. But Russians feel they are different from them. They see the Czechs as a nation of petty bourgeois – How dare they call themselves professors? We are a great nation, we have brilliance. And so no good could come of this…'[19] Apparently even Masaryk's personal commitment to the Russian exiles was at odds with his antipathy towards the general run of their arrogant and explosive countrymen.

For ordinary Russians, and for the Russian hearts which continued to beat even in the most sophisticated academics, life in Prague therefore continued to be a life in exile. Nabokov expressed an unfounded, primitive dislike of the city as 'muddy' when he visited his mother there.[20] Others more reasonably would find it provincial: not a *Weltstadt*, even though it was situated at the geographical centre of Europe.[21] The Lossky boys, having pinned their hopes on London, initially regretted their father's choice and although they seem to have benefited more than most, not least from Prague's beautiful architecture and environs in their medieval and architectural studies, they soon gravitated towards France. Meanwhile some new arrivals were particularly concerned with the effect on their younger children of the shocking change in their fates: the fact of being refugees anywhere.[22]

Emotions had to be played off against practicalities. In Zbraslav the rooms in the Velka hospoda, the Big Inn, were relatively cheap and the location idyllic. Of the many Russians attracted to settle there one was the railway engineer Nikolai Nikolaievich Ipatiev, in whose house in Ekaterinburg the Bolsheviks had murdered Tsar Nicholas II and his family. Nothing to do with the fate of his house, Ipatiev cut a slightly comic figure in emigration with his patriotic enthusiasm and his singing. Among weightier cultural residents in Zbraslav were the Lutokhins, the Stratonovs and the Valentin Bulgakovs. Meetings with singsongs, in the summer in the open-air beside the river, took place every Friday at 5 p.m. to help foster the community spirit and act as a brake against loneliness. These Fridays were so popular – more than 100 people regularly turned up – that Russians from other parts of the city came to join in. Stratonov instigated them by encouraging his fellows to present entertaining lectures for a general audience. An astronomer by training and a good communicator by nature he gave a talk on the stars considered thoroughly entertaining, as was Kizevetter's offering on literature and history. Lapshin did his lively bit on Russian music.[23]

Zbraslav, though, had its cultural limitations. One audience heard how Kizevetter took Bely's *Petersburg*, a masterpiece of Russian modernism, with him when he was arrested in August 1922 and found it such rubbish he didn't bother to read it. Perhaps politics lay behind that uncharacteristically impatient judgement. Bely, who had been in Berlin when Kizevetter and the others arrived, had by that time gone back to Soviet Russia. On the other hand, though their fate would feed the stream of modernism as an artistic and philosophical theme, Lenin's older exiles were not themselves cut out to be modernists. Less controversial was the Friday occasion when Valentin Bulgakov talked about his first meeting with Tolstoy and when he sang Schumann and Glinka.

A more central and accessible Russian communal meeting place, Russky Ochag, 'The Russian Hearth Club', was opened in 1925, with help from Masaryk's daughter Alice and other benefactors.[24] It contained a library, function rooms, a restaurant and a good ambience. Lapshin was often to be found drinking tea there, or giving another of his talks, which he would illustrate from the piano. Lapshin was a true musician through and through, and also a true bachelor. Lossky worried about how he would survive in Prague and tried to marry him off to an attractive Czech singer, but Lapshin begged his colleague to desist, if he did not want to have to fish his body out of the Vltava two weeks later.

In everything the conservative community did, the Russian Christian Student Movement, which the American YMCA sponsored, tried to keep its young people affiliated. The RKhSD, as it was known by its Russian initials, had a strong following in the Czech Russian community early on and held its first conference in Přerov in south Moravia in October 1922. Eventually it became so highly politicized that it drove the likes of Berdyaev away. But in the first years it even helped the philosophers by providing another forum in which to teach in their own language.[25]

In a freer spirit, a Czech, Anna Teskova, and her mother and sister, organized meetings at their Czech-Russian Union with Lapshin as a star performer. Teskova, who had grown up in Russia, left her most important mark in history when she became a guardian angel to Tsvetaeva. For other Russians she also provided a way into Czech society, although not many wanted it.[26] The academics met in their own professional societies. Others decided to be lonely.

The Prague Russian community had no daily newspaper until 1928, a fact which has been used to suggest the relative lack of communal feeling compared with other centres of the emigration. But one might imagine the explanation lay more with the dominance of 'The Rudder' and its journalists in Berlin. Izgoev sent regular reports there, reflecting Russian life in Prague. Instead of a newspaper in the mid-1920s Russian Prague was the point of origin of a political paper reflecting the emigration as a whole, *Volya Rossii*. The literary pages, edited by the young Marc Slonim, future author of a celebrated history of Russian literature, gave space to Tsvetaeva, Nabokov (whose penname at the time was Sirin) and others.

Russian Prague was too old and too suffused by nostalgia really to become a vibrant new community. There was something symbolic about how, after his wife and his stepdaughter died, the ageing Kizevetter used to take a fold-up chair to the Stromovka, the vast open green space adjacent to Bubeneç, and, having spread out his Russian books, pretended he was still in Russia.[27] These were not hopeless lives, but once they had achieved a measure of security nothing really remained to challenge the older Russians, whose names and careers had been made in a now vanished country.

Half a dozen of Lenin's personal expellees died in Prague in their late sixties and seventies: Zubashov (1928), Selivanov and Rozenberg (1932), Kizevetter (1933), Myakotin (1937) and Stratonov (1938). The Russian cemetery which grew up around the small church at Olšany became one of the indelible monuments of the emigration. Bursting with nineteenth-century confidence, Kizevetter's elaborate headstone, paid for by Zemgor, challenged life ever to forget men of such achievement and solidity.

For younger Russians who found themselves in Prague because, like Nabokov's penniless mother, brother Kirill and two sisters, they couldn't afford to move, life was far less grand. Nabokov considered his mother's impoverished last years pitiful.[28] Intermarriage and shared education could ease the situation by degrees. Olga Nabokova, born 1903, and Roman Jakobson, born 1896, were among two divorced exiles who remarried Czechs.

Uniquely Jakobson, not one of Lenin's exiles because he didn't stay in Russia long enough to be forced to define his loyalties, made the most of his attachment to the academic and cultural community in Prague of the 1920s. The comparison is not entirely fair, because he was so much younger than most of the men on the *Haken* and the *Preussen*. But in a positive sense Jakobson was 'one who got away'. He learned Czech, studied Czech literature, and his friends were Czech writers and linguists. Although his spoken Czech was not the best – he once said he spoke twelve languages, all of them in Russian[29] – most educated Czechs would still name Jakobson as the one who changed the course of the Czech humanities when he founded the Prague School of Linguistics and later taught at the University of Brno. Kizevetter made his mark on Russian historiography, but he was not in the same class of universal influence as Jakobson. Lossky and Lapshin will never matter anywhere but their own country.

Jakobson made something out of his love of the Russian language, which he could carry with him and build on abroad. He made the transition *in method* from the nineteenth to the twentieth century, which most of the academic émigrés and exiles could not achieve. But in substance? His project was poetry wrapped up in science, in a way which has not yet been sufficiently untangled. The findings of the science of phonology, which he founded with his friend Nikolai Trubetskoy, allowed him to explain how an essentially Russian experience of the world could be detected in sound alone. In other words, the sound of Russian poetry assured Jakobson that he had brought his Russian world with him for ever, just as Khodasevich hoped to do in his poems, and as Nabokov strained after in the intricate wordplay of his novels and stories.[30]

Jakobson's life as an émigré was subject to the same political tensions as all arrivals from Russia. He came to Prague in July 1920 with an attachment to the Soviet Red Cross Mission in Prague, 'repatriating former Russian prisoners of war who had been stranded in Czechoslovakia since Austro-Hungarian times'. This made him look suspect in the eyes of the White community and their disapproval caused him to resign.

> You ask me what I'm doing in Prague. I don't know if you know it
> or not, but in September [1920] I was strongly attacked here for my
> participation in the [Soviet] Red Cross Mission...the professors
> vacillated whether I was a bandit or a scholar or an unlawful
> mongrel*; in the cabaret they were singing little songs about me –
> all of this was not very witty. The situation was complex, but it
> seems to me my fate is to tightrope-walk in inconceivable situations.
> As a result I have left work (without tears or cursing) and entered
> university scholarship and so on.[31]

But after he resigned he went hungry and by the end of summer 1921 Jakobson was back in the Soviet mission in Prague, part-time, as 'a free-lance worker' until 1928. Nabokov claimed he was a spy.[32] This speculation remains unproven, but certainly Jakobson, having been a

Kadet in his teens, was in his early twenties pro-Soviet, even though he had had to run from Soviet power.

Fear of secret Soviet infiltration caused the same Russian community in Prague that shunned Jakobson also to turn against Lenin's patent enemy Sorokin. Despite his appointment as Professor of Sociology at the Charles University, Sorokin left in 1923 after only ten months to take up a post at the University of Minnesota.[33] Sorokin was not remotely pro-Soviet, but the letter to *Pravda* in November 1918, in which, sitting in a provincial GPU cell facing a potential bullet, he renounced his will to fight against Bolshevism, counted irrevocably against him. The book Sorokin published in 1923, *Sovremennoe sostoyanie Rossii* ('The Current State of Russia'), may have been partly an effort to establish a correct perception of his views in the wider world. Only six years after the Russian Revolution he argued that its chief consequence was the degradation of the Russian population.

Feeling the cold wind blowing from Russian Prague, Sorokin spent most of 1923 learning English. From his temporary Černošice home, ten miles from Prague, he would pace the open countryside committing long lists of vocabulary to heart. There he was observed by another misplaced man, Dalmat Lutokhin.[34]

It was even more difficult for thirty-eight-year-old Lutokhin to find a job because almost immediately he arrived he counted as a Communist. The expatriated Russians wanted him neither in Berlin nor in Prague. After giving a talk in Berlin, where he attributed his late arrival to rheumatism, Gorky's old friend was marked down as 'impossible' by Prokopovich.[35] He also didn't make the right political noises when he arrived in Prague in May. Struve and Izgoev took him to breakfast at the favourite haunt of Russians in the Czechoslovak capital, 'The Slav Hotel Beranek' on Tyl Square in Vinohrady, and came away disappointed.[36] One of the few Russians in Prague who would receive Lutokhin, apart from his host Sorokin, was Rozenberg, whom Lutokhin grudgingly called 'another old idealist'.[37] This 'white crow in the emigration' and veteran journalist and publisher declined

Lutokhin's suggestion to report positively on Communist Russia. In Prague Lutokhin sided with Sorokin until Sorokin went to America. After that Sorokin became Lutokhin's chief ideological enemy.[38]

A third character marginalized in Prague, the one man adored there by Lutokhin but whom Prokopovich likewise branded a Communist, was Peshekhonov. He was a gifted economist and quite able to head the Economic department at the Institute for the Study of Russia which he and others founded in Prague in April 1924. But the quality of the Institute's output paled beside that of Prokopovich's Economic Bureau and its ideological slant was evident. 'The institute was an SR organization', which might not have been so bad, had it not been the case that during his time there Peshekhonov 'became a Soviet employee'.[39] The real aim of the Institute was to develop agrarian policy for Soviet Russia, though its organizers would not say so directly. Lutokhin, given work at the Institute, extolled Peshekhonov for writing articles against the Whites and defending the Bolsheviks, but Prokopovich despised him for it.[40]

Lutokhin was somehow personally confused and his fate when he went back to Russia in 1927 was relatively fortunate in political terms.[41] His memoir 'Amongst Those who Fled the Revolution', written soon after his return in 1927, tried to justify his absence by stressing his closeness to and affection for Peshekhonov who, when they first met in Berlin, 'may already have spoken then, in 1923, of his underground work'.[42] But the memoir was blocked by the censor and not only was it never published in Soviet times but, had not Gorky intervened on behalf of his old friend, Lutokhin would have spent five years in the Gulag, instead of less than a year. As it was he died in the siege of Leningrad.

By contrast Peshekhonov was a tragic character. To begin, the Revolution left him with a personal burden. His only son was killed fighting with the White Army in Ukraine, and his brother, a priest, was shot as a bandit in a case of mistaken identity in the volatile weeks after Red October.[43] Further, he so much minded being forced to leave that the first thing he did abroad in November 1922 was publish a pamphlet entitled *Why I Didn't Emigrate*. He joined 'Change of Landmarks' and the Soyuz vozvrashchentsev, 'The Union of Returnees', and made his loyalties clear.[44] Such bridges once crossed could never be reversed in White eyes and Peshekhonov became caught between two Russias, neither of which had a place for him.

Despite his applications from Berlin in 1925 and from Prague in 1926 (at the consulate where Jakobson was working) the Soviet Union wouldn't have Peshekhonov back. His attempt at rapprochement was finally half-gratified in 1927 when he was offered, and accepted, the post of 'economic consultant' at the Soviet Trade Mission in Riga. (Jakobson accepted the equivalent post in Prague.) Kerensky criticized Peshekhonov for this move and Kizevetter said the fifty-nine-year-old economist 'had spoiled his obituary'.[45] Peshekhonov was a gifted, kind man who learnt Czech and German and knew some French and English. He was never allowed back to his homeland in his lifetime, perhaps because Lenin had singled him out as dangerous. After he died in Latvia in 1933, however, he was buried in the renamed city of Leningrad, where his widow, a paediatrician, was also permitted to return to live with their adopted son who became a military doctor.

Were Peshekhonov and Lutokhin GPU 'plants' abroad from the outset? Although they were arrested and listed for autumn deportation neither in fact left on the *Haken* or the *Preussen*. Lutokhin in particular just turned up in his own time. He did an odd thing by cabling 'The Rudder' from Revel (Tallinn) in February 1923 to say he was on his way to Berlin. What took place between their arrests and the arrival abroad of these two men we will probably never know. Nevertheless the exile community formed a sharp sense of who they were and they led unhappy lives abroad. Seen today from a neutral vantage point they were men who suffered internal turmoil over the right political values for Russia in the twentieth century, and their own place in the post-Revolutionary scheme of things. It's worth repeating that Peshekhonov was open about his position and nothing except an attitude has ever been pinned on Lutokhin.

As here and there someone in the community dissented, or even went home, all the exiled old guard could do was express their solidarity with pre-Bolshevik Russia and its spiritual-artistic traditions. They used literary anniversaries, like Pushkin's birthday, to renew their vows every year. The gist of their attitude was outlined by Vysheslavtsev:

> The free genius of Russia is the free genius of Pushkin which never submitted to anyone or anything...It is obedient to only one call – 'The Divine Word'...Pushkin portrays not just the tragedy of power but the tragedy of freedom...The tragedy of power is that it awakens the protest of revolutionary freedom; the tragedy of revolutionary freedom is that it awakens the innate instinct for power in the very liberators themselves...Pushkin's words of prophetic anger can be applied to every tyranny on earth, past and future.[46]

In Prague from 1925, the bard's birthday, on 8 June new style, became the annual Day of Russian Culture. Kizevetter gave a speech at the Russky Ochag, which was followed by a children's party and an evening concert.[47] Parallel events took place in Paris. Five years later the same two communities raised their glasses and instructed their orators to glorify 175 years of Moscow University. Nobly, but with increasing hopelessness and self-sacrifice, Russian Prague held out against all that was regrettable and terrible about the Revolution and the twentieth century.

A young, impatient figure like Berberova, who valued individualism and freedom no less than the old men, couldn't bear the stagnating world which the anniversaries represented.

> When we left for Prague on 4 November 1923 Marina Tsvetaeva had already been there for a long time. We could not stay in Berlin, where we had no way to live; we didn't go to Italy, because we had no visas or money; and we didn't go to Paris, because we feared Paris...So we set out for Prague...In the unstable world in which we lived at that time, where nothing had been decided and where for the second time in two years we lost people and an atmosphere I

had begun to value highly, I could not genuinely appreciate Prague; it seemed to me nobler than Berlin and more out of the way. 'Russian Prague' did not open to us its embraces; the old... were dominant there and for them I was nothing more than a small insect and Khodasevich a bug of unknown and partly dangerous origin. Tsvetaeva – already weary – [Marc] Slonim and Jakobson, men of the same stock and generation as Khodasevich, lived apart from the respectable crowd... In those weeks in Prague both Khodasevich and I, with great difficulty, could probably have latched on to something, placing one foot – like mountain climbers – tossing a rope, pulling oneself up, placing the other foot... but no one sustained us. And probably this was all to the good. Tsvetaeva and Slonim did not survive here long. Jakobson, spreading his wings, flew like a butterfly out of the cocoon.[48]

Unconnected with the internal dynamics of the exile community, Russian Action in fact went into steady decline after autumn 1924, when France joined Britain in acknowledging the Soviet Communist government. The Russian community, still expanding at this stage, and the Czechoslovaks themselves, seem to have been taken by surprise by a development which overnight gave the Czech Left a perfect reason to demand a reduction in state subsidies to the Russian community. As this began to happen from late 1924, funds for Russian enterprises and salaries diminished and had fallen to almost zero when the Russian University closed in 1928. The consolidation of Soviet Communist power under Stalin and the world economic crisis of 1929 sealed the depleted community's fate.

8

Berlin

RUSSIAN BERLIN DEVELOPED into a unique and much larger, more diverse and more vibrant community than Russian Prague ever was. The city was full of immigrants, as many as 360,000 of them, trying, like the Germans themselves, to hold their lives together.[1] The novelist and German socialist Alfred Döblin disapproved of the former Russian squierarchy living ostentatiously among the German proletariat.[2] But the White Russian general Aleksei von Lampe took the same view as Ilya Ehrenburg, that fate had pitched an extraordinary variety of Russians into a difficult life together.

In 1922 people were living for they didn't know how long in Berlin pensions [...] As fate would have it, a colourful society came together with time, of people torn from the most different Russian social strata, but who still had means (most of them lived from foreign currency which increased in value every minute). As they came down to breakfast and unfurled their napkins, every day they would ask each other: And how is the dollar today? Here there was a former director of a ship's chandlers, with his family, a sportsman, a landowner, a property owner from Ekaterinburg, the owner of the house where the family of the tsar was lodged and murdered, a forceful police captain from the imperial Duma, belonging to the Guards regiment, with his enchanting wife, a ballerina who now worked in a second-hand bookshop. Then there was a lady singer from the St Petersburg music theatre, a film commission agent who showed the young ladies how to dance the foxtrot. Anyone and everyone was here. It's impossible to enumerate them all.[3]

It's true, in Döblin's favour, that the Russian influx to Berlin was overridingly 'bourgeois' and well educated compared with the society it joined. It lacked workers and 'small men'. Nevertheless Russian prisoners of war of all classes and political persuasions made up a substantial part of the very high number of refugees.[4]

Like many left-leaning intellectuals in a generous society Berdyaev faced a dilemma. He disliked the Berlin émigrés' anti-Bolshevism and 'their stuffy, ritualistic piety' though he would have been out of a job had they not provided a Russian population to educate.[5] Von Lampe and Nabokov were more generous to the kind of Russian who in 1990 told the British historians Michael Glenny and Norman Stone about their childhood in *The Other Russia*. 'My father started several businesses in Berlin, still using money from my mother's jewellery. He tried film production... he bought two taxis...'[6] The charm of the 'Berlin Russia' of daily life, was not in the spectacle it offered of political and military losers, but in its strange juxtapositions, its estranged lives, the mixture of languages and accents and daily habits.

The intelligentsia mostly colonized an area in the southwest of the city where attractive villas enjoyed plenty of surrounding green space. They benefited from the grand standard of living Berlin enjoyed before the war. Charlottenburg attracted so many Russians it was sometimes dubbed 'Charlottengrad'. Berberova, Bely, Gershenzon and others lived on the eastern edge of adjacent Wilmersdorf, near the Russian church on the Nachodstrasse.[7] Tsvetaeva spent ten weeks of 1922, April to June, nearby. Not of interest to the atheist avant-garde, but the church on the Nachodstrasse was where Bulgakov – though not resident – held services in the German capital. Nabokov and eventually the Franks also lived in Wilmersdorf, on the western side close to the Kurfürstendamm.

Berberova drew a remarkable verbal map from her pension window.

From the window of my room in the Krampe boarding house in Berlin I can see the windows opposite. The boarding house is only the fourth and fifth floors of a huge building with a marble staircase, chandeliers, and a nude figure holding an electric torch. Our rooms lead to the courtyard: the Krampe rooms occupy both floors, and two sets of windows. All of it is Krampe. There are rooms that lead on to the square Viktoria-Luise Platz, where two floors of rooms are also Krampe (Gershenzon lives there). Krampe herself is a humourless, businesslike bald spinster, though she goes to bed with an artist about twenty years younger than her. Out of the window of my room I see them drinking coffee in the morning. In the evening she pores over her account books while he drinks Kantorowitz liqueur. Then they pull down the shades and put out the light...

Andrey Bely's room is next... [and] under Bely's window is the room of a high tsarist official's widow. She is in deep mourning either for 'his majesty' or for Rasputin, whom she knew well.

Having looked to my heart's content at strange windows, I put on Khodasevich's trousers, jacket and shoes, hide my hair under his hat, take his cane and go for a walk. I walk along the green Charlottenburg, along quiet streets where trees bend over with branches and the sky is not visible, along the quieted Wilmersdorf where in a Russian restaurant people are singing gypsy songs and cursing modern literature... where General X stands in livery in the doorway, and Gentleman of the Chamber Z is at your service. Now they are still rarities, unique. But soon there will be many of them – oh how many! Paris and London, New York and Shanghai will know them and get used to them.

Past and present interweave, fuse into one another, pour into one another. The widow and the general cursing the Revolution and the poet... welcoming it; old émigrés, that is socialists of the tsarist epoch, who have returned to their home in Europe, having happily escaped from the Revolution... The present day exists too, parallel

to this: Viktor Shklovsky and Marc Slonim come to see us, and a
little later Pasternak, Nikolai Otsup and many others come from
Russia (for a 'health cure') . . .

Russian Berlin – I knew no other. The German Berlin was only
the background for those years, ailing Germany, ailing money, the
ailing trees of Tiergarten, where we sometimes strolled in the
morning . . .[8]

The Berlin Russians, more Bohemian than their academic counter-
parts in Prague, and enjoying the cheap Reichsmark, having formed
their various political camps, often gathered in cafés and restaurants.
Berdyaev kept open house on Sundays, though he did not always like
the people who came along.[9] Through 1922–3, a transposed House of
Arts also met on Sundays at the Café Landgraf on the Kurfürstenstraße.
The other favourite venue was on the Nollendorfplatz where the
Writers' Club met at the Café Leon.[10] Aikhenvald, Frank, Berdyaev,
Osorgin and Khodasevich helped form this club at the end of 1922 and
Myakotin and above all Aikhenvald, who by now had dedicated his life
exclusively to Russian literature, kept the tradition alive by re-creating it
as the Literary Club the following year.[11] On the Nollendorfplatz the
men of the Silver Age encountered the poets of the new generation like
Mayakovsky and Esenin. One of the best Russian restaurants was on
the Genthinerstrasse just around the corner. The more avant-garde
writers and critics also had an exclusive gathering-point in the Prager
Diele on the Prager Platz, near the Pension Krampe. Someone invented
the verb *pragerdilstvovat*, which summed up all that was entailed in
going there regularly.

Berlin was a refuge for the unsettled and ousted Russian intelli-
gentsia and also an ideal place to publish their books. Because of
Cyrillic type existing from before the war, the city boasted more
Russian editorial houses than there existed writers. Some eighty-six
Russian publishers produced over 2,000 titles between 1918 and
1924.[12] Of the exiles Vysheslavtsev, Berdyaev, Stepun, Sorokin, Frank,
Aikhenvald and Novikov all published books within a year or so of

their arrival.[13] The contents varied from academic work to Russian philosophy in its characteristic style as spiritual self-help. Berdyaev, Frank, Novikov and Vysheslavtsev all contributed to this genre. Frank went through a particularly strong period of didacticism in Berlin. Theirs were not the most exciting volumes coming off the Cyrillic presses, neither visually nor in their content. The avant-garde Shklovsky, who wrote memoirs and gave his name to a book of essays on Chaplin, and beautifully produced volumes of poetry by Tsvetaeva and Esenin, left a more modern mark. But Russian philosophy had a mission it could not neglect – to carry forward the nineteenth-century tradition embodied by Solovyov, Dostoevsky, Tolstoy and others, and this it could do very well from Berlin.

Scores of the Russian classics were reprinted as part of the exiled publishers' output. Meanwhile Iosif Gessen began to put out his multi-volume *Arkhiv russkoi revolyutsii* ('Archive of the Russian Revolution') (1921–4), which was a vital source of the kind of contemporary history that might otherwise be buried, or 'lost', by Soviet historians to come. The bookshops and busy presses conveyed the sense that Berlin was ideally a refuge for the homeless Russian mind. Leading houses included Abram Kagan's Petropolis, transferred from Petrograd, Melgunov's Vataga, which was the overseas arm of Zadruga, Epokha, Neva, Helikon, Obelisk and Grzhebin. Bogolepov worked at the publishers Vozrozhdenie.

The thriving Russian-language newspaper press also benefited from the mixture of pre-war traditions and the demands and needs of a large educated community. 'The Rudder' placed itself at the centre of the community as a source of unrivalled information and a social catalyst.[14] It drew richly on Lenin's ousted Russian talent. Izgoev analysed the political situation while the literary pages were dominated by Aikhenvald and graced with poems from Bunin and Sirin-Nabokov, who also contributed crosswords. Two men from the ships, Iretsky, a writer of fiction and science fiction,[15] and the writer-painter Matusevich,[16] were also associated with 'The Rudder' and its short-lived successor *Nash Vek* ('Our Age').[17] A different stripe of Russian journalist could place and read articles in Berlin's other daily, the republican *Dni* ('Days'), founded by Kerensky.[18] On 'Days' the journalists Volkovysky, Petrishchev and Khariton all found regular work, though in Khariton's case not enough to sustain him. He quickly moved on to Riga to work for the Russian press there. Osorgin, Sorokin, Karsavin, Peshekhonov, Prokopovich and Kuskova also contributed to the political and current affairs sections of 'Days' and Stepun and many others to the literary pages.

The migrants to Berlin, including many Russians, kept on coming.[19] No sooner had the two parties from the *Haken* and the *Preussen* disembarked than the German Foreign Ministry advised its consuls to restrict entry to those 'in serious trouble'.[20] This move coincided with the new tax on furnished lodgings from Christmas 1922, which horrifed 'The Rudder'.[21] Germany's problem was the immigrants' good fortune – until the tables were reversed. The number of Russians peaked, just a few months after the German Mark was stabilized in summer 1923, after which prices started to climb and savings vanished. 'How are you living?' one immigrant asked another. 'Oh, like a moth. First I eat my trousers, then I eat my jacket.'[22] That joke characterized the second stage of Berlin Russia, when after the honeymoon of a devalued currency the Russians had to suffer the same perils of inflation as the Germans. During 1924 inflation forced most of the men from the Philosophy Steamer to move on.

The Russian academics lived in a professional and social cocoon, just as they did in Prague, bound together in Berlin by a Russian Academic Union. They matched the German government's provision of buildings and funds with enormous energy and will-power. Of two main projects one was Berdyaev's Free Religious-Philosophical Academy, which employed Karsavin, Aikhenvald, Ilyin, Stepun, Vysheslavtsev and others. The Free Academy was operational by December 1922 and perpetuated the tradition of the Religious-Philosophical Societies of Moscow and St Petersburg over the previous twenty years. At the opening gala on 26 November Berdyaev called for the spiritual regeneration of Russia as a task of universal importance.

The Revolution was not only a political and social cataclysm but also signalled the collapse of humanism.

> Efforts to found culture on purely human foundations have come to nothing...In Russia people were expecting the Third Rome and what came was the Third International, the complete negation of humanist ideals. We should remember the words of Dostoevsky, that if there is no God then there is also no humanity.

'The Third Rome' referred to the nineteenth-century Slavophile belief that as the seat of Russian Orthodoxy Moscow was poised to become the great centre of Christianity after Constantinople and Rome. Reporting the occasion, 'The Rudder' noted that 'the hall was full of Bolshevik observers...and solitary figures, open and clandestine agents...'[23]

The other almost immediate creation of the exiles in Berlin was the Russian Scientific Institute (RNI), with Yasinsky as Director.[24] Yasinsky, the steam turbine expert who had acted as group 'elder' in Moscow, sorting out problems with exit visas, was an obvious choice as a figurehead. Money and support for the RNI came from England and America, from the German Foreign Office and the Prussian Ministry of Culture in conjunction with the Red Cross. Yasinsky, Berdyaev, Ugrimov and Ilyin attended the first meeting with the sponsors on 14 November. Novikov, Stratonov and the soil scientist Odintsov, who was yet to arrive, would take over leading roles.

The aim of both institutions was to provide an unbroken education for the children of those forced into exile, as for the children of refugees, and to allow the professors to continue their writing and research. From the moment the RNI opened its doors, on 17 February 1923, to around 600 matriculated students, the list of full-time and visiting lecturers – from as far as Paris, Prague and Kharbin – read like a *Who's Who* of the ousted Russian academic world. It had three strong departments: 'spiritual-intellectual culture', which Berdyaev oversaw, law under the direction of Ilyin, and economics under Prokopovich. The staff included Karsavin, Frank, Brutskus and Kizevetter.

Bogolepov taught on the law course, as did, in addition to their usual subjects, Aikhenvald and Frank. The publisher Abram Kagan offered an extra-curricular set of lectures on 'The Archaeology of Primitive Culture in Russia'.

In Prokopovich's economics department, which boasted the highest level of expertise, Boris Brutskus was the most internationally outstanding, lecturing on agricultural economics and agrarian politics. Another of the teachers was sixty-two-year-old Efim Zubashov, former writer for Lenin's loathed *Ekonomist*, whose subject was trade and commodities. The teaching throughout the RNI, which also included language preparation in both Russian and German, was expeditious and the general ethos conscientious, though the intellectual level of the staff was considerably higher than that of the students. Volkovysky, who worked alongside the elderly Yasinsky 'in the office of the expellees' group', described him as a man of great energy, attention to detail and care when it came to distributing the charitable funds the Institute received.

By far the most popular subject at the RNI, overlapping with the output of Berdyaev's Religious-Philosophical Academy, was Russian 'spiritual-intellectual culture', that subject which made Russian pre-revolutionary culture unique, and exactly where Lenin saw his greatest rival in terms of national pride, cultural striving and social hope. The popularity of the subject caused political and academic uneasiness among the German hosts, given Germany's diplomatic ties to the new Soviet state.[25] There was also some doubt, as was also voiced in Prague, as to whether the subject was worthy of academic acceptance.[26] The German side refused to accept RNI qualifications as the equivalent of, or a qualification for, entry to German universities. But Russian 'spiritual-intellectual culture' was what the Russians deposed from pedagogical authority by the Revolution most wanted to preserve as a body of knowledge. It was the 'idealism' to which Lenin opposed dialectical 'materialism'.

The Russian 'Idea' writ large has always been difficult for outsiders, and particularly for the pragmatic Anglo-Saxon mind, to grasp. Many foreigners would like to understand it as literature, but for Russians in the religious-national tradition the distinction between literature and philosophy was immaterial in respect of a single, continuous body of writing which enshrined Russian moral values. Yasinsky explained to the Germans that it was doubly important in the face of 1917. He said the aim of RNI courses was to acquaint students 'with Russian history and Russian intellectual culture in the totality of their manifestations...It is primarily the historical-philological, philosophical and juridical faculties which have been destroyed in Russia and many thousands of students have been robbed of intercourse with their intellectual-spiritual teachers.'[27] Stepun described the Russian outlook he wanted to impart: 'It would combine the spiritual values of Orthodoxy with the social, economic and cultural benefits of a Christian socialism rooted in a personalist, spiritualist metaphysics.'[28] The Scientific Institute taught a course on 'Russia and the West' in which Kizevetter, Ilyin, Aikhenvald, Karsavin, and Frank took part. The talk, before some 250 students, was of the movements of civilizations and national cultural ideas and reflected the fascination with Spengler that the Russians had shown before they left. In essence both the Russians and Spengler were descendants of Hegel, setting out to find 'higher' meaning in history, even if Spengler found only relatively empty stories of rise and fall.[29]

The content of such courses was politically so loaded against the incipient Soviet world by virtue of being 'spiritual' and individualistic that it is not surprising that it rankled with a post-Rapallo German government keen to befriend Red Moscow. In archive material that has come to light since the end of the German Communist regime, Ilyin, Frank and Brutskus are all named on the German side as being controversial. Controversial then should not be read as unsound today. Brutskus always stressed the incompatibility of the mechanistic utopian vision of Soviet Communism with the freedom of the human person.[30] He made the point in Russia before he was forced out and repeatedly before European audiences after he arrived in the West. The lectures he gave in 1927 as part of an extra-mural Sunday series at the RNI, no doubt branched out from the general, palliative title 'Soviet Agriculture after the Revolution' under which they were billed. Berdyaev's *The Philosophy of Inequality* (1923) meanwhile set out the views, directed against cultural levelling, on which his teaching would be based.

The Germans funding the RNI had tried in autumn 1922 to combine their own political interests with honest charity. They were prepared to render humanitarian assistance to the deported professors. They were also keen to build up a centre of German expertise on Russia and Eastern Europe, but this amassing of Slavonic know-how would have to be compatible with furthering their present-day contacts with Soviet Russia. They therefore insisted that Soviet representatives in Berlin – a vast embassy of over a hundred staff – be invited to take an interest in the RNI. The Soviet cultural attaché leapt at the chance to express his sincere government's concern with the RNI professors' well-being and promised the unhampered delivery of books sent from Russia 'just as before'.[31] The German authorities asked that the exiles' teaching should not be too political, yet hesitated to impose too narrow conditions on the RNI for fear of losing these valuable men to Prague or the United States, where the new discipline of Sovietology also needed qualified staff. Some of the exiled Russians were all the more desirable because, like Stepun, an alumnus of Heidelberg, they were partly German-educated.

The possibility of concessions to Soviet pressure, even the fact that the Soviet side was consulted, may have prompted Novikov, who was also a Heidelberg graduate, Odintsov and Stratonov to move to Prague in the first months of 1923, after no more than a few weeks of the RNI's existence. The Soviet embassy at No. 11 Unter den Linden was officially obliging towards the learned Russians who set up their Institute in the old Construction Academy on the Schinkelplatz. But the strength of their objections to Berdyaev's private Academy can be seen from the otherwise bizarre inclusion of Yasinsky's name on a list of 'great books' in Russia banned as of 1923. Yasinsky's name figured alongside Kant, Schopenhauer, Taine, Ruskin, Nietzsche and Tolstoy, which made Gorky gasp.[32] Before long the Soviet diplomats succeeded in making the German side suspicious of the RNI. 'We can't rule out that a centre of anti-German and anti-Soviet agitation will develop there,' noted one of the Institute's two German founder-organizers.[33]

By the time Prokopovich, Bogolepov and Zubashov had moved to Prague in 1924 for financial reasons, the appeal of the Institute in Berlin was anyway dwindling because Russian students could no longer afford the fees. The RNI had a mere sixty students that year. From 1925 its idealistic German founders remodelled it into the Research Institute for Russia and East Europe they originally wanted, and were fortunate to retain Brutskus in a leading role, until the rise of Hitler overtook both the founders (who were sacked) and the remaining Russian staff. After that the RNI's fate was ever more unfortunate. By 1931 its work was being shaped towards the Nazi purpose of detecting the origins of Communist thinking in Germany, which did nothing for the reputation of Ilyin, and in 1932 it closed for lack of funds. As a Jew, meanwhile, by mid-1933 Brutskus was seeking with his family to leave Germany for good.

The end was sad because the early days of the RNI were so positive. Of the provision in Berlin for formal education from a parental point of view, Tatyana Frank recalled:

> Germany welcomed us, helped to build the Russian Scientific
> Institute, where not a few young Russians finished their education.
> Our children went through German schools, Victor graduated from
> Berlin University studying Russian history and became a Doctor of
> Philosophy...[34]

The best times for the RNI occurred at a time when, led by writers like Thomas Mann, German cultural life was fascinated by things Russian, and had not yet fallen into the grip of that political-nationalist mania which would regard Slavs like Berdyaev and Jews like Frank and Brutskus as *Untermenschen*.

•

When Nikolai Andreyev visited the Franks in Berlin he found that Tatyana had created a Russian home-from-home. 'In the Franks' home there was a piece of Russia both in Charlottenburg and later in France and in London and Munich – this was above all the doing of their mother, Tatyana Sergeevna.'[35] In the back of Tatyana's mind may have been the phial of earth her husband had brought from his mother's grave in Russia. The need for spiritual continuity and sacred objects to support it was very strong in religious-minded households. The Franks found security and Russianness in that religion and in their close family life. But with time they also became well established materially and professionally in secular life. Andreyev commented on their all-round prosperity as a Russian family in exile: 'Accustomed as I was to the modesty of Russian life in flats in the Baltic States and Czechoslovakia I was struck by the size of Berlin dwellings, reminiscent of the "enfilade style" of St Petersburg – at least in Charlottenburg, [also by] the Old Testament appearance of Victor's father, Semyon Lyudvigovich, and the beauty of his mother, Tatyana Sergeevna. Above all I was struck by the intensity of the Russianness of all the young Franks.'[36]

Like many families the Franks cultivated their Russianness while the question whether they would ever go home hung over them for years. In the first instance it seemed entirely rational for Russians unwillingly abroad to hope they would get back sooner or later. Whole governments, who knew as little of totalitarianism as Lenin's victims, suspected that Bolshevism would either not last or that the stringent controls the Soviets imposed would be relaxed to accommodate other views. Bunin wrote in his diary for 1 January 1923: 'We celebrated French New Year...Perhaps this year we will return?'[37] As late as 1928 Nabokov believed his hopes were based on intelligent reckoning rather than fantasy:

> In the summer of 1928...I was twenty-eight. I had been living in Berlin, on and off, for half a dozen years. I was absolutely sure, with a number of other intelligent people, that sometime in the next

decade we would all be back in a hospitable, remorseful, racemosa-blossoming Russia.[38]

Nevertheless at some level convincing themselves was not simple and required eccentric action to encourage it. Stories were told all over Russia Abroad of those who kept their suitcases packed, ready to leave.[39] Then there was the mother who never tidied her flat, for what was the point when it only existed to be left behind? Here homesickness was already becoming a neurosis.

Their complex psychology is why above all émigré communities need fiction writers to make their worlds intelligible to later generations. Nabokov is on record as hating Freud and his theories to a fanatical degree, but in my view that hatred was mainly a smokescreen, to protect his own reputation for originality. In truth, so much of his writing concerned memory of the homeland and the mind's entertaining tricks in providing the heart with satisfaction. The satisfying pictures which memory conjured and invented to keep alive the hope and heart of the exile was Nabokov's great subject matter. Think only of the novel *Pale Fire* and of his early story 'The Visit to the Museum'. The story evoked the love-object 'Russia' in just the same way the novel would evoke 'Nova Zembla', as both dream and nightmare.

Berberova's stories were much simpler in style but equally full of an originally healthy human longing for home, warped by years of frustration. A woman prepared to leave her husband when she heard that an old flame was also in exile. But when they met he failed to trigger in her the right memories and so, against an expectation which had suddenly welled up in him too, she dropped the idea. Her husband never noticed and the discarded widower fell conclusively by the wayside.

Lenin's exiles could not return, but they understood those who wanted to. Why Lenin closed the door so firmly on the shipped exiles may well have been because he knew their love was greater than their criticism, even of Bolshevism itself, and he would never get rid of them otherwise. Brutskus was another who had made no secret of not wanting to leave Soviet Russia.[40] In their café conversations and in the press the exiles expressed ambivalence and sympathy for a Russian plight of which, although they were powerless to act in their own cases, they were still part. Kuskova and Osorgin supported Peshekhonov in his very public desire to return as soon as he could. In Peshekhonov's view a good Russian did not need a guarantee of personal safety to return to his country. Osorgin and even the wise Kuskova longed to act on that heroic counsel.[41] A letter from Brutskus to Kuskova, the 'upright' woman whom Gorky called his 'lifelong friend', suggests she was still wavering in 1930.[42]

Poor Osorgin, so longing for his country, was left to create on paper an imperative he could never fulfil. If Russia was a prison, he wrote, then only the men inside it could saw through the bars. In consolation for not being an inmate he persuaded himself that one day the doors of the Russian Bastille would burst open anyway. The force of daily culture would 'strengthen the people's power and their capacity to resist and to work for the country's good'. Intellectually Osorgin disapproved of revolutionary activity, yet he ached to play an active part in Russia's fate, and renewed his Soviet passport every year until his death, just in case.[43]

The dilemma of liberal and left-leaning Russian culture in exile was that its very substance demanded self-sacrifice. The Russian intelligentsia had been bred to serve selflessly an uneasy combination of state and people. Endlessly they debated what to do. All the nuances of the Russian political and artistic scene at home were re-created in a tug-of-war in a small, intense, dynamic space abroad.

For the White activist and archivist von Lampe, those trying to pull the emigration to the left included Prokopovich and Kuskova, though he cast a beady eye over all the shipped exiles, who, because they never wanted to leave, seemed to him potential pro-Bolshevik troublemakers abroad.[44] Only a few of Lenin's exiles attracted the hopes of the generals and businessmen, public figures, wives and widows who made up the conservative community. Names were put to these hopes when the Berlin League of Russian Students held an evening in honour of Yasinsky, Stratonov, Ugrimov and Kizevetter. Later when von Lampe founded a Russian-German club to inform German social, political and industrial opinion on the real nature of Bolshevik Russia he could hardly have done better than invite Ilyin to speak there, in German,[45] for Ilyin was keen to denounce the Soviet regime's confiscation of private property. But Ilyin was a unique figure among the writers in that he moved further and further to the Right.

Something von Lampe and the conservatives could do nothing about in the earlier years was the way Russian Berlin teemed with cultural figures who, having left Soviet Russia voluntarily and legitimately, with the option to return, made it seem like a viable place. Bely, Ehrenburg, Aleksei Tolstoy, Mayakovsky, Pasternak and Gershenzon all circulated freely in Berlin. Viktor Shklovsky was there too, having fled in spring 1922 in fear of being implicated in the SRs' trial, but still nominally acting on his free choice.

In line with what was happening in Russia itself, however, the political atmosphere in Berlin was set to sharpen. The pro-Soviet Berlin paper *Nakanune* ('On the Eve') opened offices in Moscow in June 1922 and began to be distributed in Soviet Russia.[46] As a result its staff were immediately excluded from the the Union of Russian Writers and Journalists in Germany. The editor of 'On the Eve's' Literary Supplement, Aleksei Tolstoy, further revealed his pro-Soviet colours when that same June he published a 'private' letter from Chukovsky denouncing parasites at the the House of Writers. This period in the history of Berlin Russia marked an extension of the 'Janus' standards of NEP to Russia Abroad. The atmosphere seemed free but the force of repression was hovering. The sense of a Berlin Russian culture still very much counting as part of Russia in 1922 – in the eyes of those who were trying to manipulate pro-Soviet opinion – has come to light in documents recently made available in Russia.

In Berlin at the time, Tsvetaeva was incensed at On the Eve's denunciation of the House of Writers, and delivered a public reply to Aleksei Tolstoy: 'Either you are in fact a three-year-old child who does not suspect either the existence of the GPU or the *Chronicle of the House of*

Writers [*Letopis' Doma Literatorov*], or much, much else...'[47] What we can see now, with the Moscow end of the picture clear, is that Aleksei Tolstoy chose exactly the right moment to side with Lenin's plan to silence that journal which had campaigned for freedom of ideas as well as market freedom under the NEP. Three months ahead of the journalists' expulsion and several weeks before Lenin sent a crucial memorandum to Stalin, Aleksei Tolstoy backed the intention to exile the *Chronicle*'s editors Volkovysky and Khariton and others who either wrote for it or were associated with the Dom literatorov, such as Petrishchev, Aikhenvald, Osorgin and Zamyatin.[48] A member of the Petrograd literary establishment who emigrated voluntarily just in time, Nikolai Otsup, remembered Chukovsky's animosity towards Zamyatin that summer. The man who would make his reputation as a great Soviet children's writer was also detaching himself from Aikhenvald.[49] In Russia the writers sympathetic to the Soviet side had somehow been forewarned to make their position clear. As the sides sorted themselves out definitively, the unwanted men of autumn 1922 tried to settle in Berlin while Aleksei Tolstoy prepared to return. (That he didn't go until June 1923 may have been for sybaritic reasons.) With Lenin incapacitated but not yet dead, Soviet Russia was normalized along this twisted Berlin–Moscow axis.

Gershenzon, part of no conspiracy, simply speaking out of his Russian soul, decided the West was too full of 'factory-made things' and paid too much attention to luxury and convenience. He and his family left Berlin on 10 August after barely three months. Without money Gershenzon was frightened of the capitalist world: uncertain whether, if he were simply thirsty, he would be allowed to request a glass of water for nothing. Possibly he was ill and did indeed come for 'a rest cure', as he said. He died two years later, in a way, Berberova suggested, hastened by the new political status quo.[50]

The German currency reform inclined more Russians to leave in autumn 1923. In parallel, Germany and Russia were taking on the new identity which would carry them disastrously through the next twenty years. When Bely left for Russia in October he was somehow psychologically compelled to act against his own well-being, a perfect example of a Russian in the Dostoevskian mould, and therefore full of foreboding:

> Bely came in a state of fury I had never seen before. He greeted almost no one. Squeezing his huge hands between his knees, in a grey tweed suit with a jacket that hung down on him, he sat looking at no one, and when he rose at the end of the dinner, glass in hand, looking hatefully, with almost white eyes, at all those sitting at the table (there were more than twenty) he announced that he would make a speech. This was a toast, as it were, to one's self [sic]. The image of Christ in those moments came to life in this fool of a genius: he demanded that we drink to him because he was leaving to be crucified. For whose sake? For all of yours, sirs, sitting in this Russian restaurant on the Gentianerstrasse [sic]...
>
> Bely's female companion, later his second wife, sat by a window and read a book, trying not to notice that the evening was collapsing into misery.

According to Berberova, Bely broke with all his friends that autumn, declaring that 'Khodasevich was a sceptic... Berdyaev was a secret enemy.' If, however, denouncing the exiles all around him was a condition of regaining access to Russia, he quickly achieved his aim. 'At first [Bely] was refused a visa, but then the Soviet consul changed his mind.'[51]

Shklovsky's fate was different again. He could not bear life without his wife, who was a hostage being held in a Soviet prison against his return. He wrote a letter of repentance to the Central Committee of the Communist Party and Gorky and Bely vouched for him.[52]

Berlin formed this extraordinary backdrop for a second parting of the ways of the twentieth-century Russian intelligentsia, and the stragglers who parted from related centres of Russia Abroad can be counted as players on the same stage. Peshekhonov kept trying to get home from Prague because he felt he could best help a socialist Russia by being there. Lutokhin tried similarly and succeeded. One after

another Pasternak, Esenin, Mayakovsky, Ehrenburg and Gorky left
German soil and eventually even Tsvetaeva herself and the novelist
Alexander Kuprin returned to Russia from Paris, though hardly with
the intention or capacity to accommodate themselves to the regime.
Esenin, Mayakovsky and Tsvetaeva all committed suicide, and Kuprin
was dead in spirit before he got home. Their Russian home was a pool
of dark water. But still they dived in one more time. Jakobson, close
friend of Mayakovsky and Shklovsky, dipped a toe in the dark pool
when he was offered a chair in Saratov in 1924, but he was deterred
from taking the full plunge when he asked his friend Ushakov for
advice. Ushakov, with whom Jakobson and Aikhenvald had worked at
the State Institute of Public Speaking in 1919, replied unequivocally:
'When you want to dance, you have to remember not only the stove
you're dancing away from, but also the wall you're dancing towards.'[53]
The wall, of course, was the one against which men were put up and
shot by the GPU. It was prudent to suppress the Russian in oneself in
those unpredictable days. Still many could not.

Exiled hearts fluttered – perhaps Jakobson's own – when Lenin's
death was announced in the press, two days after the event, on 24
January 1924. Was life about to change? Gorky wept and asked his first
wife at home in Russia to send a wreath.[54] The inhabitants of the
Svobodarna hostel in Prague rushed out on to the staircases and joyfully clasped the hands of strangers.[55] Nabokov in Berlin forgot his
beloved Vera's telephone number.[56] Still, in the event, nothing dented
Soviet power in the run-up to its significant recognition by France,
Britain and other states seven months after Lenin's death. The exiles
turned out to have no hope.

The wise thing was to realize that the only way to retain some faith
in a good Russia was to work for a liberal country from the safe haven
of abroad. When a debate on Peshekhonov's *Why I Didn't Emigrate*
was organized in Berlin in May 1923, Brutskus used it to reject calls for
the intelligentsia to return home.[57] 'It's here abroad, and not in Russia
that the intelligentsia has a lot of work to do, to reflect on its ideology
... the return to Russia is only possible through the "Change of

Landmarks" gate, through demoralization.' The reference to 'Change of Landmarks' alluded to the idea that Russia was 'on the eve' of a prosperous period in its history, having weathered its crisis, and that, for leading this recovery, Soviet Russia should now be supported by all patriots. Tolstoy and 'On the Eve' spoke for the Change of Landmarks attitude. The liberals were right to think they represented a trap.

'Change of Landmarks', *Smena vekh*, had a certain logic, however, and created waverers. Its chronological roots lay in wartime regret for the absence of a strong Russian state under the last tsar. One of the reprieved individuals, Iosif Ozerov, had contributed to a keynote 1916 volume under the 'Change of Landmarks' title. After the Revolution 'Change of Landmarks' followers published a second collection of articles in Prague in 1921, which succeeded in rousing support in all the major exile centres. An accommodation with Soviet Russia was proposed on the grounds that Lenin had restored the might of the Russian state after the chaos of 1917–21. The NEP further provided the *smenovekhovtsy* with the argument that if Lenin could compromise his (Communist) ideals, then they too could modify their anti-Communist sentiments. The best that could happen to Russia would be for a compromise with the free market to continue. That way Russia might develop as a great power but not as a Communist power.[58]

One reason why the liberal exiles had to react was because, in a way beyond their control, they had given 'Change of Landmarks' its name. As the leading contributors to the 1909 volume 'Landmarks' in Russian, *Vekhi*, Berdyaev, Frank, Sergei Bulgakov and Izgoev were effectively invited by *smenovekhovstvo* to reconsider their discontent with recent Russian history and the role of the intelligentsia. Just as in 1909 when they had appealed to the intelligentsia to work with, rather than constantly against, the tsarist government, so now too they might themselves consider the virtues of working with Lenin and recognizing the merits of the new state.

They refused because 'Change of Landmarks' precluded Russia's development along democratic Western lines. Some of Lenin's future exiles had rejected the new ideology while still in Russia. Izgoev, Sorokin and Petrishchev made important contributions to a collection of essays opposing 'Change of Landmarks', which Dom literatorov published in December 1921. Karsavin and Lossky had also promised articles but for some reason withdrew them.[59] While welcoming the basic message of loyalty to Russia, Petrishchev warned that under no circumstances should the intelligentsia give up its moral independence. Izgoev, a Kadet and friend of Struve, agreed that the intelligentsia was a moral and spiritual force essential to Russia. Together with Frank, Berdyaev and Bulgakov, Izgoev had joined the wartime League of Russian Culture, which, inaugurated in June 1917, had emphasized patriotic duty. He was among the many centrists and conservatives who would be appalled by the premature bilateral peace with Germany, concluded by Lenin at Brest-Litovsk. Patriotism and the mystique of the state should be encouraged, Izgoev now said, but never at the cost of jettisoning moral and spiritual values.[60]

Sorokin took a different tack to deliver a powerful critique of where Sovietism was headed and why he could not support it. The *smenovekhovtsy* represented social groups 'primarily interested in a strong, stable government and [for whom] the actual nature of the regime was of no interest'. They might colour their motives with noble words about patriotism but patriotism was hardly what mattered to them. In a moment of great insight, foreseeing how the Soviet economy would function over the next seventy years, Sorokin described the 'bourgeois specialists' who decided to support it as *gosklienty*. These were essentially 'people commercially dependent on the state for orders and concessions'. Soviet jargon prefixed everything state-owned with '*gos*' from *gosudarstvo*, the word for 'the state'. Already in 1921 Sorokin envisaged what the West would come to identify fifty years later as the Soviet Union's system of 'state capitalism'. He also recognized in embryo the insincerity of that Communist economic idealism on the part of those with power.

The stances of Isgoev, Petrishchev and Sorokin, advising against any accommodation with the Soviet state, were all in their way remarkable, because they foresaw what would go wrong with Soviet Russia, and what kind of social and political reality would lurk behind the world-seducing names of Communism and socialism over the next seventy years. They made clear three things: that the Soviet state couldn't exist without a servile intelligentsia, whether conquered or capitulated; that its purported Communist moral aims would always be subordinated to the strength of the Russian state at home and abroad; and that the Soviet state was at heart, from day one, a business deal to allow Russia be run by a Party oligarchy for its own profit.

The men and women Sorokin identified as quintessential Soviet types in embryo were the future *nomenklatura* – those who wrought privileges from the economic torpor they vested on to their own country, and who, because of the material advantages to themselves, did not care what kind of state it was. What 'Change of Landmarks' accepted as a Soviet Russian reality was what would vex genuine Marxists the world over for the next seventy years: that it accepted a partnership between Communism and Russian nationalism.

The *smenovekhovtsy* envisaged a Russia with a tame intelligentsia or none at all. In effect they celebrated the moment when Lenin chopped off all the old, wild growth from the cultured classes, leaving only the new intellectual wood to grow into a predetermined shape. When the shipped philosophers and their companions arrived in Berlin in autumn 1922 'On the Eve' published a signed editorial saying the expulsions were mostly deserved. The split Lenin forced upon the intelligentsia was hailed in its servile pages.[61]

These were some of the ideas and human destinies which played themselves out against the background of Berlinskaya Rossiya, a no man's land of artistic ferment, social and political uncertainty and personal freedom. In the Academy, the RNI, the cafés, the Writers' and Journalists' Union, the Writers' Club and the Circle of Lovers of Russian Literature, what lived on for a few years was a kind of NEP Russia, which is to say a place open to the outside world and bursting with new ideas and opportunities, its cultural life stimulated by traumatic social and political experience in very recent memory. In practice Berlin Russia would soon do what a free Russia would also have done. It would graft itself on to strong, sympathetic developments across the political and cultural spectrum abroad.

Looking around for cultural allies, Berdyaev invited 'the Catholic Nietzsche' Max Scheler to give a talk at the Academy and subsequently read his work. The encounter helped him – and other Russian religious philosophers – to understand how much he had in common with religious thinkers in the West who asserted the objectivity of moral, social and aesthetic values.[62] The tide of relativism and subjectivism that the decline of religion and the rise of social science had brought about was a worry shared with Scheler. Scheler called his work 'religious anthropology' and stressed the central role of the human person, neither a purely natural being nor purely metaphysical, but capable of refined choice. The essay, 'The New Middle Ages', which Berdyaev wrote in Berlin, and which was later expanded into his book, *The Fate of Man in the Modern World* (1935), bore a similar message and became his introduction to European intellectual circles. What was true of Berdyaev was also true of Frank, Stepun, Vysheslavtsev, Bulgakov and others, though they would never become so well known abroad. '[Their] philosophical orientation converged with the religious existentialism of Kierkegaard. It helped to relieve the Russian philosophical speculation of its exclusive preoccupation with concrete social or economic and political problems...'[63]

Other Russian thinkers developed in a more progressive twentieth-century mould. Brutskus met the Austrian philosopher and free-market economist Friedrich von Hayek, future author of the anti-socialist *Road to Serfdom* (1944). Brutskus as Hayek's senior by thirty years made the same connections between the free market and personal freedom and sensed a kindred spirit. Besides being a market economist and a Soviet expert, Brutskus became a campaigner for human rights and, as reports of Stalin's and Hitler's brutality reached him in Berlin and later in Palestine, he appealed respectively for Einstein's and for Hayek's support in rousing world protest.[64]

Different again in making a universal mark were Jakobson and Nabokov. They became figures of the avant-garde, of modernism abroad. Yet, as I suggested earlier, in the Russian context their achievements were coloured with nostalgia, which actually put them in a similar position to Lenin's expelled religious philosophers. As contemporary émigré Russians knew him, Nabokov was not so much a Western modernist as the last representative of the Russian Silver Age longing for that mystical Symbolist Russia he had left behind.

Consider two sentences written by Mary McCarthy about *Pale Fire*:

> Whether the visible world, for Nabokov, is a prismatic reflection of
> eternity or the other way around is a central question that begs itself
> [*sic*] but that remains, for that very reason, moot and troubling…
> it is one of the very great works of art of this century, that modern
> novel that everyone thought was dead…[65]

What the American critic was actually describing was a world-view rooted in the Russian poetry fashionable when Nabokov was coming of age.

Nabokov left Russia three years before the shipped-out mystagogues. To deride them, which he did in his autobiography, was another part of his self-reinvention abroad: a smokescreen, a disguise, an aesthetically justified lie.[66] He was right, he had to get away. They are almost forgotten, whereas he is still known. Yet they had so much in common.

I make these observations to show where the act of exiling the philosophers, and the founding of the Soviet state, fitted in the phenomenon of cultural modernism of which Berlin of the 1920s was the great showcase. Berlin itself was receptive to Russian experimentation and allowed modernism to continue when the constraints of socialist realism were already being imposed in the Soviet Union. The men on the boats had nothing to do with the visual worlds of Tatlin and Malevich, nor the poetic worlds of Khlebnikov and Mayakovsky. But they had the Russian Idea in common with Bely and Pasternak, and with Kandinsky, which leads us to understand them as a general conduit for Russian-European ideas that were essentially anti-rationalist and mystical, even if the word 'modern' was applied to them. Berdyaev's rambling and repetitive *The Meaning of the Creative Act* (1915), for all its faults, set out the foundations of a new religion of 'creativity'. In the words of the historian Marc Raeff: 'In some respects the experimentation of the early years of the Soviet regime, to about 1925, was a direct continuation of the Silver Age, and so was the cultural activity of Russia Abroad in the 1920s and 1930s.'[67]

Collectively the Russian literary intelligentsia abroad made one of its firmest foreign marks with a special variation of modernism, bearing the name of Dostoevsky. The philosophers' interpretations of Russia's great nineteenth-century metaphysical novelist struggling with the atheistic twentieth-century soul of man impacted directly on the modern novel and on existentialism. In 1922–3, as Aikhenvald lectured at Berdyaev's Academy on 'The Philosophical Motifs in Russian Literature', Berdyaev, Vysheslavtsev and Lapshin all published books on Dostoevsky and Frank illustrated many of his articles and lectures with Dostoevsky's work. When Berdyaev's friend, Konstantin Mochulsky, an émigré who preceded Myakotin at the University of Sofia before moving to Paris, published a major study on Dostoevsky, reflecting 'the shattering of idealism' which equally convulsed Russia and the West, his work, building on the thinking of his generation, became a definitive authority for Western readers.[68] And it emerged out of the Silver Age milieu, out of the idealism that Lenin buried under official 'materialism'.

Some great discussions on the future of man and culture – to which I will return – took place in Russian Berlin against the background of shabby cosmopolitanism, Expressionist art, edgy cinema, and German food and landscape which many of us have come to love and admire as one of the most seductive moments in modern European cultural history. The downside of the era was that already too many Russians were trying to rescue an exalted, spiritual notion of Russia, just as too many Germans were trying to recover their nation on the basis of quasi-mystical principles.

One reason for this historical parallel, in the years immediately preceding the twin evils of Stalinism and Nazism, was surely that the Germans at home and those Russians abroad who represented Russian nationalism in a naked, undisguised form, had a similar sense of being convulsed. Recent memories had turned those living in Berlin circa 1923 into

> distraught souls caught in the web of fate... the delirium and hallucination, stemming from a much wilder time, darkened streets, the shouted commands of republican troops, from somewhere the harsh screeching of street-corner rhetoricians – a city clothed in the deepest darkness, occupied by radical revolutionaries, with the rattle of machine guns, chains, rooftop snipers and hand grenades.[69]

These words, taken from a review of the film *The Cabinet of Dr Caligari* (1919) by a recent historian of the city to encapsulate the mood of post-war Berlin, defined the felt world of everyday which German artists reconfigured as Expressionism. As an artistic idiom it immediately recalled the graphics and linoprints of extraordinary Russian responses to revolution in 1905 and 1917. This felt world was also the same one which religious thinkers like Berdyaev and Scheler, Frank and Heidegger saw as alarmingly godless, with men simply 'thrown' into existence to cope as best they could.

Let Nina Berberova paint a final picture, however, not of eternal metaphysical discomfort but of stalled Russians biding their time:

> In the summer of 1923... [at] the seaside spot of Prerow, where the Zaitsevs, the Berdyaevs, the Muratovs and we were staying... It would rain. I would play chess with Muratov and have long conversations, then light the stove, go for walks on the shores of the Baltic in a raincoat in wind and rain, and in the evening watch Doctor Mabuse at the movies. At the Zaitsevs' as always it was bright, warm and lively. With a heavy walking stick Nikolai Berdyaev would leave on his daily walk along the dunes. His wife and mother-in-law were both sick with whooping cough.[70]

Lack of work in Berlin, and therefore lack of purpose, drove Khariton to Riga and Brutskus's friend Pumpyansky to Estonia after only a few months. Inflation moved on most of their shipped peers two years later. Berdyaev and Osorgin resettled in Paris where before long Karsavin and others joined them. Stepun took up a chair in Dresden via Paris. As Berlin Russia shrank to a relic of its former self, Frank took over the sole running of the Academy, and Yasinsky remained a lonely figure at the RNI. Aikhenvald kept busy writing for various émigré publications, teaching and running a Russian literature circle in Berlin with Nabokov.

Aikhenvald represents Berlin Russia's gravestone. He was perhaps the sole remaining jewel in the expatriate crown until, in one of the tragedies of Russia Abroad, almost on a par with the murder of Nabokov's father, he was run over by a tram and killed in 1928. 'The Rudder' kept going until 1931, still with its pre-revolutionary type. It used that old type not for ideological reasons but because it was available and cheap. Idealism refused to be silenced, but died anyway.

9

Paris

B Y 1926 THERE was a single Russian cultural mecca abroad and that was in Paris. The émigré community, which according to official figures doubled between 1911 and 1931, grew to at least 82,000 souls but is generally thought to have totalled many more. It was socially more diverse and more affluent than anything Prague or Berlin had fostered. Cultural life could flourish on a much larger scale and the substantial pre-war Russian artistic and aristocratic presence in the French capital – the world of Stravinsky and Diaghilev's *Ballets russes*, – and even the *fin de siècle* salon of the already out-of-fashion Merezhkovsky and Gippius – provided a ready-made foundation. The same was true of academic life. A Russian People's University founded in 1921 was followed, in rapid succession, by the transfer of Berdyaev's Religious-Philosophical Academy from Berlin in 1924, and the founding of a partly vocational Franco-Russian University and an Orthodox Theological Institute and Seminary in 1925. The arrival of Lenin's exiles boosted almost every aspect of educated life.

Paris's own University of the Sorbonne admitted refugee scholars to lecture on Russian history and literature, and much extra-mural Russian teaching took place on its premises. People's University lectures were given in the evenings and at weekends, respecting the needs of a working population. No sooner had he arrived than Berdyaev was lecturing almost every evening of the week, including Sundays. The crowded calendar of lectures and talks competed with nightly theatrical performances in Russian, poetry readings, opera and song recitals and exhibitions. Books could be consulted in the extensive Turgenev library, a monument in itself to continuity with the great Russian tradition of the nineteenth century. The collection totalled 100,000 volumes on the eve of the Second World War. Russian Paris would never be the academic centre that Prague was, but unlike Russian Prague it was a cultural presence in the international stream, a place where many more people would come across Russian ideas and Russian art would enter into reciprocal relations with a larger world.[1]

The themes of the Sorbonne Russian lectures on historical-philological subjects were diverse and inviting. In the 1924–5 academic year they included Lev Shestov on Pascal and Dostoevsky and Alexandre Koyré on 'Vladimir Solovyov and his Contemporaries'. In the same week as Konstantin Mochulsky lectured on 'Pushkin and his Pleiad' there was a stage production in Russian of Tolstoy's last novel, *Resurrection*. Osorgin read one of his short stories at a concert-ball arranged by the Union of Russian Students in France on 15 November. The location was central, at the town hall in the 6e arrondissement, Place Saint-Sulpice, and the organizers hoped to attract custom by featuring 'top literary and artistic figures'. In fact the biggest attraction was a writer little known to non-Russian readers, Aleksei Remizov, who had played his part in liberal-conservative enthusiasm for a new Russia after the Revolution but emigrated in good time when he saw the form the Bolshevik state was taking. While Remizov and Osorgin were reading at Place Saint-Sulpice, the Russian Dramatic Theatre was staging an Ostrovsky play, and in yet another venue someone was offering lectures on Tolstoy. More informally, on the fringes of French café society, Nikolai Bakhtin spoke on 'The Crisis in Poetry' at the Brasserie Steinbach, Boulevard Saint-Michel. The brother of the more famous Mikhail, Nikolai Bakhtin would later emigrate to England and teach at the University of Birmingham.

In December, Osorgin read from the Russian original of his future bestseller, *A Quiet Street*, at the Café Voltaire, Place de l'Odéon, and before the end of the month he opened an evening at the Union of Russian Journalists with reminiscences from his journalistic past. Berdyaev meanwhile gave his Religious-Philosophical Academy inaugural lecture on 9 November 1924 at the Salle de l'École des hautes études sociales, 16 rue de la Sorbonne. 'The Religious Sense of the World Crisis' was followed by a panel discussion with Vysheslavtsev, former Provisional government minister A. V. Kartashev, the leading White military figure and monarchist, Prince Grigory Nikolaevich Trubetskoy and others. A week later Berdyaev delivered the first instalment of a systematic course entitled 'Russian Spiritual Tendencies (The History of our Religious and National Awareness)'. Vysheslavtsev followed the next evening with the first lecture in his series on 'Good and Evil in Christian Teaching (The Individual, Society and The State)'. Another lecture on 13 December, followed by a panel discussion of the same experts, was based on a talk by the émigré historian of Russian philosophy Vasily Zenkovsky: 'The Collapse of Belief in Man and the Crisis of Culture'. The following week, just two days after Christmas, Sergei Bulgakov led the panel on the question of 'The Immaculate Church'.

Like Berlin Russia, Russian Paris mapped a dizzying range of cultural activity, taking in every artistic endeavour from naturalism via symbolism to modernism. Peasant socialists in literature and philosophy rubbed shoulders with Marxists and postmodernists in all but name. Russian music could mean anything from Balakirev to Tchaikovsky to the contemporary Cherepnin and Stravinsky, and painting embraced styles from the realism of the Wanderer school (*Peredvizhniki*) to the modernists Sonya Delaunay and Natalya Goncharova. Philosophy spoke with competing enthusiasm for a continued nineteenth-century scientific positivism and a range of East-West mysticisms from Bergson to Berdyaev, Shestov to Sartre and Heidegger. That there were hundreds of Russian painters in Paris alone followed from the Bolshevik ban on abstract art in 1922, the year that freethinking was also banished.[2]

Because the Soviet regime was anti-conservative in politics but disconcertingly and unexpectedly anti-modernist in art, the unwanted Russia that took on a new life in Paris was equally mixed. Where it was radical it developed more freely than in Russia itself, which is to say that artistic modernism on French soil remained in a fertile relationship with the revolutionary political focus on the rights of the worker. The goal of social equality went hand in hand with artistic experiment. At the same time those determined to cling on to an old, hierarchical world fixed by monarch and Church, like Bunin, found renewed strength to make poetry out of memory. The link between the traditional art forms Bunin preferred and the cultural-political beliefs he held was an equal and opposite gesture to what was happening on the left-wing stage, and the two attitudes coexisted. In many ways in a parallel venture to that of the philosophers, Bunin pursued a deliberate old-fashionedness in literature which Stepun endorsed when he called Bunin's writing 'the sacred scripture of Life itself'.[3]

For its social life the old Russia and most of the non-intellectual middle-class emigration tended to converge on the Russian church, the Alexander Nevsky cathedral on rue Daru, behind the Étoile. Russian restaurants opened nearby. The area is still a focus for Russian life in Paris, with a noticeboard crammed with advertisements from new arrivals seeking jobs and accommodation. The radicals preferred to gather in their cafés or round the papers and journals they wrote for; publications which in fact functioned like clubs.

Russian culture in Paris more or less flourished in this diverse form until the war. Yet inevitably with time some conservative causes were lost. Education and the need to find their social place encouraged the rising Russian generation to shed their parents' exclusive Russian allegiance. The contradictions of the Paris intellectual scene were obvious to outsiders. Though a Russian secondary school was created and would continue until 1961, by 1939 nine-tenths of Russian children were receiving a French education. One by one, writers born to Russian parents in Russia – Henri Troyat (b.1911), Joseph Kessel (b.1898), Romain Gary (b.1914) – crossed the cultural divide, changing their names and languages. Their careers were paralleled by two Russsian émigré philosophers who were not on the ships because they emigrated earlier and had effectively become French. Alexander Koyransky (b. 1884) took the name Alexandre Koyré and the much younger Alexander Kozhevnikov (b. 1902) metamorphosed into the École normale instructor and French Finance Ministry diplomat Alexandre Kojève.

The expelled intelligentsia, devoted to retaining Russian thought in traditional Russian forms, found refuge in Paris because the city was large enough to provide multiple opportunities. Nevertheless, despite the welcoming cultural embrace, they had perhaps their hardest task surviving in the French capital because of the peculiarity and exclusiveness of French regulations. Post-war France could absorb large quantities of manual workers but had less room for professionals. Booming industry had to contend with the fact that many French young men had been lost. Many jobs were to be had at the Renault factory in Billancourt – *Bil'yankur* as it came out in Russian – at Citroën and elsewhere. But candidates for the professions had to pass French examinations and take French citizenship.[4] Under these circumstances middle-aged White generals had no alternative but to become taxi-drivers and gardeners – Nabokov wrote about Colonel Taxovich – while the writers and academics, funded by well-wishers, barely scraped by.

Berberova and Khodasevich together, and Tsvetaeva with her young daughter, endured extreme poverty in Paris.[5] Berberova inscribed greetings cards and fourteen-year-old Ala Tsvetaeva knitted bonnets to enable her mother, brother and herself to survive. Even though Berdyaev was the most active and successful of the Russian academics, even ten years after their arrival his wife's diary showed their lives to be a model of frugality, dented only by the generosity they showed to worse-off Russian friends such as Osorgin's wife Rachel. After the couple divorced in 1923, Rachel Ginzburg could not find work, despite a university degree and fluency in several languages. She fared better when in 1935 she emigrated to Palestine.[6] Another beneficiary of the Berdyaevs' charity was a Russian tramp, invited to lunch every day because he was one of them.

Besides Berdyaev, Mikhail Osorgin was one of the few exiles of his generation to make the transition to French culture. He wrote now and again for *Le Figaro*.[7] But family connections cushioned his existence. His third wife came from an already established Russian family, who had settled in France before the Revolution and now ran an old people's home for Russians. The location was a pleasant village about twenty miles outside Paris called St Geneviève-des-Bois, soon to become the site of the most famous cemetery of Russia Abroad. The cemetery would be built on land bequeathed to the Russian community by Berdyaev's English benefactress, Florence West. The Osorgins had one address in the country and another in Paris, although this is not to say that Mikhail ever really exempted himself from the culturally rich but financially unpredictable existence most of his intelligentsia compatriots led.

Their material situation was made worse by the 1929 Depression which also hit Russian workers. The extent of the Depression probably explains the financial clamour which surrounded the passing international success of Osorgin and even more of Bunin in the early 1930s. When Bunin won the Nobel Prize for Literature in 1933 he set up a 100,000 French francs fund with his prize money to help fellow émigré writers. In addition he was bombarded with requests from Russians he had never met for money to buy, amongst other things, a new flat or a set of false teeth.[8] They presumed upon the legendary Russian sense of community and Bunin, mostly out of weakness of character, was unable to refuse them. According to his biographer he was the first Nobel laureate to die in poverty, as well as being the first prizewinner without a country. For a short time, when *A Quiet Street* became a National Bookclub selection in America in 1931, Osorgin too enjoyed a period in the black. But like Bunin he responded to appeals for charity and soon reduced himself to his usual straitened circumstances.[9]

In the absence of sudden boosts of good fortune the Russian writers in Paris lived on limited fees received for articles, stories, talks and so on, and the Russian academics existed similarly. Astonishingly prolific between the wars, the Russian press in Paris was large enough to support many of them at a basic level. The daily *Poslednie novosti* ('The Latest News') had been founded by the first wave of émigrés in 1920 with the republican Milyukov as its editor. Of the same high quality as 'The Rudder' in Berlin, 'The Latest News' published, amongst the figures whose fates have been followed in this book, Kuskova, Myakotin, Petrishchev, Prokopovich, Berberova, Bunin, Sirin-Nabokov, Osorgin and Khodasevich. In the 1930s its circulation reached 30,000. From 1925 right-wing competition came from the alternative Paris Russian daily *Vozrozhdenie* ('Rebirth'), a monarchist paper edited first by Pyotr Struve and after 1927 by Yury Semenov. Khodasevich and Berberova ran the literary pages and Ilyin contributed to the political section. The ubiquitous Osorgin and Khodasevich also wrote for Kerensky's 'The Days' when it transferred from Berlin in 1925 and lasted another seven years in Paris.[10]

When the ousted intelligentsia were not writing to order to survive, what mattered to them was the maintenance of journals to perpetuate Russian high culture. *Sovremennye Zapiski*, created in 1920 in the tradition of the 'thick' journal in which the classic nineteenth-century writers published, ran to seventy volumes before it was closed down by the German invasion in 1940. The name, meaning 'Contemporary Notes', was an amalgam of the two most famous nineteenth-century Russian literary journals.[11] Founded with Czech money and appearing three or four times a year, it defined itself as a socio-political and literary journal publishing the best writers of Russia Abroad.[12] Vysheslavtsev, Zamyatin, Osorgin, Sirin-Nabokov, Stepun, Khodasevich, Berdyaev, Kizevetter and Kuskova all appeared there at some time. The chief philosophical journal meanwhile was Berdyaev's own highly successful *Put* ('The Way').

Officially 'The Way' was the organ of the Philosophical-Religious Academy. It concerned itself with the development of the Russian Church abroad but it had wide horizons in religious and cultural matters and is now an interesting record of the times. With a title carried over from the pre-revolutionary world, it defined its purpose in a mission statement ahead of the first issue:

> 'The Way' is an organ of Russian Orthodox thought. It aims to follow the tradition associated with the names of Khomiakov, Dostoevsky and Solovyov and it believes in the possibility of a creative development within Orthodoxy. The catastrophe which has taken place in Russia, the crisis which has gripped the whole world, changes the position of the Christian Churches and places a new responsibility on Orthodoxy. The journal 'The Way' will try to give answers to these new creative questions. At the same time it will acquaint Russians with new spiritual-intellectual tendencies in Europe and with the life and thought of other Christian faiths.[13]

'The Way' published nearly all the philosophers shipped out by Lenin: Berdyaev, Lossky, Bulgakov, Frank, Ilyin, Vysheslavtsev, Karsavin and Stepun.

'The Way' was financed by the Paris-based YMCA press, which played a major role publishing Russia Abroad before the war and went on to support dissident writers throughout the Soviet period. After it was founded in Prague in 1921, it transferred to Paris in 1924. Its early funds came from the American Young Men's Christian Association, which began its European activities by providing text-books and mainly religious reading matter for prisoners of war. The subsidy for *Put* lasted until mid-1936.[14]

The significance of American charity can't be overestimated in the functioning of Russia Abroad once it was concentrated in France. It helped to keep the ousted conservative community alive, gave it the means to publish its thoughts and in its general role prefigured the division of the world after the Second World War. America did not recognize the Soviet Union until 1934, and only then because of the rise of Hitler. Through the 1920s and early 1930s the stand-off between America and Russia took the form of a struggle, government-sponsored on both sides, between Christianity and atheism, and between liberty and tyranny. The basis for this stand-off was integral to everything the Russian religious philosophers believed in. As Bulgakov put it in a book written in 1935:

> Orthodoxy can only have a negative attitude towards the Russian communism of today; in spite of certain social achievements communism does tyrannical violence to personal liberty; it is a direct denial of personality...[15]

But undeniably, because of Lenin and the Revolution, the Christian faith itself had acquired a political edge, and so it was Christianity which pre-war America sponsored.

Many of the contributors to 'The Way' were on the staff of the Orthodox Theological Institute of St Sergius. The Christian face of the journal was paramount, and one of the roles 'The Way' took upon itself was to modernize the Russian Church and to encourage in the up-and-coming priesthood an intellectual resistance to Bolshevism and an openness to dialogue with other faiths. A major problem was the fact that the Church in exile under political pressure was in as much disarray as the Church in Russia. As a result Russian Paris became an ecclesiastical battleground.

The Orthodox Church had a history of collaboration with the state which it had only begun to rebel against when the Soviet regime took over. In exile, principally in Czechoslovakia, Serbia and France, it was riven by its own conservative and progressive factions. The issue of political affinity was forced to a head when Patriarch Tikhon, debilitated by the year he spent in prison and subsequently worn down by the GPU, died in 1925. His successor in Moscow, Metropolitan Sergei, was compelled to subordinate his church to the Soviet authorities and to call upon the Church abroad to recognize the jurisdiction of the Moscow Patriarchate. The ecclesiastical drama of 1926–8 was a drive towards intensified monological control under Stalin. One ought not to be surprised, but it is nevertheless astonishing how closely the battles within the Russian Church, both in Russia and Russia Abroad, replicated those of the Soviet Communist Party, as it ousted first Trotsky then Zinoviev.[16] The core of the drama pitched resistance to totalitarian pressure against the need for meaningful Russian community. It was the perennial Russian problem, heightened by the new era of Soviet repression, and now its ecclesiastical version was played out on the pages of 'The Way'.

In the Orthodox Church drama the bishopric of Karlovac in Serbia broke with both Moscow and Paris. The Paris episcopate eventually aligned itself with Constantinople, but meanwhile congregations of every kind established themselves in the French capital, together with their respective churches.[17] Unusually perhaps, Vladimir Lossky, now a theologian, favoured ties with Moscow, but this was more than Berdyaev, Vysheslavtsev and Bulgakov, on the Paris ecclesiastical left, could accept. Rebelling against both Moscow and Karlovac, they formed their idea of the modern church as one which could give the younger Russian generation guidance. It would need to be open to other faiths and less authoritarian. As church politics replayed the secular political events of 1922 the Karlovac patriarchy excommunicated Bulgakov for heresy.

The name of Vysheslavtsev is still hardly known in the West, but he played an important part in the Russian Orthodox world centred on Paris. A compelling writer and an influential religious personality within the small circle of those who knew him, he was Berdyaev's deputy at 'The Way', and also taught ethics at the St Sergius Theological Institute. Yet another of his jobs was deputy director of the YMCA press. His work led him to reflect on the Russian religious-philosophical tradition and the 'Russian Idea' and he wrote about it with brevity and clarity, explaining for instance how 'the Russian truth' had to be religious because the truth of philosophy could not be interpreted by Russians in a purely intellectual way. 'Russian truth' had to be felt and intuited, and, even in the age of Einstein, its goal was the Absolute. Much of Vysheslavtsev's message overlapped with that of Berdyaev and Frank, but what stood out was his excellent style coupled with a rather modern interest in psychoanalysis. With a deeper interest in Freud than most of his contemporaries, Vysheslavtsev wrote enlighteningly about Russia:

Psychoanalysis clarifed a great deal about the Russian way of philosophizing: the collective unconscious of the Russian people lies, as it were, closer to the surface of consciousness; it is not so displaced from consciousness, not so worked over by consciousness as in the West. We are a younger, more barbaric nation and thus, to be sure, more like philosophical apprentices. Yet a little something may be learned from us. Otherwise the Western interest in Dostoevsky, Tolstoy, even in Chekhov and Leskov, would be incomprehensible.[18]

What Vysheslavtsev grasped, unfortunately without taking the idea further, was why the Russian psyche, as it erupted into politics and worship alike, was passionate, querulous, immoderate and 'barbaric', and yet still expressed the deepest human truths as they are illuminated by the need for love and the propensity for conflict.

A Russian concept to which Vysheslavtsev returned over and over was of the 'person' of Russian religious thought as opposed to the 'individual' of Western philosophy. The idea of the person was designed to safeguard the dignity and integrity of individual souls whilst avoiding the assertive subjectivity of Western individualism. The need to safeguard the individual led Vysheslavtsev to see clearly what was wrong morally with Marx.

Marxism moralizes in its exposure of 'exploitation' while simultaneously being immoral in its social and political practice. Moral protest makes an appearance in order to provide a basis for and justify hatred, only to vanish again so as not to interfere with the workings of that hatred.

Why didn't Marx deepen his concept of 'exploitation' and realize that it is based on an admission of the value of the person as an end in himself. Because the idea of the person is essentially Christian in origin and bound up with an ethic of love, Marx found all that repulsive and antipathetic. What he needed was an ethic of hate. Positive values were unnecessary and dangerous for him. They could lead him to the 'sacred' and force him to bow down before it. He needed a negative value to underpin hatred and negation, and he found it in exploitation.[19]

With their Russian personalism, Vysheslavtsev and his colleagues strengthened the value of a liberty rooted in Christian responsibility. That was what, pre-1936, American charity supported in 'The Way' and Berdyaev's Religious-Philosophical Academy. The Russian philosophers cultivated what would become after the 1939–45 war the politics of human rights, but they did so in a religious rather than a legal framework.

Bulgakov's chief achievement was within the Church. His 'sophiology', a fresh exposition of Orthodox teaching, responded to the threat of the Russian Church's homelessness.

> At the present time, historical Orthodoxy is passing through a crisis. Its enemies see in this crisis death and destruction but we Orthodox should see in it the beginning of a new era. This crisis is connected with the Russian Revolution, with the fall of the Russian Orthodox empire...[20]

For Bulgakov the Revolution of 1917 was an event equal to the sack of Constantinople by the Turks. He had to fight back. But sophiology was also proposed as a response to the atheism sweeping Russia and the West alike. In 1934 Bulgakov travelled to America, lecturing on 'the curse of secularization' but also delivering the broad Christian socialist message of 'social Christianity or Christian humanism'. The message was liberty in a hierarchy of spiritual, not secular, values.[21] He was loved in America and loved and revered in the Russian community abroad.

The message of social Christianity or Christian humanism spread by Lenin's ousted idealists was decent and genuine. It was what they preached and how they lived. They acquired a role in the West, as well as in Russia Abroad, because their aim was much wider than the defeat of Communism. Berdyaev found common ground with French Catholics between the wars, while his wife, herself a Catholic, set down in her diary the kind of modern world she would like to see flourish everywhere. She wrote, for instance, on 27 October 1934 of her consternation that in such a beautiful free country as France people could live in poverty. There seemed to be rich and poor whatever political system was practised, which made her wonder if spiritual values – which would bring with them fairness and restraint – would ever triumph over worldliness. She wanted to see the religious outlook triumph and she feared that if religion disappeared then nothing would prevent society becoming just a brutal contest of strength.

In general, Nikolai Berdyaev felt very well in Paris. The couple lived in the hilly, southern, then working-class suburb of Clamart, where they rented and eventually received a house as a gift from the religious-minded Florence West. 'I am very much attached to my study in the Clamart house, with its windows opening on to the garden and its library, which I managed to collect in the course of my years of exile,' Berdyaev wrote.[22] Vysheslavtsev commented, with just a hint of acid: 'In a nice private house, Yasnaya Polyana, lives a Russian *barin*, afraid of draughts, who likes to practise philosophy and has decided to become a prophet and has achieved success in this area.'[23] With occasional breaks to visit the local cinema, Berdyaev worked extraordinarily hard, riding into central Paris several evenings a week to give lectures to upwards of a hundred people, on such topics as 'Bakunin and Herzen' and 'Dostoevsky and Solovyov'. The couple kept up their tradition of open house and hosted many discussions among French and Russian friends over Sunday tea. On one such occasion, in November 1934, the Catholic thinker Jacques Maritain and his Russian wife Raisa, the Catholic philosopher Gabriel Marcel, the Russian philosopher Lev Shestov, Yelena Izvolskaya, daughter of the last tsarist ambassador to France, and 'a young Dutchman with a letter from Remizov' foregathered in the Berdyaevs' inviting little house. Tsvetaeva who lived nearby came and read her poems.[24]

But they were not well off. Until the Popular Front government of socialist Prime Minister Léon Blum was elected in 1936 the economic times were especially difficult for the Russians in France because foreigners were not entitled to social benefits. Part of Lidiya's diary was given over to a routine complaint about the French state being increasingly inhospitable. And yet, 'after what we suffered in Russia for five years I'm not afraid of anything'. Lidiya devoted her life to charity. She became a hospital visitor and and sent food parcels to Russia. She remembered that it was the suffering she noticed when she was a child that made her grow up a Populist, a Christian and a revolutionary in tsarist Russia, and determined her life.

In their two decades together in Clamart, the Berdyaevs discussed many political, ethical and religious issues together and with their friends. One of the most interesting was the question of Eurasianism, which became a new way of looking at Russian history and Russia's place in the world. Like 'Change of Landmarks', Eurasianism suggested a way in which the exiles could accommodate Soviet Russia. It was a movement, and a set of ideas, which responded to and embraced all the dangers of the period, including the rise of Hitler and what began to seem to many at the time the more attractive world of Stalin's Russia. It tried to invent the idea of a non-Western but Christian civilization centred on Russia – but it needed to be treated with caution.

The movement began in Prague in 1921 when an émigré called Pyotr Savitsky responded to the ideas of Roman Jakobson's friend and colleague, Nikolai Trubetskoy. Trubetskoy, cousin of the Prince of the same name who sailed from Russia on the *Haken*, was at the time teaching Russian literature in Sofia. He and Savitsky contributed essays to a book called *Izkhod k vostoku*. The title, which meant both 'Exodus to the East' and 'Solution to the East', was as ambiguous as the movement itself.[25]

Eurasianism asserted Russia's non-Western essence and unique geo-cultural position. The geography of Eurasia was roughly that of the Russian Empire before 1914, including the Baltic States in the West and Central Asia in the East. The basis of cultural unity was not racial – neither Russian nor pan-Slav – but a matter of envisaging Eurasia as a unique, economically self-sufficient continent dominated by Russia.

With a confidence based on the recent history of the Russian Empire, Savitsky wrote of Orthodox-Muslim and Orthodox-Buddhist cultures playing their part in the Eurasian whole. (His prediction was fulfilled when Russia's guiding 'Orthodox' hand became the Soviet Communist hand. A comparison of what Eurasianism envisaged and what the Soviet Union became suggests it could have developed along similar lines without adopting a veneer of Marxism at all.)[26] Trubetskoy matched his vision of what in practice the Soviet Union largely became with a fierce ideological thrust against Eurocentrism.

One of the most interesting features of Eurasianism was its anti-Westernism. The impulse to confine 'the West' qua Europe to the dustbin of history had been strong in Russia throughout the nineteenth century and anticipated the West's sense of its own downfall at the beginning of the twentieth century. When it emerged in new packaging in the 1920s, therefore, Eurasianism had the name of Spengler's *Decline of the West* written all over it. Like Spengler the Eurasians looked to a changed balance of global power. They predicted that Russia and America, but not Europe, would play the major parts in the twentieth century order.

The new movement required Russia to adopt a non-Western conception of itself and thus find a greatness that way. It should disdain 'Romano-Germanic ethnocentricity' and Western claims to speak for universal humanity. Eurasianism's anti-Western project made novel sense of the Revolution. Trubetskoy saw 1917 as Western-influenced Russia's moment of self-destruction, prior to a new Eurasian start. He said that measuring itself against Europe had always been detrimental to Russia and produced derogatory notions of Russian backwardness and imitativeness. Eurasianism's rethinking of Russia's achievement would underscore its uniqueness and strength.

Because Eurasianism would change the balance of the world, Savitsky claimed that the Russian Revolution was not just a Russian event, nor just a European one, but a moment of global shift. 'After the Bolshevik Revolution Russia in a certain sense becomes the ideological centre-point of the world.'[27]

Berdyaev said Eurasianism was 'the only post-revolutionary intellectual movement to arise out of the émigré milieu', a description which has been subsequently endorsed by historians. One reason why its promptings could be taken seriously was the scholarly programme it proposed: a different way of seeing Russian history, economics, culture and so on. Eurasianism gave émigré scholars a reason to exist and defined projects they could work on from abroad. Marc Raeff has stressed how difficult it was for exiled historians to continue their work without access to sources in Russia.[28] The problem of sources did not apply to philosophers, theologians, economists and scientists, and arguably not to writers either, but what the Revolution meant mattered to all of them. If they could understand their fate and work on it as the fate of modern civilization, then they would have a boundless new subject to explore. The emotional and psychological appeal of Eurasianism landed a rich catch of émigrés and exiles in its net, though almost as many jumped out again, including, eventually, Trubetskoy himself and Jakobson.

The problem with Eurasianism was the incitement it gave to political extremism, the last thing the liberal exiles wanted to encourage. It is in this sense that it has been labelled a fascist movement. Most interesting, I think, was the way it made the Russian post-revolutionary shock its starting-point, because this set up a parallel with the German inter-war problem, as historians would later analyse it. Trying to understand how Nazism grew out of the unhappiness of Germany's devastated, deposed capital after the First World War, Golo Mann wrote forty years ago:

> By its very existence Berlin raised the question of how an
> undisciplined society, estranged from its own past, should live.
> We all have base instincts only too easily exploited for business or
> political profit. The time was to come when the stimulation of
> sensationalism and hate would overcome all counter elements,
> destroy the old system and on its ruins establish an authority which,
> while originating in the masses, loathed humanity. Of all the great

scholars who in the twenties had concerned themselves with the problems of society, no one had predicted this.[29]

No one predicted the German situation, but in the case of Eurasianism many in the Russian emigration saw that it was potentially exploiting 'base instincts'. They were immediately on the alert against crypto-Nazi excesses. 'Contemporary Notes' published ten articles on the new ideology and 'The Way' returned again and again to the subject. Not the least hurdle raised by the elevation of the October Revolution to universal significance was that the event and its violence, which equally produced 'an undisciplined society, estranged from its own past', was justified in the Eurasian outlook by a kind of Hegelian-Spenglerian necessity. Russia had a unique task and the Bolsheviks had played a useful role in revealing it. As one liberal critic after another rose up in rebellion against these views, one compared Trubetskoy furiously to Lenin while another identified in Eurasianism a school of scholarship designed to return Russia to the Middle Ages.

The Soviets were keen to encourage Eurasianism in any way they could, which eventually produced a backlash. The Paris left-Eurasians pitched themselves against the right-wing in Prague. Nikolai Trubetskoy became strikingly pro-Soviet, while Berdyaev steered a neither/nor course characteristically of his own. He wisely discouraged all speculation on building a perfect world. That wasn't a job for human beings, he said.

The best critics of the new ideology kept their eyes on how much was at stake in Eurasianism for the future of mankind, not just for Russia, with its destructive quest for self-definition.[30] Kizevetter denounced the Eurasians for their cultural relativism. Izgoev considered an abyss lay between him and the Eurasians.[31] Berdyaev in 'The Way's' first number also pounced on the lack of universalism, the hatred of Catholicism and the misuse of Orthodoxy. But his overall point was the most important. It was that the emotions and the activity, rather than the reasoning that Eurasianism was stirring in young émigrés, raised the danger that the movement would turn into a 'Russian fascism'.[32]

Eurasianism rejected all forms of Western parliamentarianism as unsuitable to the Russian-Eurasian essence. It disliked socialism, cosmopolitanism and internationalism. Berdyaev, with his hopes of a spiritual Russia raised above the politics of left and right, began to notice unhappy references all around him to 'foreigner' and 'alien' and growing nationalisms and by that route identified Eurasianism with the worst developments in Europe of the late 1920s and after. The sting in the tail of the story of Eurasianism, however, was that it pushed Berdyaev, like many Westerners on the left, to side with Marxism because it was an international movement.

For all his irritating knowingness Berdyaev was never a man to avoid or deny inevitable contradictions. He summed up:

> [The Eurasians] were in tune with the events and tendencies inside
> Russia…for them Russia was to be re-created in relation to the far-
> reaching spiritual, social and political changes brought about by the
> Revolution. This had a considerable appeal to me…[but] they
> showed too little appreciation of freedom. Neither could I identify
> myself with their extreme 'Asiatic' nationalism and with their
> interpretation of Russia as a cultural world wholly apart from and
> standing over against the West. I was also not happy about their
> rather deliberate and pious churchmanship [and] I was equally
> apprehensive of the importance they attached to the state.[33]

A factor that lurked behind much of the discussion, and which in Marxist disguise also underpinned the Soviet outlook, was the nineteenth-century idea of Russian culture's *vsechelovechestvo*. The word meant Russia's 'capacity to embrace and express all humanity' by pursuing *its own* self-understanding. It was the tendency to see 'universalism as a specifically Russian quality'. The fact that not only Dostoevsky championed it but also Berdyaev and even Lossky shows that if it was politically dangerous in its paradoxical Eurasian form, the idea was nevertheless difficult to give up culturally, for it summed up all that was felt about the superiority of the 'Russian Idea'. It was of course also dangerous in its Soviet form, and here once again was one of those instances of a phenomenon in Soviet Russia finding a *Doppelgänger* in Russia Abroad. Whereas the Soviets adopted 'Russia's capacity to embrace and express all humanity' in a left-wing, Marxist guise, some of the exiles adopted it in a right-wing ecclesiastical form where it looked ugly but did less harm.

The only exception was the case of the shipped philosopher Lev Karsavin, whose life it would eventually destroy. Though he was not in the first rank, Karsavin contributed to Eurasian journals in Paris and when he too moved to Clamart in 1926 his home became the headquarters of Eurasianism.[34] Karsavin sided with the religious right which believed itself above politics, at the same time as he drew political conclusions from Eurasianism's severe doctrines. As one of his colleagues expressed their vision for Russia: 'The future of [post-Communist] Russia belongs to a lawful Orthodox state, which will be able to combine unshakeable power (the principle of dictatorship) with the people's self-government (the principle of freemen) and service to social justice.'[35] Eurasianism expressed the kind of society Soviet Russia truly was, with the sole difference that in place of the 'lawful' Orthodox Church stood the law-giving Communist Party.

For Karsavin, whom the Revolution turned into a passionate Orthodox believer and scholar, it was a great temptation to believe in a Russia regenerated by religion, and leading the world in that capacity.[36] The Eurasian vision gave his own historical experience meaning and showed a way forward for Russia at large. The argument went that an entire old world had collapsed, not just in Russia, and that with the new dawn visible in the East, the Bolshevik Revolution cleared the way for a Greater Russia to emerge as the dominant world culture.

Karsavin struck others as a man of vacillating views, at the same time as he was untethered and recalcitrant.[37] In Berlin when the first book he published was a study of Giordano Bruno, the sixteenth-century Italian philosopher who was burned at the stake for heresy, the degree of personal association was evident. Karsavin had the autobiographical impulse of a personality that longed to confess and be affirmed by the outside world. He had even fictionalized the end of his affair with Yelena while it was still flourishing. In Paris, where he had a large family to support and no real job, his money problems played on his weaknesses. Like Nabokov in both cases, he looked good, and tried to earn something as a film extra.[38] He was vain and circumstances made him trivial. The émigré writer Don Aminado recalled him making a fuss when a newspaper published a photograph of him bearded after he had become clean-shaven and how they responded by asking whether he wanted an apology in print.[39]

Karsavin's position in Paris went from bad to worse when he failed to get a job at the Theological Institute because he came over as a 'heresiarch' – the leader or founder of a heresy, presumably Eurasianism. He struck the panel as a man full of ambiguity and artificiality.[40] His political ideals were predicated on the fact that he loved culture more than he loved freedom. He would have approved of Nietzsche's admiration for Renaissance despotism, for as Nietzsche said, at least despotism ensured the architecture of a city was all of a piece, not democratically chosen and messy. An affinity has also been suggested between Karsavin and the extreme but gripping conservative Joseph de Maistre.[41]

Karsavin must have been tempted by the money available for Eurasian thought when no other source of income presented itself. An English philanthropist, Henry Spalding, offered £10,000 to fund Eurasian enterprises, a huge sum at the time. (The price of a Remington typewriter was about 26 shillings, with twenty shillings to the pound.) Karsavin saw his book *Tserkov', lichnost i gosudarstvo* ('Church, Personality and State') appear under the Eurasian imprint in 1927 and he continued to work for the journal *Versty*, the lifespan of which, 1926–8, lasted as long as Spalding's endowment.[42]

When Eurasianism lost its funding, he could no longer survive in Paris but was able to secure a chair at the university in Kaunas, Lithuania's second city, and he moved there with his family the same year, 1928. He learned Lithuanian and for the next ten years taught a much-admired course in the history of European culture, drawing on his extensive knowledge of medieval France and Italy, and of the Renaissance. He was an expert on art history and knew many languages. In his first Lithuanian years he produced a book of religious-cultural thought and, pursuing his parallel belletristic career, an idiosyncratic book-length poem on death. His lectures were also published in their entirety in Lithuanian. But his life was doomed to founder on the contradictions inherent in his Eurasianism.

It is a remarkable truth that emerges from the history of its ideas and the histories of its individual members that, despite Lenin's action in 1922, the twentieth-century Russian intelligentsia could not be split. The painful reality was that thinking, feeling Russia was one entity in two places: home and abroad. Because Russia Abroad was entirely formed by its awareness of the other Russia left behind it became by far the more traumatized of two unhappy twins split at birth. Unable to accept the forced break with Russia, many of the exiles and émigrés suffered nightmares of disinheritance and dangerous thoughts of reconciliation and self-sacrifice. A striking feature of memoirs and stories from between the wars is the recurrent sense of Soviet Russia and Russia Abroad as always aware of the other and thinking similar thoughts, whether or not they were actively watching over or intervening in each other's lives.

In *Pravda* some time in April 1935, Berdyaev was amused to read that he was a 'White guard'. In December, Lidiya recorded how they then pored over a copy of *Izvestiya*, which had a long feuilleton article by the Bolshevik theorist Nikolai Bukharin devoted to Berdyaev's *The Fate of Man in the Modern World*, while on the other side of the looking-glass Nadezhda Mandelstam wrote that she and Osip had heard that Berdyaev's thinking had matured in exile and 'Mandelstam was always asking about him'.[43] In official circles around Stalin, Soviet Russians read the émigré press to know what 'they' thought of 'us'.[44] Soviet libraries kept copies of émigré journals like 'The Way' in special restricted collections. And, if their editors were clever, even apparently critical articles in newspapers could actually inform the Soviet public about Russia Abroad.

But bonds between the two sides went deeper than consciousness, because what the exiles felt about their homeland went far beyond curiosity. Bunin dreamed he received a postcard with Stalin's signature.[45] Berberova dreamed of a coffin going home to St Petersburg.[46] Nabokov's story, 'The Visit to the Museum', showed a man opening door after door in a provincial French museum until finally he found himself back on a Moscow street where it was snowing. These tales were signs of a twisted and troubled psychological reality among the émigrés.

At the same time there was a real basis for feeling unsafe. The French capital had a strong Soviet secret police presence. Many felt they were living in Soviet times, and were subject to the whims of tyranny, whether or not they dwelt beyond Russian borders. As one member of the community observed:

> Those who have not lived under the Soviet regime must find it hard to imagine the psychology of persons who left that paradise during the first decade of the new order... but at that time nobody who had previously belonged to the old Russia could be sure of his life and well-being, right down to the last minute of his existence. A careless word... a sharp knock at the door... A carelessly written letter. We could not shake off our instinctive reaction of fear.[47]

When faced in the cold light of day this fear remained particularly pronounced in those who still had family in the Soviet Union, against whom reprisals could be exacted. It was why Aikhenvald wrote under a pseudonym when contributing political articles to the Baltic Russian press.[48] Though many Russians lived for more than twenty years in France, the atmosphere of ordinary freedom that the French knew was something they could never assimilate.[49]

Through the 1920s those mentally still fighting the Civil War heightened the tension for the rest. If von Lampe, the White general who was otherwise quietly documenting the emigration in a way that would be invaluable to historians, was one who could be blamed for creating conspiracy fever, so was one of Lenin's shipped exiles about whom little is known, I. I. Lodyzhensky. Having settled in Geneva, Lodyzhensky was in correspondence with von Lampe and played an active part in organizing the remnants of military resistance.[50] The White move responded to, or provoked, a mirror move by the Politburo on the other side. The Soviet leadership instructed the GPU, now renamed for a second time the OGPU, 'to organize the disintegration of the White Guard emigration and to use some of them in the interests of the Soviet regime'.[51] Soviet tactics included targeting specific journals for infiltration. According to one source this was when the top Bolshevik agent in Paris, Georgy Piatakov, met Karsavin to investigate his Eurasian views.[52]

The French found that the Russian émigrés behaved oddly, and who could blame them? They brought a strange cloak-and-dagger world with them. This was not an explanation of why a deranged émigré assassinated the French President, Paul Doumer, in 1932, a deed which appalled both the French and the Russian community. But nor did this sensational event help the popular image of Russia Abroad. Meanwhile, in the 1930s, Stalin raised the stakes in the battle with the émigrés and provided a spectacle to make France gape. The details read like a *roman policier*. One day the head of Lodyzhensky's and von Lampe's White military organization ROVS, General Miller, was abducted from the streets of Paris and bundled on to a Soviet warship anchored off Le Havre. The crime, which Nabokov immortalized in a story called 'The Assistant Producer', seemed all the more daring for virtually repeating the kidnap of Miller's predecessor, General Kutepov, seven years earlier.

Another scandal broke out within the Russian community when two of its members had to escape to Russia after committing a murder in Switzerland on behalf of the Soviet police. One was Tsvetaeva's husband Sergei Efron, a co-editor of Eurasian journals with Karsavin. The other was Nikolai Klepinin, a colleague of Vysheslavtsev at the YMCA press. Both were shot in Moscow's Lefortovo prison in 1941. This second drama reflected the unacceptable separation that plagued so many Russian psyches. The historian of the emigration, Nikita

Struve, suggests that Eurasianism was a way out for those ousted Russians who could not bear to live 'outside history' in that non-country called Russia Abroad. They hurled themselves back in and paid the ultimate price.[53] Berdyaev worried for the rootless new generation of Russians growing up abroad, prone to these temptations. 'Life among the émigrés came to be dominated by every kind of reaction, by obscurantism, clericalism, authoritarianism, servility and the rest.'[54]

Non-violent, moderate Russians Abroad took refuge in their classical culture, their last home from home, but even that culture worship became tinged with mania, as when a centenary edition of Pushkin was printed on Bible paper bound in leather. Pushkin was Russia Abroad's patron saint of freedom, but did he really have a political public worthy of him? Nabokov, Stepun, Kizevetter, Vysheslavtsev, Aikhenvald, Bulgakov, Berdyaev and Frank, Yasinsky and Ilyin all stepped forward to praise him, even while the souvenir culture created a 'very critical, nervous and uneven bond between people who, during fifteen years, travelled life's road together'. Berberova despaired of

> the banquet of *Poslednie novosti*, the fifth or tenth anniversary of the newspaper, the thousandth number, the five thousandth; Bunin's Nobel Prize, its celebration in the Théâtre des Champs-Elysées … meetings of the newspaper 'The Days' … [and] the banquet of 'Contemporary Notes', to which several hundred people were invited, on 20 November 1932, on the publication of the magazine's fiftieth issue … [It] left a rather sad impression in me of the concentrated but airless space in which we lived, the artificial union at these dinner tables of people who for the most part had not managed to and did not want to change, compromise or unite, and did not even know if this was necessary…[55]

She left Khodasevich a few years before the war, and longed to get out of a community made hateful by its shabbiness and its wretchedness and its insularity.[56] The 1939–45 conflict, about which she wrote memorably, delayed her escape, and prolonged the agony, but still she was relatively young. There was time for another life, whereas for many of the passengers on the Philosophy Steamer the passing of the years and the arrival of yet another European catastrophe this time truly spelt the end.

10

Ending Up

D URING THE 1930s leading exiles died or reached the effective end of their lives. Of the six who died in Prague before 1939, Stratonov commited suicide.[1] The reason why is not known, but clearly many elderly Russians more or less isolated abroad faced poverty and loneliness. Volkovysky commented on Yasinsky's last days, still at the helm of the RNI in Berlin in 1933, that 'He was a thoroughly lonely person about to be swallowed up in the hundreds of graves of a dying Russian Berlin.'[2] When Izgoev died in the Estonian town of Haapsalu Volkovysky also wrote a tribute, while their old colleague Khariton mourned 'a knight without fear and beyond reproach'.[3]

Natural deaths were only to be expected, but the rise of Hitler was not. Nazism brought new difficulties for men who were already exiles from one tyrant and were about to be pursued by another. Volkovysky, 'son of Moses', moved from Berlin in 1933, citing Hitler as the reason, and thinking he would be safe in Warsaw.[4] Of the other Jews among Lenin's exiles in Berlin, Brutskus left safely for Palestine in 1935, but Iosif Matusevich, the painter-journalist whose one Berlin exhibition was reviewed for 'The Rudder' by Nabokov, did not. He was arrested by the Nazis in 1938 and is presumed to have died some time after 1940.[5] Stepun was not Jewish but, suspect to the Nazis as a Russian, he was removed from his chair at the Dresden polytechnical institute in 1937. His eviction from his job was, as he observed, 'on remarkably similar grounds as the Bolshevik ousting of its unwanted intellectuals'.

He refused to think and teach in the National Socialist racist spirit. When Stepun went to visit Berdyaev in Clamart for what was to be their last meeting, they discussed 'Hitler and the night that hung over humanity'.[6]

During the war Stepun remained in Dresden, lecturing and enduring as best he could. He lost all his possessions in the Allied bombing. After the war the German government, unlike the Russian, keen to make amends, created a new replica chair for Stepun at the University of Munich, where he remained until his (natural) death. Stepun, like Berdyaev, was relatively lucky to survive two instances in his life of totalitarian persecution.

The Franks left Berlin in 1938–9. Semyon went ahead to Paris, followed by Tatyana, while the children left for England. Victor remained in Berlin the longest, until the German police wanted to expel him as a Soviet citizen back to the Soviet Union. The exiles had only been issued with Soviet passports and he had not applied for any other nationality. In danger of his life, Victor was rescued by friends, principally the historian Bernard Sumner, who enabled him to become a doctoral student in Oxford.[7] Almost as soon as the BBC Monitoring Service was created, in summer 1939, Victor joined as a Russian expert, which exempted him from military service, unlike his brother Aleksei, a year younger. Aleksei Frank would be called up in the war, receive his commission and suffer from his wounds for fifteen years before he died of them. Natalya's English husband was also killed in 1943.

In many ways the Franks were lucky to survive as well as they did. The Czechoslovak presidency continued to give them and the Losskys occasional support. Frank received the money even though he was not resident in Czechoslovakia.[8] Semyon was Jewish by blood, but he and Tatyana saw out the war in semi-hiding in the south of France and the family was subsequently reunited in London for Semyon's remaining years.

When war broke out, the first shock for many Russians abroad was the Molotov–Ribbentrop pact between Russia and Hitler.[9] Many feared Hitler and Stalin in equal measure, and could never understand why the West was soft on Stalin. Others, notably Merezhkovsky and Ilyin, had looked to Hitler as the last possible hope for destroying Soviet power.[10] In a letter to Hitler in 1934, Ilyin appealed to the Führer to deliver the world from both Bolshevism and Mammon. An implacable enemy of totalitarian systems of any description, who evidently misjudged Hitler in his first year in power, Ilyin later came under constant surveillance by the Gestapo. In 1938 he escaped to Switzerland with financial help from the composer Sergei Rakhmaninov.[11]

Before France was occupied in June 1940 the Nabokovs, who had no interest in Hitler's redemptive powers, all the more so as Vera Nabokov was Jewish, just managed to escape with visas for the United States, praying that their sick son wouldn't die on the way.[12] When the Nazis arrived in Paris, Alexander Ugrimov, aged seventy, joined the French Resistance.[13] Boris Lossky was called up into the French Army. Vladimir Lossky, by now also a French citizen married to a Jewish émigré, spent the war in hiding with his family in a Catholic convent. Andrei Lossky, a US citizen, entered the war on the American side.

In Czechoslovakia, where the Lossky parents Nikolai and Lyudmila still lived, and in neighbouring Poland, the Jews among the Russian exiles faced the worst problems. Jakobson left Brno before the Germans arrived, in great bitterness at losing yet another homeland. He went to Sweden via Vienna and from there to the United States. The previous year he had lost his friend Nikolai Trubetskoy, who suffered a heart attack after being searched by the Germans in Vienna. Jakobson called these years the worst in his life and an Italian writer who interviewed him in 1968 began his article with the observation that here was a man who had suffered.[14] From occupied Prague, meanwhile, Alexander Izyumov was sent in 1941 to a concentration camp, while from Warsaw, Volkovysky, on the run in the direction of the Soviet Union, disappeared in Ukraine. The last sighting of him was in 1941.[15] The Russian Jews who lived in Riga would surely also have fallen victim to the Nazis if the Red Army had not arrived first and despatched them to the Gulag. Khariton, one of the editors of 'Today', died en route, also in 1941, and a similar fate befell Pumpyansky in Tallinn.[16]

In occupied Prague Nikolai Lossky remembered coming out of a seminar on 17 November 1939 to find German soldiers guarding university buildings beside the river. Taking command of the Slavonic Library in the Klementinum, the Germans, driven by Hitler's anti-Bolshevik crusade, ordered that no Russian book published after 1900 should be loaned, while to consult any book published before 1900 the reader had to provide a reason. The time was not propitious for Russian studies. The Losskys moved to the easier circumstances of Bratislava, where the breakaway independent state of Slovakia was cooperating with the Germans. Lyudmila Lossky died of natural causes in Bratislava in 1942. Nikolai worked on at the university until the moment when, at the end of the war, the Red Army arrived to liberate a country which had finally turned against the Germans. The liberators sent many Russians and Slovaks to the Gulag, but according to Lossky left the Russian professors in Bratislava untouched. A political policeman, his organization now known as the NKVD, even expressed admiration for Lossky's religious philosophy. Lossky had difficulty getting a foreign passport from the Slovaks but was helped in Prague by the French embassy and a Czech politician in New York. He left Prague, en route for the United States, in a French aeroplane.[17]

The Red Army was less merciful when it arrived in Prague. Its major target was the Russian émigré archive, the entire contents of which were loaded into seven goods wagons and sent by rail back to Moscow, together with the archive staff. These men included Sergei Postnikov, who featured by mistake on Boris Lossky's list of those who sailed on the *Haken*. Having left Russia voluntarily for Prague in 1921, Postnikov remained in a Soviet camp from 1947 to 1950 and then lived in internal exile in Nikopol. Amnestied in the early 1960s, he made his way back to Prague and lived a few more years.[18] Another Russian sent to the Gulag from Prague was the Eurasian Pyotr Savitsky, who also survived and returned in 1956, only to be rearrested by the

Communist Czechoslovak authorities in 1961. Other Russians, including distinguished professors, died, either from being shot or sent east.[19] Yelena Nabokova wrote to her brother in a clever code which invoked Cincinnatus, the name of the protagonist of his 1935 novel, *Invitation to a Beheading*. In this way she let him know what was happening in 1945.[20] But another lucky man, Lapshin, was left in peace and died naturally in 1952, while Valentin Bulgakov returned to the Soviet Union and the job for which he was made, curator of the Lev Tolstoy museum.[21]

Izyumov, who had worked in the Prague archive of the emigration, survived his time in a German concentration camp and when Europe was liberated he left for the United States, as did Bogolepov, Odintsov and Novikov, all of whom the war apparently left unscathed. Bogolepov taught Russian in Berlin in 1941–6, an unexplained story, while Odintsov and his wife and son left Prague for Berlin before the Red Army arrived. Novikov was one of Lossky's colleagues in Bratislava and in his case it was said to have been the Germans who encouraged the Russian professors to go west in good time.[22]

In occupied Paris, Ugrimov worked with two other Russian figures, the nun known as Mother Maria (Elizaveta Skobtsova) and the priest Dmitry Klepinin, brother of Nikolai who had committed murder on behalf of the OGPU. Ugrimov, whose knowledge as a professor of agronomy had landed him a job in a flour mill, supplied food to Jews whom Mother Maria, the first wife of the shipped poet and future Catholic bishop Dmitry Kuzmin-Karavayev, and Father Klepinin were sheltering. Mother Maria, a frequent visitor to the Berdyaevs in Clamart before the war, died in Ravensbrück while Klepinin perished in another camp, along with other distinguished figures from the Paris Russian community. Ugrimov was captured by the Nazis in 1944 and tortured, but survived.[23]

The fate of an unknown number of anonymous Russians on the periphery of the present story was sealed by the Allied bombing of the industrial area of Billancourt. Nina Berberova left a harrowing account of this devastation of the Paris landscape which had been home to a ragged, displaced Russia from the end of the Civil War. She herself was almost murdered by a French neighbour in the anarchic last days of the war, because she was Russian.

Possibly one or two of Lenin's exiles collaborated with the Germans. The finger of suspicion has been pointed at Vysheslavtsev, who, having spent the war in occupied France, left for Switzerland in 1944, it is said out of fear of French reprisals. But the story is not confirmed and it is also suggested that he spent the war in Germany.[24]

When Hitler broke the pact of 1940 and invaded Russia in June 1941 a wave of relieved emotion swept over the exiled community, dissolving their resistance to Sovietism and Stalin in a wave of sympathy for the Russian people as Hitler's victims.[25] Milyukov, eighty-three years old and destitute, the man who never became leader of Russia Abroad, wrote an article entitled 'The Truth of Bolshevism'.[26] Victor Frank was part of a singsong among Russian exiles in England, at an all-night picnic on the banks of the river Avon near Evesham.[27] Berdyaev, who had felt some sympathy for Stalin's Russia from before the war began, despite the show trials, saw the world situation now fall into place for him. By the end of the war he was praising socialism and the Red Army which the Revolution had made invincible. Semyon Frank thought he had gone mad.[28] Before he died in 1942 Osorgin also called for support for the Soviet Union and held out the prospect of reconciliation between Russia Abroad and Soviet Russia. For a man who feared prison, fate dealt Osorgin a final round of suffering when he was once more jailed, this time by the Germans, in his last months.[29]

When the Nazis were defeated and Paris was free the Soviets took advantage of this climate of support and after twenty-one years of closed doors triumphantly opened their embassy at 78 rue de Grenelle to the exiles and the émigrés. They offered Soviet passports and visas home to all who wanted them. None of Lenin's exiles accepted an offer they distrusted, although some émigrés did, to their cost. Incomprehensibly Berdyaev said Russians ought to go, but didn't go himself. Tatyana Frank called Ugrimov a Bolshevik in her memoirs, presumably because she thought he returned to the Soviet Union by taking advantage of this diplomatic overture. But in fact when Ugrimov the agronomist (the professor who had taught his children to appreciate the German style of agriculture in the train from Stettin to Berlin) returned to Russia with his daughter the move was not voluntary. In 1947, fearing Communist influence, the French government forcibly repatriated Russians, including the Ugrimovs.[30] Subsequently he worked as an agronomist in the provinces and was allowed back to Moscow in 1957. He lived to be a hundred years old. His daughter, still in Russia, published her memoirs in 1993.

The year 1947 was also the year in which Berdyaev received an honorary doctorate in divinity from Cambridge University. The citation called him 'another Socrates, an imperturbable spirit' and remembered 'Caesaribus patriam suam regentibus exilio affectus est' ('He was sentenced to exile by the despots ruling his homeland'). Berdyaev died at his desk the following year, 1948, Lidiya having died of cancer three years earlier. Frank died in Hendon, north London, in 1950, while Victor was working for the BBC Russian Service in London and freelancing for *The Tablet*. The meagreness of a BBC behind-the-scenes income then forced Victor, as the sole breadwinner for his mother and his own family, to move to Germany, where he became the chief broadcaster, in the Russian language, for the then Munich-based American radio station Radio Liberty. He gave weekly talks on literature, poetry and current affairs.

But surely the most vividly unhappy end was Karsavin's.[31] In 1940, when the Red Army arrived in Lithuania and the country once represented by Jurgis Baltrusaitis, poet, ambassador and saviour of lives, was once more unhappily swallowed up into the Russian Empire, the university at Kaunas was transferred to Vilnius, the capital, and Karsavin followed. (Baltrusaitis himself died in poverty in Paris.) Karsavin didn't try to get to the West. Often he tried to give up his hopes that the Soviet Union would abandon its repressive ideology, but perhaps because he was a Eurasian who believed in his country's mighty destiny, those hopes revived in 1940, and again in 1944, sufficiently to keep him in the Soviet orbit.

The first result of Karsavin's decision to stay in the East was that he had to give up teaching history but could continue lecturing on aesthetics. Then his contribution to both subjects was banned and he had to leave the university altogether. His next two years as Director of the Vilnius Museum of Art must have been relatively pleasurable. They were also a sign of the esteem in which he was held locally. But in May 1949, after ridiculing an election in which there was no choice, he was sacked. Too late he discovered that he did prefer Western freedom to Eurasian political originality. He was arrested two months later.

A. A. Vaneyev got to know Karsavin in a camp in Abez, a village on a railway line not far from the Arctic Circle in the Autonomous Soviet Republic of Komi. Just over 100 miles from the well-known Gulag town of Vorkuta, it was a camp for those whose health or age made them unsuitable for work in the mines. Karsavin was sixty-seven. 'The search for an affirmation of truth, of spiritual integrity, the need for which Karsavin as a Russian always felt in his soul, was characteristic of him,' wrote Vaneyev, who became his disciple and helper. Karsavin died of tuberculosis in 1952, in the camp hospital.

Karsavin was officially sent to the Gulag, according to his police file, because of his alleged support for the Whites and his Eurasianism, but fundamentally because he was a Russian in the wrong place at the wrong time. After the war Russians found outside the country for whatever reason were regarded as traitors by Stalin, just as were foreigners caught by chance inside the Soviet Union. The two-way purge came in a ferocious wave of arrests in 1949, by which time, happily, most of Lenin's original victims were either safe or safely dead.

PART III

'Sixty years ago metaphysical theorizing was declared meaningless on the sweeping grounds that its results were neither true by virtue of meaning alone nor confirmable or disconfirmable in experience. But metaphysical theorizing of the proscribed kind was involved in reaching that very conclusion. It proved to be essential to philosophy then just as it is today.'

Barry Stroud, *The Quest for Reality*

'It is just as impossible to expect that the human spirit will some day completely renounce metaphysical speculation as to expect that we would sooner not breathe at all than breathe unclean air.'

Immanuel Kant, *Prolegomena to Any Future Metaphysics*

11

The Sense of What Happened

THE SAILING OF the Philosophy Steamer signalled to millions of Russians over the next four generations that in 1922 their country began to shut the door to the outside world. When Glavlit, the censorship agency, was founded on 6 June it was the first attempt by the Soviet state to bring literature under state control. Together with the GPU, Glavlit would henceforth control newspapers and publishing within Russia and prevent undesirable ideas getting in. Having banished the unwanted thinkers, the regime now made sure that their words also could not return. The implementation wasn't perfect, but it was enough to ensure that in its key discourses as well as its geographical location Soviet Russia remained a separate country from 'Russia Abroad' for the next seventy years.

Though the Soviet regime's control of its citizens' thoughts would grow immeasurably worse after 1929, already in 1922 all academic and literary organizations – with the exception of the Academy of Sciences – were brought under state surveillance. Zinoviev closed the House of Writers, the House of Arts and the House of Scholars, all of which were independent bodies, even as the second boat sailed. The Institute of Red Professors was urged to educate an intelligentsia more representative of workers and peasants. Crowning these actions a new state, the Union of Soviet Socialist Republics, the USSR, was founded on 30 December.

Of the principal targets of Lenin's 1922 action two Russian professions in particular would not fare well in the depleted, chimeric form they were left behind: agriculture and philosophy. Soviet agriculture, subjected by Stalin to a collectivization that killed millions in the 1930s, never truly flourished and one of the great embarrassments of the Cold War from the Soviet side was the annual need to buy grain from the Americans to feed Russia. It's a moot point whether any of the agricultural economists on the ships could have staved off the disaster of the next decade and collectivization generally, but at least Brutskus and Sorokin, Zubashov and all the team at *Ekonomist*, Zvorykin, Odintsov and Ugrimov and many others would have argued against the underlying agronomic and economic principles. It is a sad irony of the expulsion story that the one prominent agriculturalist reprieved, Nikolai Kondratyev, became one of the leading architects of collectivization in the remainder of his career. Soviet agricultural and general economic inefficiency meanwhile merged with the disillusion of the mass of the populace to ensure decades of consumer shortages.

Philosophy was a very different business from agriculture, and not everyone noticed, or mourned, its absence. Nevertheless, in both its Western and traditional Russian form it shrivelled in Soviet Russia. The academic subject was built, from the early 1930s, on a foundation which entirely ignored the 'bourgeois' and 'religious' past. It was effectively ideology, which ensured that generations of Russians would grow up hating 'philosophy'. Meanwhile representatives of the old school disappeared. The art historian and religious thinker Pavel Florensky and the phenomenologist Gustav Shpet were both shot in Stalin's purges, and another important philosopher, Aleksei Losev, was sent to a camp. Exiled to the provinces, Mikhail Bakhtin kept a low profile and disguised his real interests.[1]

Literature was more difficult to control, but writers could be oppressed and frightened into silence. After 1922, and even more effectively after 1929, they either expressed themselves tamely or indirectly or not at all. If they were brave, which usually meant getting themselves published in the West, the reprisals were severe. The KGB, latest heir to the Cheka/GPU/NKVD mantle, may have tried to murder Solzhenitsyn in 1971,[2] and they nearly destroyed the poet Joseph Brodsky before they expelled him in 1972. Many others could be named.

The mistreatment of the intelligentsia led to great confusion on the part of the Soviet Union's sympathizers abroad during the Cold War. Leading figures in France like Sartre and Simone de Beauvoir had to deny they had any prior inkling of the truths Solzhenitsyn told after his two major novels were published in the West in 1968. But in this case the politicians were more alert, and among the Soviet Union's antagonists art and literature became major weapons in the propaganda struggle between a repressive regime and a West that was proud of its civic freedom.[3]

As for the Russian populus at large, *The Times* in September 1922 was quite right that 'the stubborn remnant of the Russian educated class... [was] being eliminated' and it was a bad augury for the rest of the century. On the other hand, the stubbornness endured, both in those expelled and, in the end more importantly, in those who remained. Post-Soviet Russia has rushed to embrace its lost heritage. After the end of 1991 the former Red Army colonel who turned historian and became Lenin's greatest critic welcomed back the shade of Berdyaev in triumph.[4] Public awareness of the story of the Philosophy Steamer has spread with recurrent newspaper articles and even a small exhibition. Yet once Russia Abroad has been reincorporated in the minds and hearts of Russia at home, perhaps two things remain to be pondered. One is the schismatic nature of modern Russian history, which suggests Lenin's 'surgical intrusion into the body of Russia'[5] was the outcome of more than the Revolution of 1917. The other challenge is the meaning of an event which, as I suggested in my introduction, while it happened bodily in Russia, simultaneously symbolized a change of outlook which affected the entire Western heritage.

Modern Russian culture has been a struggle to prevent rupture between the people and the intelligentsia, and between intellectual factions. The forced exodus of 1922 was one result. But the truth was that the two halves of Russia had begun to break apart already in the mid-nineteenth century. Turgenev's novel *Fathers and Sons* (1862) named the two Russias that were parting company. It was not just a matter of the usual generational tensions but of two completely opposed philosophies of life, both in the narrow and the popular sense of philosophy. Nabokov forged a brilliant link with Turgenev's understanding of modern Russia when some years after he arrived in Berlin – but reflecting his first years there – he began to write *his* novel of the great modern schism, whose consequences forced him to live abroad. *The Gift*, largely written in 1935–7, was not about the men on the Philosophy Steamer, but it commemorated their loss of Russia and Russia's loss of them:

> The tremendous outflow of intellectuals that formed such a prominent part of the general exodus from Soviet Russia in the first years of the Bolshevist Revolution seems today like the wanderings of some mythical tribe whose bird-signs and moon-signs I now retrieve from the desert dust. We remained unknown to American intellectuals (who, bewitched by Communist propaganda, saw us merely as villainous generals, oil magnates and gaunt ladies with lorgnettes). That world is now gone.[6]

Why had the old Russia disappeared? Because at that point in history when Turgenev was writing a new utilitarian generation emerged determined to reform a backward country. The social atmosphere in Russia began to change irrevocably, almost as if a revolution had already happened. If one wanted to feel what was at stake one might meditate upon the life and career of Nikolai Chernyshevsky, a thinker of humble origin who spent the greater part of his career in prison and Siberian exile, and epitomized the 'new men' of the 1860s whose atheistic and materialist thinking clashed with the more idealistic and sentimental Russia of earlier years. Not by coincidence Chernyshevsky was Lenin's favourite writer. There Nabokov had his theme. *The Gift* became, superficially, a novel about how a young writer of aristocratic background like himself, Fyodor Godunov-Cherdyntsev, struggled to complete a brilliant first novel on the life of Chernyshevsky and its impact on Russia.

Dense, enigmatic, full of Proustian memories of childhood and all the more significant for the fact that it was the last novel Nabokov wrote in Russian, *The Gift* was a leavetaking of great intensity and camouflaged emotion, by a master who seemed to be recording why he would never tell the story of Russia straightforwardly again, but that everything he wrote would be symbolic of the great parting of ways. Fyodor Godunov-Cherdyntsev felt the split had so deformed his country that he couldn't bear to contemplate what it had really become.

> Suddenly [Godunov-Cherdyntsev] felt a bitter pang – why had everything in Russia become so shoddy, crabbed and grey...? Or had the old urge 'toward the light' concealed a fatal flaw, which in the course of progress toward the objective had grown more and more evident, until it was revealed that this 'light' was burning in the window of a prison overseer, and that was all? When had this strange dependence sprung up between the sharpening of the thirst and the muddying of the source? In the forties? In the sixties? And 'what to do' now? Ought one not to reject any longing for one's homeland...? Some day, interrupting my writing, I will look through the window and see a Russian autumn.[7]

I've tried to evoke that last Russian autumn in this book and to be one of its chroniclers. It was in the mid-1960s when Nabokov also wrote that the Russian emigration 'still awaits its chronicler'.[8]

While Nabokov blamed the generation of Chernyshevsky and their utilitarian mentality, Berdyaev blamed the schism on the 'rational' Petersburg mentality. Both men were thinking symbolically at that moment, Berdyaev of Petersburg's ethos as a city conjured up out of marshland according to a rational and foreign plan. Peter the Great, when he built his perfect city from scratch, in defiance of nature, stood for Westernization in the name of reason, just as Lenin would do. There was a link between blaming Russia's fate on a utilitarian and on a despot, and that link was rationalism. Lenin's project was to forge a modern, efficient and coherent country and to make the Soviet Union a world power. It entailed forcing less-than-rational, unkempt, spontaneous, spiritual Russia into a harness, and of course the dissidents had to go, if the harness was to be effective. But, as I have repeated, it was the ideological nature of the religious thinkers' beliefs, their 'idealism', which actually had to go. Seen in the best light, the action Lenin called a 'cleansing' was an attempt to rationalize Russia and make the new proletarian, materialist-minded nation an efficient business. At least one man on the Philosophy Steamer acquired a grudging respect for what Lenin did. Izgoev wrote in 1932 that Lenin understood the nature of power in Russia, which required stability and systematic organization. Further, he saw how Marxism could help him get a grip on that power.[9]

It was always a Western fancy to see Lenin and Stalin as 'Oriental' despots. The great Russian tyrants in the eighteenth and the twentieth century were Westernizers. But precisely because the ethos of Petersburg was 'Western' and 'rational', in the sense that first Peter and then Lenin practised it, Berdyaev began to doubt the function of reason in modern civilization. He wondered how much could be invented, how far civilization could move away from the constraints of nature. St Petersburg has been called 'the crucible of cultural revolution' and 'the laboratory of the modern' for the way it carried before it the idea of reason as an unlimited creative force independent of everything apart from its own logic.[10] In that city where a revolution took place, every 'modern' value had to be redefined. But in this definition of modernity what one sees is that the expulsions were part of a twentieth-century cultural experiment which happened in the West as well as Russia. The sailing of the Philosophy Steamer had a universal symbolic significance. Its status in history deserves to become mythical.

Modernity was a battleground for the right way to live. What was at stake was vast but can be roughly grasped as the clash of three sets of values. The three debates in which the Russian philosophers were so clearly represented were over the value of moral individualism compared with the collective benefit, over liberalism versus Marxism, and over absolute truth versus relativism. These debates were of universal significance, but each took on a special colouring and significance in the Russian context, where battle was joined over 'reason'.

Lenin embodied a modernity that was not dissimilar from Peter the Great's three centuries before. He conceived of reason as a tool to improve and perhaps perfect social reality. Russia needed to become a coherent, secular, literate, egalitarian society with an efficient economy, and something fine in the impulse to rationalism and secularism makes one think that, in theory at least, discounting the means he used, Lenin got some things right. The modern world does not need religion to make it a decent place. It needs to focus its energies on real projects which make human lives better. Against the Communists, who were rationalists and progressives, Berdyaev and his kind were the Russian religious fundamentalists of their day, who could be accused of cultivating darkness and superstition in place of reason and light. Architecturally they belonged under the great domes of Russian churches, in an esoteric candlelit darkness filled with spiritual longing, whereas Lenin was a modernist, a man who, had his vision been translated into architectural terms, would have believed with Le Corbusier in efficient living, in open, bright, communal spaces, and the conversion of mathematically precise theories into daily practice. Since Le Corbusier was an artist who deviated from his own norms the comparison can only go so far. But the idea of life as an efficient machine was certainly his, as it was Lenin's. I would also add to the positive characterization of Lenin's historic role that Sovietism was Russia's version of 'the Enlightenment project' – much under attack now in some quarters but a dream which entirely underpinned social hope in Europe until thirty or forty years ago.

Lenin's world was anti-metaphysical, anti-individualistic, atheist and materialist. The idealists whom Lenin despised for their 'superstitions' believed by contrast in transcendental values, moral individualism, faith, idealism and, resting on all these things and indissoluble from them, freedom. The freedom they defended was not a political answer to the coerciveness of the totalitarian state Lenin was inventing; its essence was spiritual. For the Russian idealists freedom was possible because God existed and in the divine order of things human beings had the gift of free will. What the idealists would have wanted to prove to Lenin, had they been invited to a debate, was that moral individualism and belief in God were not irrelevant to 'the real world' but kept it human. Second, they would have wanted to assert that a rational world, however it was defined, was nothing without individual 'inner' freedom.

Both Lenin's belief in a self-sufficient materialist world and the idealists' Christian spiritual outlook went into the crucible of the modern which they shared with Western thinkers, along with a third element, humanism. But different results obtained in the West because Russia and the West had different needs. For instance, while in Russia Frank and Lossky spent their lifetimes arguing that God was the highest form of reason both because that was what they believed and because it delivered a message of the inviolable sanctity of the person, Western humanists didn't need to prove the existence of God to persuade people to believe in free will and the dignity of man. These liberal values could equally stand without a belief in God in the twentieth century, whereas in Russia, because of the long history of tsarist despotism, political liberalism had very little ground of its own to stand on and had to be either spiritualized or poeticized. The Western situation meant that humanist values could coincide with atheism and rationalism and thus with the social and moral hopes of the same Enlightenment project of which Lenin practised a version. This was the point where Western humanists and Russian religious idealists were bound to part company. The expelled Russian philosophers could not accept secular liberalism, just as, by the same token, Western liberals would find redundant the idea of religious metaphysics as the necessary component of morality.

It seems to me that this difference, the result of the anti-totalitarian Russians' quite different historical provenance, underlay much confusion east–west as to what 'socialism' was and who was a 'socialist' during the Cold War years. In the first half of the twentieth century the Jewish-born British publisher Victor Gollancz, founder of the Left Book Club, for instance, was a socialist who believed in 'man' and who read Berdyaev and loved to quote him. When in 1950 Gollancz made a speech in Germany on 'Religion and Humanism', praising 'man's potentialities' and advocating humanist faith, he ended with quotes from Beethoven, Rilke, Berdyaev's friend Jacques Maritain and Berdyaev himself.[11] What Gollancz didn't see was that 'man' was endangered by both the socialism of Lenin's kind and the more liberal forms of secularism practised in the West, because liberalism could only supply relative values. It was not possible to discard the metaphysical arguments for moral aspiration without losing the very possibility of ethics. 'If there is no God then all is permitted,' as Dostoevsky said. This at least is how Berdyaev would have seen the problem.

Those opposed to a metaphysics of morals would say Berdyaev was talking nonsense, that the moral impulse of human beings is located in the will, not in a perception of God or 'higher reality' of some kind. Berdyaev would have replied that the will without God was hubristic. It was that tendency of the human will to err, if unchecked by any force morally greater than itself, which Goethe created *Faust* to show. (The Russian tradition was illuminated by German insight, as all the philosophers knew.) As Berdyaev, Frank and their kind saw it, what men needed to be moral was to perceive a truth of existence greater than themselves, in which their single will and their single existence was relatively insignificant. They needed to perceive a greater 'Other'.[12] This is why Stepun referred to Bunin's fictional-poetic world as 'the sacred scripture of life itself' because it opened up a spiritual dimension to human existence and created metaphysical-moral imperatives to conserve nature and personhood and love, and not to destroy life.

Lenin's sense of 'man's potentialities' rested on the boundless application of human will to the problems of society and the resources of nature. There was no sense in Lenin's world of listening to reality as an 'Other' whose existence might be respected as a limitation. For Lenin the human mind conceived a plan and acted upon it. He agreed with the liberal humanist world that the concept of God was redundant in modern times.

The problem for liberal humanists of the mid-twentieth century, like Gollancz, though they could not see it at the time, was how they could agree simultaneously with a rationalist like Lenin and a non-rational Russian-style Christian socialist like Berdyaev. The discrepancy between these overlapping views came down to what atheism meant for society. Did it really mean progress? Should it be encouraged? The answer to that question was unequivocally yes, if belief in God was a mere supersitition as Lenin said it was, but it was more uncertain if religious belief meant something more. That something more might amount to the question whether 'man' was capable of truth and goodness for their own sake, or whether truth and goodness were relative by-products of making use of the world for material benefit.

The line the idealists would have taken in a debate with Lenin would have been to explain the difference between supersitition and religious faith. They would have said that superstition merely creates fear and prejudice, whereas Christian belief creates a moral environment in which the 'inner life' of the individual person is respected and seen as the source of responsibility.

The truest indication of what Lenin was about with his vision of modern Russia was that he had no grasp of this distinction, at the same time as he operated with a concept of reason much narrower than the Western humanist vision. Leszek Kolakowski has shown how Lenin's view of reality, aside from the influence of Marxism, derived from European positivism, which defined reality as what could be known to and demonstrated by science.[13] The positivist definition of what was real ruled out all that was uncertain and all that was unprovably 'inner' and 'private', including the experience of God.

When Lenin got rid of the religious thinkers he was acting on this philosophy. He believed that the inner world didn't exist and to talk about it was to talk about phantoms. He might just as well have been expelling madmen.

Lenin had a great deal of support in Russia for his rejection of superstition, as did Marxism across the world. Progress meant atheistic rationalism, and evidently not only for Marxists and Leninists. In 1926 the Futurist poet Mayakovsky said good riddance to the 'idealists' in thoroughly Lenin-like terms. Kindred Russians of his day like Roman Jakobson and Viktor Shklovsky were of the same mind, as some Western historians still are, that in this sense at least the expulsion of the religious idealists was justified, because the ideas they stood for were rubbish. As Mayakovsky put it:

> The burbling of the intelligentsia with their vocabulary of castrated words like 'ideal', 'principles of justice', 'the divine origin', 'the transcendental countenance of Christ and Antichrist' – all this kind of talk, once mouthed in restaurants, has been wiped out...[14]

The personal tragedy of Mayakovsky was the way he embodied this misconceived hope for modern rationality and efficiency and light. When he killed himself the loss of humanity in the Russian situation was becoming clear.

Not perhaps the West, but Russia needed its religious philosophers because only they could uphold values for individuality and freedom in the Russian tradition where historically and politically time and again these values came under threat. The idealist philosophers stood for an untouchable inner space, an imagined seat of Personhood, which, even if it was only imagined as an actual location, like God on high and the soul in the breast, nevertheless had a vital moral and political function in Russia. It was the absence of these values which made Lenin's world totalitarian. Had Mayakovsky not lost the will to live he might have agreed with the substance, if not the language, of the idealists' arguments.

Since spiritual values are difficult to illustrate without reference to real lives, I'm tempted here to record the despair of another poet of the day, another future suicide, Sergei Esenin. These sentiments were expressed in a letter he wrote to a friend in 1921, with a passing reference to Napoleon's final prison on St Helena:

> Forgive me, my dear, once again, for alarming you. I feel very sad at
> this moment when history is undergoing a difficult epoch, in which
> the individual as a living organism is targeted for destruction.
> Indeed what's going on is not the socialism I envisaged at all, but a
> definite and deliberate thing like some island of St Helena, stripped
> of glory, drained of dreams. You feel cooped up if you're truly alive,
> if you build bridges to the invisible world, for they sever and
> detonate these bridges from under the feet of future generations. Of
> course, the man for whom this invisible world unfolds will be able
> to see these bridges, even when they have become rotten, but in the
> end it's always sad to build a house no one will live in, to hollow out
> a boat no one will sail in.[15]

Is the meaning of this letter clear? When Lenin banished the inner man he took the decisive step towards making the Soviet world an inhuman world without 'bridges to the invisible'. It was to be a place in which socialists and non-socialists alike would feel 'cooped up' and less than alive because there was insufficient provision in its reality for what was poetic, but not untrue.[16]

Lenin defined the modern effectively as totalitarian, and the result was the banishment of inwardness not only from philosophy, but from life itself. It became the task of propaganda and the political police in Russia to disallow individuality and privacy – the sources of imagination – in daily life and in the political lives of individuals. Under the Soviet version of totalitarianism there was no such thing as private thoughts; no possibility of an inner space in which a man might commune with himself. When Soviet citizens were interrogated they were told what they thought and what their motives were, and they couldn't prove otherwise. It's significant that when Western political theory fought back against totalitarianism, the concept it reached for – at least when the Russian-born Isaiah Berlin considered the problem – was an idea of individual integrity, both of the individual in answer to his own 'inner' sense of himself and of society in recognizing the inalienable right of this person to be himself and not to be invaded.[17] The contemporary concept of human rights rests on an essential privacy which can be construed as an inner space in which every man is free to think his own thoughts and be 'himself'. The religious idealists expelled from Russia would hardly have rejected 'human rights'. They would only – and once again because of Russia's impoverished political experience in the past – have distrusted the capacity of secular law to defend those rights.

As Berlin went on to observe, the freedom he wanted to define, which was a definition explicitly made with the totalitiarian threat in mind, ran into a problem with the mere idea of liberty as 'the ability to do what one wishes' without the intervention of the state or other men.

One problem with this 'negative' definition of freedom is the extent to which we have the right to remove some or all of the barriers and constraints to the realization of our wishes. Given that we all have wishes these are bound to conflict. But another problem Berlin noticed, and which is more relevant here, concerned the shortcomings of a definition of freedom entirely based upon the freedom of the human will. It is an insufficient definition because will can be manipulated:

If I find that I am able to do little or nothing of what I wish, I need only contract or extinguish my wishes, and I am made free. If the tyrant (or 'hidden persuader') manages to condition his subjects (or customers) into losing their original wishes and embrace ('internalize') the form of life he has invented for them, he will, on this definition, have succeeded in liberating them. He will no doubt have made them *feel* free... But what he has created is the very antithesis of political freedom.

The distinction Berlin drew here, between real political freedom and the illusion of enjoying it that can be induced in people, was, I think, the same one that Nabokov was aiming at with his double image of the 'light' of Western reason and the 'light burning in the window of a prison overseer'. It was also the gap between delusion and reality which Solzhenitsyn explored in his novel *The First Circle*. In Dante's 'First Circle of Hell' the light is bright and appears to be unending. But there is a limit and beyond that limit is infinite darkness.[18]

For Berlin what follows from the possibility of real political freedom is how we can recognize the inadequacy of fake political freedom, which would include all the many forms of social conformism, some of them brutally and some of them subtly imposed. We can only look towards real political freedom if we recognize that the freedom of the individual will, precisely because it can be endlessly manipulated, is not a sufficient basis either for the experience or the definition of true freedom. So it seems Berlin is saying there must be some positive constraint on our right to assert ourselves. 'When I induce somebody to make room for me in his carriage, or conquer a country which threatens the interests of my own ... what gives me the right to say you must hold back, rather than me?' The law, which may deter some and not others, offers only an interim solution to a question that can't be solved politically. It seems to me that three Russians thinkers as different as Nabokov, Solzhenitsyn and Berlin are, in the light of their Russian experience, all asking if in the end some metaphysical constraint is the only possible basis for the good life, even if, in the way of modern thought, it is barely credible outside imaginative literature and private faith.

Here I rest my case for the Russian philosophers. As idealists they were not modern enough to doubt the reality of the metaphysical imperative. But what they could see, in a way that Nabokov, Solzhenitsyn and Berlin inherited, was that it was necessary.

Freedom for the Russian idealists of the Silver Age was defined as the integrity of the individual's inner space. At the same time, unlike the Oxford-educated émigré Isaiah Berlin, they were accustomed to separating the realms of God and Caesar and to retreating from the political realm, when they had to, in order to survive. Theirs was a pre- or non-political definition of freedom in a world of 'hidden persuaders'. In fact they belonged in a world which *in extremis* touched the frontiers of medieval martyrdom. They believed that the will was a moral will which could only be kept on track through knowledge of goodness or godliness, whatever happened in the political sphere.

Not many readers will find the idea of God-given inner freedom and moral guidance convincing today. At the same time they may well find equally unconvincing an idea of morality as only a matter of will. There is a need for guidance from a source outside ourselves. But all secular guidance – which also means the institutions of the churches, which also means education – is open to manipulation, so where can that guidance come from? The most we can hope for is to trust our own discrimination, but to hope such a thing begs the question of how discrimination is educated, because education is also potential manipulation. The idealists didn't succumb to these terrible post-modern, post-rational problems because they thought a Christian education taught the right kind of discrimination.

Generally the twentieth century in Western thought took an atheist, rational and anti-inward course in pursuit of the good society. There is a strong sense, I think, that when Lenin defined the modern as non-inward and non-individual, albeit unconsciously he was not acting alone. He was in fact acting out a moment in history which was not his to choose. The idea of a historical process greater than any of those who participate in it and try to shape it may be greeted with scepticism, if not horror, by most contemporary readers who value their autonomy. But the two positions don't cancel each other out. One can act on a belief in one's own freedom and still find that history carries one along in a certain direction. At the very least there are always remarkable coincidences in the way similar ideas are effected in quite different situations and parts of the world at any one time.

An example of an idea taking shape in history regardless of human direction is atheism. It spread in the twentieth century more or less through state decree in Russia. Churches were closed, genuine priests were outsiders and dissidents. There has been a religious revival in post-Soviet Russia just because religion was suppressed by state ordinance, but in effect most people live without practising a faith, just as they do in the West. In the West the churches are empty not under government pressure, however, but because atheism has freely taken hold. History has no explanation for how these things have happened in parallel, but they have done, and the result is the twenty-first-century 'West', including Russia. Two related worlds arrived at roughly the same social juncture by a different course. The outcome doesn't seem to have been affected by whether or not human beings have actively intervened in one interest or another.

Modern Russia has tried to intervene. There has been a remarkable readiness to take on 'History' as if it were a contest between David and Goliath. Ideas which other cultures have left as theoretically debatable on the page, Communist Russia took up as real challenges. Russia conducted experiments which have served in the West as a warning. Behind the Revolution lay the idea, for instance, that there was something called 'History', which had a particular course, and that this course could be speeded up. It was a Western idea, originating with Hegel and Marx, but it was in the Russian intellectual-political context, a world of extremes and of faith in metaphysical ideas as real guides as to how to live, that it became possible to act on Marx's idea. The banishment of inwardness was another idea which modern Russia through Lenin was prepared to enact. It marked a historical milestone at the beginning of the twentieth century.

In what sense was the banishment of inwardness a modern idea? The coincidence is a fact of history. While Lenin was galvanizing the GPU into making reservations on the *Haken* and the *Preussen*, Western philosophy was also casting out metaphysics and heralding a new age of social philosophy.

The French thinker Auguste Comte did the groundwork for

positivism and the German Avenarius and the Austrian Mach developed it in a way that would specifically determine Lenin's thought though Lenin would move on. Their empiriocriticism aimed at ruling out metaphysics – any experience of a 'beyond' – from the definition of reality. In Anglo-American philosophy the early Wittgenstein, fresh from Vienna, where the views of Mach had stimulated logical positivism, equally insisted that metaphysics was nonsense. The Wittgenstein of the *Tractatus* would just as readily as Mayakovsky have referred to idealism as 'burbling'. For Wittgenstein the first-order questions metaphysics tried to answer couldn't even be posed intelligibly and therefore should be set aside. Philosophy should rather do an efficient and useful job in society, clarifying meaning and possibility. It should not bother itself with 'higher reality' and it should regard the distinction between an outer world and an inner mind, or self, as misleading. Wittgenstein predominated over Ango-American attitudes to philosophy for almost the next sixty years. He helped underpin the idea of philosophy as science, and of ethics as the science of how ethical concepts are applied. I don't think it is a coincidence that these sixty years were also the durée of the 'short century' of the Soviet Union and the era when Marxism retained its credibility.[19]

What Lenin did in politics and society was the equivalent of Wittgenstein's sophisticated achievement in philosophy. To put those two names together sounds like a terrible injustice to Wittgenstein, who outside philosophy profoundly appreciated 'things whereof we cannot speak'. But the comparison helps us understand why the author of *Materialism and Empiriocriticism* should feel it legitimate to expel from society the idealists who contributed to *Landmarks*. Like the metaphysics Wittgenstein rejected this philosophical nonsense, the work of men like Semyon Frank and Sergei Bulgakov could be seen as not doing a useful job in the world. They were parasites on efficiency, as well as talking nonsense. Lenin banished these men who based their values upon inwardness and 'higher reality'. And it's why, to this day, it is possible to take the view that he did a good, Wittgensteinian thing.

•

Rational, anti-metaphysical, anti-religious, anti-idealist twentieth-century society took different forms in Russia and the West over the short century, but what happened resulted from a small number of well-defined cultural choices that were shared, even if they were not perceived to be shared at the time. What happened in philosophy, for instance, also happened in literature. The ousting of Yuly Aikhenvald symbolized a turning point for literary humanism.

When the literary-critical space Aikhenvald was forced to vacate was invaded by the concept of socialist realism as the single permissible school of art, Lenin's ideal society officially banned inwardness not only from the minds of its philosophers but also from literature, painting and music.

Aikhenvald was a critic oriented to the 'common reader'. He believed that literature had a moral and social meaning which the gifted critic could tease out and make clearer to readers. One might compare Aikhenvald variously with Matthew Arnold, with Virginia Woolf and with F. R. Leavis. Nabokov compared him to Walter Pater. Aikhenvald was modern but not a literary theorist, not a structuralist and not a relativist. He called his method 'principled impressionism' and it enabled him to write appreciations of poetry and prose which fitted as readily into intelligent newspapers like 'The Rudder', where his reviews appeared every Sunday, and 'Today', where they were almost as frequent, as into academic volumes. Of the first edition of *Siluety*, Aikhenvald's classic collection of essays on Russian writers and poetry that in its final three-volume form went into six editions before he died, reviewers noted that 'Aikhenvald didn't so much analyse as set out his impressions – his was the method of the heart; his task [was] to grasp subtle, deep aesthetic and emotional impressions.' His main question was: 'Is it art, or is it merely writing?' Aikhenvald looked for the unique spirit in each writer and his commentary was a form of critical friendship. He admired the 'ethical pathos' of Christianity, attached particular value to personality and believed every person was creative. 'Literature is for me,' he wrote, 'not merely an art amongst other arts, but something else, a kind of intimacy, bringing closer to me its abstract idea out of the concrete warmth of life.'[20]

Not everyone liked Aikhenvald's work, including those who were his friends in the Berlin Russian Writers' Club. Khodasevich found it dilettantish and unoriginal. He called it simple-minded aestheticism. Bely spoke of Aikhenvald's 'saccharine liberalism'. But everyone admired the man. Aikhenvald was quiet, even-tempered, tender, attentive, mild, steady. Nabokov, Frank and Stepun were amongst the Berlin friends who showered praise on him and genuine pity. 'In Berlin, in a lonely, rented cupboard-of-a-room he led an ascetic life which strengthened the self-containedness of this dedicated, refined and morally gifted man.'[21]

Aikhenvald more than anyone supported 'the high mission of the emigration to preserve cultural traditions uprooted by the Soviet regime', said Frank.[22] Diligently he attended those anniversary evenings and jubilees which made others gasp for cultural air, and supported the reprint of the Russian classics to keep what was best about old Russia alive. In 1925, with another Russian émigré in Berlin, Raisa Tatarinova (Raisa Tarr), Aikhenvald formed a literary circle, Arzamas, in which Nabokov and others took part. After Nabokov read them a chapter of *Mashen'ka* ('Mary') Aikhenvald declared that a new Turgenev had appeared. A week later he described Nabokov's art exactly:

> He sees clearly, he has a fine ear, and every incidence of time and place is for a keen observer like him far richer in content and more interesting than for us. What is microscopic, scattered details and the splendid way they come into being and develop, are accessible to him; he saturates trivial things with life, sense and psychology and gives a mind to objects; his refined senses notice colorations and nuances, smells and sounds, and everything acquires an unexpected meaning and truth under his gaze and through his words.[23]

Meaning and truth were words Aikhenvald dared to use. He pro-moted modernism in literature, but without ever losing his common sense in the deep meaning of that eighteenth-century term which concerned the social traditions which bind people together. He had a sense of universal humanity and of what belonged to 'mankind'.

Several things happened to the humanist view of literature in both Russia and the West which coincided with Aikhenvald's expulsion by Lenin. The Marxist theory of the cultural superstructure saw literature as primarily political, as the expression of particular socio-economic class interests, and therefore not universal at all, but middle-class, proletarian and so on. This was the theory Trotsky put into practice when he ridiculed Aikhenvald in the pages of *Pravda*. The Marxist attitude was so violent, so slippery, so carpingly strange and so philistine. Reading Trotsky today it is as if he had invented a new school of rhetoric. His eloquence used artistic ridicule as class revenge.

So Aikhenvald the humanist was middle class. But another thing: the values he teased out of literature were too subtle for the mass of mankind. Thus what also coincided with the expulsion of Aikhenvald was that literature was suborned as a didactic-political tool with unique zeal in Communist Russia, which still wanted to educate its people, but only so far. Third, Aikhenvald's expulsion also symbolized a revolution in culture, roughly after 1922, for literature professionals, critics and theorists. The structuralist vantage point opened up, whereby literature become text, an autonomous system of signs and sounds, whose value was self-contained within its structure and did not point to anything outside itself.

The structuralist view of literature, pioneered by Jakobson and his 'Formalist' contemporaries Shklovsky, Yury Tynyanov and Boris Eikhenbaum, made claims for literary criticism that were the exact opposite of Aikhenvald's method. (That they were beyond the Soviet pale is another matter.) Against Aikhenvald, the Formalists championed an impersonal and scientific procedure in literary criticism as opposed to one friendly and impressionistic. They followed structural-rational principles rather than moral principles. For Aikhenvald, art comprised universal meaning and consolation. It was a comment on the human condition and a relief from it. But for Jacobson and others text was a system of expression, a kind of statement of the cultural balance of power which, like a snapshot, a burst of written or spoken language could embrace at any one moment. Lenin literally sent Aikhenvald out of his ideal world, and metaphorically Jakobson and his colleagues also did not want him in theirs.

The upheaval experienced by Russian literary criticism in the immediate pre-revolutionary years was deeply symbolic of how ideas of culture and civilization would be revised everywhere in the twentieth century. Lenin and Communism in practice reinstated the dominant Russian realist tradition, the old nineteenth-century Civic School of Belinsky and of Chernyshevsky. They held literature to its social function and discounted aesthetic considerations. But at the same time they dehumanized humanist literature by making a simplified version of it compulsory. This world of socialized literature was at once humanist and antipathetic to humanism. It revered the artist as a moral figure in society, but it stopped modernist literature – and subjectivity – from coming into being. Art for art's sake, aesthetic and linguistic experimentation, symbolism, individualism, stream of consciousness narrative, anti-social values, existential speculation, subjectivity, tragedy – all these aspects of modern and modernist writing were officially banned in Soviet Russia.

But Soviet society also banished the 'Formalism' which referred to the method of Jakobson, Eikhenbaum and others, because Formalism threatened Communist domination of the meaning of literature from another direction. Formalism gave the text autonomy. It also suggested another way of analysing the meaning of culture and society in competition with Marxist method, and, worst of all from a Marxist-Leninist viewpoint, it suggested that cultural meanings were relative to the context of their expression.

What one therefore sees with the expulsion of Aikhenvald, the emigration of Jakobson and, to utilize as a symbol an actual event, the formation of the Soviet censorship agency, Glavlit, in June 1922, is the formation of three competing fronts in the domain of twentieth-century culture. One, the Official Realist, belongs to a totalitarian political world and is aesthetically childish, but has the possible merit of delivering meaning and encouraging social coherence because it draws on a fixed and universal scale of values, in the Soviet case Marxist-Leninist. The second, Formalist front is aesthetically sophisticated, impersonal and subversive of all universal values, including the political universals. The third, Humanist front, is aesthetically imaginative and morally committed but in its very assets 'old-fashioned' and vulnerable to mockery. This is because the claim that spiritual values – the world of the good – are knowable, underlying it, can seem quite fantastic.

The culture wars of the twentieth century which were the result of these three competing ideas catered for three broad kinds of reader – although by reader here I mean something as broad as the individual with a certain expectation of life and therefore of culture, and by literature I almost mean life. Of these three kinds of 'reader' the first, the conventional reader, is less interested in art (and culture) than in a happy ending. He wants a safe society. He is the ideal subject/customer, whose will, to endorse Berlin's point, can be manipulated without his feeling anything wrong. He feels 'free'. The second kind of 'reader' is the humanist of the old school who historically felt increasingly undermined by theories which relativized his values and made them expressions of his social class, skin colour and so on, as the century progressed. He wanted literature and his own life to have a moral meaning. The third kind of 'reader' is the Formalist/structuralist/professional decoder of texts who would remove the pleasure from reading and relativize the power of art to manipulate the will, to save it from potential political misuse, but at the same time take literature down the postmodernist road to nowhere.

To these three cultural fronts, which were in place in Russia by 1922 on behalf of the whole Western world, corresponded three basic kinds of society: the first morally protective on the part of the state, the second liberal-humanist and the third anarchic-subversive-anti-humanist-postmodern. It seems to me we have not settled for any one of them today.

Of these three contemporary inheritances the line from the Russian structuralism of the 1920s to the postmodernism of Western thought from around 1970 is the most difficult to understand.[24] But it seems to be marked by a concealed emotional element accompanied by a feeling of disinheritance and exile. For Western thinkers like Derrida this disinheritance was principally an exile from reason, whatever personal elements were also involved. It proceeded from the horror of the Second World War and the Holocaust and, despite what Communism did to prolong hope in French minds, from the collapse of faith in 'man'. As against this example Jakobson was simply a real exile, a man deeply hurt by being cut off from his country and from seeing his closest friends, Mayakovsky and Nikolai Trubetskoy, fall victim to the two forms of twentieth-century tyranny: Soviet and Nazi. Attitudes to literature and to culture were formed by these two plights, world-historical and personal, which came to overlap.

In the case of Jakobson, this creator of a 'formal' critical method was creating his own kind of profoundly encoded literature to express a real human plight. In the postmodern, or post-structural world, the misery of disinheritance became amplified into a literary trope and a cultural value in itself – exile. In Jakobson, whose work laid the foundation for later developments, his version of structuralism was an attempt to create a portable home in language. He created a theory of language which answered the same need that Khodasevich felt when he too was expelled from his homeland.[25]

Russia for Jakobson was the sound of the native language, the associations and their interplay, something he didn't even need a backpack to take with him. No one could take the Russian language away from a Russian speaker.[26] But, at the same time, science could begin to theorize about 'homelands' and their discourses, and a scientist of language could be at home anywhere.

The Symbolist Merezhkovsky said emigration was not a one-way street out of one's country but also a means of return, a road that leads back to one's country.[27] Jakobson, who began as a poet and became a theorist, created a way back in theory. He avowed that life, work and poetic language were, for him, all part of the creation of a personal mythology.[28]

In the beginning, before he was exiled, Jakobson's fascination with language and the meanings it could express was part of an optimism to create a wholly new society from scratch. Structuralism could seem like a kind of innovatory brutalism in sociology and literature, the equivalent of erecting concrete skyscrapers in the belief that their functional qualities alone would make human beings want to live in them. But the emphasis on the autonomy of the text was a positive expression of freedom, of the kind Mayakovsky hailed as Futurist. It had something to do with the enormous enthusiasm with which the young Mayakovsky and also the young Jakobson greeted Einstein's Theory of Relativity. Jakobson wrote:

> There suddenly appears the science of relativity. For yesterday's physicist, if not our earth, then at least our space and time were the only possible ones and imposed themselves on all worlds; now they are proclaimed to [be] merely particular instances. Not a single trace of the old physics has remained ... In all the domains of science there is the same total rout of the old, the rejection of the local point of view, and new, giddy perspectives. One's most elementary premises, which were unshakeable not so long ago, now clearly reveal their provisional character.[29]

Structuralism in Jakobson's hands showed how language expressed relative, temporal meanings, though language itself was a realm of science and hardly a local matter.

Jakobson's 'Futurist' outlook bound him to Lenin and Mayakovsky. But when Mayakovsky was dead and Lenin had corrupted utopia and Jacobson was homeless the structural theory of language and literature which grew out of Russian Futurism became a compensation for loss of homeland and loss of meaning as such. It was what Nietzsche, identifying key aspects of the modern world, had called a 'superabundant substitute'. With complex terminology Jakobson's poetic science kept any personal cultural loss disguised, as a defence against political manipulation and intrusion. Jakobson wanted the freedom of the inner space, and found it in a new place: in the poetic ear.[30]

Structuralism was both elitist and anti-collectivist. It was an esoteric modernism designed to keep out the simple minds who wanted a happy ending and the prying attention of political manipulators who wanted mind-control. On all these counts, none of them insignificant, all of them painful for the home-loving human heart, structuralism stripped out the gentle and personal pleasures of literature.

Aikhenvald the humanist was by contrast on the side of 'Her Majesty, Life'.[31] He never gave up his concern with the writer's conscious craft, nor his conception of human beings as sensibilities who would suffer in too functional and too mechanized a world where they did not have art to guide them. Aikhenvald was a classic 'Life and Work' man who taught that the relationship between art and life was morally significant. He defended 'Her Majesty, Life' against the scientific pretensions of Bolshevism and he would have taken up arms against structuralism equally, had it come of age as a critical method in his day. Like Nabokov, Aikhenvald was part of Russian conservative and liberal opposition to the stiflingly narrow, mechanistic application of 'science' and 'scientific' values to life. Aikhenvald called the Bolsheviks' adherence to theory an insult to life.

He held common ground with Nabokov here, as, against both structuralists and Bolsheviks, he rejected the imposition of any a priori critical apparatus on the art of the written word. Readers of Nabokov will recall how he hated and parodied the way critics, editors and scholars vulgarly processed something they called truth. Nabokov was a complex case, like Jakobson. It was not that there was no truth, but that it was in the verbal and symbolic play of the text, a kind of amalgamation of what Nabokov might have taken from a Jakobson and what he might have taken from a Russian Symbolist like Blok or Ivanov or even Merezhkovsky.

In early Soviet Russia Lenin created a threefold negative world: one in which Nabokov could not live (no symbolism, no freedom of imagination), one in which Jakobson could not work (no independent human sciences), and one where Aikhenvald was condemned to death (no respect for the integrity of life) if he did not leave for ever.

The thinkers on the ships stuck to their open-hearted defence of the person, their call for a society of moral individuals, and their sense of reality as a sacred otherness in which the individual mind plays its small part. The religious philosophers were not burblers, but if they used words in a way Wittgenstein disallowed, then their burbling had a moral point which an alternative, repressed Russia would continue to practise and encourage all century. Looking back from the 1970s to Stalin's purges, when her husband was taken away and died in a camp in 1938, Nadezhda Mandelstam conceded that it was already hard, given the course the short century had taken in both Russia and the West, to believe in the old religious idealism such as Berdyaev taught, based as it was on the 'optimism' of the nineteenth-century philosopher Vladimir Solovyov, but 'I still cling to a very faint hope,' she wrote.[32] This faith helped to fuel the political dissent for which Mrs Mandelstam became famous in the West during the Cold War. Through her, as through the quite different figure of Mikhail Bakhtin, and through various dissident writers and artists, spiritual opposition to the subverted Enlightenment project in Russia remained alive through Soviet times, even though its last exponents were banished in 1922. Significantly, the film-maker Andrei Tarkovsky cited Karsavin and Frank as amongst the most important influences on the thinking which eventually made him break with the Soviet establishment.[33] The Nobel prize-winning poet Joseph Brodsky, tortured and driven out of Soviet Russia, was fascinated by Berdyaev.[34] To help him resist Sovietism Solzhenitsyn steeped himself in the antidote of the tradition of Russian religious idealism created by Solovyov.[35]

The confusion which arose in Europe and America over what spiritual dissent from Soviet totalitarianism consisted in is part of the still undistilled history of the Cold War. That dissent never amounted to Western liberalism, not in the 1920s and not in the 1970s. In the form anti-totalitarianism was expressed by Solzhenitsyn, it hurt and disappointed 1970s liberal America. Solzhenitsyn defended persons, but he was not egalitarian. He was a religious-minded authoritarian. By the same token the expelled 1922 idealist generation which helped inspire Solzhenitsyn was humane and politically liberal, but it wasn't morally liberal; it sought spiritual authority. Berdyaev defended a notion of 'spiritual aristocracy'. Sergei Bulgakov wanted to realize with his philosophy the dreams 'of the best Russian people'.[36] Nabokov wondered at the terrible drabness and mediocrity which the 'new men' ushered in and looked back to his own nostalgic version of the aristocratic which he might re-create in literature. In that sense Lenin did expel 'aristocrats' on the ships.

He also expelled true philosophers in the sense that these were men prepared to think on behalf of humanity at large. Unlike Nabokov and Jakobson, the expelled philosophers were too old to change their idiom and even their mental tactics, but they understood that their task was to preserve meaning, and to do it without disguise. As universalists they perceived that Europe was just as much in crisis around 1920 as Russia was. Everywhere idealism had been shattered by the First World War. The modern world was a place from which the gods, and God, had departed. Whether socialism in some form could make good the loss of God for the majority of people was an unresolved question. Berberova remarked in her memoirs that 'though it uplifted people spiritually, Christianity did not free them socially and only the democracy of the nineteenth and twentieth centuries taught people not to preen themselves on wealth, not to scorn poverty, and gave everyone the right not to be bought and sold'.[37] Socialism made people more tolerant of each other and less materialistic, Berberova felt, implying that a charitable secular society in which men and women were kind to each other, unselfish and attentive to the needs of strangers, would be enough. But the exiles, who were mostly a generation older than her, disciples of Dostoevsky, and witnesses of the first Soviet years, were not so sure.

What they knew for certain was that Lenin's Russia was not a socialist country, and that Europe had formed an erroneous impression of its political merits. In this they were one with Nadezhda Mandelstam when she cursed prominent Soviet apologists abroad, like the French writer Louis Aragon.[38] Both Russians abroad and dissident Russians at home knew that Western Soviet sympathizers like H. G. Wells and Romain Rolland were deluded. They fought the same battle in pre-war France in respect of a wrong-headed sympathy with Marxist-Leninism as Nabokov did in post-war America. Berdyaev was delighted when André Gide returned from the USSR disillusioned and came to him for advice. Alexandra Tolstoy despised Rolland for siding with Leninist tyranny: '[he] found excuses for Bolshevism and violence by maintaining that people must be led against their will to happiness and prosperity.'[39] Nabokov later agonized in his correspondence with the American critic Edmund Wilson over how such an intelligent man could be so misled.[40]

In France the man who spearheaded the positive view of Lenin's creation was the mayor of Lyons, Eduard Hérriot, who, after a visit to Russia organized by Aleksei Tolstoy and the 'On the Eve' team in pro-Soviet émigré Berlin,[41] published *La Russie nouvelle* in 1923. The émigrés were enraged when the progressive Frenchman dismissed 'old Russia' as a submissive and religious culture oriented towards the peasantry, and which history had now left behind. It was Hérriot who, in 1924, having become the President of France, brought about his country's recognition of the Soviet Union. Into the 1930s the name Hérriot conveyed to Russians abroad the sense of someone who knew nothing of what present-day Russia was really about. When socialists in the West began to denounce Hitler, many Russians abroad wondered why the same socialists should think Stalin worthy of their friendship.

Historians and writers will continue to try to explain why Western sympathies went the way they did. One cogent answer for the general anti-establishment fascination with Communist Russia was given by Romain Rolland to Gorky early in their friendship and even earlier in the history of the West's infatuation with the world of Lenin and Stalin: 'Despite my disgust, despite my horror...I accept the new-born.'[42]

Something about the Russian Communist world was just too exciting, too bold an experiment, with all the right moral excuses on its
side. It made rational men suspend their judgement.

At the round-table discussion with Stepun, Aikhenvald, Berdyaev,
Kuskova and Bely, which took place in Berlin on 11 December 1922,
the positions taken raised such questions as whether metaphysical
'meaning' mattered, whether it wasn't idle talk and whether socialism
promised something better.

The Revolution, said the chairman in his introduction, had no
precedent in history and raised a mass of questions to which everyone
would find his own answers. Stepun stood up to clarify some of the
issues as he saw them. He defended the spiritual integrity of the person
–'personhood' – as an aspect of the 'Russian Idea' and twinned with it
an interpretation of the Revolution as an event which trampled over
the person. Here was a tragedy the intelligentsia must make sense of
and out of which it must create new meaning. 'The creator of tragedy
is always God,' he said. Stepun's speech had much in common with
ideas that would develop abroad as German Existentialism. In 1922
they were embryonic in the mind of Heidegger and Martin Buber.

The danger with the public debate on 11 December was its potential unintelligibility. Here were huge ideas which tailed away into
vagueness. Bely seemed to agree with Stepun, but no one in the Berlin
audience that evening could be sure. There was no Wittgenstein to
heckle, a relief for the panellists, but also no Wittgenstein to chair the
session, no relief for the audience. Happily the three other panellists
spoke more straightforwardly. Berdyaev stressed individual responsibility for the events of history. But otherwise, uncharacteristically, he
did not say much. Aikhenvald struck the right note with the audience
when he defended Life – 'full of depth, sense, beauty and meaning' –
against the encroachments of absolute art or absolute anything. 'Not
to regard [life] as authentic is a sin and a mistake. Real life stands
higher than the most artistic work.'[43] And higher than politics in its
Russian sense, he would need to have added.

Most striking for understanding the range of mentalities of the day, however, was Kuskova's answer to what the Revolution meant, for, as a left-wing thinker, Kuskova was closest to Lenin. At the same time, with an extraordinary naivety, she unconsciously invoked the same Christian spirit of 'through a glass darkly' as Stepun. The difference was only in her vocabulary devoted to the new society and the new man. Nothing is clear now, she told the Berlin audience, but 'from the moment that individuals arise out of the chaos and set definite goals, so that people can strive to fulfil them, then the decisive break will come, the revolution will begin. Then Russia will speak of the forms of life in which she wants to live, the meaning of the past will be revealed and we will see the shape of the concrete new man who has passed through the profound experience of war and revolution.' Here was the socialist project expressed overtly as hope. It was Christian metaphysics reborn.[44]

I cite this occasion to make clear that it was not only the Russian idealists who thought of themselves as apolitical but found themselves inevitably caught up in politics. Those on the socialist side, who believed themselves only political, were in addition old-style idealists. They were not 'rationalists' at all. The Enlightenment project in Russia – as in the West – didn't really get rid of metaphysical hope. It reconceived it as social hope. What was cast out, though, was faith in the moral value of suffering: everything that was meant when the idealists used the word 'tragedy'. That was the corner they tried to defend. They pinpointed the one value about to be lost. Berberova thought socialism would make people less materialistic. Kuskova thought it would provide the great goal to strive for, and in that striving the meaning of life would be revealed. But the idealists insisted on the idea that these goals and satisfactions could never be met outside of the Christian spiritual life which invited modesty rather than Faustian striving. The idealists belonged to a world in which good and evil did not equate with material success and failure, not even when the project was socialism.

When Vysheslavtsev wondered in Paris how to explain the old way of Russian philosophy to a contemporary Western audience, he decided on one occasion to talk about Grigory Skovoroda, an eighteenth-century Russian thinker, theologian and poet:

> I will allow myself [he said] just two citations: 'That most primary, ecumenical, invisible Force... [which]...endows humanity with its most noble benefit: free will'. And here is a passage...'We've measured the depth and height of the seas, the earth and the heavens, we've discovered a countless multitude of worlds; we construct "incomprehensible machines". But something is missing. You can't fill up a vacuum in the soul with the limited and the transitory.'

Vysheslavtsev went on:

> The figure of Skovoroda embodies, in essence, all the sacred aspirations and sympathies of Russian philosophy...later... [as] in Solovyov...and in some of us who can still remind a new generation of the spirit and tragedy of Russian philosophy, and who are trying to perpetuate that philosophy in our works abroad.[45]

The Russian religious philosophers set themselves against the modern in the sense that they disliked the idea of a mankind which, having rejected God, was arrogantly self-sufficient. They sought a principle of metaphysical modesty to counteract both the 'egoism' of individuals in a liberal society and the arrogance of socialism, as they saw it. Berdyaev often referred to Faust. But these were not only Russian ideas. Berdyaev shared many values with his Catholic friends in France, and there was an interesting overlap between his thought and that of the ascetic Simone Weil.

Essentially what the expelled Russians said was that human beings needed a higher incentive to be moral. Pragmatism and other forms of utilitarianism were something less. Many people have felt, from generation to generation, the same gap in Western values, despite recognizing the merits of a universal quest for what politicians glibly call 'freedom and prosperity'. Iris Murdoch's generation was disappointed with Communism, 'the God that Failed', while in the same era, the mid-twentieth century, the height of the Cold War, Rory Bruce Lockhart felt a parallel disappointment with the Western alternative: not because he was Communist but because the West lacked moral appeal:

> What is wrong with the world is not the strength of Communism which Stalin and Co. have perverted into an instrument of Slavist expansion … but the moral and spiritual weakness of the non-communist world.[46]

Like several generations of Russians, from Berdyaev to Solzhenitsyn, the Russian religious philosophers hoped the Western world would have a place for them and endorse this sense of something missing. But the West was too liberal to find the moralism of the idealists bearable.

It may be that their story has been ignored because their message was unacceptable.[47] But their story is extraordinary and their view of ethics as compelling as it ever was. The weakness of their political position, which is neither liberal nor repressive, is balanced by their vision of a quality of life which is not cultivated in the service of any political or national goals. They have no truck with a consumer world of modern comforts. They believe not in the much-touted, much-debased contemporary 'freedom to choose' but in free will. They are a good prescription to make us uncomfortable.

The Russian idealists have been rediscovered on a vast scale since the end of the Soviet Union. Much of the material used to write this book is contained in recent Russian publications and some of it only exists on the worldwide web. The banished idealists are inevitably misused as figureheads to attack the Communist past and invoke a messianic-mystical Russian future. They are not insipid, and therefore not undangerous figures.

And so it is important that they re-enter Western history too, where it would be best for them to be reincorporated into the broad corpus of philosophy. They should be appreciated and criticized alongside Weil, Buber and Levinas – religious thinkers who worked on the margins of philosophy. They should be understood with regard to Nietzsche, and the once Catholic Heidegger. In that way their graphic role illustrating what the rationalist twentieth century rejected can be more deeply understood.

Appendix One

GPU Report on the Arrests of 16/17 August 1922

23 August 1922
Secretariat of the [GPU] Collegium

Comrade Stalin,

On the instructions of Comrade Unshlikht I enclose a report on the state of the operation concerning the deportation of anti-Soviet intelligentsia as of 23 August 1922.

Enclosed: as mentioned above

Secretary of the GPU Collegium Ezerskaya

1) In the two days the report covers, according to our telegrams, two people were arrested and despatched: Bulatov from Vologda and Shishkin from Novgorod.
2) Of the people we hadn't been able to find until now we've arrested three: L. N. Yurovsky, Osorgin and Izyumov and Professor Velikhov has been transferred from house arrest to the inner prison.
3) In all, of the 67 people on the Moscow list subject to arrest and deportation abroad, we have arrested

a) 11 people at home

> Maloletnikov Nikolai Vasil'evich
> Lyubimov Nikolai Ivanovich
> Rybnikov Aleksandr Vasil'evich
> Novikov Mikhail Mikhailovich
> Kizevetter Aleksandr Aleksandrovich
> Fomin Vasily Emel'yanovich
> Ozerov Ivan [*sic*] Khristoforovich
> Ugrimov Andrei [*sic*] Ivanovich
> Izyumov Aleksandr Filaretovich
> Yurovsky Leonid Naumovich
> Osorgin Mikhail Andreevich

b) 14 people have been arrested and are being held in the inner prison

> Tyapkin Nikolai Dmitrievich
> Briling Nikolai Romanovich
> Kravets Tarichan Pavlovich
> Trubetskoy Sergei Evgen'evich
> Bakkal Il'ya Yur'evich
> Kil'chevsky Vladimir Agafonovich
> Ushakov Ivan Ivanovich
> Kondrat'ev Nikolai Dmitrievich
> Velikhov Pavel Apollonovich
> Peshekhonov Aleksei Vasil'ievich
> Korobkov Nikolai Dmitrievich
> Uspensky Aleksandr Ivanovich
>   (temporarily in Smolensk at the trial of
>   the church ministers)
> Bulatov
> Shishkin

c) 21 people have been released after declaring their willingness to go abroad at their own expense

> Arbuzov Aleksandr Dmitrievich
>
> Sakharov Andrei Vasil'evich
>
> Kuz'min-Karavaev
>
> Baikov Aleksandr L'vovich
>
> Abrikosov Vladimir Vladimirovich
>
> Matveev Ivan Petrovich
>
> Zvorykin Vladimir [*sic*] Vasil'evich
>
> Kukolevsky Ivan Ivanovich
>
> Parshin Nikolai Evgrafovich
>
> Matusevich Iosif Aleksandrovich
>
> Kudryavtsev Vasily Mikhailovich
>
> Frank Semyon Lyudvigovich
>
> Tsvetkov Nikolai Nikolaevich
>
> Bordygin Vasily Mikhailovich
>
> Yasinsky Vsevolod Ivanovich
>
> Fel'dshtein Mikhail Solomonovich
>
> Berdyaev Nikolai Alekseevich [*sic*]
>
> Rozenberg Vladimir Aleksandrovich
>
> Artobolevsky Ivan Alekseevich
>
> Aikhenval'd Yuly Isayevich
>
> Stratonov Vsevolod Viktorovich

All undertook to wrap up their affairs and leave within a week

d) 8 people in the Moscow area have not been arrested

> Izgaryshev Nikolai Alekseevich
>
> Ozeretskovsky Veniamin Sergeevich
>
> Il'in Ivan Aleksandrovich
>
> Sigirsky Aleksandr Ivanovich
>
> Stepun Fyodor Avgustovich
>
> Loskutov Nikolai Nikolaevich

Myakotin Venedikt Aleksandrovich

Pal'chinsky Pyotr Ioakimovich

e) 11 are in other towns

Tver' – Klevetsky

Kaluga – Romodonovsky

Orel' – Izrail'son

Saratov – Rozanov

Petrograd – Yushtin, Vainberg, Kozlov

Batum – Oganovsky

Gomel' – Charnolussky

A second request has been made to the Provincial Departments in the area for the results of the arrest.

f) Thus overall two people on the list remain unaccounted for – Falin, who was arrested earlier and [internally] exiled under GPU surveillance and Efimov who is being held in the Taganka prison.

4) Of the 14 held in the inner prison Tyapkin, Kravets, Briling and Velikhov have been handed over together with their files to the Counter-Espionage Department [KRO] of the GPU. The remaining 10 people are subject to deportation abroad at the GPU's expense and by convoy.

5) No information has arrived from Ukraine. A second telegram has been sent suggesting they hurry up with an answer.

6) The Petrograd Department has presented the following summary of results of the operation: on the night of 16/17 August, in accordance with the list of anti-Soviet intelligentsia in the city of Petrograd we arrested 30 people.

Stroev Vasily Nikolaevich

Savich Konstantin Ivanovich

Zubashyov Sergei Luk'yanovich

Selivanov Dmitry Fyodorovich

Ermolaev Nikolai Nikolaevich

Evdokimov Pyotr Ivanovich

Lapshin Ivan Ivanovich

Kartel's Nikolai Konstantinovich

Lutokhin Dolmat [*sic*] Aleksandrovich

Kozlov Nikolai Pavlovich

Ostrovsky Andrei Andreevich

Petrishchev Afanasy Borisovich

Yushtin Ivan Ivanovich

Brutskus Boris Davydovich

Kogan [Abram] Saulovich

Polner Sergei Ivanovich

Tel'tevsky Aleksei Vasil'evich

Gusarov Iganty Evdokimovich

Eremeev Grigory Alekseevich

All the above-named people will be exiled abroad in convoy at the GPU's expense.

Punpensky [*sic*] Leonid Alekseevich

Zamyatin Evgeny Ivanovich

Kharitonov Boris Iosifovich

Izgoev-Lande Aleksandr Salomonovich

Karsavin Lev Platonovich

Volkovyssky [*sic*] Nikolai Moiseevich

Lossky Nikolai Anyfrievich [*sic*]

The seven above named in accordance with their wishes will be allowed to go abroad at their own cost.

Sadykova Iul'ya Nikolaevna

Kantsel' Efim Semenovich

Gutkin Abram Yakovlevich

Bronshtein Isai Evseevich

The four above named will be sent to the Eastern provinces where their specialities can be of use in combating epidemics.

7) Entry visas for Germany for all those subject to foreign exile have already been obtained. As long as the money is received in good time all those subject to foreign exile at the GPU's expense can be sent very soon.

Samsonov Chief Administrator GPU Secret Department
I. Reshetov Chief Administrator 4th section GPU Special Department

Appendix Two

The Lists of Deportees from Moscow and Petrograd

LISTS OF THE intellectuals scheduled to be deported from Russia in autumn 1922 exist in at least four different archives which were opened to researchers after 1991: the Russian State Archive for Social and Political History (RGASPI), the Archive of the President of the Russian Federation (APRF), the Russian Centre for the Conservation and Study of Documents of Contemporary History (RTsKhIDNI) and the Central Archive of the FSB, the present-day 'Federal Security Service' which has inherited the records of the Cheka, the GPU and subsequent Soviet security organizations. Most of these documents have now been published and give a clear account of who and how many people were arrested. The names, grouped according to three places of residence – Moscow, Petrograd and 'Ukraine' – total 174 in the State Archive version and and 197 or 'as many as two hundred' in the Presidential Archive, as of 2/3 August.[1] The Presidential Archive lists 66 names for deportation from Moscow and 51 from Petrograd. The sample document, translated here as Appendix One, was compiled for the GPU chief Dzerzhinsky at his request on 7 September, and adjusts the number to sixty-seven for Moscow and thirty for Petrograd, citing figures from 23 August.[2]

It has become clear, however, that a final assessment of numbers actually expelled, based on these lists, is unreliable. They have given a vastly inflated impression of the number of individuals who actually left the country as a result of the police action of August 1922. The commentary accompanying the most recently published documents, from the FSB Archive, observes that the GPU lists of scheduled deportees were not a guaranteed record of who left.[3] In the most obvious instance, with the exception of three individuals, none of those named on the Ukrainian list were sent abroad but exiled internally.[4] The historian A. V. Florovsky was among the exceptions.[5]

The size of the police operation throughout the summer and autumn of 1922 was without doubt considerable. Documents in the FSB Archive testify to the arrest of 228 individuals, 225 of whom can be definitely identified, including thirty-four students. But of those 225, only sixty-seven were actually expelled. Some forty-nine were sent into internal exile, thirty-three were reprieved and the outcome in the remaining cases is unclear.[6]

Since this book is devoted to the Moscow and Petrograd expulsions, the list presented here includes all the individuals I have been able to trace who were expelled from the two cities within the time frame that seems to me to embrace the Philosophy Steamer as a phenomenon: that is, from mid-May 1922, when Lenin wrote his letter to Dzerzhinsky outlining the forthcoming police operation, to 1 March, 1923, when the Moscow-registered Tolstoyan Valentin Bulgakov and two others left Russia from the Black Sea port of Odessa. Their departure was belated and the last to take place.[7] Otherwise the last party to leave went on the *Preussen*. V. G. Makarov bases his alternative figures on a period up to 20 January 1923.

One researcher has suggested going back to summer 1921 to the departure of Maxim Gorky to take in the full scope of those pressed to depart by Lenin, but given the many pressures and fears which led individuals to turn their backs on Soviet-Russia-in-the-making, but which did not amount to an active police campaign to oust them, this kind of notional extension of the idea of the Philosophy Steamer does not seem practicable. A study of the expulsions with slightly different parameters might well want to include the deportations special to Kazan, and to single out the Vice-Chancellor of the University,

Alexander Alexandrovich Ovchinnikov, and the psychiatrist and Dean of the Medical Faculty, Grigory Yakovlevich Troshin, as among Lenin's most interesting victims in the professions. But here I am confining myself to Moscow and Petrograd, above all to draw attention to the handful of Lenin's expellees who are known internationally.[8]

Given that whatever parameters one sets this chapter in Russian history is difficult to quantify, in my list I have included

i) individuals who, like Valentin Bulgakov and his namesake Sergei Bulgakov, although they were originally sought by the GPU on the basis of Moscow or Petrograd residence, were eventually deported from elsewhere

ii) individuals who might otherwise have travelled on the *Haken* and the *Preussen* but in fact, for various reasons, left Russia by independent means, both before and after the departure dates of these two ships.

iii) the poet Khodasevich, who left Russia because he believed he had been marked out for arrest and whatever might follow.

Lists for Moscow and Petrograd compiled in the West, based on émigré sources, and in the first case drawn up by one of the actual deportees, have long been substantially shorter than those worked with by post-Soviet Russian historians. The one that appeared in 1981, compiled by Boris Lossky in conjunction with Tatyana Osorguina and the first historian of the expulsions Mikhail Heller, had omissions but has proved a useful yardstick by which to judge the GPU schedules which have been published more recently.[9] A list previously viewed with some circumspection, but which now turns out to be indispensable to establishing who actually arrived from Russia, was published in the émigré newspaper 'The Rudder' soon after the *Haken* docked. One of the expellees, Venedikt Myakotin, gave the paper an interview immediately on his arrival in Berlin from Moscow.[10] Incidental comments in a variety of autobiographies and memoirs have also brought into question the large numbers arising out of purely archival research in Russia.[11]

Myakotin said in October 1922 that thirty to thirty-five individuals were in the process of being expelled from Moscow of whom he named twenty. Petrograd was expelling thirty-four *intelligenty*, of whom he named seven. These figures amount to less than half the number of candidate expellees suggested by GPU documents published in Moscow. For the whole of Russia in 1922 and early 1923 a figure approaching seventy-five to eighty expulsions from the intelligentsia suggests itself. V. G. Makarov from the FSB Archive, whose work has reversed the trend towards inflated figures, puts the number even lower, at sixty-seven. Lenin's 'cleansing' of Russia in 1922, to purge it of men and women whose views would be unacceptable in the new Soviet Union, was no less shocking for involving a greater or lesser number of leading figures. But the facts demand a sense of proportion.

But then again, if one wants to arrive at a complete numerical picture of the expulsions, as well as take in their human aspect, one has to remember accompanying family. For instance, Myakotin put the total number of Moscow deportees, *including* family, at one hundred, roughly three times the number of named expellees for that city alone. I would therefore suggest an overall figure of around 220 people deported from Russia, men and women of all ages, and children, all of whose lives were violently disrupted by an unprecedented state action.

My figure for the number of named individuals expelled from Russia's two capitals meanwhile rests at sixty-nine. The notes explain where my compilations for Moscow and Petrograd diverge from the FSB finding. I must stress that they are my compilations, arranged in alphabetical order and numbered, for ease of reference. They do not correspond to any existing historical document. Nor are they replacements for the passenger lists of the *Haken* and the *Preussen*, which have never come to light. Clearly it would have been impossible to get all the Moscow-listed names and their families on board the *Haken* on one sailing. Even Myakotin's one hundred people from Moscow comprised far more people than the ship could take. Berdyaev said twenty-five families were on board and it was full.[12] Similarly the *Preussen* could only have carried about seventy-five passengers. So not all the notional passengers on the Philosophy Steamer actually sailed on the ships of 28 September or 16 November and we are stretching the facts into a legend if we suggest they did. Nevertheless, this list represents, to the best of my knowledge, the Russians resident in Moscow and Petrograd who were driven out of their country by the 1922 purge.

THE MOSCOW LIST

1. Vladimir Abrikosov – Uniate priest, disciple of Tolstoy
2. Yuly Isayevich Aikhenvald – literary critic
3. Aleksei Dmitrievich Arbuzov – member of Abrikosov's religious study group
4. Aleksandr L'vovich Baikov – member of the Abrikosov group
5. Il'ya Yur'evich Bakkal – publicist, political activist, SR[13]
6. Vasily Bardygin – member of the Archeological Institute
7. Nikolai Alexandrovich Berdyaev – philosopher
8. Aleksei Alekseevich Bulatov[14] – journalist, economist, partner in the Zadruga publishing co-op
9. Valentin Feodorovich Bulgakov[15] – former secretary to Lev Nikolaevich Tolstoy
10. Semyon Lyudvigovich Frank – philosopher
11. Ivan Alexandrovich Ilyin – philosopher
12. 'Intetsky'[16]
13. Alekandr Filaretovich Izyumov – archivist, partner in the Zadruga publishing co-op
14. Alexander Alexandrovich Kizevetter – historian
15. Vasily Mikhailovich Kudryavtsev – deputy head of the Zadruga publishing firm
16. Dmitry Vladimirovich Kuz'min-Karavaev – poet, former SR
17. Nikolai Ivanovich Lyubimov – cooperativist
18. Nikolai Vasil'evich Maloletnikov – cooperativist
19. Iosif Alexandrovich Matusevich – painter and journalist
20. Venedikt Alexandrovich Myakotin – historian, writer, editor of *Russkoe Bogatstvo* ('The Wealth of Russia')

21. Mikhail Mikhailovich Novikov – Vice-Chancellor ('Rector') Moscow University

22. Mikhail Andreevich Osorgin – writer

23. Veniamin Sergeevich Ozeretskovsky – partner in the Zadruga publishing co-op. Popular Socialist

24. Nikolai Pavlovich Romodanovsky – cooperatist

25. Vladimir Alexandrovich Rozenberg – editor, *Russkie vedomosti* ('The Russian Gazette') and publisher

26. Matvei Dmitrievich Shishkin – cooperatist

27. Aleksandr Ivanovich Sigirsky – cooperatist

28. Vsevolod Viktorovich Stratonov – Dean of the Maths Faculty

29. (Prince) Sergei Evgenevich Trubetskoy – historian, philologist, White activist

30. Nikolai Aleksandrovich Tsvetkov – archivist at the Museum of the Red Army and Navy

31. Sergei Nikolaevich Tsvetkov – member of the Archeological Institute

32. Alexander Ivanovich Ugrimov – agronomist

33. Ivan Ivanovich Ushakov – agriculturalist, jurist, professor

34. Boris Petrovich Vysheslavtsev – philosopher

35. Vsevolod Ivanovich Yasinsky – agronomist

36. Nikolai Nikolaevich Zvorykin – economist

37. Aleksei Vasilievich Peshekhonov[17] – economist, Minister of Food in the Provisional government

Total: 37

THE PETROGRAD LIST

38. Sergei Nikolaevich Bulgakov[18]

39. Alexander Alexandrovich Bogolepov – Deputy Vice-Chancellor ('Pro-Rector'), University of Petrograd

40. Boris ('Per') Davidovich Brutskus – economist

41. Viktor Yakovlevich Iretsky[19] – writer, journalist

42. Alexander Solomonovich Izgoev – writer, journalist

43. Abram Saulovich Kagan – publisher
44. Lev Platonovich Karsavin – philosopher
45. Boris Osipovich Khariton – journalist
46. Nikolai Pavlovich Kozlov – civil engineer
47. Ivan Ivanovich Lapshin – philosopher
48. I. I. Lodyzhensky[20] – economist
49. Nikolai Onofreievich Lossky – philosopher
50. Dalmat Alexandrovich Lutokhin[21] – economist
51. Boris Nikolaevich Odintsov – soil scientist
52. Afanasy Borisovich Petrishchev – journalist
53. Sergei Ivanovich Polner – maths teacher
54. Leonid Moishevich Pumpyansky – journalist
55. Dmitry Fyodorovich Selivanov – mathematician
56. Stanislav Mikhailovich Visloukh – professor of Botany
57. Nikolai Moiseevich Volkovysky – journalist
58. I. M. Yushtim or Yushtin – agronomist
59. Efim Lukyanovich Zubashov – agronomist

Total: 22

Also expelled, but travelled independently:

60. Pitirim Sorokin[22] – sociologist
61. Fyodor Stepun – writer and philosopher

Also departed independently:

62. Sergei Melgunov[23] – historian and White activist
63. E.D. Kuskova – economist
64. Sergei Prokopovich[24] – economist
65. Anatoly Eduardovich Dyubua – writer and jurist[25]

Also departed, fearing he was listed:

66. Vladislav Khodasevich – poet, with his partner Nina
    Berberova, a writer[26]

Also expelled, by special order:

    67.   Vladimir Filimonovich Martsinkovsky[27]
    68.   Vladimir Petrovich Poletika[28]

Also expelled on the *Haken*:

    69.   Vadim Dmitrievich Golovachev – student[29]

Reprieved:[30]

    Yakov Markovich Buchspan – economist
    Vladimir Grigorevich Chertkov – former secretary to Tolstoy,
       leading Tolstoyan
    Mikhail Solomonovich Feldstein – jurist, professor at Moscow
       State University
    Vasily Emilianovich Fomin – professor of Histology at Moscow
       University No 1.
    Nikolai Dmitrievich Kondratyev – professor of agronomy
    Ivan Ivanovich Kukolevsky – professor at the Higher Technical
       Institute, specialist in theoretical hydraulics
    Ivan Khristorovich Ozerov – economist, banker
    Pyotr Ioakimovich Palchinsky – engineer
    Aleksandr Alexandrovich Rybnikov – economist, agrarian
       reformer
    Gustav Shpet – philosopher
    Evgeny Zamyatin – writer

Listed and refused the offer to go abroad:

    Leonid Naumovich Yurovsky[31] – financier, pupil of Struve,
       released, later perished in Stalin's purges.

Detained in prison:

    Pavel Apollonovich Velikhov – agronomist

Appendix Three
The Lives

Vladimir Abrikosov (1880–1966) Uniate (Eastern Catholic) priest, expelled on the *Haken*. Organized committee for Russian Catholics in Rome, provided information for papal inquiry, *Pro Russia*, into imprisoned priests in Russia. Moved to Paris in 1926 under unclear circumstances and spent rest of life in seclusion.

Yuly Aikhenvald (1872–1928) Literary critic expelled on the *Haken*. A rabbi's son, born in Odessa, converted to Christianity. Studied philosophy, translated Schopenhauer's *The World as Will and Representation* into Russian. Author of three-volume *Silhouettes of Russian Writers* and many essays and articles on literature. First discovered Vladimir Nabokov. Myopic. Run over by a tram in a Berlin street.

Yury Annenkov (1889–1974) Writer, painter, member of House of Writers. Close to Gumilyov. Emigrated 1924 and published two volumes of richly detailed literary memoirs.

Aleksei Arbuzov (1859– ?) former director of the Department of General Affairs, Ministry of Internal Affairs, and senator. Expelled on the *Haken*.

Aleksandr Baikov (1874– ?) Lawyer and professor at the Moscow Institute for Oriental Studies. From 1914 professor of international law, Moscow University. From October 1921 head of the archive of the Red Army and Navy. Expelled on the *Haken*.

ILYA BAKKAL (1983–after 1950) SR since 1906, from October 1917 to July 1918 chairman of the Left SR faction on the VTsIK. From 1920 chairman of the Central Office of Left SRs. Expelled on the *Haken*. In Berlin after the Second World War became director of the German theatre of Comic Opera in the Soviet zone. He was arrested by the Red Army in 1949 and sentenced to ten years in a labour camp, where he probably perished.

JURGIS BALTRUSAITIS (1873–1944) Lithuanian-born Russian Symbolist poet. Became Lithuanian ambassador to Moscow in 1920 and helped persecuted Russian artists and intellectuals to leave.

VASILY BARDYGIN (1893– ?) Professor at the Moscow Archeological Institute. Son of a factory owner. Accused of holding anti-Soviet views and supporting monarchist activists. Expelled on the *Haken*.

ANDREI BELY (1880–1934) Writer, mystic, author of groundbreaking modernist novel, *St Petersburg*. Lived in Berlin 1921–3, then returned to Russia.

NINA BERBEROVA (1901–93) Writer. Emigrated with the poet Khodasevich, lived in Paris and in United States after the war. Author of many stories of émigré life and exceptional memoirs. Professor of Russian literature.

NIKOLAI BERDYAEV (1874–1948) Leading Russian idealist philosopher expelled on the *Haken*. Lived in Berlin and Paris, established worldwide reputation before his death.

PYOTR BITSILLI (1879–1953) Literary critic, emigrated and lived in Paris. Admirer of Karsavin, author of memoirs.

ALEXANDER BOGOLEPOV (1885–1980) Specialist in law and the history of the Church, university professor, Deputy Vice-Chancellor of Petrograd University. Expelled, settled in Berlin. After the war moved to the United States where he became Professor of Canon Law at St Vladimir Academy in New York. Wrote a study of Russian lyric poetry and several volumes on Orthodoxy.

BORIS ('PER') BRUTSKUS (1874–1938) Born in Kurland of Jewish parents in the fur trade, came to Moscow as a child. Anti-Jewish pogroms forced the family to leave Moscow in 1892. Brutskus studied in Warsaw where he became interested in Zionism. Returned to St Petersburg in 1908. An 'economic individualist' opposed to socialist ideas, expelled in 1922. Worked in Berlin until forced to leave for Palestine in 1935.

ALEKSEI BULATOV (1877– ?) Economist, co-operatist. Expelled in 1922 and settled in Reval (Tallinn), Estonia, where he edited a Russian agricultural-cooperative journal.

SERGEI BULGAKOV (1871–1944) Idealist philosopher, Orthodox priest, expelled via Constantinople. Ministered in Prague and Paris. Author of major works of theology.

VALENTIN BULGAKOV (1886–1966) Secretary to Lev Tolstoy in 1910, director of Tolstoy Museum at Yasnaya Polyana before expulsion from Odessa in March 1923. Head of Russian cultural-historical museum in Zbraslav, Czechoslovakia. Returned to the Soviet Union in 1948 and again worked as a curator at Tolstoy Museum in Yasnaya Polyana.

IVAN BUNIN (1885–1953) Writer. Emigrated 1920, lived in Paris. Winner of Nobel Literature Prize 1933. Strongly disliked both modernist and socially committed Russian literature.

KORNEI CHUKOVSKY (1882–1969) Famous Soviet children's writer, member of the House of Writers in Petrograd and the Serapion Brotherhood of avant-garde writers. Broke with many former literary friends who emigrated or who were expelled in 1922.

DON AMINADO (A. P. Shpolyansky) (1888–1957) Writer, editor, satirist. Emigrated 1920 and lived in Paris. Author of colourful memoirs.

FELIKS DZERZHINSKY (1877–1926) Polish-born head of the Cheka, later the GPU, oversaw the expulsions. Dzerzhinsky spent a quarter of his life – eleven years – in tsarist prisons and Siberian exile, including three years of hard labour. 'His identification with, and championship of, the underprivileged and the oppressed' (Leggett) was unquestionable. Dzerzhinsky remains an enigmatic figure.

SERGEI EFRON (1892–1939) Husband of Marina Tsvetaeva. Became Soviet police agent and fled back to Russia where he was shot.

ILYA EHRENBURG (1891–1967) Soviet writer who partly lived abroad. From 1923, European correspondent of *Izvestiya*.

ANTON FLOROVSKY (1884–1968) Historian, Professor at Novorossisk. Deported 1922 and settled in Prague.

GEORGY FLOROVSKY (1893–1979) Priest. Emigrated in 1920 to Prague. Head of St Sergius seminary in Paris, 1926–39. After the war, in the United States at Harvard and Princeton. Author of major work on Russian religious thought.

SEMYON FRANK (1877–1950) Jewish-born, converted to Christianity. Religious thinker, writer on literature and poetry. Expelled on the *Haken* with his family, lived in Berlin, Paris and London.

VICTOR FRANK (1909–72) Eldest son of Semyon, converted to Catholicism. Historian, broadcaster for BBC Russian Service and Radio Liberty, literary critic. Lived in Berlin, London and Munich.

ZINAIDA GIPPIUS (1869–1945) Poet, wife of Dmitry Merezhkovsky. Emigrated in 1919. Hostess of the Green Lamp salon in Paris.

MAXIM GORKY (1868–1936) Writer close to Lenin. Pressed to leave Soviet Russia in 1921, returned in 1928. Gorky helped the stricken intelligentsia from after the Revolution until he left and wrote a superb trilogy of autobiographical novels about his difficult early life of poverty and manual work. His reputation has suffered from his collaboration with the regime after his return to Russia.

NIKOLAI GUMILYOV (1886–1921) Acmeist poet, monarchist. First husband of Anna Akhmatova. Arrested and shot as part of the Tagantsev Affair in August 1921.

IVAN ILYIN (1883–1954) Philosopher, specialist in Hegel and Fichte at Moscow University. Expelled 1922 and settled in Berlin. Teacher, journalist, polemicist, monarchist and passionate believer in the unique Russian path. Moved to Switzerland in 1938. Ten volumes of his works have been published in post-Soviet Russia. His cousin Vasily Sergeevich Ilyin (1882–1957) was an émigré professor in Prague.

VIKTOR IRETSKY (1882–1936) Self-described as 'Jew and petty-bourgeois from Shlissel'burg'. Minor writer of fiction and science fiction, contributor to conservative press, director of the House of Writers Library from 1918. Also wrote under pseudonyms I. Ya. Glikman and Ya. Erikson. Expelled in 1922. Contributed to Russian press worldwide and was close to Nabokov and Aikhenvald. Died in Berlin.

R. V. IVANOV-RAZUMNIK (1878–1945) Literary critic, sociologist and author of a two-volume *History of Russian Social Thought* (1907), very popular before the Revolution. Implacable opponent of Marxist ideas. Arrested in 1919, then released. Allowed to continue working 'in the field of literature though far from freely'. His memoirs, also translated in English, were published posthumously.

ALEXANDER IZGOEV-LANDE (1872–1935) Journalist, writer, editor, political moderate and contributor to *Landmarks* (1909) which made him a close associate of the idealist philosophers, also of P. B. Struve. After expulsion in 1922 worked in Berlin. Published a conspectus of the state of Russia over the fifteen years after 1917 and wrote frequently for the Riga-based *Segodnya* ('Today'). Died in Estonia.

ALEXANDER IZYUMOV (1885–1951) Expelled on the *Haken*. Friend of Kizevetter, worked on the Historical Archive of Russia Abroad (RZIA) in Prague from 1925. Interned by the Nazis in 1941 and sent to a concentration camp. Freed by US troops in 1945. Retained his Soviet citizenship.

ROMAN JAKOBSON (1896–1982) Poet, literary theorist, linguist, close to the Futurist poets Mayakovsky and Velimir Khlebnikov before emigration in 1920. Founder of Moscow and then Prague Linguistic School, collaborator with Nikolai Trubetskoy on new science of phonology. Worked at Soviet consulate in Prague until 1929, professor in Brno until the war. Emigrated to the United States and taught at Harvard and MIT.

ABRAM KAGAN (1889–1983) Founder of Petropolis publishing house in Petrograd and after expulsion in Berlin. Moved to Brussels in late 1930s and in 1941 to the United States where he became a director of the Russian Mutual Aid Society, *Nadezhda*.

LEV KAMENEV (1883–1936) Founding Bolshevik, with Lenin, abroad, supporter of Provisional government in 1917, critical of Lenin's revolutionary extremism and Cheka violence. Central Committee member. Berdyaev observed that Kamenev 'had a pleasant way with him; he invariably defended the interests of scholars and writers and did a great deal on behalf of the persecuted intellectuals'. Zamyatin was one beneficiary.

LEV KARSAVIN (1882–1952) Medieval historian, art historian, writer, academic, defender of the Orthodox Church. Expelled 1922, lived in Berlin and Paris, active in Eurasian movement. Moved to Chair of cultural history in Kaunas, Lithuania, in 1927. Arrested in 1949 and sent to the Gulag.

TAMARA KARSAVINA (1885–1978) Ballerina, emigrated to England in 1918. Author of memoirs in English.

BORIS KHARITON (1876–1941) Journalist, manager of the House of Writers 1918–22. Expelled and worked as a journalist in Berlin and Riga, where he became editor of *Segodnya* ('Today'). Deported by the Red Army to the Soviet Union.

VLADISLAV KHODASEVICH (1886–1939) Classical-style Russian poet. Emigrated with Nina Berberova in 1922.

ALEXANDER KIZEVETTER (1866–1933) Distinguished historian, leading Kadet, outspoken Bolshevik critic. After expulsion lived in Prague.

NIKOLAI KOZLOV (? – ?) Civil engineer. Expelled with his family in 1922, lived in Berlin

VASILY KUDRYAVTSEV (? – ?) Deputy director of the cooperative Zadruga. Colleague of Melgunov. Expelled in 1922.

IVAN IVANOVICH KUKOLEVSKY (? – ?) Professor at the Moscow Higher Technical Institute. Reprieved from expulsion and later won a Stalin Prize for his specialization in theoretical hydraulics.

EKATERINA KUSKOVA (1869–1958) Economist, socialist, wife and professional colleague of Sergei Prokopovich. Pressed to leave in 1922, they established themselves in Berlin and from 1924 in Prague as expert analysts of the Soviet economy. Kuskova died in Geneva.

DMITRY KUZMIN-KARAVAEV (1886–1959) SR in 1905, suffered from imprisonment in solitary confinement in 1907. Minor Acmeist poet active in Gumilyov's Guild of Poets, married Elizaveta Pilenko (later Mother Maria) in 1910, divorced 1916. Medical orderly at the front during First World War, active in the Red Cross. Attended the classes of Vladimir Abrikosov and converted to Eastern Catholicism. Expelled in 1922, went to Rome in 1923 and studied at the Papal Oriental Institute Russikum. Taught the history of Russia and the Russian Church. Head of the Russian Catholic Mission in Berlin and from 1931 student chaplain in Louvain, Belgium. Become a bishop. His father, Vladimir Kuzmin-Karavayev, was a distinguished Moscow professor of law who emigrated and taught in Paris until his death in 1927.

IVAN LAPSHIN (1870–1952) Philosopher, musicologist, psychologist, St Petersburg academic, studied in England. Expelled in 1922 and rebuilt his career in Prague.

VLADIMIR LENIN (ULYANOV) (1870–1924) Revolutionary, founder and
leader of the Bolshevik Party. First leader of Soviet Russia. Prime mover
behind the 1922 expulsions.

I. I. LODYZHENSKY (? – ?) Economist expelled in 1922. Coordinated
White military resistance to the Bolsheviks. Lived in Geneva.

ANDREI LOSSKY (1917–   ) Third son of Nikolai Lossky. Studied
European and Russian history in London. Studied and taught at Yale,
became a US citizen.

BORIS LOSSKY (1905–   ) second son of Nikolai Lossky. Studied
architecture then history of art in Paris. Became a French citizen and
distinguished art historian and curator. Has published several sets of
memoirs.

NIKOLAI LOSSKY (1870–1965) Russian-style philosopher at St
Petersburg University for many years. Fabian Socialist linked to the Kadet
Party but not drawn to political activity. Claimed he taught his students
to dislike capitalism but respect the personality of the capitalist. After
expulsion, moved with his family to Prague where his academic career
flourished. After the war lived in the United States. Author of specialized
books and articles and a history of Russian philosophy.

VLADIMIR LOSSKY (1903–1958) First son of Nikolai Lossky. Studied in
Prague and Paris. Became distinguished Orthodox theologian and French
citizen. Died in a car accident.

ANATOLY LUNACHARSKY (1875–1933) Dramatist, journalist, pioneer
Bolshevik. Longstanding friend of Lenin in exile and after. People's
Commissar for Education and the Arts (1917–29). Uncomfortable with
post-revolutionary violence but not tempted to leave. Quoted as saying
that it is irrelevant to wonder whether the power of lightning to kill
people is immoral, and so also with the power of Marxism. Died en route
to taking up post in Madrid as Soviet ambassador to Spain.

DALMAT LUTOKHIN (1885–1942) Landowner, publicist, economist, journalist, editor of *Ekonomist*. Expelled in 1922, went to Prague, returned to Russia in 1927. Saved from arrest in Stalin's purges in 1935 by Gorky. Author of autobiography, unpublished in his lifetime. Died in the siege of Leningrad.

NIKOLAI LYUBIMOV (? – ?) Member of the All-Russia Union of Cooperatists. Expelled on the *Haken*.

NIKOLAI MALOLETNIKOV (? – ?) Fellow of the Moscow regional agricultural research station. Expelled in 1922.

OSIP MANDELSTAM (1891–1938) Great twentieth-century Russian poet, who died in a labour camp. His wife Nadezhda wrote unique memoirs.

VLADIMIR MARTSINKOVSKY (1884–1971) Writer, teacher and priest. From 1913 Secretary of the Russian Christian Student Movement. Expelled 27 December 1922. Lived in Poland, in Prague, and from the early 1930s in Palestine (Israel).

IOSIF MATUSEVICH (1879– after 1940) Studied fine art in Odessa and Moscow, became a painter, journalist, editor and critic. Expelled in 1922, contributed widely to émigré newspapers and journals. A Jew, arrested by the Gestapo in 1938.

IVAN MATVEEV (1880– ?) Member of the All-Russian Union of Agricultural Cooperatives. Expelled on the *Haken*.

VLADIMIR MAYAKOVSKY (1894–1930) Futurist poet, close friend and protégé of Roman Jakobson. Briefly in Berlin, but returned to Russia. Committed suicide.

SERGEI MELGUNOV (1879–1956) Historian, professor, publisher, anti-Bolshevik activist, emigrated in autumn 1922. Author of *The Red Terror* (1925), the first book about Lenin's Russia, which became a world bestseller.

DMITRY MEREZHKOVSKY (1865–1941) Poet, critic, mystic, writer of historical novels acclaimed in their day, and religious biographies. Emigrated in 1919 and settled in Paris in 1920. With his wife, Gippius, co-host of the Green Lamp salon from 1926.

PAVEL MILYUKOV (1859–1943) Co-founder of Kadet Party, Duma deputy, leading figure in the Provisional government of 1917. Emigrated in 1918 and settled in Paris. Failed to establish himself as liberal leader of the emigration. Founded and edited the weekly *Poslednie novosti*. The bullet which killed V. D. Nabokov was intended for Milyukov.

VENEDIKT MYAKOTIN (1867–1937) Journalist, Populist, editor of *Russkoe Bogatstvo*. Expelled 1922, lived in Berlin, Prague. Held Chair of East European history in Sofia 1928–37.

VLADIMIR DMITRIEVICH NABOKOV (1869–1922) Father of the novelist, Kadet leader, Duma deputy, newspaper editor. Emigrated in 1919, co-founded the newspaper *Rul*, killed by a stray bullet in a terrorist attack in Berlin.

VLADIMIR VLADIMIROVICH NABOKOV (1899–1977) Novelist in Russian and later in English. Emigrated in 1919, studied in England, lived in Berlin, wrote under penname Sirin. Emigrated to the United States in 1940.

PAVEL NOVGORODTSEV (1866–1924) Moscow history professor, co-founder of the Kadet Party who became a minister in Kerensky's government. Emigrated and became first head of Russian Law Faculty in Prague.

MIKHAIL NOVIKOV (1876–1965) Biologist, Vice-Chancellor of Moscow University, public figure distinguished for wartime work with the Red Cross. Worked in Berlin, Heidelberg and for sixteen years in Prague. Aged seventy-three became leading figure in Russian academic community in New York. Wrote his autobiography.

BORIS ODINTSOV (1882–1967) Soil scientist, agronomist, expelled in
1922. Lived and worked in Prague and after the war in the United States.

MIKHAIL OSORGIN (1878–1942) Leading SR in his youth, imprisoned
after 1905 Revolution. Self-exiled to Italy, as foreign correspondent for
Russkie vedomosti until 1916. Minor writer of historical novels and
autobiographical fragments. Settled in Paris.

NIKOLAI OTSUP (1894–1958) Poet, active at House of Writers 1918–22.
Close to Gumilyov, Volkovsky and others. Emigrated in 1922. Edited
Paris periodical *Chisla* and wrote many poems and richly informative
memoirs.

ALEKSANDER OVCHINNIKOV (1874– ?) Statistician, professor, Vice-
Chancellor of Kazan University. The son of a village priest. Not arrested
but expelled to Germany in autumn 1922.

VENIAMIN OZERETTSKOVSKY (1888– ?) Writer, member of the Zadruga
publishing co-op. Member of the Popular Socialist Party and the Juridical
Society. Expelled on the *Haken*.

IVAN OZEROV (1869–1942) Economist, university professor, banker,
reprieved from expulsion in 1922, rearrested in 1930 and sentenced to ten
years in a labour camp.

ALEKSEI PESHEKHONOV (1867–1933) Economist, socialist, sympathetic
to Soviet Russia. After expulsion became a Soviet agent, applied to return
and was eventually rewarded with a post at the Russian consulate in Riga,
where he died.

AFANASY PETRISHCHEV (1872–1951) Writer, journalist and editor for
Populist papers, close to the House of Writers where his brother was a co-
manager, and to Khariton, Melgunov, Myakotin, Pumpyansky and
Peshekhonov. Cooperatist. After expulsion worked in Berlin for émigré
press, moved to Paris where he monitored the Soviet press and became a
prominent commentator on Soviet affairs and daily life through the
1930s. In Russia his son was sent to a labour camp because Petrishchev

was an émigré, according to fellow émigré Roman Gul, after which Petrishchev 'capitulated'. From 1945–7 wrote for the Paris-based *Sovietsky Patriot* ('Soviet Patriot').

VLADIMIR POLETIKA (1888– ?) Meteorologist, professor at the Petrograd Geographical Institute. Expelled by special order on 3 February 1923.

SERGEI POLNER (? – ?) Mathematician and cooperativist, founder member of the publishing house Zadruga. Expelled in 1922. Lived in Berlin, where he became director of the Financial Department of the publishing house Vataga.

SERGEI POSTNIKOV (1883–1965) Historian, bibliographer, journalist, Socialist Revolutionary. Emigrated 1921. Leading figure in the Russian community in Prague, author of a history of the community's activities, historian with the Historical Archive of Russia Abroad (RZIA). Survived Gulag sentence and died in Prague.

SERGEI PROKOPOVICH (1871–1955) Economist, Kadet, later independent socialist, Minister of Trade and Industry and later of Food in Kerensky's Provisional government. Pressed to leave with his wife Kuskova in 1922, established Economic Bureau specializing in Soviet affairs, first in Berlin and after 1924 in Prague. Moved briefly to the United States, died in Geneva.

LEONID PUMPYANSKY (1889– after 1940) Economist and journalist expelled in 1922. Friend of Brutskus. Moved from Berlin to Tallinn where he became director of the Shelye Bank (1924–34). A victim of the arrival of the Red Army in Estonia.

NIKOLAI PAVLOVICH ROMODANOVSKY (1876– ?) Member of the council of the All-Russia Society of Agronomists. Expelled on the *Haken*.

VLADIMIR ROZENBERG (1860–1932) Socio-political activist, economist, journalist, editor of *Russkie Vedemosti* ('The Russian Gazette') from 1907, historian of the Russian press. After expulsion in 1922 lived in Berlin.

Moved to Prague in 1924 to work on the Historical Archive of Russia Abroad (RZIA).

ALEXSANDR RYBNIKOV (1877–1938) Economist, arrested and reprieved, shot in 1938.

DMITRY SELIVANOV (1855–1932) Mathematician of international repute. One of the oldest expellees. Lived in Prague

LEV SHESTOV (CHESTOV) (1866–1938) Russian philosopher. Emigrated to Paris. Close to Berdyaev.

MATVEI DMITRIEVICH SHISHKIN (1886– ?) Cooperatist, Menshevik, expelled on the *Haken*.

VIKTOR SHKLOVSKY (1893–1984) Critic, literary theorist, pioneer 'Formalist', friend of Roman Jakobson. Detested 'old-fashioned writers'. Fled Russia for Berlin in spring 1922, fearing arrest in conjunction with the SRs trial. Returned to Russia in 1923. Author of *A Sentimental Journey. Memoirs 1917–1922.*

ALEXSANDER SIGIRSKY (? – ?) Cooperatist, took part in the 1921 All-Russia Congress of Agricultural Cooperativism, leading figure in the Agronomists' Union. Expelled in 1922.

PITIRIM SOROKIN (1889–1968) Russian sociologist and culturologist, active SR in his youth, active anti-Bolshevik and open critic of Lenin in the press after 1917. Pressed to leave with his wife in September 1922. After brief period in Czechoslovakia emigrated to the United States where he founded the Sociology Department at Harvard University in 1931 and became its head from 1942. President of the American Sociological Association in 1964. Author of many books, including memoirs of his life in Russia.

FYODOR STEPUN (1884–1965) Writer, critic, minor novelist, Russian and German philosopher. Strong connection to Heidelberg where he studied and contributed to the international periodical *Logos* 1910–14. Fought and wounded in First World War. Expelled in 1922. Held Chair in Dresden 1926–37. After the war resumed his academic life in Munich. Author of many books, including memoirs.

MARIYA STOYUNINA (1846–1940) Founder with her husband of the Stoyunin Academy, one of St Petersburg's top girls' schools before the Revolution. Expelled on the *Preussen* with her daughter, her son-in-law Nikolai Lossky and their family.

VSEVOLOD STRATONOV (1869–1938) Astronomer, astrophysicist, banker, publisher, dean of Maths Faculty at the University of Moscow. Lived in Prague after being deported in 1922.

PYOTR STRUVE (1870–1944) Journalist, political activist, early Marxist who in emigration both before and after the Revolution became a 'liberal on the Right'. White supporter and ardent anti-Bolshevik. Lived in Paris, Prague and later in Belgrade. Dominant figure who coined the phrase 'Russia Abroad' and campaigned in vain for its political organization under an effective leadership.

ALEXANDRA TOLSTOY (1884–1977) Daughter of the writer Lev Tolstoy. Tolstoyan, social campaigner, several times arrested and released. Escaped from Russia in 1929 and settled in New York. Author of memoirs in English.

ALEXSEI TOLSTOY (1883–1945) Novelist, author of three-volume *Road to Calvary*, whose literary reputation was irreparably besmirched by collaboration with the Soviet authorites. After brief sojourn in Berlin returned to Russia. Winner of the Stalin Prize.

LEV TROTSKY (1879–1940) Bolshevik, People's Commissar for War during the Civil War, writer and intellectual. Kept close watch on the literary world, ardent supporter of the 1922 expulsions.

GRIGORY NIKOLAVICH TRUBETSKOY, PRINCE (1873–1930) Scion of distinguished conservative family close to Church and tsars. When the White Army was routed in southern Russia, escaped to Paris and continued organizing the military effort against the Reds until his death. Prominent figure in the conservative emigration.

NIKOLAI SERGEIEVICH TRUBETSKOY, PRINCE (1890–1938) Linguist, pioneer of phonology. Emigrated 1920, taught in Sofia and Vienna. Close friend and collaborator with Roman Jakobson.

SERGEI EVGENIEVICH TRUBETSKOY, PRINCE (1890–1949) Son of the religious thinker and one of the Kadet Party founders, Evgeny Trubetskoy. After the Revolution, head of the White underground movement, Tactical Centre. Imprisoned and released, then expelled on the *Haken*. Moved with his family to Austria. Contributed articles to the conservative émigré press, including one in 1932 warning of the danger to Russia of Hitler's eastward ambitions.

MARINA TSVETAEVA (1892–1941) Great twentieth-century poet. Emigrated in 1922 to join her husband, Sergei Efron, a White Army evacuee, in Prague. Spent the next seventeen years with her children in Prague, Berlin and Paris, in poverty. After her husband fled to the Soviet Union in 1937 she followed in 1939. Intense police pressure induced her to kill herself.

NIKOLAI TSVETKOV (1857–?) Archivist at the Museum of the Red Army and Navy. The son of a priest. Before the Revolution the Director of a Moscow merchant bank. Expelled in autumn 1922.

SERGEI TSVETKOV (1881–?) Civil servant, expelled in autumn 1922.

ALEXANDER UGRIMOV (1874–1974) Agronomist, professor. Expelled in 1922, lived in Berlin and from 1930 in Paris. During the war joined the French Resistance. Expelled in 1947 from France to Soviet Union where he was rehabilitated in 1957. His daughter Vera Reshchikova wrote interesting memoirs.

VERA UGRIMOVA (RESHCHIKOVA) (1902–) Daughter of A. I. Ugrimov. Expelled with him in 1922 and returned to Russia by the French government in 1947. Author of memoirs.

IOSIF UNSHLIKHT (1879–1938) Polish-born activist, follower of Lenin, spent time in tsarist jails. Became one of Dzerzhinsky's two deputies at the Cheka/GPU and was responsible for the day-to-day organization of the expulsions. Unshlikht has come down in Western history as a 'sombre and secretive figure' and 'a cold and calculating bureaucrat', as well as one who remembered Lenin fondly.

PAVEL VELIKHOV (? – ?) Agronomist, public figure. Arrested and kept in prison. Not sent abroad.

ROBERT VIPPER (1859–1954) Historian, specialist in religious studies, briefly head of 'The Living Church' supported by the Bolsheviks to counter the influence of the established Orthodox Church. From 1922–40 Professor of the Latvian University and from 1941 Professor at Moscow State University. Member of the Academy of Sciences. Author of school and university textbooks.

STANISLAV VISLOUKH (1885– ?) Professor of Botany from 1918 at the Petrograd Institute of Agronomy. Arrested in 1921 in connection with the Tagantsev Affair and again in August 1922. Expelled on the *Preussen*.

NIKOLAI VOLKOVYSKY (or VOLKOVYSSKY) (1881– after 1940) Educated in Kharkhov and St Petersburg. Prolific journalist both before and after expulsion. Berlin and later Warsaw correspondent for the Riga-based Russian newspaper *Segodnya* ('Today').

BORIS VYSHESLAVTSEV (1877–1954) Professor of philosophy at Moscow University, close to Frank. Strong interpreter of and contributor to the Russian tradition in philosophy. Expelled in 1922, resumed his career in Paris. Deputy editor of Berdyaev's religious-philosophical journal *Put* ('The Way') and deputy director of the Paris-based Russian-language YMCA press. Spent last decade in Geneva.

VSEVOLOD YASINSKY (1850?–1933) Professor at the Moscow technical academy, builder of steam turbines. Expelled in 1922, became a professor at the Russian Scientific Institute in Berlin

I. A. Yushtin (or Yushtim) (? – ?) Engineer expelled in 1922.

Lev Zak (1892–1980) Escaped from Russia in 1920 via Constantinople. Painter, theatre designer, poet, writer, half-brother of Semyon Frank. Lived from 1923 in Paris.

Evgeny Zamyatin (1884–1937) Writer close to the House of Writers, author of the anti-Utopian novel *We* (1921). Member with Chukovsky of the experimental literary group, Serapion Brothers. Avoided deportation in 1922 but left with permission from Stalin in 1931.

Grigory Zinoviev (1883–1936) Bolshevik, head of the Petrograd Soviet, of whom Gorky said that he was 'one of those petty, psychically unhealthy people with a morbid thirst for the enjoyment of the suffering of their fellow men'.

Efim Zubashov (1860–1928) Engineer, agricultural economist, former Duma deputy, expelled in 1922. Settled in Czechoslovakia.

Valentin Zubov, Count (1884– ?) Hereditary aristocrat, founder of the pre-revolutionary History of Art Institute in Petersburg. Museum curator, aesthete, socialite. Arrested in 1922, but released and did not leave permanently until 1925. Lived in Germany and published memoirs of the period 1917–25.

Nikolai Zvorykin (*c*.1850– ?) Economist, landowner, born into hereditary aristocracy. Taught agronomy in France before the First World War. Adviser to V. K. Pleve and P. K. Stolypin, ministers under the last tsar, on land issues and the Russian peasant question. After expulsion belonged to a group in Paris studying Russia's socio-economic development and culture.

Notes

The following abbreviations have been used for frequently cited memoirs:

Dream: Nicholas Berdyaev, *Dream and Reality. An Essay in Autobiography*, London, 1950.

Fiene: Donald M. Fiene, *Mikhail A. Osorgin,* Ann Arbor, 1982.

MIA, 11 and 12: Boris Lossky, 'Nasha sem'ya v poru likholetiya 1914–1922 godov', *Minuvshee Istorichesky Almanakh*, Kn 11, Moscow, 1992 and Kn 12, Moscow, 1993.

MIA, 16: Boris Lossky, 'V russkoi Prage 1922–27', *MIA* 16, Moscow, 1994.

NLV: Nikolai Lossky, *Vospominaniya,* Slavische Propyläen Band 43, Munich, 1968.

TFV: Tatyana Frank, *Vospominaniya* (unpublished transcript of a taped interview with Peter Scorer), Munich, 1975.

Trubetskoy: Sergei Trubetskoy, *Minuvshee*, Paris, 1989.

Ugrimova: Vera Reshchikova (née Ugrimova), 'Vysylka iz RSFSR', *Minuvshee Istorichesky Almanakh*, Kn 11, Moscow, 1993.

The following abbreviations have been used for other frequently cited works:

CW: V. I. Lenin, *Collected Works*, translated from the Russian, based on 4th edition, London, 1960–80.

Glavatsky: Mikhail Glavatsky, *Filosofsky parokhod v god 1922–i*, Ekaterinburg, 2002.

PSS: V. I. Lenin, *Polnoe sobranie sochinenii*, 5th edition, 55 vols, Moscow, 1967–73.

Volkogonov Leaders: Dmitri A. Volkogonov, *The Rise and Fall of the Soviet Empire. Political Leaders from Lenin to Gorbachev*, edited and translated by Harold Shukman, London, 1998.

Volkogonov Leaders (Russian edn): Dmitri A. Volkogonov, *Sem' Vozhdei*, 2 vols., Moscow, 1995.

Volkogonov Lenin: Dmitri A. Volkogonov, *Lenin: Life and Legacy*, translated and edited by Harold Shukman, London, 1994.

Volkogonov Lenin (Russian edn): Dmitri A. Volkogonov, *Lenin Politichesky Portret*, 2 vols., Moscow, 1994.

All first references are to the author, title and place and date of publication. Subsequent references are to the author and page number, except in the case of multiple works or editors' introductions. See the Bibliography for full details of works cited.

INTRODUCTION

1. The *Oberbürgermeister Haken* should have left Petrograd early on Thursday, 28 September, and arrived in Stettin on Saturday, 30 September, to conform to the usual Petersburg–Stettin timetable. According to S. S. Khoruzhii ('Filosofsky parokhod', *Literaturnaya Gazeta*, 9 May 1990), the expelled Russians did arrive on 30 September. Sergei Trubetskoy's account (Trubetskoy, p. 286 ff.) says the *Haken* was a day late leaving Petrograd, i.e. on Friday, 29 September, which also fits with Boris Lossky's account of embarkation only beginning in the afternoon of 28th. Lossky did not witness the *Haken*'s departure, but all other accounts agree with details advertised by the steamship company that the ships left Russia at first light. Departure from Petrograd at dawn on 29 September would have meant arrival on Sunday, 1 October, which is, I conclude, what happened. Travel guides from 1901 to 1934 vary in their estimations of the journey at between 56 and 70 hours, with a

stop at Reval (Tallinn). The direct journey, at a speed of 10 knots, can only have taken about 52 hours on this occasion.

2. The GPU, the State Political Administration, which existed from February 1922, was still better known by the name of its predecessor, the Cheka, or more properly Vecheka. The notorious acronym was based on the first three words in the name of (The) All-Russian Extraordinary Commission for Combating Counter-Revolution and Sabotage, which was founded in December 1917. See *The Blackwell Encyclopedia of the Russian Revolution*, Oxford, 1988.

3. Philip Boobbyer, *S. L. Frank. The Life and Work of a Russian Philosopher 1887–1950*, Athens, Ohio, 1995, p. 116.

4. *Pravda*, 31 August 1922. The first mention of the event by a Soviet historian, as part of the early Soviet struggle against 'bourgeois ideology', came in S. A. Fedyukin, *Bor'ba s burzhuaznoi ideologiei v usloviyakh perekhoda k NEPu*, Moscow, 1977.

5. *The Times*, 23 August 1922.

6. For a profile of Victor Frank, see Lesley Chamberlain, *Strange Meeting*, BBC Radio 3, 10 April 2002.

7. K. I. Chukovsky, *Dnevnik 1901–1929*, edited by E. Ts. Chukovskaya and with an introduction by V. A. Kaverin, 2nd corrected edition, Moscow, 1997.

8. Viktor Kagan, 'Boris Brutskus: uchenyi i pravozashchitnik' in *Evrei v kul'ture russkogo zarubezhiya*, Vyp. 1, pp. 476–84. The US economist was D. G. Wilhelm.

9. Laurel E. Fey, *Shostakovich. A Life*, Oxford, 2000, p. 11.

10. Karl Schlögel, *Jenseits des großen Oktober Das Laboratorium der Moderne Petersburg 1909–1921*, Berlin, 1988, p. 448; *MIA*, 12, p. 132. Tikhon Ivanovich Polner was a founder member of the publishing cooperative Zadruga. See *Russky Parizh*, compiled and with a foreword and commentary by T. P. Buslakova, Moscow, 1998. L. Fleishman, R. Hughes, O. Raevskaya-Hughes, *Russky Berlin 1921–1923 Po materialiam arkhiva B.I. Nikolaevskogo v Guverskom*

Institute, Paris, 1983.

11. <http://www.ihst.ru/projects/emigrants/selivanov.htm>, accessed 11 June 2004. 'Selivanov' in *Russkoe zarubezh'e. Zolotaya kniga russkoi emigratsii. Pervaya tret' XX veka Entsiklopedichesky biografichesky slovar'*, Moscow, 1997.

12. Trubetskoy, p. 287.

13. L. A. Kogan, 'Vyslat' za granitsu bezzhalostno', *Voprosy filosofii*, 1993, No. 9, p. 83.

14. Khoruzhii, *Literaturnaya Gazeta*, 6 June 1990.

15. An example is *Evangel'skaya Gazeta Mirt*, No. 5(36), Sentyabr–Oktyabr 2002 g.

16. Mikhail Geller, 'Pervoe predosterzhenie – udar khlystom', *Vestnik russkogo khristianskogo dvizheniya*, No. 127, Paris, 1978; in French as Michel Heller, 'Premier avertissement: Un coup de fouet. L'histoire de l'expulsion des personnalités culturelles hors de l'Union Sovietique en 1992', *Cahiers du monde russe et sovietique*, XX (2), 1979, pp. 131–72.

17. For Lenin and the use of reason see Lesley Chamberlain, *Motherland. A Philosophical History of Russia*, London, 2004.

18. See the severe criticism of Berdyaev in Richard Pipes, *Struve Liberal on the Right 1905–1944*, Cambridge, Mass., 1980, pp. 352 ff; G. S. Smith, *D. S. Mirsky*, Oxford, 2000, pp. 125, 160.

I THE NIGHT BEFORE

1. Nicholas Berdyaev, *Dream and Reality. An Essay in Autobiography*, London, 1950, [*Dream*], pp. 3 ff.

2 *Professiya: Zhena filosofa Lidya Berdyaeva* [Diaries], compiled and with a foreword and commentary by Elena V. Bronnikova, Moscow, 2002, pp. 5–12. It's an interesting detail that on both sides of the eve-of-revolution drama the key players married educated women who actively shared their beliefs. As Lenin had his (Nadezhda) Krupskaya so Berdyaev had his Lidiya. These couples – and of course many more – were in the front rank of an intelligentsia about to divide for a century, and both husband and wife were potential activists.

3. Ibid, p. 12.

4. N. O. Lossky, *History of Russian Philosophy*, London, 1952, p. 237.

5. 'Mariy Stoyunina', *Minuvshee Istorichesky Almanakh*, vol. 7, Moscow, 1989.

6. On the Living Church and the mistreatment of Patriarch Tikhon, see W. C. Emhardt, *Religion in Soviet Russia*, Milwaukee and London, 1929, and Matthew Spinka, *The Church in Soviet Russia*, New York, 1956.

7. *MIA*, 12, p. 189.

8. N. A. Berdyaev, 'The Pre-Death Thoughts of Faust' (1922), p. 6, <http://www.berdiaev.com/berd lib/1922> accessed on 22 July 2004. These thoughts formed part of Berdyaev's contribution to the four Russian essays on Oswald Spengler's *Decline of the West* which enraged Lenin and encouraged him to put the writers' names on the expulsion list. The four contributors to *Osval'd Shpengler i Zakat Evropy*, Moscow, 1922, were Berdyaev, Frank, Stepun and Bukshpan.

9. *MIA*, 12, p. 127 ff.

10. Bertram Wolfe, *The Bridge and the Abyss. The Troubled Friendship of Maxim Gorky and V. I. Lenin*, London, 1967, p. 51. See also Lenin to Gorky, written 13 or 14 November 1913, PSS vol. 48, p. 260, CW, p. 121.

11. A. A. Kizevetter, *Na Rubezhe dvukh stoletii Vospominaniya 1881–1914*, with an introduction by M. G. Vandalkovskaya, Moscow, 1997, p. 18.

12. Ibid.

13. *MIA*, 12, p. 110.

14. Geller, p. 223.

15. *Dream*, p. 242.

16. *MIA*, 12, p. 164. The condition is known today as Sydenham's chorea, a disturbance of the nervous system causing involuntary movements and now treatable with sedatives.

17. *Dream*, p. 242.

18. *MIA*, 12, p. 129.

2 THE PAPER CIVIL WAR

1. Kizevetter, *Na Rubezhe dvukh stoletii*, p. 17; L. M. Demina, 'Kizevetter', *Politicheskie deyateli rossii 1917. Biografichesky Slovar'*, Moscow, 1993. The article is summarized at <http://www.hronos. km.ru/ biograf/kizevetter.html>

2. Dalmat Aleksandrovich
Lutokhin, 'Alien Pastors',
*Minuvshee Istorichesky
Almanakh,* vol. 22, St
Petersburg, 1997, p. 95.

3. A. S. Izgoev, 'Tragediya i vina',
Nash Vek, 5 April 1918, quoted in
Mark D. Steinberg,
'Introduction' in Maxim Gorky,
*Untimely Thoughts. Essays on
Revolution, Culture and the
Bolsheviks 1917–1918,* translated
by Herman Ermolaev, London,
1995. On Izgoev, see also
Schlögel, 1988, pp. 392–400;
Pipes, *Struve Liberal on the Right
1905–1944,* Cambridge, Mass.,
1980, pp. 107, 108, 112;
L. Fleishman, Yury Abyzov, and
B. Ravdin, *Russkaya Pechat' v
Rige: is istorii gazety Segodnya
1930 godov,* 5 vols, Stanford,
1997, vol. 1, pp. 311–14.

4. Boobbyer, p. 117.

5. B. P. Vysheslavtsev, *The Eternal
in Russian Philosophy,* translated
by Penelope V. Burt, Grand
Rapids, Michigan, 2002, pp. 21,
68. *Russkoe zarubezh'e. Zolotaya
kniga russkoi emigratsii. Pervaya
tret' XX veka Entsiklopedichesky
biografichesky slovar',* Moscow,
1997, pp. 156–9.

6. Catherine Evtuhov, *The Cross

and the Sickle. Sergei Bulgakov
and the Fate of Russian Religious
Philosophy 1890–1920,* London,
1997, pp. 121 ff.

7. Vadim Kreid, 'Aikhenval'd',
Siluety russkikh pisatelei, I,
Moscow, 1994; F. A. Stepun
'Pamyati Yu. I. Aikhenval'da', in
ibid.; Abram Reitblat,
'Podkolodnyi estet s myagkoi
dushoi I teverdymi pravilami:
Yuly Aikhenval'd v emigratsii',
*Evrei v kul'ture russkogo
zarubezh'ya,* Vyp. 1, Jerusalem,
1992.

8. Pipes, *Struve Liberal on the
Right,* pp. 171–4.

9. V. Rozenberg, *Iz istorii russkoi
pechati: Organisatsiya
obshchestvennogo mneniya Rossii
i nezavisimaya gazeta Russkie
Vedemosti (1863–1918),* Prague,
1924. For general histories of the
press, see *Russkaya
periodicheskaya pechat'
1702–1894: Spravochnik,* edited
by A. G. Dement'ev, A. V.
Zapadov, M. S. Cherepakhov,
Moscow, 1959; *Russkaya
periodicheskaya pechat'
1895–October 1917: Spravochnik,*
edited by M. S. Cherepakhov
and E. M. Fingerit, Moscow,
1957; Charles A. Ruud, *Fighting

Words. Imperial Censorship and the Russian Press 1804–1906, Toronto, 1982.

10. Khariton, Iretsky, Petrishchev, Peshekhonov, Rozenberg, Osorgin, Kizevetter, Myakotin, Aikhenvald, Berdyaev. The founders of *Rech'* – Pavel Milyukov, V. D. Nabokov, I. A. Gessen and A. I. Kaminka – all emigrated earlier.

11. Journalists such as Osorgin and Petrishchev hovered between the Kadets and the Popular Socialists, which was the party of two other 'higher' journalists, Venedikt Myakotin and Aleksei Peshekhonov.

12. Robert Service, *Lenin: A Biography*, London, 2000, p. 122.

13. Boobbyer, pp. 38, 45.

14. FSB file No. 15374, released to the press on 15 August 2002. Commentary at <http://www. newsgala.net>.

15. Khoruzhii, *Literaturnaya Gazeta*, 6 June 1990.

16. Kreid in Aikhenvald, *Siluety*, vol. 3, p. 12.

17. Lenin made this connection repeatedly in *Materialism and Empiriocriticism* (1909) available in *CW*, vol. 14.

18. Michael Glenny and Norman Stone, *The Other Russia*, London, 1990, p. 319. *Dusha* is normally translated as soul.

19. Yury Terapiano, *Literaturnaya zhizn' russkogo Parizha za polveka*, Paris, 1987, p. 181.

20. *Dream*, p. 230.

21. Nina Berberova, *The Italics are Mine*, London, 1991, p. 141, said Gershenzon was 'forced to die'. See also A. Yu. Galushkin et al., eds., *Zhurnaly*, Moscow, 1996, p. 50.

22. *Dream*, p. 109.

23. Boobbyer, p. 116.

24. P. I. Sorokin, *A Long Journey*, New Haven, Conn., 1963. I. A. Golosenko, *Pitirim Sorokin Sud'ba i trudy*, Syktyvkar, 1991. Useful articles can be found at <http://www. hronos.km.ru/ biograf/sorokin>, <http://www. philosophy.albertina.ru> and <http://www. krugosvet.ru/ articles/77/1007787al>, accessed 24 June 2004.

25. For the family history see 'Introduction' in Evgeny Trubetskoy, *Iz proshlogo*, Tomsk, 2000; Ol'ga Trubetskaya, *Knyaz' S. N. Trubetskoy Vospominaniya sestry*, New York, 1953.

26. Trubetskoy, *Iz proshlogo*, p. 280.

27. Ruud, p. 199; V. A. Myakotin, *Nado li idti v Gosudarstevennuyu Dumu?*, St Petersberg, 1906; Dement'ev et al. (eds), *Russkaya periodicheskaya pechat' 1702–1894*, Moscow, 1959, p. 574. Lenin had already attacked *Russkoe Bogatstvo* in the 1890s: 'these gentlemen are the open enemies of social-democracy.' See Lenin, PSS vol. 1, p. 115. From 1914 to March 1917 the journal appeared as *Russkie Zapiski* before it was stifled in 1918.

28. Hannah Arendt, *The Origins of Totalitarianism*, London, 1958.

29. Orlando Figes, *A People's Tragedy: The Russian Revolution 1891–1924*, London, 1996, p. 778.

30. *Dream*, p. 227.

31. CW, vol. 28, pp. 192, 389. PSS, vol 37, pp. 195, 411.

32. Ugrimova, p. 206, uses the word '*sovdepie*', as does Osorgin quoted in Fiene, p. 99. The abbreviation *sovdep* was widely used in the first years after the Revolution, until the formation of the Soviet Union in November 1922, which officialized that term and, as a description of the state, the adjective 'Soviet'. *Sovdep* either meant a Soviet deputy or the body to which he reported, which was the Council of Deputies or 'Soviet Deputatov'. It has disappeared from modern dictionaries. '*Sovdepiye*' is an abstract noun which suggests the impromptu, unfinished nature of the Bolshevik state and mocks its love of abbreviations and acronyms.

33. Wolfe, p. 92 and passim.

34. Steinberg, p. xxii.

35. Sorokin, p. 171.

36. Ibid.

37. For Lunacharsky's rescue of Gustav Shpet, see Gustav Shpet, *Filosofskie Etyudy*, Moscow, 1994, p. 8.

38. Alexandra Tolstoy, *Out of the Past*, translated by various hands, edited by Katherine Strelsky and Catherine Wolkonsky, New York, 1981, p. 101.

39. K. I. Chukovsky, *Dnevnik 1901–1929*, p. 196 (19 March 1922).

40. Alexandra Tolstoy, p. 132. She mistakenly called him Valerian.

41. NLV, pp. 208–9

42. *Dream*, p. 230.

43. Ibid., p. 236.

44. Ibid., p. 233.

45. George Leggett, *The Cheka: Lenin's Political Police*, Oxford, 1981, pp. 308–9. Emhardt, p. 29, refers to 'execution by the hundreds [between 1918 and 1922]'.

46. M. Kulikova, 'Boris Nikolaevich Odintsov', p. 2, at <http://www.ihst.ru/projects/emigrants/odintsov> accessed 6 June 2004.

47. Anatoly Mariengof, *A Novel without Lies*, translated by Jose Alaniz, Moscow, 2000, p. 51.

48. Fiene, pp. 165–8.

49. <http://www. vgd.ru> has brief biographical details of Abram Kagan.

50. Ya. V. Leontiev, *Zven'ya Istorichesky Almanakh*, Vyp. 2, 1991, p. 469. All the expellees who were Zadruga partners are noted in Schlögel, 1988.

51. Nadezhda Mandelstam, *Hope Abandoned. A Memoir*, translated by Max Hayward, Harmondsworth, 1976, p. 79.

52. Wolfe, p. 67.

53. Ibid., pp. 71–2.

54. Tatyana Frank, *Pamyat' serdtsa*, unpublished family memoir in the possession of Peter Scorer, pp. 4–5.

55. Boobbyer, pp. 107–12.

56. TFV, p. 5.

57. Sorokin, p. 186.

58. *Zven'ya Istorichesky Almanakh*, edited by N. G. Okhotin and others, Vyp. 2, Moscow, 1992, p. 140.

59. *Dream*, pp. 231–2; Fiene, p. 221.

60. PSS, vol. 37, p. 411; CW, vol. 28, p. 389.

61. Trubetskoy, p. 174.

62. M. G. Vandalkovskaya, 'Introduction' in A. A. Kizevetter, *Na Rubezhe dvukh stoletii*. Additional material on Kizevetter from <http://www.hronos.km.ru/biograf/kizevetter>.

63. Leggett, pp. 284–7.

64. Richard Pipes, *Russia Under the Bolshevik Regime 1919–1924*, London, 1994, p. 29.

65. Leggett, pp. 287–8. S. E. Trubetskoy's leadership of this organization, aged twenty-eight, has only come to light with the publication of his memoirs. Leggett confuses him with his father.

66. Ibid., p. 287.

67. T. Ul'yankina, 'Mikhail Mikhailovich Novikov', at <http://www. ihst.ru/projects/emigrants/>.

68. Leggett, p. 288.

69. *Dream*, p. 238. This arrest has been confused with the 1922 event by Donald Rayfield, *Stalin and His Hangmen: An Authoritative Portrait of a Tyrant and Those who Served Him*, London, 2004, p. 117.

70. Leggett, p. 273.

71. Ibid., p. 327.

72. Service, p. 434.

73. Glavatsky, p. 85.

74. Volkogonov Leaders, p. 76.

75. Sorokin, p. 187. The best accounts of the Tagantsev Affair, written prior to the release of archive material in 1992, are in Leggett, p. 289, and Pipes, *Struve Liberal on the Right*, p. 344. Ten years before the end of the Soviet Union, Pipes summed up the official Soviet version and exposed it as a sham. All through the Cold War some Western historians deprived of information continued to believe the Bolshevik story, as is reflected, for example, in the notes to Nadezhda Mandelstam, *Hope Against Hope. A Memoir*, translated by Max Hayward, Harmondsworth, 1975, p. 487. Details of the archive material which led to the rehabilitation of the victims and the erection of a memorial were published in Dmitry Prokhorov, '"Zagovor" po planu vozhdya proletariata', *Gazeta Sovershenno sekretno – Versiyu v Pitere*, No. 19, 26 May 2003, at <http:// www. konkretno.ru>.

76. Berberova, *The Italics*, p. 122.

77. Michael Ossorgin, *A Quiet Street*, translated by Nadia Helstein, London, 1930, p. 171.

78. Nikolai Otsup, *Okean vremeni Stikhotvoreniya, dnevnik v stikhakh, stat'i i vospominaniya o pisatelyakh*, with an introduction by Louis Allen, St Petersburg, 1993, pp. 517 ff.

79. *MIA*, 12, p. 89.

80. Cited in Wolfe, p. 90.

81. Mandelstam, *Hope Abandoned*, pp. 153–4.

82. Volkogonov Leaders, p. 40.

83. Service, pp. 430–33.

84. Figes, pp. 778–9. An account of the clumsy way the Soviet authorities handled a visit by English well-wishers is in Vladimir Mikhailovich Zenzinov, *Deserted. The Story of the Children Abandoned in Soviet Russia*, translated by Agnes Platt, London, 1931.

85. The text of Hoover's telegram in Wolfe, p. 50. See also Marc Raeff, *Russia Abroad. A Cultural History of the Russian Emigration 1919–1939*, Oxford, 1990, pp. 27–30.

86. Fiene, pp. 218–19.

87. Fiene, p. 63. Geller, pp. 201 ff. stresses the role of Pomgol in prompting the expulsions.

88. Nikolai Dmitrievich Kondratyev (1892–1938), Professor at Moscow Agricultural Academy from 1917 and one of the founders of planned agriculture in Soviet Russia. Purged under Stalin and rehabilitated in 1963. Biographical information at <http://www.vgd.ru>. For his pardon in 1922 see Glavatsky, p. 172.

89. Roman Jakobson, *My Futurist Years*, edited by Bengt Jangfeldt,

translated by Stephen Rudy, New York, 1997, p. 324.

90. Thomas R. Beyer, 'Andrej Belyjs Rußland in Berlin' in Karl Schlögel (ed.), *Russische Emigration in Deutschland 1918–1941*, Berlin, 1995, p. 312.

91. Vitaly Shentalinsky, *The KGB's Literary Archive*, translated by John Crowfoot, London, 1995, p. 234.

92. As Figes, 1996, explains Gorky's departure.

93. Berberova, *The Italics*, pp. 140–41.

94. Ibid., p. 163.

95. Jakobson, *My Futurist Years*, p. 307.

96. Ibid., p. 326.

97. Ibid., p. 211.

98. Wolfe, pp. 136–9.

99. Glavatsky, pp. 60–61.

100. Ibid.

3 THE JANUS YEAR

1. Wolfe, p. 81; Glavatsky, p. 15.

2. The Kremlin could not afford to ignore Martov's *Sotsialistichesky Vestnik*, published in Berlin. See Nikita Struve, *Soixante-dix ans d'emigration russe 1919–1989*, Paris, 1996, p. 29; André Liebich, 'Die Menschewiki in

Deutschland 1921–1933' in Schlögel, 1995. Martov, once a friend of Lenin in tsarist exile, had left Russia a sick man but kept up the battle in print.

3. The Genoa Conference mattered greatly to Lenin as the occasion to secure foreign loans and take

steps towards international diplomatic recognition, but Soviet tactics, outlined in a letter marked 'secret' from Lenin to Molotov on 16 January, were destined to undermine the conference. Lenin urged Molotov to open separate undocumented talks with the Germans in Berlin and Moscow to predetermine 'our and their contact' in Genoa, and separate 'unofficial, secret talks giving an advance indication of their line in Genoa' with all other participating countries that are willing. Letters to his foreign minister and conference delegation leader Chicherin on 16 and 25 February further advised exploiting the bourgeois sympathy for pacifism. Russia should be presented as a peace-loving country in order to soften up its enemies. On 8 March Lenin insisted Chicherin get the right editor specifically to prepare reports to send to the *Manchester Guardian* in order to get a good press. All these letters were in print in Lenin's *Collected Works* during the Cold War.

4. Lenin, PSS, vol. 54, p. 144 (*CW*, vol. 45, p. 454) wrote to Unshlikht some time between 26 and 31 January 1922 calling for the Cheka 'to intensify the force and speed' of revolutionary tribunals and to meet 'the slightest increase in banditry etc with martial law and shootings on the spot'. Nevertheless, what followed was 'a soft-paw' policy of deporting troublemakers abroad.

5. Quoted in Glavatsky, p. 17, from A. M. Gak, A. S. Masal'skaya and I. S. Selezneva, 'Deportatsiya inakomyslyashchikh v 1922 g. (Positsiya V.I. Lenina)', *Kentavr*, 1993, No. 5, p. 79.

6. Fyodor Dan, *Dva goda skitanii 1919–21*, Berlin, 1922, and Theodor Dan, *Letters 1899–1946*, edited by Boris Sapir, Amsterdam, 1985, p. 320. Glavatsky, p. 88, cites the forced exile of Martov already in 1920, but not the expulsion of Dan, as a precedent for the autumn 1922 expulsions.

7. Lenin to Gorbunov, 6 February, PSS, vol. 54, p. 155; *CW*, vol. 45, p. 461.

8. PSS, vol. 54, p. 182. *CW*, vol. 45, p. 484.

9. Ibid., 21 February to Kamenev and Stalin, PSS, vol. 54, pp. 177,

480. In CW, vol. 45, the phrase is wrongly translated as 'fooling us'.

10. *Pravda*, 31 August 1922.

11. B. Bronshtehn, 'Stratonov Vsevolod Viktorovich', at <http://www.ihst.ru/projects/emigrants/stratonov> accessed on 11 June 2004. 'Bogolepov Aleksandr Aleksandrovich' at <http://www.zarubezhje.narod.ru> accessed on 19 June 2004. See also Robert Paul Browder and Alexander F. Kerensky, *The Russian Provisional Government of 1917 Documents*, vol. 1, Stanford, 1961, p. 469.

12. Sorokin, p. 186.

13. 'On the Significance of Militant Materialism', PSS, vol. 45, pp. 23–33; *CW*, vol. 33, pp. 227–36.

14. Yakov Markovich Bukshpan (1887–1939) was born either in St Petersburg or the Polish city of Lodz, according to conflicting accounts, and worked at the St Petersburg Polytechnical Institute. He was to be purged by Stalin.

15. PSS, vol. 54, p. 198; CW, vol. 45, p. 500.

16. *Pravda*, 10 May 1922.

17. Quoted in Glavatsky, p. 104:

'In respect of the impossibility of bringing about a whole raft of matters through the courts and at the same time the necessity of getting rid of nasty and harmful elements the GPU is proposing to introduce the following amendments to our regulations [*Polozhenie*]: "As an amendment and development of the regulations concerning the GPU of the Republic from 6 February 1922 to give the GPU the right: to carry out sentences of exile [*vysylka*] beyond the frontiers of the RSFSR for up to two years in the case of ill-intentioned Russian or foreign persons."'

18. George Kennan, *Siberia and the Exile System*, 2 vols, London, 1891, vol. 1., p. 242.

19. Ibid., p. 247.

20. Ibid., p. 274.

21. Glavatsky, p. 62. For Russian historians Lenin's words to the Tenth Party Congress reverberate with the same political spirit as words spoken by Catherine the Great almost two centuries before. Catherine allowed the formation of a 'Free Economic Society' in 1765 on condition that its members remained *blagonadyozhny* –

trustworthy and reliable.

22. PSS, vol. 45, p. 189, not available in *CW*.

23. Volkogonov Leaders, pp. 71, 76.

24. Lenin's meticulous approach to pro-Soviet propaganda, even by spring 1922, set the standard for the Soviet century. Yury Steklov was a propagandist writer for *Soviet Russia*, published in the United States and aimed at the English-speaking world in 1922.

25. Lenin hesitated over *Novaya Rossiya* because it was a *Smena Vekh* publication (see pp. 220 ff.), whose Russian patriotism was potentially useful.

26. The cover of *Ekonomist* featured the names of B. D. Brutskus, A. I. Bukovetsky, S. I. Zverev, D. S. Zernov, E. L. Zubashov, A. S. Kagan, V. I. Kovalevsky, D. A. Lutokhin, N. V. Monakhov and A. L. Rafalovich. Lenin would single out another contributor, Ozerov, in his letter of 16 June to Stalin.

27. L. A. Kogan, *Voprosy filosofii*, 1993, No. 9, p. 61.

28. NLV, p. 216. Raeff, p. 209, interviewed Abram S. Kagan (1889–1983), one of the expellees, who told him that after Rapallo German authorities were most cooperative and helpful in granting visas and arranging transportation.

29. Glavatsky, p. 177, and Unshlikht's 'top secret' memorandum to Stalin of 6 January 1923, pictured in Glavatsky, p. 95. The text reads: 'In view of the difficulties that have arisen in sending the Ukrainian anti-Soviet intelligentsia abroad, in connection with the refusal of a series of countries to let them on to their territory the GPU considers it most expedient in order not to delay carrying out the sentences of exile any longer to replace foreign exile for the Ukrainians with exile to distant places in the RSFSR.'

30. Schlögel, *Russiche Emigration in Deutschland 1918–1941*, Berlin, 1995, p. 48.

31. Glavatsky, pp. 94 ff., details this campaign against the professions.

32. Ibid., p. 102, in the form of a memorandum on 1 June.

33. Volkogonov Leaders, p. 7: 'Lenin's assault on the intelligentsia was directed not against their ideas, but against

them personally' is surely wrong. Slavoj Zizek, 'Revolution must strike twice' (review of Hélène Carrère d'Encausse, *Lenin*, translated by George Holoch, London, 2001), *London Review of Books*, No. 25, July 2002, p. 14, approves the opposite view, in Carrère d'Encausse's words: 'this was another example of Lenin's singular method, consisting of eliminating not his opponents but their ideas, allowing the losers to remain in the governing bodies.' Zizek's enthusiasm for this view, however, is in direct proportion to the degree to which it shows Lenin in a good light compared with Stalin. The comparison is odious so far as the present author is concerned. Lenin's view was a composite of his Russian background, his Marxist ideology and his personality. He distrusted the intelligentsia to which he belonged, because he knew it to be non-compliant. Glavatsky, p. 19, cites many instances of its activities that had recently provoked him. He hated the class enemy from a Marxist point of view. Personally, as Copleston,

Philosophy in Russia, p. 292, and Pipes, *Russia under the Bolshevik Regime*, p. 507, note, he hated intellectuals. The negative term he coined in 1909 to describe the contributors to 'Landmarks' was *intelligentshchina*: 'O "Vekhakh"',PSS, vol. 19, pp. 167–75; CW, vol. 16, pp. 123–31. The English edition contains a misleading translation above all of the crucial term '*intelligentshchina*' which is closer to today's 'chattering classes'.

34. Leggett, p. 114. At the time Lenin publicly disagreed with Latsis, to put a distance between himself and the execution of such ruthless policies as took the lives of thousands of innocent intellectuals and clerics when it was implemented by an unruly political police. But class remained Lenin's yardstick.

35. Quoted in Glavatsky, p. 62 (see above, note 21).

36. Volkogonov Lenin, p. 358, has details of this report.

37. Glavatsky, p. 160.

38. Volkogonov Lenin, p. 367. Volkogonov Lenin (Russian edn), vol. 2, p. 194, lists all the doctors. The greater number

were exiled later.

39. Pipes, *Russia under the Bolshevik Regime*, pp. 403–9.

40. For this translation see Volkogonov Lenin, p. 362.

41. Glavatsky, p. 108. Both letters were headed 'On the Question'.

42. Service, pp. 443–9.

43. On 'cleansing' the churches, see Lenin to Trotsky, 11 March 1922, quoted in Volkogonov Leaders (Russian edn), vol. 1, p. 40. The verb was *ochistit'*, the noun *ochishchenie*.

44. Trotsky's authorship of this article has been established for the first time in Glavatsky, p. 76.

45. See above, note 32.

46. Glavatsky, p. 124.

47. 'Berdyaevs' in Volkogonov Leaders, p. 16.

48. Glavatsky, p. 150.

49. Volkogonov Lenin (Russian edn), vol. 2, p. 181.

50. Volkogonov Lenin, p. 358. Comparing the translation of this note with the original Volkogonov Lenin (Russian edn), vol. 2, p. 179, I have made a slight but significant change from 'idealistic' to 'idealist'. Lenin did not expel people because they were 'idealistic' but because, philosophically, they were idealists, not dialectical materialists.

51. Even strained by illness, the process of the expulsions, coupled with the double-edged sword wielded as a result of NEP, economic liberalism and political terror, a socialist face abroad and a tyrannical one at home, Lenin showed he was constantly capable of the double-bluff. His readiness to change policy, should a revolution suddenly happen in Europe, a remark of Lenin's about NEP never published but quoted by Service, p. 431, was par for the course.

52. The literature is extensive on Lenin's capacity to detach himself from his emotions. Service, p. 7: 'he was an able suppressor of outward emotion' and p. 59: 'he suppressed his emotions more effectively than his sisters'. Gorky described him as 'cold-blooded', 'pitiless' and 'lacking in morality', see Steinberg (ed.), Maxim Gorky, *Untimely Thoughts*, p. x.

53. *Pace* Volkogonov he was not 'a gibbering wreck' and it was not a fair survey of the situation (Volkogonov Lenin, p. 360) to

surmise that 'the future of an entire generation of the flower of the Russian intelligentsia was being decided by a man who could barely cope with an arithmetical problem for a seven-year-old'. No doubt Lenin failed certain medical tests but the letter of 16 June shows him in astonishing command of the situation.

54. Volkogonov Leaders, p. 7; Volkogonov Lenin, p. 363. See also Lenin, *CW*, vol. 45, Letter of 30 March 1922: 'We must strive at all costs not to lose this worker.' Leggett, p. 169. Glavatsky, p. 175, notes that many post-Soviet historians have omitted Lenin's insistence that Rozhkov, a man whom he detested and distrusted and had scheduled for deportation, once he was known to be ill, be reprieved from exile abroad and sent instead to Pskov, with explicit instructions that he should have a comfortable place to live and sufficient money to keep himself.

55. Maksim Gorky, *Selected Letters*, edited by Andrew Barratt and Barry P. Scherr, Oxford, 1997, p. 233.

56. Pipes, *Russia under the Bolshevik Regime*, p. 408.

57. Volkogonov Lenin, p. 359, notes that the dossiers were submitted to Lenin several times in his Gorky convalescence through June, before going on to the GPU, Dzerzhinsky, Stalin and Unshlikht for completion.

58. Glavatsky, pp. 154 ff.

59. Ibid., p. 160.

60. Ibid. pp. 180–82.

61. See chapter 2, p. 63.

4 ARREST AND INTERROGATION

1. Kogan, pp. 73–4.

2. Glavatsky, p. 108.

3. Glavatsky, p. 163.

4. Glavatsky, pp. 192 ff. See Appendix 1.

5. TFV, p. 6.

6. *NLV*, p. 217.

7. Ugrimova, p. 204.

8. TFV, p. 7.

9. Fiene, pp. 65–8.

10. Sorokin, pp. 192–5.

11. Leggett, p. 9. The Bolshaya Lubyanka No. 2. 'accommodated a whole complex of Cheka and NKVD departments and associated

units'. It housed 'the NKVD HQ and the Vecheka OO (Special Department), with its inner prison.' This inner prison was notorious. (ibid., p. 20).

12. NLV, p. 218.

13. *Rul'*, No. 603, 22 November 1922.

14. Graf Valentin Zubov, *Eine Welt ändert ihr Gesicht Erinnerungen aus den Jahren der russischen Revolution 1917–1925*, Munich, 1967, p. 142.

15. Boris Lossky, 'K izgnaniyu lyudei mysli v 1922g.' in *Russkii Almanakh*, compiled by Zinaida Schakovskoy, René Guerra and Eugène Ternovsky, Paris, 1981, p. 358.

16. Zubov, p. 142.

17. Trubetskoy, p. 280.

18. NLV, pp. 217–18.

19. Tamara Karsavina, *Theatre Street*, revised, enlarged edition, London, 1947, pp. 266–7.

20. Gorky described Zinoviev as one of those 'petty, psychiatrically unhealthy people with a morbid thirst for the enjoyment of the suffering of their fellow men'. Quoted in Wolfe, p. 98.

21. NLV, p. 219.

22. *MIA*, 12, p. 123.

23. Zubov, p. 139. Schlögel, 1988, p. 481, lists some of the university teachers arrested, plus one student, but only about half of these were deported on the 1922 ships and may not have left Russia at all. Sorokin, p. 197, noted that 'many' students were also arrested on 16 / 17 August, and these too were not deported.

24. Zubov, ibid.

25. 'Beseda v [*sic*] Myakotinym', *Rul'*, No. 560, 1 October 1922.

26. A transcript of Berdyaev's interview is printed in Glavatsky, pp. 166–9.

27. Trubetskoy, p. 280.

28. Glavatsky, pp. 182–92; FSB files on Peshekhonov, Iretsky and Prokopovich and Kuskova at <http://www. gala.net>.

29. Glavatsky, p. 157.

30. S. S. Khoruzhii, 'Zhizn' I uchenie L'va Karsavina' in *L. P. Karsavin Religiozno-filosofskie sochineniya*, T.1, Moscow, 1992; Boris Lossky, *MIA*, 12; Solomon Volkov, *St Petersburg. A Cultural History*, London, 1996, pp. 256–60; Zubov, p. 138. Not only was Karsavin related to Khomiakov but physically he resembled the pioneer Russian

philosopher Vladimir Solovyov, the inspiration of so much of the Symbolist poetry and philosophy of the Silver Age. This added to his mystique.

31. *MIA*, 12, pp. 126–7, 163. Yelena Chaslovna Skrzhinskaya (1897–1981) followed Karsavin to Berlin. Coinciding with his move to Paris she returned to Russia in 1926, where, like him, she became a distinguished medievalist.

32. Zubov, p. 138; Boris Lossky in *Russkii Almanakh*, p. 356.

33. *Dream*, p. 239.

34. Volkgonov Lenin (Russian edn), vol. 2, p. 181.

35. The word for 'far-sighted', *predusmotritel'nyi*, which could also be translated as 'prudent', echoed the idea of preventative justice embodied in the practice of administrative exile.

36. Louise Bryant, author of *Six Red Months in Russia*, New York, 1918, worked for the Hearst press in Moscow when she could get there and otherwise filed stories without datelines. Under political suspicion in her native United States, she was forced to travel without a passport. She was certainly in Russia in summer 1922, probably June to September. See Virginia Gardner, *Friend and Lover. The Life of Louise Bryant*, New York, 1982, pp. 228–30. Gardner does not mention the Trotsky 'interview' but notes on p. 229 that Bryant thought Trotsky 'a passionate and thorough soul'. Bryant commented on Lenin's desire to allow his political enemies to leave Russia, over which he was at odds with the GPU: 'His stance shows an unexpected softness in his make-up which only those who know him will comprehend.'

37. Fiene, p. 64, confuses the two.

38. A brief news gency report headed 'Over 200 Intellectual Leaders Arrested' appeared in the *Manchester Guardian* on 24 August 1922. For Lenin's view that the *Manchester Guardian* would print favourable reports if fed the right information from Moscow, see his letter to Chicherin, 8 March 1922: 'I'm very afraid that if we don't appoint the right editor – very reliable and very clever – for all that we place in the British newspapers, that we'll get trash in the *Manchester Guardian*

which can only harm us.'

39. *Soviet Russia*, 15 October 1922.

40. Volkogonov Lenin, p. 360–61.

41. Ibid., p. 359.

42. Ibid.

43. NLV, p. 216.

44. Volkogonov Lenin, p. 358; Volkogonov Lenin (Russian edn), vol. 2, p. 179. See also *Rul'*, No. 603, 22 November 1922.

45. Fyodor Stepun, *Byvshee i Nesbyvsheesya*, 2nd expanded edition, St Petersburg, 2000, p. 622. According to *Rul'*, op.cit., the one-way Petrograd–Berlin ticket cost £6. Boobbyer, p. 116, writes: 'They had to cover all expenses themselves, including fees for passports. The British Foreign Office estimated that "those who have worldly goods can thus, in the most favourable circumstances, cross the frontier with a capital of 25 pounds; most of them have next to nothing."' Schlögel, 1988, p. 480, put the allowance at US$20. Makarov, pp. 111–12, reproduces a GPU document of 22 August 1992, setting out the official view in Moscow of the costs of expulsion, said to be 212 million roubles per person.

46. Trubetskoy, p. 285.

47. For details, see Appendix 2.

48. Kazys Norkeliunas, 'Jurgis Baltrusaitis as Rescuer of Russian Poets and Artists from the Bolshevik Persecution', <http://www.academic.marist.edu/nork/jurgis.htm>, accessed 21 June 2004. Norkeliunas was a pupil of Nina Berberova in New York, who encouraged him to pursue the subject. Baltrusaitis also offered Gustav Shpet citizenship and passports for his family, see Gustav Shpet, *Filosofskie Etyudy*, Moscow, 1994, p. 8.

49. Sorokin, p. 197.

50. Berberova, p. 144.

51. Stepun, p. 622 and pp. 626–7.

52. For details, see Appendix 2.

5 JOURNEY INTO EXILE

1. *MIA*, 12, pp. 136–7.

2. Ibid., p. 135.

3. Trubetskoy, p. 286.

4. Ugrimova, p. 204.

5. Yury Annenkov, *Dnevnik moikh vstrech*, 2 vols, New York, 1966, vol. 1, p. 261. An exact date is not given.

6. See A. Yu. Galushkin, 'E. I. Zamyatin Pis'mo A. K. Voronskomu k istorii aresta i nesostoyavsheisya vysylki E. I. Zamyatina v 1922–1923gg.', *De Visu*, No. 0, Moscow, 1992, pp. 112–24.

7. The evening at the House of Arts (Dom iskusstv) was recorded by Kornei Chukovsky in his diary. See K. I. Chukovsky, *Dnevnik 1901–1929*. The entry for 30 September 1922, which the editors have unfortunately abridged, suggests the pro-Bolshevik Chukovsky and the future émigré Annenkov both doubted Zamyatin's seriousness. Without clear attribution of whose judgement this was, it called Zamyatin's ideological 'struggle' sham and bogus (*butaforskaya i margarinovaya*).

8. Chukovsky, op.cit; Galushkin, *De Visu*, p. 17.

9. Zamyatina's view was expressed by Alex M. Shane, *The Life and Works of Evgenij Zamjatin*, Berkeley, 1968, p. 40, and notes 48, 49. For Trotsky's opinion see Galushkin, *De Visu*, p. 18. Another poet who emigrated, Nikolai Otsup, expressed Zamyatin's dilemma: 'Everyone was expecting [Zamyatin] in Berlin with the first deportation. It was known that like others, he longed for the European air. They didn't realize how strongly he was bound to Russia.' *Okean vremeni Stikhotvoreniya, dnevnik v stikhakh, stat'i i vospominaniya o pisatelyakh*, St Petersburg, 1993, p. 544. Unlike Chukovsky, who certainly distrusted Zamyatin, Otsup stressed how straightforward and honest Zamyatin was with the Bolsheviks at a time when many of their early followers were wrestling with their consciences and deceiving themselves.

10. The word *taksomotor*, in use in 1922, didn't catch on. The modern word for taxi is just that, *taksi*.

11. Trubetskoy, p. 288.

12. TFV, p. 8.

13. Ugrimova, p. 204.

14. Berberova, p. 147.

15. *Dream*, p. 244.

16. Kurt Pittelkow, Reinhard Schmelzkopf, *Heimathafen Stettin*, Cuxhaven, 1987, pp. 112, 342, 374.

17. *Dream*, p. 244.

18. Ibid., p. 27.

19. Solomon Volkov, *St Petersburg.*

A Cultural History, London, 1996, pp. xiv–v and passim. See also Katerina Clark, *St Petersburg Crucible of Cultural Revolution*, London, 1995.

20. Marcus Aurelius, *The Meditations*, edited by Maxwell Staniforth, London, 1964, 7:21. For Osorgin's preference see Fiene, p. 78, 'My Library'.

21. *The Meditations*, 5:16.

22. *Professiya: Zhena filosofa Lidya Berdyaeva* [Diaries], p. 139.

23. The complex evolution of Ilyin's thought, from tolerance of revolution to a complete identification with the White cause is mapped in I. I. Evlampiev, 'Filosofskie I pravovye vzglyady I. A. Il'ina', accessed on 16 June 2004 at <http://humanities.edu.ru/db/msg/25101>.

24. Boobbyer, p. 40.

25. Semyon Frank, *Reality and Man*, translated by Natalie Duddington, London, 1965, p. 70.

26. Ibid., p. 227.

27. Compare *Dream*, p. 227 and p. 241.

28. Spinoza became very popular in Russian philosophy after the Revolution, as the basis of a determinist alternative to Marxism-Leninism. It was stamped on after 1929. See George L. Kline, *Spinoza in Soviet Philosophy*, New York, 1952, and Chamberlain, *Motherland*, p. 214.

29. *Dream*, p. 81; Boobyyer, p. 90.

30. Boobbyer, p. 23.

31. Ibid., p. 139.

32. Kreyd in Aikhenvald, *Siluety*, vol. 1, p. 4.

33. Nikita Struve, p. 13. Frank apparently converted to Orthodoxy for the utilitarian reason of getting a university job.

34. Trubetskoy, p. 288.

35. I. V. Gessen, *Gody izgnaniya*, Paris, 1979, pp. 164–5. Chukovsky, *Dnevnik 1921–1929*, 22 March 1922, mentions that Aikhenvald's wife was working for the Americans in Moscow in 1922. 'She says they call us Russians "natives".'

36. The term belongs to V. D. Nabokov, *Vremennoe pravitel'stvo i bolshevistskii perevorot*, London, 1988, p. 168.

37. For Frank's parodies of Soviet neologisms, see Boris Lossky in *MIA*, 11, p. 186. The widespread, coarse-sounding use of

acronyms was generally greeted ironically and negatively by the educated public. As Roman Jakobson pointed out, the telegramatic tendency to shorten words came into Russian with the First World War, but it was associated with Sovietism, as was the renaming of Petersburg as Petrograd. See Roman Jakobson, 'Vliv revoluce na rusky yazyk', *Nové Atheneum*, III, Prague, 1921, pp. 203–4. A Nabokov character saw initial-letter acronyms like TASS and couplings of first syllables like NARKOMPROS moving like trains across the page. 'The agonizing constructions of capitalized abbreviations, carried like doomed cattle on frieght cars (the barging of those buffers, the clanking, the hunchbacked greaser with a lantern, the piercing melancholy of godforsaken stations, the shudder of Russian rails, infinitely long-distance trains).' *The Gift*, p. 158. The speed element in the new style of Soviet speech was deliberate, theorized by the worker-poet Aleksei Gastev when he applied Frederick Taylor's time-motion methods of industrial production to improving efficiency in everyday life. Gastev, a metal-worker turned poet, proposed to 'mechanize speech' by replacing long expressions with shorter ones. See Pipes, *Russia under the Bolshevik Regime*, pp. 288–90. Zamyatin and Mayakovsky satirized the political trend which abused the language. Nabokov also detested the simple-mindedness and superficiality of what he called the Soviet KOM-POM-POM (Andrew Field, *Vladimir Nabokov*, London, 1967, p. 182, from his article 'An Anniversary', *Rul'*, 18 November 1927). André Mazon, *Lexique de la guerre et de la revolution en Russie*, Paris, 1920 (see Jakobson's review above), said it was designed to catch the imagination of simple people. The simplifications – though the crucial '*Sov*' and also *tovarishch* (comrade) were introduced by Kerensky's Provisional government in February 1917 – offered themselves as a new opportunity for totalitarian theorizing in the

1930s, ultimately by Stalin himself. For an introduction to this vast and volatile subject, see Clark, *St Petersburg*, esp. Chapter 9, 'Promethean Linguistics'.

The cultural upheaval as it applied to poetic language, of which the poets Velimir Khlebnikov and Mayakovsky were the leaders, was of a different and higher order, creative and inventive. It would be the foundation of Roman Jakobson's enthusiasm for the difference between poetic and natural language and surely also for his intense focus on the communicative power of the phonetic syllable. See Roman Jakobson, *My Futurist Years*. Nevertheless the initial influence of Futurism was visible in both the higher poetic and the less exacting political spheres. Over the next two to three decades the latter became cruder, while the former became more and more esoteric.

38. Sorokin, p. 176.
39. Jakobson, *Nové Atheneum*, p. 205.
40. Jakobson, *My Futurist Years*, p. 85.

41. Roman Jakobson and Krystyna Pomorska, *Dialogues*, Cambridge, 1984, p. 22.
42. For the musicality of the family, see Boobbyer, pp. 10, 81, and communication to the author of Peter Scorer.
43. Ugrimova, p. 204.
44. Boobbyer, pp. 24–5, 52.
45. TFV, p. 9; Tatyana Frank, *Nasha Lyubov*, p. 2.
46. Trubetskoy, p. 288.
47. Fiene, p. 15.
48. NLV, p. 216.
49. B. O. Khariton, *Dni* (Berlin), 13 February 1923, reprinted in Glavatsky, pp. 202–6.
50. Osorgin remembered Trotsky's involvement in the 1922 expulsions, and when Trotsky was himself expelled Osorgin felt justice had been done. See Osorgin, *Vremena. Romany i avtobiograficheskoe povestvovanie*, Ekaterinburg, 1992, p. 597. See also Boris Lossky, 'K izgnaniyu lyudei mysli v 1922g.' in Zinaida Schakovskoy, René Guerra and Eugène Ternovsky (compilers), *Russkii Almanakh*, p. 356; Aikhenvald correctly discerned Trotsky as the author of the *Pravda* article against him and thus inferred him as a prime

mover behind the expulsions. He also believed Bryusov had a hand in things. See Geller, pp. 220–22.

51. <http://www.ihst.ru/projects/emigrants/> 'Zubashin' [sic] accessed September 2004.

52. S. S. Khoruzhii, 'Zhizn' I uchenie L'va Karsavina' in *L.P. Karsavin Religiozno-filosofskie sochineniya*, T.1, Moscow, 1992, p. xvi.

53. *MIA*, 12, p. 142.

54. Volkogonov Lenin (Russian edn, vol. 2), p. 190.

55. *MIA*, 12, p. 143. Boris Lossky seemed to remember the newspaper carried an article about Hitler's founding of the National Socialist Party the previous year.

56. See Tatyana Frank, *Pamyati Viktora Franka*, London, 1974; Victor Frank, *Izbrannye stat'i*, London, 1974; and *Po suti dela*, London, 1977, and Introduction, note 6.

57. Robert H. Johnston, *New Mecca, New Babylon*, Montreal, 1988, p. 188. For Osorgin's fondness for the 'yat' see *Vremena*, pp. 515, 537 and 606 note.

58. Nikolai Andreyev, 'Bluzhdayaushchaya sud'ba' in Tatyana Frank, *Pamyati Viktora Franka*', p. 27.

59. This poem was recited by the émigrés on their way to Kharbin. See Glenny and Stone, p. 223.

60. Sergei Esenin (1895–1925) moved to Berlin with his wife, the dancer Isadora Duncan. The relationship ended and back in Russia he slipped into heavy drinking and committed suicide. Duncan appeared on the Mariinsky theatre stage in the spring of 1921 for only the fourth time that century and came into people's lives with the promise generally swept in by NEP. See *MIA*, 12, p. 110.

61. 'The Tram that Lost its Way' was published in the first number of Gorky's House of Arts journal in 1921. In his revised essay for the 1923 edition of *Siluety* on Gumilyov, Aikhenvald quoted the prophetic stanza 'In a red shirt...'

62. *Dream*, p. 226.

63. Adapted from Kizevetter, *Istoricheskie siluety*, 1931.

64. For the idea of the Russians as a wandering people, see

Merezhkovsky quoted in Nikita Struve, p. 24. Henriette Mondry, 'Are there Jews in the History of Russian Culture'. *Russia and Euro-Asian Bulletin*, 9:3, 2000, pp. 1–9, calls Aikhenvald 'the famous Jewish Expressionist critic of the Silver Age'. See also Reitblat, op.cit., in *Evrei v kul'ture russkogo zarubezh'ya*, Vyp. 1, Jerusalem, 1992.

65. Stettin is today the Polish city of Szczecin. For the city before it was largely destroyed by Allied bombing, see *Stettin Ansichten aus 5 Jahrhunderten*, Stettin, 1991, and Tadeusz Bialecki, *Stettin auf alten Abbildungen*, Szczecin, 1995.

66. *Dream*, p. 244.

67. *MIA*, 12, p. 142.

68. TFV, p. 8.

69. Ugrimova, p. 205.

70. *Professiya: Zhena filosofa Lidya Berdyaeva* , p. 52.

71. Compare *Dream*, p. 51

72. Nabokov, *The Eye*, translated by Dmitri Nabokov in collaboration with the author, New York, 1965 (1990), p. 29.

73. NLV, p. 220.

74. Sorokin, p. 197.

75. Fiene, p. 65.

76. Tatyana Frank, 'Kratkaya biografia Viktora' in *Pamyati Viktora Franka*, p. 8.

6 JOINING THE EMIGRATION

1. Gessen, p. 54.

2. *MIA*, 12, p. 144.

3. Alexandra Richie, *Faust's Metropolis. A History of Berlin*, London, 1998, p. 247. If this really happened then the London bus drivers twenty years later who hailed 'Finchleystrasse!' to alert the high number of Hitler refugees when they got home to Hampstead, behaved according to type.

4. *Dream*, p. 244.

5. Boobbyer, p. 122.

6. Tatyana Frank, *Pamyat' serdtsa*, p. 5.

7. *MIA*, 12, pp. 143–4.

8. NLV, p. 221.

9. See the missing handkerchief in the final paragraph of Nabokov's *Speak Memory*, ch. 9, and Brian Boyd, *Vladimir Nabokov. The Russian Years*, London, 1990, p. 83.

10. 'The Congress of the Russian

Émigrés in Paris by our Paris correspondent', *Soviet Russia*, August 1921.

11. Schlögel, *Der große Exodus*, p. 549.

12. Quoted in Richie, p. 288.

13. A. S. Izgoev, *Rozhdyonnoe v revolyutsionoi smute (1917–1932)*, Paris, 1933, p. 3.

14. S. S. Ippolitov, V. M. Nedbaevsky, Yu. I. Rudnetsova, *Tri stolitsy izgnaniya Konstantinopol, Berlin, Parizh*, Moscow, 1999, p. 16. The upper range of figures for 1921 were landowners 17 per cent, officers 12 per cent, nurses, soldiers, technicians 8 per cent, students 9 per cent, teachers 4 per cent, illegal workers 4.2 per cent. By contrast the figures were low for performing artists (1 per cent), clergy (0.5 per cent), painters (0.5 per cent) and journalists and writers (0.1 per cent).

15. Raeff, pp. 22–3. Karl Schlögel (ed.), *Der große Exodus, Russische Emigration und ihre Zentren 1917–1941*, Munich, 1994, contains informative essays on all the major centres.

16. Pipes, *Struve Liberal on the Right*, pp. 336–7 and 328–9.

17. Nikita Struve, *Soixante-dix ans*,

'Chapitre II: la Vie politique' is gripping on both the infighting and the penetration of Soviet agencies.

18. *Dream*, p. 236.

19. *Dream*, p. 245.

20. Nikolai Andreyev, *To chto vospominaetsya*, Tallinn, 1996, vol. 1, pp. 243–4.

21. Ugrimova, p. 207.

22. Boobbyer, pp. 134 ff.

23. Nabokov, Foreword to *The Gift*.

24. Boobbyer, p. 134; *Dream*, p. 245, Frank 'Vospominaniya o P. B. Struve' in *Neprochitannoe*, Moscow, 2001, pp. 498–9. *MIA*, 12, p. 148.

25. S. P. Postnikov, 'The beginning of the Czechslovak Republic and its hopes coincided with the Russian emigration', *Russkie v Prage 1918–1928gg.*, Prague, 1928. See also Johnston, Foreword to *Russkie v Prague*, p. 124.

26. NLV, p. 221.

27. See Postnikov op. cit.; Zdenek Sladek, 'Prag: Das Russische Oxford' in Schlögel, 1994; Boris Lossky, 'V russkoi Prage 1922–27', *MIA*, 16, Moscow, 1994; Catherine Andreyev and Ivan Savicky, *Russia Abroad. Prague and the Russian Diaspora*

1918–1938, London, 2004. Many other distinguished Russian émigrés like Struve, S. I. Gessen, the historians G. V. Florovsky and G. V. Vernadsky, the Byzantine specialist N. P. Kondakov and the Ukrainian Dmitry Chyzhevsky, not directly expelled by Lenin, also settled in Prague. Sladek, pp. 219–21, identifies five waves: prisoners of war; refugees from the Soviet regime; including, but not only, SRs and monarchists; the repatriated Czech legions and their Russian followers and others connected with them for a total of 100,000; the recipients of Russian Action; with students, agricultural workers and the intelligentsia given priority.

28. Sorokin, p. 197.

29. Lutokhin, 'Alien Pastors'; *MIA*, 22, pp. 20, 28, 35.

7 PRAGUE

1. Andreyev and Savicky, *Russia Abroad*, challenges this view. See below note 14. See also Hans Lemberg, 'Masaryk and the Russian Question against the Background of German and Czech attitudes to Russia' in *T. G. Masaryk (1850–1937)*, vol. 1, *Thinker and Politician*, edited by Stanley B. Winters, London, 1990. Masaryk's great work on Russia was published in German as *Russland und Europa* (1913) and much later in an expanded three-volume English edition as *The Spirit of Russia* (1967).

2. Glenny and Stone, p. 255. Katkov added: 'The Czechs were always afraid of the Germans.

That's the only reason they helped us.'

3. The clearest versions are in Pipes, *Russia Under the Bolshevik Regime*, pp. 30–3, 114–17, and Figes, pp. 658–9.

4. Pipes, *Russia Under the Bolshevik Regime*, p. 33.

5. Andreyev and Savicky, pp. 39–40. Russian Action left behind the unsolved question of whether Masaryk also funded the attempt by Russian terrorist Boris Savinkov on the life of Lenin, a theory propounded in Communist anti-Masaryk times. Andreyev and Savicky believe it to be a red herring. Lemberg, p. 295, suggested the answer

might lie in the newly opened archives but nothing has emerged in the last fifteen years.

6. *Rul'*, No. 583, 17 October 1922.

7. Lemberg, pp. 292–4.

8. Thomas Gaiton Marullo, *Ivan Bunin: From the Other Shore 1920–1933. A Portrait from Letters, Diaries and Fiction*, Chicago, 1995, p. 79.

9. Maria Razumovsky, *Marina Tsvetaeva*, translated by Aleksei Gibson, Newcastle upon Tyne, 1994. Chapters 16 and 17 are richly informative.

10. Andreyev and Savicky, pp. 109–10; Svetlana Tejchmanová, *Rusko v Çeskoslovensku (Bilá emigrace v ČSR 1917–1939)*, Prague, 1993, pp. 49–50.

11. Andreyev and Savicky, p. 86.

12. The complex political foundations on which Zemgor rested, which shielded the pro-SR Czechoslovak government from direct subsidy of that cause, didn't detract from its wider humanitarian and cultural mission.

13. *MIA*, 16, Moscow, 1994, p. 43.

14. Andreyev and Savicky, p. 64: 'Masaryk's great merit was not that he initiated Russian Action but that he correctly assessed the rapidly changing situation, the realistic opportunities available to Czechoslovakia and her various allies among the Russian emigration, and put his ideas into practice.'

15. Glenny and Stone, p. 254.

16. In 1929 Lossky received 12,000 crowns from the President's Office. NLV, p. 250.

17. The Professors' House was at Buçhkova St. 27–29. Today Ul. Rooseveltova.

18. Bradford, *Roman Jakobson*, p. 24.

19. Glenny and Stone, p. 255.

20. Boyd, *The Russian Years*, p. 235.

21. Berberova, p. 201.

22. V. V. Zenkovsky, *Deti emigratsii*, Prague, 1925.

23. *MIA*, 16, pp. 32–4.

24. The address was Krementsova St. No. 8.

25. See Andreyev and Savicky, p. 121, and Raeff, p. 61.

26. See Razumovsky, especially p. 176.

27. Vandalkovskaya, 'Introduction' to Kizevetter, *Na rubezh'e dvukh stoletii*, p. 5.

28. Vladimir Nabokov, *Speak Memory*, London, 2000, p. 40.

29. Cesare Segre, 'Da Mosca a

Harvard via Praga – conversazione con Roman Jakobson', *La Fiera letteraria*, 1968, 4 Luglio, pp. 14–15. The poet Jaroslav Seifert, however, congratulated Jakobson on his good Czech: Oleg Malevich, 'Roman Jakobson v Chekoslovakii' in *Evrei v kul'ture russkogo zarubezh'ya*, Vyp. 2, Jerusalem, 1993, p. 72.

30. 'I was struck by the profound unlikeness in structure between iambic tetrameter in Russian and in Czech, and I was particularly astonished by the variety of rhythmical deviations from the metrical pattern that the Czech iamb permitted, but which in Russian were totally impossible.' Roman Jakobson and Krystyna Pomorska, *Dialogues*, Cambridge, 1982, p. 22. What followed was Jakobson's comparative study of Czech and Russian poetry, published in 1923: 'O cheshskom stikhe, preimushchestvenno v sopostavlenii s russkim' ('On Czech Verse, Primarily in Comparison with Russian'), see Roman Jakobson, *Selected Writings*, vol. 5, The Hague,

1978, pp. 3–121. That this study formed a foundation for one of the two major branches of Jakobson's work – in founding the Prague School of Linguistics and for the rest of his career – is well known.

That 'other' branch of Jakobson's work was 'his idea that speech sounds (phonemes) are not atomic entities devoid of further analysis but complexes of phonetic properties (distinctive features)'. '[This idea] inhabits the same sphere of perception and analysis as his studies of Pushkin's obsession with statues, Pasternak's poetic prose and prosaic poetry, and his theory of the relation between poetry and history: all are founded upon the conviction that the material substance of the sign is never fully distinguishable from its signifying properties.' See Richard Bradford, *Roman Jakobson. Life, Language, Art*, London, 1994, p. 3.

To this scholarly picture of what Jakobson's work in comparative poetry and linguistics was doing I would add the following anecdote told by Berberova in *The Italics are Mine*, p. 205, about advice given by Jakobson, also in 1923, to fellow Russian exile and poet, Khodasevich. It concerned how to survive life abroad psychologically. 'Jakobson suggests to Khodasevich that he translate into Russian a long poem of the Czech romantic Maha. Perhaps "from Maha to Maha you could set yourself up in Praha?" he says pensively. But Khodasevich is not enchanted by Maha…' Khodasevich was not enchanted by Maha, but we have the evidence of his own words that Jakobson was.

The effect of Jakobson's work was therefore twofold. He became 'the major theorist and practitioner of formalist literary criticism and structuralist linguistics in the West yet [also] he was very much – and remained so – a citizen of Russia Abroad, not only by his background but also by his lifelong preoccupation with Russian poetics and the common Slavic heritage.' Raeff, p. 107.

31. Jakobson, *My Futurist Years*, p. 117. *'Unlawful mongrel' seems to allude to Blok's poem 'The Twelve', in which the Revolution is led by Jesus Christ with an 'unlawful mongrel' – *bezrodny pes* – following behind.

32. Brian Boyd, *Vladimir Nabokov The American Years*, London, 1992, p. 311.

33. See 'Pitirim Sorokin' at <http://www.hronos.km.ru> citing A. P. Shikman, *Deyateli otechestvennoi istorii. Biografichesky Spravochnik*, Moscow, 1997.

34. Lutokhin, 'Alien Pastors', *MIA*, 22, p. 35.

35. Ibid., p. 104.

36. Ibid., p. 30. The setting of this meeting was of no consequence to Lutokhin but much loved by the Russian expatriate establishment. See Anastasie Kopřivová, *Strediska ruského emigrantského zivota v Prate (1921–1952)*, Prague, 2001, pp. 104–5. The russophile proprietor of the Beranek' advertised his hotel and restaurant as 'The Centre of the Russian Emigration' and made available without cost the 'Japanese Room' and the 'Russian Room'. The address gave a number of émigré organizations their

headquarters. Czech-Russian meetings took place every Friday from 1919 till 1939, as well as celebratory dinners and gatherings. From the mid-1920s until the mid-1990s, when the building was made available 'in an abrupt fashion' to an investment bank, a marble plaque with a portrait of Gorky marked his visit to the hotel.

37. Lutokhin, *MIA*, 22, p. 49.

38. Ibid., pp. 41 ff. The tone of Lutokhin's memoir, commented upon with regret by his post-Soviet editors, was one of pathbreaking Soviet nastiness and sarcasm.

39. Andreyev and Savicky, p. 107-8.

40. Ibid., p. 108. Lutokhin, *MIA*, 22, p. 77, refers to his underground work and p. 85 to his 'illegal work'; on p. 57 Prokopovich calls him a Communist. His FSB File No.

15374 was released on 15 August 2002 to coincide with the eightieth anniversary of the deportations and comments on it dated 7 July 2003 can be downloaded at <http://www. news.gala.net>. See also the profile of Peshekhonov at <http://www.gallery. economicus.ru>.

41. Lutokhin, *MIA*, 22, p. 85.

42. Ibid., p. 77.

43. Lutokhin, *MIA*, 22, p. 82.

44. Ibid., p. 82.

45. Raeff, pp. 63, 84; Hilde Hardeman, *Coming to Terms with the Soviet Regime*, De Kalb, 1994, pp. 163, 268.

46. Vysheslavtsev, *The Eternal in Russian Philosophy*, translated by Penelope V. Burt, Grand Rapids, Michigan, 2002, p. 29.

47. Postnikov, p. 126; Tejchmanová, p. 43.

48. Berberova, pp. 200–201.

8 BERLIN

1. Karl Schlögel, 'Berlin: Stiefmutter unter den russischen Städten' in Schlögel, 1994, p. 237, citing German Foreign Ministry figures. German estimates, however, were higher than outside assessments. See Ippolitov et al., p. 62. J. H. Simpson, *The Refugee Problem*, London, 1939, estimated 250,000 Russians in Germany as a whole, compared

with a German government figure of at least 600,000. Of those 250,000 around three-quarters were in Berlin. The lowest figures for Berlin are given by Richie, p. 287: 100,000 Russians in 1922 and 300,000 by 1924.

2. Richie, p. 288.

3. L. K. Skarenkov, 'Die Materialien des Generals Aleksey A. von Lampe' in Schlögel, 1995, p. 70.

4. Schlögel, 1994, p. 236–40.

5. *Dream*, p. 248.

6. Glenny and Stone, p. 263.

7. The Russian church on Nachodstrasse no longer exists. See Razumovsky p. 149. The Russian Orthodox cathedral on the Hohenzollerndamm near Fehrbellinerplatz was not consecrated until 1938.

8. Berberova, pp. 151–3, 165. I have slightly amended the translation.

9. *Dream*, p. 249.

10. For the House of Arts see V. V. Sorokina (compiler), *Russky Berlin*, Moscow, 2003, pp. 74 ff; Schlögel, 1988; Thomas R. Beyer, 'The House of Arts and the Writers' Club Berlin 1921–1923' in Thomas R. Beyer, Gottfried Kratz, Xenia Werner,

Russische Autoren und Verlage in Berlin nach dem ersten Weltkrieg, Berlin, 1987, pp. 9–38. *Berlin–Moskau 1900–1950*, edited by Irina Antonova and Jörn Merkert, Moscow/Berlin/ Munich, 1996, has a map of Russian Berlin on the inside front cover.

11. 'Aikhenvald' in *Russkoe zarubezh'e. Zolotaya kniga russkoi emigratsii. Pervaya tret' XX veka Entsiklopedichesky bigrafichesky slovar'*, Moscow, 1997, and Abram I. Rejtblat, 'Julij Ajchenval'd in Berlin' in Schlögel, 1995, pp. 359–60; Berberova, pp. 168–9; Schlögel, 1994, p. 258.

12. Schlögel, 1994, p. 241–4; see also Claudia Scandura, 'Die Ursachen für die Blüte und den Niedergang des russischen Verlagwesens in Berlin in den 20er Jahren', one of several articles in Schlögel, 1995, collected under the heading 'In der Gutenberg-Galexis. Russische Verlage und Zeitungen in Berlin' and Sorokina, pp. 120 ff. Karl Schlögel, *Berlin Ostbahnhof Europas Russen und Deutsche in ihrem Jahrhundert*, Berlin, 1998,

pp. 104–5, contains a list of Russian publishers and Russian bookshops.

13. M.M. Novikov, *Problemy zhizhni* ('Problems of Life'); Berdyaev, *Mirosozertsanie Dostoevskogo* ('Dostoevsky's World-Outlook') and *Filosofia neravenstva* ('The Philosophy of Inequality'); Frank, *Zhivoe znanie* ('Living Knowledge'); and *Vvedenie v filosofiyu* ('Introduction to Philosophy') 2nd edn; Stepun, *Zhizn i tvorechestvo Solovyova* ('The Life and work of Solovyov'); Vysheslavtsev, *Russky element v Dostoevskom* ('The Russian Element in Dostoevsky'); Shklovsky, *Zoo, ili pis'ma ni o lyubvi* ('Zoo or Letters not about Love'); Sorokin, *Sovremennoe sostoyanie Rossii* ('The Present Condition of Russia'); Tsvetaeva's collections included *Remeslo* ('The Craft') and *Psikheya; Romantika* ('Psyche: Romantic Verse'). Peshekhonov's political confession *Pochemu ya ne emigriroval* ('Why I Didn't Emigrate') was also published in Berlin 1923. A new, fifth edition of volume 2 of Aikhenvald's *Silvety* also appeared.

Melgunov's classic *Krasny Terror v sovietskoi Rossii* ('The Red Terror in Soviet Russia') appeared in 1924 and Aikhenvald's *Dve zheny* ('Two Wives') in 1925. Iretsky published stories in the Berlin journal *The Russian Echo* and in 1924 a play *The Mousetrap*, which ran on the Berlin Russian stage (Sorokina, *Russky Berlin*, p. 345).

14. Mark R. Hatlie, 'Die Zeitung also Zentrum der Emigrations-Öffentlichkeit: Das Beispiel der Zeitung *Rul'*' in Schlögel, 1995.

15. Viktor Iaklevich Iretsky also wrote under the pseudonyms I. Ya. Glikman and Ya. Erikson, causing confusion as to his real name. See entry under 'Glikman' at <http://www.vgd.ru>; under Iretsky in the 'Tsentralnyi Evreisky Resurs' at <http://www.SEM40.ru>; under Iretsky in *Russkaya pechat' v Rige*, vol. 1.

16. *Russkaya pechat' v Rige*, vol. 2, p. 104.

17. Amory Burchard, 'Die russische Emigrantenzeitung *Naš Vek* 1931–1933', in Schlögel, 1995, pp. 447–57.

18. Vladislav Moulis, 'Die

russische republikanische
Tageszeitung *Dni'*, in Schlögel,
1995, pp. 439–446; *Russky
Parizh*, p. 515.

19. The number of Russians in
Berlin was about 150,000 in 1928
and 100,000 in 1933. See
Schlögel, 1994, p. 238. Raeff has
90,000 in 1930 (in *Russia
Abroad*, p. 37).

20. *Rul'*, 8 October 1922, No. 566.

21. *Rul'*, 20 December 1922, No.
627.

22. Glenny and Stone, p. 270.

23. *Rul'*, Nos 608 and 609, 28, 29
November 1922.

24. Raeff, p. 60. The Institute was
the product of the Russian
Academic Union, and the
initiative came from England
where Sir Paul Vinogradov
chaired a committee of well-
wishers and émigré scholars
including Pavel Milyukov. See
also 'Russischer Geist in
deutscher Umgebung' in
Schlögel, 1995, pp. 262–3, and
Gerd Voigt, 'Otto Hoetzsch,
Karl Stählin und die Gründung
des Russischen
Wissenschaftlichen Instituts' in
Schlögel, 1995, pp. 267–78;
Sorokina, pp. 284 ff., *Russkaya
pechat' v Rige*, vol. 2, pp. 80, 98.

25. Voigt in Schlögel, 1995,
pp. 275–7.

26. Lossky was regarded by some as
'a mystic…whose work had no
part in serious academic
philosophy'. See Andreyev, vol.
1, p. 322, vol. 2, p. 6.

27. Ibid., p. 275.

28. Quoted in Raeff, pp. 153–4.

29. Voigt in Schlögel, 1995, p. 275.
For the attraction of Spengler,
for example, to Frank, see
Boobbyer, pp. 129–30.

30. Viktor Kagan, 'Boris Brutskus:
unchenyi i pravozashchitnik',
*Evrei v kul'ture russkogo
zarubezhya*, Vyp. 1, Jerusalem,
1993, pp. 476–84; see also the
excellent digest at <http://www.
economicus.ru>, galleryeya
ekonomistov by N. L. Rogalina,
based on her monograph *Boris
Brutskus – Istorik narodnogo
khozyaistva Rossii*, Moscow, 1998.
The lectures were advertised in
Rul'.

31. Voigt in Schlögel, 1995, p. 273.

32. Wolfe, p. 143.

33. Voigt in Schlögel, 1995, p. 273.

34. 'Kratkaya biografia Viktora' in
Pamyati Viktora Franka,
London, 1974, p. 8.

35. *Pamyati Viktora Franka*, p. 23.

36. Ibid., p. 33.

37. Marullo, p. 100.

38. 'Foreword' (1967) to Vladimir Nabokov, *King, Queen, Knave*, London, 1968.

39. Johnston, p. 32.

40. Rogalina, p. 11.

41. Hardeman, pp. 163 and 268.

42. Wolfe, p. 59; Rogalina, p. 15.

43. Berberova, p. 399.

44. L. K. Skarenkov, 'Von Lampe' in Schlögel, 1995, p. 73.

45. Ibid., p. 54. His lecture was part of the 1927/8 programme.

46. *Russky Parizh*, p. 517. For the close links between *Nakanune* and 'Change of Landmarks' see Hardeman.

47. Razumovsky, pp. 145–6.

48. The key archive document is Lenin's memorandum to Stalin of summer 1922, published by Glavatsky, p. 108, and Volkogonov Lenin, p. 362, and Pipes, *The Unknown Lenin From the Secret Archive*, New Haven and London, 1996, pp. 168–9. Glavatsky dates the document 16 July, Pipes 17 July. Volkogonov is surely wrong with 'autumn'.

49. Otsup, p. 544. Chukovsky's diary for 15 December 1922 contains a sly denunciation of Aikhenvald's talent. See *Dnevnik*

1901–1929, p. 219.

50. Berberova, p. 167; Aleksandr Bakhrakh, *Po pamyati, po zapisam*, Paris, 1980. Gershenzon's letters are available in *Minuvshee Istorichesky Almanakh*, [MIA] 8.

51. Berberova, pp. 163–4

52. Berberova, pp. 194–5; Jakobson, *My Futurist Years*, p. 307. Viktor Shklovsky, *A Sentimental Journey. Memoirs 1917–1922*, translated by Richard Sheldon, London, 1970, p. xv, omits the crucial factor of emotional blackmail by the state.

53. Jakobson, *My Futurist Years*, p. 88.

54. Berberova, p. 189.

55. *MIA*, 16, p. 41.

56. Stacy Schiff, *Véra (Mrs Vladimir Nabokov)*, London, 1999, p. 35.

57. On 22 May 1923 as reported in *Dni*. Rogalina, p. 14.

58. Hardeman, pp. 93–107. For an interesting commentary on *Smena Vekh*, see also also Nikita Struve, pp. 51–4.

59. Hardeman, pp. 93–107.

60. Pipes, *Struve Liberal on the Right*, p. 236.

61. *Nakanune*, 26 November 1922.

See also Hardeman, p. 155.

62. For the Russian interest in Scheler cf. Boobbyer, p. 125, and Frank's review of Scheler's latest book *Vom Ewigen im Menschen* ('On the Eternal in Man') for a collection, edited by Berdyaev, *Sofia: Problems of Spiritual Culture and Religious Philosophy*. Here was yet another book published in 1923. See also Schlögel, 1995, p. 265, and *Dream*, p. 248.

63. Raeff, p. 104.

64. He failed with Einstein, who had fallen prey to Soviet propaganda. See Kagan, 'Boris Brutskus' in *Evrei v kul'ture russkogo zarubezh'ya*, Vyp. 1, pp. 480–8. and Rogalina, p. 19.

65. Mary McCarthy, 'A Bolt from the Blue' (1962), reprinted in *Pale Fire*, London, 1991.

66. Nabokov, *Speak, Memory*, p. 218 (Chapter 14, Section 2) seems to be an attack on a composite personality of Nabokov's invention. It has many, though not all, of Berdyaev's characteristics, plus those of the minor poet and literary critic Georgy Adamovich, who disliked Nabokov's work. Another attack on 'mystagogues' follows on p. 220.

67. Raeff, p. 101.

68. Joseph Frank, *Dostoevsky: The Stir of Liberation 1860–65*, Princeton, N. J., 1986, p. 119.

69. Quoted in Richie, p. 313. See also Schlögel, 1995, p. 266.

70. Berberova, pp. 162–3.

9 . PARIS

1. *La vie culturelle de l'émigration russe en France: chronique (1920–1930)*, compiled by Michèle Beyssac, Paris, 1971, lists daily Paris-wide Russian-language lectures and cultural events. For a general survey of Russian life in France, see Robert Harold Johnston, 'Paris: Die Hauptstadt de russischen Diaspora' in Schlögel, 1994. Catherine Triomphe, *La Russie à Paris*, Paris, 2000, is an excellent practical guide.

2. Marullo, *From the Other Shore*, p. 74.

3. Nina Kandinsky, *Kandinsky and Ich*, 2nd edn, Munich, 1976, p. 88. Evidently this ban excluded Constructivism and

Suprematism at this stage. See also Christopher Read, *Culture and Power in Revolutionary Russia: The Intelligentsia in the Transition from Tsarism to Communism*, Basingstoke, 1990, p. 178 and pp. 183–5. Also p. 91 on the economic crisis for artists under the NEP: 'Such state support as there was began to be channelled more frequently to members of the realist school and less frequently to any of the avant-garde.'

4. Raeff, pp. 37–8.

5. Berberova, pp. 215 ff., 277. Johnston, pp. 73–81.

6. *Professiya: Zhena filosofa Lidya Berdyaeva*, [Diaries] p. 89; Fiene, p. 43.

7. see Fiene; Leonid Livak, *How it was Done in Paris. Russian Émigré Literature and French Modernism*, Madison, Wisconsin, 2003, p. 217.

8. Marullo, *From the Other Shore*, pp. 284, 288; Berberova, pp. 282–3. Zinaida Shakhovskaya, *Une Manière de vivre*, Paris, 1965, p. 237.

9. Fiene, p. 124.

10. *Russky Parizh*, pp. 519–20; p. 513.

11. Ibid., pp. 522–3. The older journals were *Sovremmenik* and *Zapiski otechestva*.

12. Raeff, p. 87.

13. Antuan Arzhakovsky, *Zhurnal 'Put' 1925–40 Pokolenie russkikh religioznykh myslitelei v emigratsii*, Kiev, 2000, p. 114, quoted from the Paris YMCA Press Archive. The title echoed that of the journal *Novy Put'* of pre-1914.

14. Johnston, p. 54; Raeff, p. 78. Arzhakovsky has made extensive use of the YMCA archives to compile a picture of how the Russians, and Berdyaev in particular, were supported by the American organization. See also *Professiya: Zhena filosofa Lidiya Berdyaeva* diary entry for 3 June 1936, p. 149.

15. Sergei Bulgakov, *The Orthodox Church*, translated and edited by Donald A. Lowrie, London, 1935, p. 201.

16. Raeff, pp. 123–30; Arzhakovsky, pp. 125–33.

17. Triomphe, pp. 79–88.

18. Vysheslavtsev, p. xv.

19. Ibid., p. 21.

20. Bulgakov, 1935, p. 219.

21. For the sermon Bulgakov preached when he went to America in 1934 (the year the

United States recognized the Soviet Union) see *A Bulgakov Anthology*, London, 1976, pp. 163 ff. It included (p. 180) the ecumenical sentiment that 'The West may find a complement to its dryness in the free spirit of Orthodoxy; and the Orthodox East may learn from the Christian West many things in regard to the religious organization of everyday life.'

22. *Dream*, p. 284.

23. *Russkoe zarubezh'ye. Zolotaya kniga russkoi emigratsii*, p. 80.

24. Berdyaev was particularly close to Jacques Maritain and his Russian wife Raisa, Gabriel Marcel, Wilfred Monod and Emmanuel Mounier. He returned many years running to the Décades de Pontigny, an international intellectual gathering and retreat founded by Paul Desjardins in an old Cistercian monastery in southern France.

25. Andreyev and Savicky, pp. 135–48. For the full text, see Petr Savitskii, *Exodus to the East: Forebodings and Events: An Affirmation of the Eurasians*, translated by Ilya Vinkovetsky, Afterword by Nicholas V.

Riasanovsky, Idyllwild, 1996. The other authors of *Exodus* were P. P. Suvchinsky and G. V. Florovsky. Nikita Struve, pp. 54–60, gives an excellent account of Trubetskoy's thought.

26. Lasha Tchantouridze, 'Eurasianism in Russia', *Perspectives. The Central European Review of International Affairs*, Institute of International Relations, Prague, 16, Summer 2001, pp. 73, 75.

27. Quoted by Andreyev and Savicky p. 138; the same passage is cited by Tchantouridze p. 72 though I have modified her translation.

28. Raeff, pp. 163–9.

29. Golo Mann, *The History of Germany since 1789*, Harmondsworth, 1968, p. 607.

30. Nikita Struve, pp. 58–9.

31. Andreyev and Savicky, p. 148.

32. Arzhakovsky, p. 70.

33. *Dream*, pp. 265–6.

34. See Arzhakovsky, pp. 135 ff.; A. Z. Shteinberg, *Druz'ya moikh rannykh let 1911–1928*, Paris, 1991.

35. Arzhakovsky, p. 136.

36. S. S. Khoruzhii, 'Zhizn' i uchenie L'va Karsavina' in L. P. Karsavin, *Religiozno-filosofskie*

sochineniya, T. 1, Moscow, 1992, p. xxxvii.

37. Ibid., pp. viii, xv, lxvi.

38. Ibid., p.xv.

39. *Russky Parizh*, pp. 107–8.

40. Khoruzhii, p. lxvi. The Chair of Patrology went instead to the great historian of the Orthodox Church, Georgy Florovsky.

41. Maistre was an ultra-conservative Jesuit thinker and antagonist of the French Revolution. See S.S. Khoruzhii, 'Karsavin i de Mestr', *Voprosy filosofii*, 1989, No. 3.

42. Andreyev and Savicky, p. 119.

43. Mandelstam, *Hope Against Hope*, p. 288.

44. Simon Sebag-Montefiore, *Stalin at the Court of the Red Tsar*, London, 2003, p. 16. Through the 1930s the Soviets and the émigrés sniped at each other like warring family members in their respective presses, according to Marullo, *Ivan Bunin*, p. 134. See also Schögel, *Der große Exodus*, p. 415.

45. Marullo, ibid, p. 277.

46. Berberova, p. 290.

47. Glenny and Stone, p. 289.

48. Boyd, 1990, p. 201.

49. The view of Vasily Yanovsky quoted in *Russky Parizh*, p. 172.

50. Schlögel, 1995, p. 66.

51. Volkogonov Lenin, p. 366; Volkogonov Lenin (Russian edn), vol. 2, p. 192, contains a list of émigré journal targets.

52. Nikita Struve, p. 59.

53. Ibid.

54. *Dream*, p. 254.

55. Berberova, p. 282.

56. Ibid., p. 387:'The destitute, stupid, stinking, despicable, unhappy, base, deprived, harassed, hungry Russian emigration (to which I belong)!'

10 ENDING UP

1. Stratonov commited suicide. <http://www.ihst.ru/projects/emigrants/stratononov>; <http://www.vgd.ru>.

2. Fleishman et al., *Russkaya pechat' v Rige*, vol. 2, p. 98.

3. *Segodnya*, 1935, Nos 192 and 195, cited in Yury Abyzov, *Russkoe pechatnoe slovo v Latvii 1917–1944gg. Bibliografichesky Spravochnik*, Stanford, 1990, vol. 3, part 2.

4. *Segodnya*, 1934, No. 1013, cited in Abyzov, vol. 1.

5. *Russkaya pechat' v Rige*, vol. 1, p. 104; vol. 2, p. 376; *Evrei v kul'ture russkogo zarubezh'ya*, Vyp. 1, pp. 46, 53.

6. Stepun, pp. 640–41.

7. *Pamyati Viktora Franka*, p. 9.

8. NLV, p. 252.

9. Johnston, p. 151; Ilyin's letter in Burchard, 'Die russische Emigrantenzeitung *Naš Vek* 1931–1933', in Schlögel, *Der große Exodus*, 1995, p. 451.

10. Johnston, p. 166; Pipes, *Struve. Liberal on the Right*, p. 413

11. 'Ilyin', *Russkoe zarubezh'e. Zolotaya kniga russkoi emigratsii*, p. 266; Ippolitov et al., *Tri stolitsy izganiya*, pp. 94, 106. N. P. Poltoratsky, *I. A. Ilyin: Zhizn' I trudy mirovozrenie*, New York, 1989; I. I. Evlampiev, 'Filosofskie I pravovye vzglyady I. A. Il'ina' <http://www.humanities.edu.ru/db/msg> accessed 16 June 2004, p. 10.

12. Stacy Schiff, *Véra (Mrs Vladimir Nabokov)*, London 1999, p. 103–6.

13. Nikita Struve, p. 147.

14. Cesare Segre, 'Da Mosca a Harvard via Praga – conversazione con Roman Jakobson', *La Fiera letteraria*, 1968, 4 Luglio, pp. 14–15.

15. Alexander (Aleksandr) Filaretovich Izyumov retained his Soviet citizenship abroad and called himself a convinced Stalinist. His papers are in the Nicolaevsky collection in the Hoover Institute, Stanford, California. See Fleishman et al., *Russkaya pechat' v Rige*, vol. 4, pp. 122–3. For Nikolai Moiseevich Volkovysky, see entry in *Bibliografichesky Spravochnik Abyzov*; Fleishman et al., *Russkaya pechat' v Rige*, vol. 1, pp. 299–307.

16. For Boris Osipovich Khariton, see Fleishman et al., *Russkaya pechat' v Rige*, vol. 1, pp.79–82. Details of Leonid Moishevich (Maximovich) Pumpyansky in the same volume and also at <http://www. vgd.ru>.

17. NLV, pp. 292–3.

18. <http://www.vgd.ru>; Andreyev and Savicky, p. 197.

19. Andreyev and Savicky, p. 197.

20. Vladimir Nabokov, *Perepiska s sestroyu*, Ann Arbor, Michigan, 1985, letter of Yelena Nabokova to her brother, 1 October 1945.

21. Valentin Feodorovich Bulgakov (1886–1966) served as Tolstoy's secretary in 1910 and published his diary of that year. It

appeared in English as *The Last Years of Tolstoy* and was last reprinted in 1971. His *Tolstoy, Lenin and Gandhi* was published in 1930. For his career in Czechoslovakia and return to the Soviet Union see Fleishman et al., *Russkaya pechat' v Rige*, vol. 4, p. 33. Valentin Bulgakov has been subject, more than most, to minor confusion about his identity, being called variously 'Valerian' and 'Venyamin' and being confused with Vladimir Feodorovich Bulgakov, author of *Slovar' russkikh zarubezhnykh pisatelei*, New York, 1993.

22. For Izyumov, see above, note 15. For Aleksandr Aleksandrovich Bogolepov, see Fleishman et. al., *Russkaya pechat' v Rige*, vol. 2, pp. 112, 114, and N. M. Zernov (compiler), *Russkie pisateli v emigratsii: Biograficheskie svedeniya i bibliografia ikh knig po bogosloviyu, religiosnoi filosofii, tserkovnoi istorii I pravoslavnoi kul'ture 1921–1972*, Boston, 1972. Mikhail Mikhailovich Novikov and Boris Nikolaevich Odintsov both have entries at <http://

www.ihst.ru/projects/ emigrants>. Novikov also wrote his autobiography: *Ot Moskvy do Nyu-Yorka Moya zhizn' v nauke i politike*, New York, 1952. His papers are in the Bakhmetev Archive at Columbia University.

23. Nikita Struve, p. 147; Sergei Hackel, *Pearl of Great Price: The Life of Mother Maria Skobtsova 1891–1945*, London, 1981. Hackel quotes from a memoir by Ugrimov 'deposited with the author'. Ugrimov was at some time accused both of slandering the Third Reich and being in Soviet pay, see Schlögel, 1995, p. 463.

24. *Russkoe zarubezh'e. Zolotaya kniga russkoi emigratsii*, pp. 156–9.

25. Johnston, pp. 168 ff.

26. Ibid.

27. 'Listening to the War', *Testimony of Lorna Swire*, BBC Radio 4, 14.01.1980.

28. Nikita Struve, p. 149.

29. Fiene, p. 218.

30. Nikita Struve, p. 152.

31. Karsavin in *Russky Parizh*, p. 444; <http://www.hronos.ru ; www.repherat.ru>.

II THE SENSE OF WHAT HAPPENED

1. See Chamberlain, chapter II, 'How the Long Tradition Survived'.

2. D. M. Thomas, *Alexander Solzhenitsyn. A Century in his Life*, London, 1998, p. 376.

3. The 1922 purge set the precedent, cf Volkogonov Lenin, p. 368. David Caute, *The Dancer Defects. The Struggle for Cultural Supremacy during the Cold War*, Oxford, 2003, is the first instalment of a projected two-volume history of the cultural Cold War.

4. Volkogonov Leaders (Russian edn) and Volkogonov Lenin (Russian edn) passim. The quotations from Berdyaev which preface every chapter of these major revisionist histories are not included in the English editions.

5. Schlögel, 1988, p. 480.

6. Nabokov, *The Gift*, p. 8.

7. Ibid., p. 162.

8. Foreword to *The Eye*.

9. Izgoev, p. 19.

10. Catriona Kelly, *Petersburg. Crucible of Cultural Revolution*, London, 1995; Schlögel, 1988.

11. Ruth Dudley Edwards, *Victor Gollancz*, London, 1987, p. 550. For his fondness for quoting Berdyaev, see also Victor Gollancz, *The New Year of Grace. An Anthology for Youth and Age*, London, 1961.

12. For this argument I am guided by Iris Murdoch in *The Sovereignty of Good*, London, 1970.

13. Leszek Kolakowski, *Positivist Philosophy. From Hume to the Vienna Circle*, Harmondsworth, 1972.

14. Mayakovsky, 'How are Verses to be Made', quoted in Sinyavsky, p. 197.

15. Mariengof, pp. 104–5, my amended translation.

16. See below, note 19.

17. Isaiah Berlin, *Two Concepts of Liberty*, Oxford, 1969, pp. 139–41.

18. Chamberlain, pp. 135–6.

19. Kolakowski, pp. 150–155, 210–11.

20. Quoted in Reitblat, 'Podkolodny estet' in *Evrei v kul'ture russkogo zarubezh'ya*, Vyp. 1, Jerusalem, 1992, p. 41.

21. Kreyd, in Aikhenvald, *Siluety*, vol. 1, pp. 8–9.

22. Quoted in Reitblat, p. 48.

Frank's obituary of Aikhenvald appeared in *Rul'*, 17 December 1929.

23. Reitblat, p. 49; Boyd, *The Russian Years*, p. 257; Abram I. Rejtblat, 'Julij Ajchenval'd in Berlin' in Schlögel, 1995, p. 465.

24. J. G. Merquior, *From Prague to Paris: A Critique of Structuralist and Post-Structuralist Thought*, London, 1986, is a wonderful attempt to make sense of it.

25. See above, p. 137.

26. When Khodasevich first arrived in Berlin, Jakobson proposed that he support himself by translating Czech poetry into Russian. This was exactly the route Jakobson himself took and which became inordinately productive: the difference between the way in which Czech and Russian worked, as signifying systems, gave him the beginning of his structuralist method.

27. Nikita Struve, p. 23.

28. Bradford, p. 5: 'his idea of the poetic speaker, text and biography as a form of mythology in which life and work are intermingled'.

29. Roman Jakobson, *Language in Literature*, edited by Krystyna Pomoska and Stephen Rudy, Cambridge, 1987, pp. 35–6.

30. After interviewing Jakobson, the critic Cesare Segre made the sense of his suffering his opening remark in his article in *La Flera letteraria*, 4 July 1968, pp. 14–15. Segre felt, trying to understand the new science, that Jakobson was 'ubiquitous, including in a metaphorical sense'. Bradford underscores in conjunction with the creation of a mythology 'his avoidance of the first person singular…'

31. Part of Aikhenvald's contribution on the tragedy debate. See *Rul'*, 10 December 1922.

32. Mandelstam, *Hope Abandoned*, p. 581.

33. I. I. Evlampiev *Khudozhestvennaya filosofia Andreye Tarkovskogo*, St Petersburg, 1991, p. 9.

34. Volkov, p. 515.

35. Alexander Solzhenitsyn, *Cancer Ward*, translated by Nicholas Bethell and David Burg, London, 1975, p. 515 (see translator's note).

36. Evtuhov, p. 122.

37. Berberova, p. 6.

38 Mandelstam, *Hope Against*

Hope, p. 436.

39. Alexandra Tolstoy, p. 336.

40. *Dear Bunny, Dear Volodya, The Nabokov–Wilson Letters 1940–1971*, edited, annotated and with an introductory essay by Simon Karlinsky, revised and expanded edition, Berkely, 2001. See Karlinsky's 'Introduction', pp. 21–26 and Letters 6 and 7.

41. Johnston, p. 63–4.

42. Romain Rolland, *Voyage à Moscou Juin–Juillet 1935*, Paris, 1992, p. 53.

43. *Rul'*, 10 December 1922.

44. Ibid.

45. Vysheslavtsev, p. xiv.

46. Quoted in Francis Stonor Saunders, *Who Paid the Piper?*, London, 1999, p. 58.

47. Mark Kulikowski, 'Eine vernachlässigte Quelle' in Schlögel, 1994, p. 373.

APPENDIX TWO

1. See Glavatsky, p. 151; Kogan, *Voprosy filosofii*, 1993, No. 9, p. 67.

2. This document is reproduced in Glavatsky, pp. 192–7.

3. V. G. Makarov, V. S. Khristoforov compilers, *Vysylka vmesto rasstrela Deportatsiya intelligentsii v dokumentakh Vecheka-GPU 1921–1923*, with a commentary by V. G. Makarov, Moscow, 2005, pp. 109–111. See also the commentary on the lists held in various archives pp. 39–42. An earlier version of this research was also published in *Voprosy filosofii*, 2003, No. 7, pp. 113–37, and can be accessed at <http://russcience.chat.ru/papers/mak)3vf.htm>.

4. Glavatsky, pp. 176–7, cites sources saying the Ukrainians were offered asylum in Prague but the Soviet authorities declined to strengthen the Ukrainian university in the Czechoslovak capital. A memo from Unshlikht to Stalin of 5 January 1923 (Glavatsky p. 95), however, speaks of a change of plan 'in view of the difficulty of putting into practice the decree on exiling abroad the Ukrainian anti-Soviet intelligentsia, in connection with the refusal of various countries to admit the exiles on to their territory'.

5. *Rul'*, No. 560, 1 October 1922; Makarov, *Vysylka vmesto*, p. 175.

6. Makarov, *Vysylka vmesto*, p. 41.

The students are listed by name on pp. 118–19.

7. Khoruzhii, *Literaturnaya Gazeta* No. 19, 9 May 1990, cites the words of the Moscow prosecutor; for Valentin Bulgakov see Fleishman et al., *Russkaya pechat' v Rige*, vol. 4, p. 33; Makarov has 30 March.

8. For Gorky see Geller, p. 224. For the Kazan expulsions see S. Yu. Malysheva, 'Kazanskie professora-passazhiry "filosofskogo parokhoda"', *Kultur'naya missiya Rossiiskogo Zarubezh'ya: istoriya i sovremennost'*, Moscow, 1999, pp. 53–60.

9. B. Lossky, 'Ki zgnaniyu lyudei mysli v 1922g.' in *Russkii Almanakh*, Paris, 1981, pp. 351–62.

10. *Rul'*, No. 560, 1 October 1922.

11. Makarov, *Vysylka vmesto*, p. 40.

12. *Dream*, p. 244.

13. *Rul'*, No. 566, 8 October 1922, records Bakkal's arrival in Berlin. When he was arrested in the Soviet sector of Berlin and subjected to questioning before being deported back to Russia, Bakkal attested to the first years of his life in enforced exile, when he met with fellow deportees Matveev, Romadonovsky, Shish'kin and Kuz'min-Karavayev in Berlin cafés. See Makarov, *Vysylka vmesto*, pp. 33–4. This evidence corroborates the expulsions of the first three names mentioned here. Bakkal also refers to others – 'Smirnov' and 'Novosel'sky' – who do not appear on any expulsion lists I have seen.

14. Bulatov probably travelled overland because 'he got stuck in Riga or Reval', according to *Rul'*, No. 566, 8 October 1922.

15. See above note 7.

16. Intetsky arrived on the *Haken*. See *Rul'*, No. 560, 1 October, 1922.

17. Peshekhonov travelled overland, via Riga. See the frontespiece to his book *Pochemu ya ne emigriroval* dated Riga November 1922.

18. S. N. Bulgakov left Russia on 1 January 1923 via Constantinople. See Boris Yakim's introduction to Sergei Bulgakov, *The Friend of the Bridegroom. On the Orthodox Veneration of the Forerunner*, Grand Rapids, Michigan, 2003, p. viii, and *Russkoe zarubezh'e. Zolotaya kniga russkooi emigratsii Pervaya*

tret' XX Veka Entsiklopedichesky bigrafichesky slovar', p. 116.

19. According to Fleishman et al., *Russkaya Pechat' v Rige*, vol. 1, 1997, Iretsky was left behind in Petrograd on orders from Moscow, and then expelled three weeks later overland.

20. Lodyzhensky's expulsion as part of the 1922 action is not corroborated by the final GPU list of 20 January, cited in Makarov pp. 173–5, although his name occurs on other lists and he certainly emigrated.

21. Lutokhin 'telegraphed from Reval, Estonia that he was arriving in Berlin in February 1923'. See Lutokhin, p. 99 fn. 93.

22. Sorokin travelled from Moscow with his wife on 23 September by rail via Sebezh to Riga.

23. 'I contrived to leave that country during October of 1922. Scarcely had I broken my journey at Warsaw…' S. P. Melgunov, *The Red Terror in Russia*, London, 1925. Melgunov left on 10 October. His name is not included on the GPU list of 20 January 1923.

24. Kuskova and Prokopovich left for Riga in June. The GPU file on their expulsion is held at the Obshchii Sledstvenny Fond M[inisterstva] B[ezopasnosti] SSSR R-31759. See 'Prokopovich, S. N.' at <http://www.gallery. economicus.ru>.

25. Anatoly Eduardovich Dyubua (1882– ?) was arrested in July and sentenced to expulsion on 14 August 1922. See Makarov, *Vysylka vmesto*.

26. Khodasevich and Berberova left in late May 1922. See Berberova, pp. 144, 214.

27. Martsinkovsky, not earlier noticed by the GPU, was expelled from Moscow as a unique case on 27 December 1922. See Makarov, *Vysylka vmesto*.

28. Poletika was arrested 8 September 1922 and expelled from Petrograd by special order on 3 February 1923. Another straggler. See Makarov, *Vysylka vmesto*.

29. Golovachev's arrival was noted in *Rul'*, 1 October 1922. See also Makarov, *Vysylka vmesto*.

30. For Chertkov's reprieve see Khoruzhii, *Literaturnaya Gazeta*, 9 May 1990. For Gustav Shpet see above p. 50 and for Zamyatin p. 132–4. For

Feldstein, Fomin, Kukolevsky, Ozerov and Rybnikov see Makarov. All others are in Glavatsky, p. 172.

31. Yurovsky was on the GPU's Moscow list but reprieved. He was shot in Stalin's purges in 1938. See also Tatyana Frank TFV, p. 6.

Bibliography

Abyzov, Yury, *Russkoe pechatnoe slovo v Latvii 1917–1944gg. Bibliograficheksy Spravochnik*, vols 1–, Stanford, 1990–.

Aikhenvald, Yuly, *Siluety russkikh pisatelei*, 3 vols, Moscow, 1909–1910, reprinted with a foreword by Vadim Kreid, and a biographical article by F. A. Stepun, Moscow, 1994.

Andreyev, Catherine, and Ivan Savicky, *Russia Abroad. Prague and the Russian Diaspora 1918–1938*, London, 2004.

Andreyev, Nikolai, *To chto vospominaetsya*, 2 vols, Tallinn, 1996.

Annenkov, Yury, *Dnevnik moikh vstrech*, 2 vols, New York, 1966.

Antonova, Irina, and Jörn Merkert (eds), *Berlin–Moskau 1900–1950*, Moscow/Berlin/Munich, 1996.

Arzhakovsky, Antuan, *Zhurnal 'Put' 1925–40 Pokolenie russkikh religioznykh myslitelei v emigratsii*, Kiev, 2000.

Bakhrakh, Aleksandr, *Po pamyati, po zapisam*, Paris, 1980.

Baron, Samuel H., *Plekhanov: The Father of Russian Marxism*, London, 1963.

Berberova, Nina, *The Italics are Mine*, London, 1991.

Berberova, Nina, *Billancourt Tales*, translated by Marion Schwarz, New York, 2001.

Berdyaev, Nicholas, *Dream and Reality. An Essay in Autobiography*, London, 1950.

Beyer, Thomas R., Gottfried Kratz, Xenia Werner, *Russische Autoren und Verlage in Berlin nach dem ersten Weltkrieg*, Berlin, 1987.

The Blackwell Encyclopedia of the Russian Revolution, Oxford, 1988.

Boobbyer, Philip, *S. L. Frank. The Life and Work of a Russian Philosopher 1887–1950*, Athens, Ohio, 1995.

Boyd, Brian, *Vladimir Nabokov. The Russian Years*, London, 1990.

Boyd, Brian, *Vladimir Nabokov. The American Years*, London, 1992.

Bradford, Richard, *Roman Jakobson. Life, Language, Art*, London, 1994.

Browder, Robert Paul, and Alexander F. Kerensky, *The Russian Provisional Government of 1917 Documents*, 3 vols, Stanford, 1961.

Bulgakov, Sergei, *The Orthodox Church*, translated and edited by Donald A. Lowrie, London, 1935.

—*The Wisdom of God. A Brief Summary of Sophiology*, New York, 1937.

—*Avtobiograficheskie zametki*, Paris, 1948.

—*A Bulgakov Anthology*, edited by James Pain and Nicolas Zernov, London, 1976.

—*The Friend of the Bridegroom. On the Orthodox Veneration of the Forerunner*, translated and with an introduction by Boris Yakim, Grand Rapids, Michigan, 2003.

Chamberlain, Lesley, *Motherland. A Philosophical History of Russia*, London, 2004.

K. I. Chukovsky, *Dnevnik 1901–1929*, edited by E. Ts. Chukovskaya, with an introduction by V. A. Kaverin, 2nd corrected edition, Moscow, 1997.

Clark, Katerina, *St Petersburg. Crucible of Cultural Revolution*, London, 1995.

Clarke, Oliver Fielding, *An Introduction to Berdyaev*, London, 1950.

Dan, Fyodor, *Dva goda skitanii 1919–21*, Berlin, 1922.

Dan, Theodor, *Letters 1899–1946*, edited by Boris Sapir, Amsterdam, 1985.

Emhardt, W. C., *Religion in Soviet Russia*, Milwaukee and London, 1929.

Evlampiev, I. I., *Khudozhestvennaya filosofia Andreye Tarkovskogo*, St Petersburg, 1991.

Evrei v kul'ture russkogo zarubezh'ya, Vyp. 1 (1919–39), Vyp. 2 (1919–39), Jerusalem, 1992.

Evtuhov, Catherine, *The Cross and the Sickle. Sergei Bulgakov and the Fate of Russian Religious Philosophy 1890–1920*, London, 1997.

Fey, Laurel E., *Shostakovich. A Life*, Oxford, 2000.

Fiene, Donald M., editor and translator, *Mikhail A. Osorgin. Selected Stories, Reminiscences and Essays*, Ann Arbor, Michigan, 1982.

Figes, Orlando, *A People's Tragedy: The Russian Revolution 1891–1924*, London, 1996.

Fleishman, L., Yury Abyzov, and B. Ravdin, *Russkaya pechat' v Rige: is istorii gazety Segodnya 1930 godov*, vols 1–5, Stanford, 1997.

Fleishman, L., R. Huges, O. Raevskaya-Hughes, *Russky Berlin 1921–1923 Po materialiam arkhiva B. I. Nikolaevskogo v Guverskom Institute*, Paris, 1983.

Frank, Semyon L., *Reality and Man*, translated by Natalie Duddington, London, 1965.

—*Neprochitannoe Stat'i Pis'ma, Vospominaniya*, Moscow, 2001.

Frank, née Bartseva, Tatyana, *Vospominaniya*, recorded by her grandson Peter Scorer, Munich, 1975, unpublished.

—'Kratkaya biografia Viktora', *Pamyati Viktora Franka*, London, 1974.

—*Pamyat' serdtsa*, undated, unpublished memoir in the possession of Peter Scorer.

—*Nasha Lyubov*, Munich 1958–9, unpublished memoir in the possession of Peter Scorer.

Frank, Victor, *Izbrannye stat'i*, London, 1974.

—*Po suti dela*, London, 1977.

Galushkin, A. Yu., 'E. I. Zamyatin Pis'mo A. K. Voronskomu k istorii aresta i nesostoyavsheisya vysylki E. I. Zamyatina v 1922–1923gg.', *De Visu*, No. 0, Moscow, 1992, pp. 112–24.

Galushkin, A. Yu., G. A. Grikhanov, N. S. Dvortsina, L. A. Skvortsova, compilers, A. Yu. Galushkin, editor, *Zhurnaly*, 'Vestnik Literatury' (1919–22), 'Letopis Dome liberatoror' (1921–22), 'Leteraturnye zapiski' Anntirovanny ukazatel', Moscow, 1996.

Gardner, Virginia, *Friend and Lover. The Life of Louisa Bryant*, New York, 1982.

Geller (Heller), Mikhail, 'Pervoe predosterzhenie – udar khlystom', *Vestnik Russkogo khristianskogo dvizheniya*, No. 127, Paris, 1978.

Gessen I. V., *Gody izgnaniya*, Paris, 1979.

Glavatsky, Mikhail, *Filosofsky parokhod v god 1922–i*, Ekaterinburg, 2002.

Glenny, Michael, and Norman Stone, *The Other Russia*, London, 1990.

Golosenko I. A., *Pitirim Sorokin Sud'ba I trudy*, Syktyvkar, 1991.

Gorky, Maxim, *Untimely Thoughts. Essays on Revolution, Culture and the Bolsheviks 1917–1918*, translated by Herman Ermolaev, with an introduction and chronology by Mark D. Steinberg, London, 1995.

Gorky, Maksim, *Selected Letters*, edited by Andrew Barratt and Barry P. Scherr, Oxford, 1997.

Hardeman, Hilde, *Coming to Terms with the Soviet Regime*, De Kalb, 1994.

Ippolitov, S. S., V. M. Nedbaevsky, Yu. I. Rudnetsova, *Tri stolitsy izgnaniya Konstantinopol, Berlin, Parizh*, Moscow, 1999.

Ivanov-Razumnik, R. V., *The Memoirs of Ivanov-Razumnik*, London, 1965.

Izgoev A. S., *Rozhdyonnoe v revolyutsionoi smute (1917–1932)*, Paris, 1933.

Jakobson, Roman, 'Vliv revoluce na rusky yazyk' in *Nové Atheneum*, III, Prague, 1921 (a review of André Mazon, *Lexique de la guerre et de la revolution en Russie*, Paris, 1920).

—'On a Generation that Squandered its Poets' (1931) in Edward. J. Brown (ed.), *Major Soviet Writers Essays in Criticism*, Oxford, 1973.

—*Une Vie dans de langage Autoportrait d'un savant*, préface de Tzvetan Todorov, Paris, 1984.

—*My Futurist Years*, edited by Bengt Jangfeldt, translated by Stephen Rudy, New York, 1997. This volume also contains Brown's translation of the essay 'On a Generation...', slightly revised by Stephen Rudy.

Johnston, Robert H., *New Mecca, New Babylon – Paris and the Russian Exiles 1920–1945*, Kingston, Montreal, 1988.

Karsavin, L. P., *Religiozno-filosofskie sochineniya*, T.1, Moscow, 1992.

Karsavina, Tamara, *Theatre Street*, revised, enlarged edition, London, 1947.

Kelly, Catriona, *Petersburg. Crucible of Cultural Revolution*, London, 1995.

Kennan, George, *Siberia and the Exile System*, 2 vols, London, 1891.

Khechinov, Yu., *Krutye dorogi Aleksandrei Tolstoi*, Moscow, 1995.

Khodasevich V. F., *Nekropol: Vospominaniya*, Brussels, 1939.

Khoruzhii, Sergei, 'Filosofsky parokhod', *Literaturnaya Gazeta*, 9 May and 6 June 1990.

Kizevetter, A. A., *Na rubezhe dvukh stoletii Vospominaniya 1881–1914*, with an introduction by M. G. Vandalkovskaya, Moscow, 1997.

—*Istoricheskie siluety lyudi i sobytiya*, Berlin, 1931.

Kogan, L. A., 'Vyslat' za granitsu bezzhalostno', *Voprosy filosofii*, 1993, No. 9.

Kolakowski, Leszek, *Positivist Philosophy. From Hume to the Vienna Circle*, Harmondsworth, 1972.

Kopřivová, Anastasie, *Strediska ruského emigrantského života v Praze (1921–1952)*, Prague, 2001.

Lapshin, I. I., *Estetika Dostoevskogo*, Berlin, 1923.

—*Filosofia izobreteniya I izobretenie v filosofii: Vvedenie v istoriyu filosofii*, Moscow, 1999.

Leggett, George, *The Cheka: Lenin's Political Police*, Oxford, 1981.

Lenin, V. I., *Collected Works*, 47 vols, London and Moscow, 1960–80.

—*Polnoe sobranie sochinenii*, 5th edition, 55 vols, Moscow, 1967–73.

Livak, Leonid, *How it was Done in Paris. Russian Émigré Literature and French Modernism*, Madison, Wisconsin, 2003.

Lossky, Boris, 'K izgnaniyu lyudei mysli v 1922g' in *Russkii Almanakh*, compiled by Zinaida Schakovskoy, René Guerra and Eugène Ternovsky, Paris, 1981, pp. 351–62.

—'Nasha sem'ya v poru likholetiya 1914–1922 godov', *Minuvshee Istorichesky Almanakh*, Kn 11, Moscow, 1992, and Kn 12, Moscow, 1993.

—'V russkoi Prage 1922–27', *MIA* 16, Moscow, 1994.

Lossky, N. O., *Vospominaniya*, Slavische Propyläen Band 43, Munich, 1968.

Lossky, V. N., 'Vstrecha s russkim narodom', *Minuvshee Istorichesky Almanakh*, Kn 12, Moscow, 1993.

Lutokhin, Dalmat Aleksandrovich, 'Alien Pastors', *Minuvshee Istorichesky Almanakh*, vol. 22, St Petersburg, 1997.

Makarov, V. G., V. S. Khristoforov, 'Passazhiry "Filopofskogo Parokhoda' (Sud'by intelligentsii, repressirovannoi letom-osen'yu 1992g.), *Voprosy filosofy*, Moscow, 2003, pp. 113–37.

Makarov, V. G., V. S. Khristoforov, compilers, *Vysylka vmesto rasstrela Deportatsiya intelligentsii v dokumentakh Vecheka – GPU 1921–1923*, with a commentary by V. G. Makarov, Moscow, 2005.

Mandelstam, Nadezhda, *Hope Against Hope. A Memoir*, translated by Max Hayward, Harmondsworth, 1975.

—*Hope Abandoned. A Memoir*, translated by Max Hayward, Harmondsworth, 1976.

Mariengof, Anatoly, *A Novel without Lies*, translated by Jose Alaniz, Moscow, 2000.

Marullo, Thomas Gaiton, *Ivan Bunin: From the Other Shore 1920–1933. A Portrait from Letters, Diaries and Fiction*, Chicago, 1995.

—*Ivan Bunin: The Twilight of Émigré Russia 1932–53*, Chicago, 2002.

Merquior, José Guilherme, *From Prague to Paris: A Critique of Structuralist and Post-Structuralist Thought*, London, 1986.

Misonzhnikova, Maria E. I., 'Zamyatin i K.I. Chukovsky v petrogradskoi periodike pervoi poloviny dvadtsatikh godov', <http://chukfamily.ru/Kornei/Biblio/Zamyatin.htm>.

Murdoch, Iris, *The Sovereignty of Good*, London, 1970.

Nabokov, Vladimir Dmitrievich, with an introduction by Mikhail Geller, *Vremennoe pravitel'stvo i bolshevistsky perevorot*, London, 1988. (First published in *Arkhiv russkoi revolyutsii I*, Berlin, 1921.)

Nabokov, Vladimir, *King, Queen, Knave*, translated from the Russian by Dmitri Nabokov in collaboration with Vladimir Nabokov, London, 1968.

—*Mary*, Harmondsworth, 1973.

—*The Gift*, translated from the Russian by Michael Scammell in collaboration with Vladimir Nabokov, London, 1981.

—*Perepiska s sestroyu*, Ann Arbor, Michigan, 1985.

—*The Eye*, translated by Dmitri Nabokov with the author, New York, 1990.

—*Pale Fire*, with an introduction by Mary McCarthy, London, 1991.

—*Speak Memory*, reprinted with a new appendix, London, 2000.

O'Connor, Timothy Edward, *The Politics of Soviet Culture. Anatolii Lunacharsky*, Ann Arbor, Michigan, 1983.

Osorgin, Mikhail A., *Vremena: Romany i avtobiograficheskoe povestvovanie*, Ekaterinburg, 1992.

Ossorgin, Michael, *A Quiet Street*, translated by Nadia Helstein, London, 1930.

Otsup, Nikolai, *Okean vremeni Stikhotvoreniya, dnevnik v stikhakh, stat'i i vospominaniya o pisatelyakh*, with an introduction by Louis Allen, St Petersburg, 1993.

Pamyati Viktora Franka, by various hands, with a Preface by Leonard Schapiro, London, 1974.

Pipes, Richard, *Struve Liberal on the Left 1870–1905*, Cambridge, Mass., 1970.

—*Struve Liberal on the Right 1905–1944*, Cambridge, Mass., 1980.

—*Russia Under the Bolshevik Regime 1919–1924*, London, 1994.

Pipes, Richard (ed.), *The Unknown Lenin From the Secret Archive*, New Haven and London, 1996.

Piskunov, V. M., *Russkaya Ideyav krugu pisatelei I myslitelei russkogo zarubezh'ya*, 2 vols, Moscow, 1994.

Pittelkow, Kurt, and Reinhard Schmelzkopf, *Heimatshafen Stettin (Strandsgut)*, Cuxhaven, 1987.

Postnikov, S. P., *Russkie v Prage 1918–1928gg.*, Prague, 1928.

Professiya: Zhena filosofa Lidya Berdyaeva [Diaries], compiled and with a foreword and commentary by Elena V. Bronnikova, Moscow, 2002.

Raeff, Marc, *Russia Abroad. A Cultural History of the Russian Emigration 1919–1939*, Oxford, 1990.

Razin, Alexander V., and Tatiana J. Sidorina, 'The Philosophers' Ship', *Philsophy Now*, March–April 2001.

Razumovsky, Maria, *Marina Tsvetaeva*, translated by Aleksei Gibson, Newcastle upon Tyne, 1994.

Renier, Olive, and Vladimir Rubinstein, *Assigned to Listen!*, London, 1986.

Reshchikova, Vera Aleksandrovna, 'Vysylka iz RSFSR', *Minuvshee Istorichesky Almanakh*, Kn 11, Moscow, 1993.

Richie, Alexandra, *Faust's Metropolis. A History of Berlin*, London, 1998.

Rogalina N. L., *Boris Brutskus – Istorik narodnogo khozyaistva Rossii*, Moscow, 1998.

Russkaya periodicheskaya pechat' 1702–1894: Spravochnik, edited by A. G. Dement'ev, A. V. Zapadov, M. S. Cherepakhov, Moscow, 1959.

Russkaya periodicheskaya pechat' 1895–October 1917: Spravochnik, edited by M. S. Cherepakhov and E. M. Fingerit, Moscow, 1957.

Russkoe zarubezh'e. Zolotaya kniga russkoi emigratsii. Pervaya tret' XX Veka Entsiklopedichesky bigrafichesky slovar', Moscow, 1997.

Russky Parizh, compiled and with a foreword and commentary by T. P. Buslakova, Moscow, 1998.

Ruud, Charles A., *Fighting Words. Imperial Censorship and the Russian Press 1804–1906*, Toronto, 1982.

Scherr, Barry, 'Notes on Literary Life in Petrograd 1918–1922. A Tale of Three Houses', *Slavic Review*, 1977, vol. 36, No. 2, pp. 256–67.

Schiff, Stacy, *Véra (MrsVladimir Nabokov)*, London, 1999.

Schlögel, Karl, *Jenseits des großen Oktober Das Laboratorium der Moderne Petersburg 1909–1921*, Berlin, 1988.

Schlögel, Karl (ed.), *Der große Exodus, Russische Emigration und ihre Zentren 1917–1941*, Munich, 1994.

—*Russische Emigration in Deutschland 1918–1941*, Berlin, 1995.

Service, Robert, *Lenin: A Biography*, London, 2000.

Shakhovskaya, Zinaida, *Une Manière de vivre*, Paris, 1965.

Shane, Alex M., *The Life and Works of Evgenij Zamjatin*, Berkeley, 1968.

Shentalinsky, Vitaly, *The KGB's Literary Archive*, translated from the Russian, abridged and annotated by John Crowfoot, with an introduction by Robert Conquest, London, 1995.

Shklovsky, Viktor, *A Sentimental Journey. Memoirs 1917–1922*, translated by Richard Shelden, with a historical introduction by Sidney Monas, London, 1970.

Shpet, Gustav, *Filosofskie Etyudy*, with an introduction by M. K. Polivanov, Moscow, 1994.

Shteinberg, A. Z., *Druz'ya moikh rannykh let 1911–1928*, Paris, 1991.

Sinyavsky, Andrei, *Soviet Civilization*, New York, 2000.

Sorokin, P. I., *A Long Journey*, New Haven, Conn., 1963.

Sorokina, V. V., compiler, *Russky Berlin*, Moscow, 2003.

Spinka, Matthew, *The Church in Soviet Russia*, New York, 1956.

Steinburg, Mark D. See Gorky, Maxim.

Stepun, Fyodor, *Byvshee i Nesbyvsheesya*, 2nd expanded edition,

St Petersburg, 2000.

Stonor Saunders, Francis, *Who Paid the Piper? The CIA and the Cultural Cold War*, London, 1999.

Stroud, Barry, *The Quest for Reality*, New York, 2000.

Struve, Gleb, *Russkaya literatura v izgnanii*, New York, 1956; 2nd edn, Paris, 1994, 3rd edn, Moscow, 1996.

Struve, Nikita, *Soixante-dix ans d'emigration russe 1919–1989*, Paris, 1996.

Tait, Arch, *Lunarcharsky: Poet of the Revolution*, Birmingham, 1984.

Tejchmanová, Svetlana, *Rusko v Československu (Bilá emigrace v ČSR 1917–1939)*, Prague, 1993.

Terapiano,Yury, *Literaturnaya zhizn' russkogo Parizha za polveka*, Paris, 1987.

—*Vstrechi 1926–1971*, Moscow, 2002.

Thomas, D.M., *Alexander Solzhenitsyn. A Century in his Life*, London, 1998.

Tolstoy, Alexandra, *Out of the Past*, translated by various hands, edited by Katherine Strelsky and Catherine Wolkonsky, New York, 1981.

Triomphe, Catherine, *La Russie à Paris*, Paris, 2000.

Trubetskoy, Evgeny, *Iz proshlogo Vospominaniya iz putevykh zametok bezhenstva*, with an introduction by S.M.Polovinkin, Tomsk, 2000.

Trubetskoy, Sergei Evgenievich, *Minuvshee*, Paris, 1989.

Vadimov, A., *Zhizn' Berdyaeva*, Oakland, California, 1993.

La vie culturelle de l'émigration russe en France: chronique (1920–1930), compiled by Michèle Beyssac, Paris, 1971.

Volkogonov, Dmitri A., *Lenin Politichesky Portret*, 2 vols, Moscow, 1994.

—*Lenin: Life and Legacy*, translated and edited by Harold Shukman, London, 1994.

—*Sem' Vozhdei*, 2 vols, Moscow, 1995.

—*The Rise and Fall of the Soviet Empire. Political Leaders from Lenin to Gorbachev*, edited and translated by Harold Shukman, London, 1998.

Volkov, Solomon, *St Petersburg. A Cultural History*, London, 1996.

Vysheslavtsev, B.P., *The Eternal in Russian Philosophy*, translated by Penelope V. Burt, Grand Rapids, Michigan, 2002.

Williams, Robert C., *Culture in Exile – Russian émigrés in Germany*

1881–1941, Ithaca, London, 1972.

—*Artists in Revolution. Portraits of the Russian Avant-garde 1905–1925*, Bloomington, Indiana, 1977.

Winters, Stanley B. (ed.), *T. G. Masaryk (1850–1937)*, vol. 1: *Thinker and Politician*, London, 1990.

Wolfe, Bertram, *The Bridge and the Abyss. The Troubled Friendship of Maxim Gorky and V. I. Lenin*, London, 1967.

Zenzinov, N. A., compiler, *Pavel Apollonovich Velikhov Uchenyi i Chelovek*, Moscow, 1994.

Zenzinov, Vladimir Mikhailovich, *Deserted. The Story of the Children Abandoned in Soviet Russia*, translated by Agnes Platt, London, 1931.

Zubov, Graf Valentin, *Eine Welt ändert ihr Gesicht Erinnerungen aus den Jahren der russischen Revolution 1917–1925*, Munich, 1967.

Zven'ya Istorichesky Almanakh, edited by N. G. Okhotin and others, Vyp. I, Moscow, 1991, Vyp. 2, 1992.

USEFUL WEBSITES:

<http://www.economicus.ru>
<http://www.hronos.km.ru/biografichesky>
<http://www.ihst.ru/projects/emigrants>
<http://www.istina.rin.ru>
<http://www.krugosvet.ru>
<http://www.persona.rin.ru>
<http://www.rulex.ru>
<http://www.rusphil.albertina.ru>
<http://www.SEM40.ru>
<http://www.vgd.ru>, Vserossiiskoe genealogicheskoe drevo (All-Russian Genealogical Tree)

Index